AF575387

A STRANGER AMONG US

A STRANGER AMONG US

A Novel

By
Conor Gallagher

TAN Books
Gastonia, North Carolina

Unless otherwise noted, Scripture quotations are taken from the Douay Rheims Bible, in the public domain.

Cover design by David Ferris—www.davidferrisdesign.com

Cover images: "Hooded figure and background texture" by Raggedstone / Shutterstock. "Church" by JunYi Chow Photography / Shutterstock. "Tree Silhouttes" by Anna L-G / Shutterstock.

Library of Congress Control Number: 2024945397

ISBN: 978-1-5051-3306-6
Kindle ISBN: 978-1-5051-3308-0
ePUB ISBN: 978-1-5051-3307-3

Published in the United States by
TAN Books
PO Box 269
Gastonia, NC 28053
www.TANBooks.com

Printed in India

To my late editor and friend, John Moorehouse.
Though he is no longer my editor, he is still my friend.

Contents

Part One

Part Two:

Part Three

PART FOUR:

Chapter:

PART FIVE

Chapter:

"Lord, I know not how to lead this young man, a giant among men, a saint among sinners, a stranger among even those who love him."

The Journal of Abbot Ambrose, May 1, 1925

"Who is this stranger among us, distracting us from the Rule, bringing disorder to our community, contaminating our proper view of all things of the highest importance?"

The Journal of Father Vincent Roth, May 5, 1925

Part One

Chapter 1

Teach Us to Number Our Days

May 21, 1924

"You think you rich!" said a loving yet strong voice. "Never let the sun catch you in the bed!"

Most kids dreaded climbing out of bed. But not Hack. Any day with his Pa—even if filled with backbreaking work—was a good day.

"I tell you boy, these pancakes gonna get ate if your fanny don't get to the table."

An idle threat if he ever heard one. He'd have to steal a man's horse for Pa to eat his pancakes. Nonetheless, Hack hustled to throw his britches on and slide a pair of raggedy suspenders over his boney shoulders. He pulled on one of the floppy shoes that was too big for his feet and hopped the whole seven steps from his bed to the kitchen table while trying to get his other shoe on.

"The Good Lord gave ya two feet, boy. Sorta an insult not to use them," Pa said, pouring a glass of milk.

"Gave me the ability to hop on one foot too."

Pa shook his head. "Hack, your brain don't work like none I've ever seen. You just see it different, don't ya?"

"Don't know, Pa. Don't know what others see."

Pa poured the syrup a little more generously today.

"I'm thinkin' you ain't missin' much."

"But I ain't educated, like them boys at the school—reading books and all."

"Son," Pa said leaning in, "we's behind on book reading. I knows it. But don't forget, book smarts ain't the same as wisdom."

"But I ain't old either."

"Who said you've got to get old to get wise?"

Pa looked up and away—the telltale sign a verse was on its way.

"*Teach us to number our days so that we'll have a heart of wisdom,* says the psalms . . . somewheres."

"You mean count how many days we've lived?"

"Uh-huh. The Good Book means live like it's your last, son. You might choke to death right there on that pancake. If you know you's gonna die soon, your heart will be *filled* with wisdom; a wisdom not found in them books at Good Shepherd. Lots of them boys you'll see tonight—partying all up like them kings—they's thinkin' they gonna live forever. Books ain't gonna fix that, except the Good One."

Hack thought about the men of Good Shepherd College. At least they looked like men to a twelve-year-old boy, but he wasn't really sure. When he worked the grounds with Pa, he saw them in their suits and ties flying in and out of huge brick buildings; he saw their flashy baseball uniforms and heard the clatter of cleats walking on the pavement to and from practice. Even more, he heard their laughter.

He never had a bad experience at the college other than being totally ignored—not such a bad deal, Pa taught him, for a negro in a white world.

As Hack envisioned the college men in his head, he found that Pa was right: they looked like they believed they would live forever. If money and education and good looks and energy and friendships could keep your heart bumping for eternity, the men of Good Shepherd would never die.

But right next to such a vision of the young and invincible were the monks. To Hack, they looked like wizards in their Benedictine habits, especially the old ones—with wild hair and warts and bad teeth poking through creepy smiles. In the beginning, Hack was afraid of them. But as time passed, he saw them for what they were, both good and bad.

"What about the monks, Pa? They think they gonna live forever?"

Pa thought for a moment and bobbed his head side-to-side. "Some. Some don't. I've learned that them monks are just normal folks. Some are Christian-like . . . Bible Christian-like . . . with kindness and patience. Humble . . . humble is the word." And he looked away for the verse: "*With humility comes wisdom.* Proverbs somewheres." He kept looking for it in his mind but shook it off and continued, "One thing I know when a man speaks to me is his humility. Any negro knows that from the ways he spoken to. Some of them monks are good as gold. Others . . ." He stopped and sipped on his coffee.

"Others what?"

Pa smiled and shook his head. "Here I am talkin' humility just as I'm about to use my tongue to lash others? No sir."

And that was enough. Hack understood.

"It's time. Let's get a move on. The dance hall ain't gonna deck itself out. Brother Bruno's gonna be waitin'. I don't like gettin' a giant German all riled up."

Brother Bruno! Hack thought to himself. His favorite of all the monks. *A day with Pa. A day with Brother Bruno the Bavarian. It don't get much better than this.*

The walk to Good Shepherd was a few miles with a convenience store along the way. They needed a few supplies for their preparation of the graduation dance later that night. One would think such a purchase would be a simple task, but if humanity's history teaches nothing else, it teaches that we are inclined to make everything difficult on at least one group of people in society. What culture has not had a victim of oppression due to its insecurities, its wrath, its self-righteous indignation? The Egyptians made the Jews stomp their lives away in the mud pits to make bricks; the Romans held them beneath the edge of the sword; even Aristotle believed that all barbarians were slaves by nature. Mankind has never been too friendly to the outsider walking into town, and neither was the general public in Capstone, North Carolina all too kind to a black man and his son walking into a convenience store.

A local farmhand, lingering in the store and visiting with the cashier, saw the man and son enter.

"What the hell is this!" the man said to the cashier. "You lettin' negros infest your store?"

"It's just Percy and his boy," the cashier objected. "He works at the abbey . . . and is a dern good customer. Leave him be."

Percy tipped his hat at the farmhand despite his insolence, shouting to the cashier, "Mornin' Jimmy." Percy and Hack gathered up their items as quickly as possible.

"So now Capstone has niggers working for papists," said the farmhand, spitting. "They got Jews in the basement counting gold coins?"

"Leave him be, I said." Jimmy didn't want to offend a good customer like Percy, who placed most of his orders for his groundskeeping job through him. Jimmy didn't care if Percy or the monks or the alleged Jews working in the basement were white, black, yellow, or red. He just wanted a good paying customer.

"You stinkin' up this fine store. You know that?" the man said to Percy, shooting a glance at Hack.

Percy kept a smile on his face as he approached the register. "Gonna be a hot one today, huh Jimmy?"

"Believe so. Big dance tonight?"

"Yes, sir. These here supplies will help spruce up the place."

"Hey, I was talking to you," interjected the man at the counter.

"Leave him be, I tell ya," Jimmy repeated.

Hack was amazed at how his Pa didn't seem to be bothered in the least. After Jimmy loaded up his supplies in a brown paper bag, Percy put his hat back on, looked at the man at the counter, and said, "God bless your day, sir." He tipped his hat and smiled.

As the door swung closed behind them, Hack could hear the man continue on. "Don't care what he pretends to be. They infestin' the whole damn town."

"Pa?" asked Hack. "What'd he mean about Jews in the basement?"

"Jews are good with money. And that old boy don't like Jews any more than he likes blacks. And he don't like Catholics much more than he likes us."

"But I heard someone does live in the basement."

"Some monks live there from time to time. They gots something called a hermitage."

"What's that?"

"It's where a hermit lives, I reckon."

"What's a hermit?"

"I don't rightly know. . . . He prays a lot, I guess. But he stays away from people."

"Why would you stay away from people?"

"Some stays away from people to stay closer to God."

"Does it work?"

"Alls I can say is the more you go out around men, the less of a man you are when you get home."

They walked along in silence. The abbey bell towers had come into full view. For a small southern town, the brick architecture was rather spectacular. Hack had wondered many times, however, why one tower was taller than the other. *They must have run out of bricks,* he thought to himself.

"Pa?"

"Yes son?"

"How come that man don't get you all mad?"

"Oh, he does, son. He does."

"But you don't show it."

Percy looked up and away.

"*A fool utters his mind, but the wise keeps all up inside till afterwards,* or something like that. . . . Proverbs somewheres. The Book speaks lots on wisdom. And it never says *Open your dern mouth.* It always says, *Shut yer dern mouth . . . so saith the Lord.*"

"But aren't we supposed to preach to others?"

"Some. But there's a good chance, son, them boys are Klan. I ain't gonna go pickin' a fight with no Klan. Sure, I like to preach. But don't be so heavenly minded you ain't no Earthly good. Besides, sometimes we get to leave our troubles up to God. He don't need yer jibber-jabber to change that man's heart. He needs yer patience. He needs yer humility. It's hard for God's gospel to squeeze in when we fills up the day with our own gospel. Come to think of it, I can't remember a time I regretted holding my tongue. Well . . . that ain't totally true."

Percy went silent. But Hack had to know.

"Wutcha mean, Pa?"

"I wish I'da told your momma I loved her ten times a day. Shoulda told her how beautiful she was ten times a day. Shoulda said, 'Thank you for being my wife' ten times a day."

Hack had plenty of memories of her. He wished he had a picture. The most vivid of memories were of her final days, five years ago. She suffered for a few weeks with a fever making her delirious, making her moan and weep and shake her head left and right for hours on end. And the adults made him sleep outside to keep him away from her. But he would look at her through the window until his knees began to buckle. Later on, his Pa said it was something called a Spanish Flu, and it took lots of mothers away from lots of boys his age.

"I wish I woulda told her 'Thanks for being my momma.' Not sure I ever did."

"Oh, she knew. She knew you loved being her son."

"She told you that?"

"Well . . ." Percy looked around for a moment, "in ways. Yes, son. She told me many times, *Hack makes me feel so good to be a momma.*"

That was good enough for Hack.

"But look here now, boy: We gots lots of work today. We ain't mopin' around."

Hack nodded as they entered the gymnasium.

"Hack!" a deep, bellowing German accent came from across the room. Brother Bruno was already busy unfolding tables and chairs. His six-foot five, barrel-chested frame intimidated anyone who met him, especially with his conspicuous limp that caused his body to lurch with each step. But Hack had learned that the Great Bavarian was the friendliest of monks at the abbey. His Pa speculated that being German helped; after the Great War, Germans were lumped into the group of untouchables in their small southern town. Bruno didn't have to put up with much, however, for his stature alone seemed to keep most tongues in their place.

"If you catch it, you can eat it." And he threw a piece of chocolate candy thirty some feet, as if he were a catcher picking off a runner stealing second—though the Great Bavarian knew nothing of America's pastime. Hack had to move fast but caught it just in time.

Two other young monks were hanging a sign above the doors: *Class of 1924.*

They spent the morning decorating for the dance. Hack overheard some of the monks expressing their disapproval of such dances.

"Just asking for trouble," Father Henry said.

"When I want the opinion of the sub-prior," said the prior, Father Vincent Roth, "I will ask for it."

It was uncanny how much these two men were alike, which explained why Father Roth made sure that Father Henry be named sub-prior just a few months before. Although Father Henry was in his early thirties, his premature curmudgeonly spirit made him seem even older. But to those who knew him, it was obvious that he acted far harsher than he actually was. It was as if he was trying to live up to the gold standard of curmudgeons personified in Father Roth. As prior, Father Roth was in charge of discipline, and he relished it. With his tall stature and long, thin face, he looked like a whip about to crack down on anyone standing before him. To those who knew him, it was obvious that he acted exactly as he was: cold, harsh, and unforgiving.

"You could have used a few dances in your time," Bruno said to Father Henry. "You'd be easier to live with now."

"Nonsense." He huffed through his nostrils like an angry horse.

Bruno waited for Father Roth to move on. "You know, Henry, if you aren't careful, you're going to end up just like Father Roth."

"You mean become prior of a great Benedictine monastery? Why, thank you, Brother Bruno."

"Sure, you might be something like that. But you'll be bitter and nasty . . . and worst of all, no damn fun to be around."

"There are more things in life than fun, Brother Bruno."

"There's more things in life than water, but you still need it."

Percy wisely pulled his curious son away from the two monks who could argue all day, every day just for the sake of it.

After a long day of groundskeeping, they had no reason to return home. Percy had been asked to stay on the grounds to help clean up after the dance. It would be a long night. He settled into the groundskeeper's shed where a few chairs provided a nice place to relax during down times.

The shed had been converted from the original brick kiln. Every one of the bricks of the abbey and college had been quarried from the seemingly useless red clay spread beneath the farmland of the entire region. Thus, the monks who settled here in 1874 made every single brick by hand. The firing of the bricks was most suitable next to the natural pond fed by a nearby river. The homemade bricks were a badge of honor for the monks of Good Shepherd. In fact, every graduating student was given an original brick left over from its founding. It was here, around the pond, that bricks were piled and scattered all over the place. As the monks grew older, they seemed to complain more and more about these tripping hazards. It was on the abbot's list of projects for Percy: clean up the old pond and kiln. Not today though. Today, they decided to go fishing. Down by the pond, it was not uncommon for them to encounter a monk sitting on the shore with a long pole lying next to him on the ground, his hands occupied with a drink. Hack loved seeing the fat, red-cheeked, balding monks wave from across the pond, nearly rolling to their side in doing so. He noticed, in fact, that most of them were a great deal more pleasant when tipsy. Today, however, there were no monks to be found.

"We gonna throw the first back to Saint Peter, as always."

"I know Pa."

After a few minutes of silent casting, Percy began one of their favorite games. "Different word for fishing . . ."

"Hmm . . ." *Why was it named for the fish?* he wondered. *You don't call it doving for dove hunting or turkeying for turkey hunting.*

"Lining."

"Good one."

"Wanna rhyme?"

Hack gave his Pa a nod.

"I-love-to-fish . . ."

"Oh, how I wish . . ."

Pa hesitated.

". . . to catch one now . . ."

Hack seemed stumped. *Now . . . Mow . . . Cow . . .Bow . . . How?*

"Saint Peter, show me how."

"Dern boy. That's good. You gettin' better every time. Your turn."

Hack smiled. *"Bruno is funny . . ."*

". . . and he sweats when it's sunny . . ."

Hack laughed. "He sure does."

"Keep it goin' . . ."

"Sorry. Umm . . . *his belly can jiggle . . ."*

". . . and that makes me giggle!"

And giggle they did.

It was the first time they remembered not getting even a nibble. It mattered not to the father and son, for as any father and son know, fishing is not about the fish. But for years thereafter, Hack would wonder if it was an omen of what was to come a few short hours later.

CHAPTER 2

No Greater Love

9:30 p.m.

Hack sat close to his father in the shed, holding the Good Book by the dim light of the lantern.

"Behold, what manner of love the Father ha . . . hath be . . . besto . . ."

"Bestowed."

"Bestowed upon us, that we should be called the sons of God."

"Sons of God . . ." Percy repeated, like sweet music to his ears.

"Is this here why you say I'm a son of God?"

"It's all through the book, son. You remember that. You my Earthly son. But you God's heavenly son. He's your real father because heaven is more real than Earth. Now keep on reading. The dance'll be over in an hour or so."

Hack continued on through the First Letter of John. He was surprised at the strong language in this letter. He would have thought the beloved disciple only wrote about pleasant things. But he did not. He wrote about the most real of all things. And while Hack struggled over a few of the words, he did not struggle over their meanings in the least.

"Who . . . so . . . ever hateth his brother is . . . is a murderer: and ye know that no murderer hath eternal life a . . . abi . . . abiding in him."

"That's good. Keep on now," his Pa said.

A sound from outside broke Hack's attention.

"Keep on now . . . just an animal or somethin'. This line here . . . one of the best in the whole Good Book."

Hack cleared his throat. "*Hereby per . . . perceive we the love of God, because he laid down his life for us: and we ought to lay down our lives for the brethren.*"

Hack looked up at his Pa. "Who's our brethren?"

"If your Pa had more sons, would you have brethren?"

"Yes, sir."

"Well then, your heavenly Pa has lots of sons and daughters. That means you got lots of heavenly brethren."

"How many?"

"Everyone, son. The kindest. The meanest. The best. The worst. Them who love you. Them who hate you. Everyone, son. Every last person walking God's green Earth." He looked away and closed his eyes: "*Greater love hath no man than . . .*"

A young woman's voice outside—distressed—interrupted him.

"Hold on, son. Stay here." Percy stood up, placed his hand on Hack's shoulder, grabbed the lantern, and walked out the door.

Hack followed but stopped at the threshold, peaking around the doorframe.

"Hello?" Percy yelled into the dark, walking toward the pond, holding the lantern out as far as his arm would reach.

The girl's voice came again, but this time more clearly. "Stop it, please!"

Hack saw his Pa quicken his pace.

"Hey! Hey there! You get off her!" Percy placed the lantern down next to the couple lying on the ground. Hack could see his Pa grab the young man's arm and throw him back like a rag doll.

Hack left the shed and inched closer, closer, hiding behind a tree here, another there. His Pa knelt down on one knee beside the young girl. She sat upright now with his help. She was crying, heaving for air, pushing down her dress, which had been bundled up around her waist.

"It's all right now, Miss. It's all right."

The young man struggled to rise to his feet, swerving, leaning. He was bigger than Pa, looming like a shadow behind him. He reached for something on the ground. A look of horror came into the young woman's eyes. "Walter! No!"

The young man swung a brick down upon Percy's head. Percy dropped to the ground instantly.

The air in Hack's lungs left him. He began to yell, but nothing came out. He started running toward his Pa but froze in fear.

"Stupid nigger!" the young man yelled at Percy, standing over him. "Why didn't you mind your own damn business?"

He stumbled again, leaning in to take a closer look at Percy. He stood silently, a look of uncertainty. The young girl stared at the body lying next to her, then to the man. Then, she let out a deafening screech—a sound that only comes from the deepest parts of the soul, the place where raw emotion resides.

"Shut up!" the young man yelled. "Shut the hell up!"

But she did not. She stared at Percy's body, screamed until out of breath, inhaled, and screamed again. The young man jumped on her and covered her mouth. And they struggled. Hack could hear her muted scream beneath his grip. "Shut up!" the man said. "Shut up! I told you! Shut up!"

The girl's flailing legs kicked the lantern over. All went black, except the slightest outlines of the three bodies by the moonlight. The movement of the woman's legs began to wane, give up completely. Hack looked for something—anything—to use as a weapon. *There!* He picked up a nearby log, running toward the grapple. Stopping just short, he threw the log with all his might at the back of the young man. It hit him square between the shoulders. The young man stood and turned toward Hack.

"Who's there?"

Hack darted behind another tree, hiding in the dark. The man approached, leaving the motionless girl behind. Hack struggled to control his breathing. He decided he must get help. And he knew one person a whole lot bigger than the attacker.

Hack ran off in the dark.

"Hey! You! Get back here!" the young man yelled. And he took off after Hack.

Hack ran as fast as he could, but those long legs behind him were faster than his own. It came to him instantly: *Pray Hack. Pray.* And so he said between breaths, "Make me fast, Lord. Make me fast to help Pa."

His pace quickened. He ran like he had never run before. There was no fatigue. He felt a boundless energy throughout his body that seemed to make him as swift as a buck running through the woods. His eyes seemed to adjust instantly to the darkness; he saw every branch along his path, every bramble, every stump with perfect clarity. His pursuer was not so lucky. He heard the young man trip and fall behind him. The odious cursing faded in the distance as Hack fled through the woods and toward the main entrance of Good Shepherd Monastery.

"Brother Bruno!" Hack cried as he banged on the monastery door. "Brother! Please!"

The young porter, Brother Matthias, opened the door.

"Hack? What on Earth . . . ?"

"Need Brother Bruno. Pa's hurt. A girl's hurt!"

Brother Matthias wrapped his hands around both the boy's shoulders trying to quiet him down as he gently brought him inside the monastery.

"He . . . he hit him with a brick. And he's hurting the girl. And . . ."

"Please, Hack. Slow down. Who hit who?"

The newly elected Abbot Ambrose came around the corner.

"I heard someone banging on the door. What is all this about?"

His mere presence, perhaps embellished with the large gold crucifix dangling around his neck, forced Hack to gather himself and to speak clearly.

"Pa needs help. He's hurt."

"Where is he, son?" the abbot asked, walking out the front door, unflinchingly ready to go himself.

"Abbot, wait," Matthias said as he grabbed the abbot's arm. "Hack here said something about Percy was hurt by someone. And a girl was hurt?"

The abbot paused. "Hack?"

"A man—a student I think—hit him with a brick, real mean like. And he hurt this girl too. And he chased me, but I gots away. Abbot, we need Brother Bruno. He's real big and strong and . . ."

As if God had heard a prayer, Brother Bruno appeared. The abbot turned. "Brother, something has happened. It sounds like both Percy and a young lady have been attacked." He turned to Hack again. "Where are they?"

"Our fishing spot at the pond. Outside the groundskeeper's shed."

The abbot looked back and forth between Bruno and Matthias, finally saying to both of them. "Go. Run. I'll stay with Hack."

Bruno dashed out the door, running like a man on a life-or-death mission, despite the limp that turned his run into more of a strategic hop. Matthias followed but lagged behind despite having two perfectly healthy legs.

The abbot put his arm around Hack and led him into the parlor. "Sit down, son. They'll be back soon." And he paced the room. Other brothers came in, surprised to see Hack sitting quietly in the high back chair usually occupied by the abbot himself. But there sat a lanky, dirty, black boy, shaking in fear.

The abbot shooed away the interested spectators. "Back to your cells, Brothers. Immediately." They scattered like mice, all except the prior, Father Vincent Roth. He made his way into the parlor, rightly assuming the instruction did not apply to the second most powerful man in the abbey. For it was he who regularly instructed the young abbot in the ways of governance according to the Rule of the Founder. It was he who had been novice master when Ambrose entered years ago, and he who took credit for his ascension to the abbot's chair, despite his well-known but failed lobbying for his own election. The bitterness of defeat no doubt emboldened his demeanor and assertiveness toward the young abbot.

When Father Roth stepped into the parlor, he gave the boy a look of disapproval. Hack suddenly felt as though he was trespassing. "What's *he* doing here?"

"Something has happened to Percy and to a girl," the abbot said. "Bruno and Matthias have just gone to see what was going on."

"Hmmm." He shook his head and plopped down with a sigh.

After a moment of silence, the abbot stopped his pacing and turned to the boy. "Hack, do you know who hit your dad with a brick?"

Hack paused and thought through the moments of horror. He could hear the girl's scream. He could hear his Pa's words of comfort to the girl. And then he remembered. "Walter! The girl called him Walter!"

The abbot looked at Father Roth, who seemed to be shaken out of his annoyance, even if momentarily. The abbot then slowly moved to a seat, sat down, and rubbed his face with both hands.

"Walter Brooks . . . Dear Lord . . ."

As every culture in every land has discovered, there are not only the untouchables at the bottom of the economical and societal scale but also the untouchables at the top. In more ancient and medieval times, the divine right of kings gave (though with misapplication of principle) an indemnity from unbecoming accusations. Yet if some credible grievance managed to creep through the ranks of safeguarding, ecclesial and societal absolution was almost certain, not for the offender's sake, but for the institution's preservation and continuity despite the misdeeds of the fallen man enjoying the chair for (what is truly) a fleeting moment.

In modern times, there is a decreasing presence of relevant royalty in the industrial world. Society, however, seems compelled to thrust someone atop a pedestal for us to gaze upon, for man is not comfortable looking upward and seeing God alone. It is as if the fallen man yearns to see the glorified man yet lacks the patience to wait for resurrection on the last day. Man must see himself glorified in this life by merit and strength and grit and ingenuity. Perhaps this is due to man's worship of his own innate abilities; perhaps it is man's desire to fit within a holistic structure of the rich, the poor, and everyone else in the middle; perhaps it is unadulterated boredom with the simple life. Whatever the cause, man seems more content being an indentured servant than being ignored.

Thus, in these modern times, it is not kings, princes, or dukes elevated to the heights of the untouchable; rather, it is the captains of industry.

It is he who gives sight to the blind with innovative medicine or multiplying loaves and fishes by the power of mass production. Yes, the miraculous powers of he who weaves God-created raw materials with man-created technology. And no wonder it is the captain of industry who is worshipped: the consumer sees his creation as a perfection of God's imperfect world. What good is oil resting beneath our feet in a pit of darkness? But when man brings it out of the darkness and into the light, he can bring a true light to all nations. What good is cotton, snug in its boll, sprouting in a lonely field? But when man brings cotton through his innovation gin, on massive scales of productivity, he can clothe the naked—technicolor coats for all.

In 1924, particularly in the southeast, the captains of industry clothed the naked on an unprecedented scale with their miraculous textile mills. As Rockefeller did with oil, Carnegie with steel, and Ford with the automobile, so the textile owners did the next best thing to giving people trees upon which money could grow—they dramatically reduced prices.

As in all industries, there could not be too many captains in textiles at once. And the one in the Carolinas that reigned above all others was Leopold Brooks of Brooks Textiles. One of the largest mills south of the Mason-Dixon line, it employed over four thousand workers at any given time. A third of Capstone was employed as his openers, pickers, slubbers, speeders, spinners, doffers, spoolers, twisters, warpers, and weavers. Oddly enough, these people were gainfully employed somewhere and somehow before the entrepreneurship of Mr. Brooks took root in Capstone, but now, if he were to call it quits, they would have no place to turn.

Every facet of the town, save for Good Shepherd, depended on Brooks Textile. Not only did the people work there, but many lived in "mill homes" and shopped at the "mill stores" where groceries were deducted from one's meager paycheck; even schools and churches were built by the millowner as a magnet for out-of-state migrant workers.

While neither the captain himself nor the wage-slaves filling his multi-floor mill would want to admit it, the lifestyle of the worker was not all that different from a peasant in the feudal system working his king's land. Thus, a weaver was no more likely to challenge the millowner than a serf would likely challenge his lord. The population of Capstone was no different. Everyone knew of Mr. Brooks. They knew of his only son. And they knew that his inheritance grew with every rotation of the cotton gin rollers.

But why would a staunch Presbyterian millionaire, with a good dose of anti-Catholicism in his belly, send his son to study under Catholic monks? Why not send Walter to a northeastern Ivy League college like the rest of the oligarchy? The answer rested in conspicuous nepotism. He simply wanted his son as close as possible. As a star athlete and valedictorian of his class, Walter would, however, be departing for Yale Law School eventually; there was no way around this conundrum for Mr. Brooks if Walter was to have a preeminent pedigree in the eyes of northern elites. All the townspeople knew that Walter was destined for greatness.

All of this and more came to mind when Abbot Ambrose heard the name *Walter* emerge from the mouth of the little boy. He knew the challenge that lay before Hack—indeed, that lay before the brothers of Good Shepherd—and he felt the eternal weight of this moral conundrum dropped on his shoulders.

Bruno returned with sweat pouring down every inch of his face. He breathed with a frenzy in part from the run but mostly from the terror he had just encountered. Matthias followed, making his way up the steps. Bruno gave the abbot a nod to enter the hall, at which both the abbot and the prior complied, shutting the door behind them. Hack's stomach churned. He couldn't sit still. He stood up from the grand chair and crept over to the door, pressing his ear against it, listening to the muffled voices.

"He's dead, Abbot. Lost too much blood from the head wound. And the girl next to him—dead. No blood. Just dead. No pulse. Both of them. Eyes wide open."

"Oh, dear Jesus," said the abbot, crossing himself.

Matthias's footfall could be heard entering the monastery.

"I told him," Bruno said.

"What about Walter?" the abbot asked.

"Walter?" Mathias asked.

"Walter Brooks?" Bruno followed.

"Hack said the girl called him Walter."

Bruno grunted. "That dirty bastard. I'm going to find him."

"No," the abbot objected. "If they're dead, there is nothing we can do for them. We must think about this. You know who we're dealing with here."

"I'll bust every last one of them!" Bruno said.

"Quiet, Brother! This isn't time for bluster. Let me think."

Hack heard the pacing steps of the abbot, then felt the door opening toward him. He shot back to his seat. The abbot sighed, then turned and said, "Brother Bruno, would you please join us?" When Father Roth followed Bruno in, the abbot gave him a small wave, stopping him. The abbot shut the door and approached Hack, sitting across from the boy with Bruno. He searched for words, dropping his head. Hack relieved him of the burden.

"He's dead."

The abbot nodded. "Yes, son. He is. And so is the girl."

Hack stared into his own lap, rubbing his hands together. He began rocking back and forth as a small whine began to creep from his closed mouth. Brother Bruno slid from his chair to his knees, wrapping his giant arms around him, nearly pulling him out of his chair. Hack fell into his arms like a baby and buried his face in the thick of the Great Bavarian shoulder. Finally, Hack heaved out a moan . . . and another . . . and another. It was the sound of a twelve-year-old boy having his life stripped away yet using every ounce of inner strength to hold in a wailing of sadness that would shatter the walls. Bruno squeezed him so tightly it looked like Hack would shatter into pieces.

"I'm so sorry, Hack. I'm so sorry," Bruno said over and over again.

The abbot did not know what to say. He determined to balance Bruno's tender love with practical matters. "Hack, did Walter see you?"

Hack pulled back from Bruno, wiped his face, and said, "He chased me for a while."

"Dear Lord," the abbot said under his breath.

Just then, Brother Matthias entered the parlor.

"Abbot, the police are here."

"What?" The abbot jumped from his seat. "Did we call them?"

"No. But they said they got a call from a student."

The abbot looked at Bruno. "Take him to the hermitage. Now. Go!"

"Good evening, Officer Andrew," Abbot Ambrose said to the older of the two officers standing on the steps. Thankfully, the abbot had known Officer Andrew's family for years—one of the benefits of a small town. But there was no affection between them. Andrew's family were well-known Klan members who had made it clear they were not particularly fond of the papists infiltrating their town. The relationship, however, had been largely peaceful, for the previous abbots always made sure to steer clear of certain families in town. Abbot Ambrose made sure to continue the tradition. He had recently, however, been forced to interface more than he wished due to a few fist fights between Brother Bruno and some local folks who did not take a liking to a German or a Catholic—certainly not a German monk.

The abbot closed the great door with the stained-glass window featuring an elaborate Benedictine medal. The abbot gave the medal an extra look, knowing tradition taught it protected its devotees from the evil one.

Officer Andrew tipped his hat. "Father Ambrose . . . oh . . . *Abbot* Ambrose, excuse me." The sarcasm in his tone bespoke of his disdain for the papists, a not-too-uncommon feeling among families tied to the Klan.

"What can I help you with?" the abbot said.

"We received a call tonight from a student of yours."

"Goodness . . . I hope everything is all right."

"Can we come in and talk before we . . . well . . . before we take a little walk to show you something?"

The abbot wondered if Hack was down in the hermitage yet, and if Officer Andrew would sense the unusual amount of activity for a monastery at this time of night. He would surely wonder why there were so many lights on, and why the prior and the porter—and the abbot for that matter—were up so late.

"Forgive my lack of hospitality, Andrew, but it is strictly against our Rule to have guests in the monastery at this hour. I will gladly meet with you in another building?"

"No time for that," said Officer Andrew. "Come with me."

"Let me grab my porter, Brother Matthias." He cracked open the door and waved for Matthias to join him.

Walking in the darkness, the abbot finally asked, "What's this all about?"

"I'm sorry to say, abbot, but you've had a murder on your campus tonight."

"What on Earth are you talking about?" the abbot said, gasping.

"Well, I guess I should say *a* murder, but two deaths."

The abbot said nothing as his face twisted in confusion.

"And you have a very brave young man," the officer continued. "A real hero."

"A hero?" the abbot asked.

"Mm-hmm. Walter Brooks."

"Walter Brooks? How . . . how do you mean?"

"You're gonna see soon enough."

As they approached the scene, Walter stood next to two more officers. The abbot saw him shake hands with one while the other patted him on the back.

The abbot's eyes, however, left Walter and fell upon the large corpse. Percy. One of the finest men the abbot knew. Blood spilled over the grass. A brick lay next to his head. His eyes had not even been closed. His pants had been pulled down around his knees. And the young lady laid next to him, her beautiful yellow dress was hiked up around her waist. Her under garments had been torn off and thrown next to her. Her eyes had been closed; her face beaten. A broken nose, gashed lips . . . her hair pulled in every direction.

Brother Matthias leaned over to the abbot's ear and whispered, "This is all different." A slight move of the abbot's head communicated both that he knew and that it wasn't the time.

The officer began to speak, but Abbot Ambrose silenced him and all those around with a simple, "Quiet." Not knowing how long he had been dead, the abbot knelt down on one knee next to Percy's head and administered Last Rites in the ancient tongue of the Church.

There was a mumble from one of the officers. "Niggers goin' to hell no matter what . . ."

The abbot spun around a moment later in the grass and repeated the same over the young lady. He paused, looked up at the crowd of men next to him, and said, "What's her name?"

"Catherine," Walter said. "Catherine Smith."

He finished giving the last bit of grace available to the poor girl. He stood and turned toward the officers.

"Now. What did you want to tell me?"

"You have a brave young man here," and Officer Andrew placed his hand on Walter's shoulder. "Go on, Walter. Tell him what happened."

The abbot stood perfectly still, like a statue of an ancient saint, staring at the face of evil without a flinch.

"Ah . . . right. Okay. So I was at the dance with my friends. We were having a great time, but Catherine and I walked outside. We walked a little ways from the dance. I wanted to speak privately with her, ya see, so she wouldn't be embarrassed in front of her friends.

"Anyhow . . . I told her that I cared a lot for her, but that I had to go off to law school soon—Yale School of Law, that is. I said she needed to move on from me. She argued. She wouldn't listen to reason. So I told her, probably too bluntly, that she couldn't be my girl any more. She got awfully upset. She smacked me hard, and her nails cut me." He leaned toward the abbot to show the nail marks running down his face. "And then she ran off. I sat there for a minute. But after a while, I decided I should go look for her.

"I walked around calling her name. I must have walked for fifteen or twenty minutes until I heard her scream. She screamed so loud, over and over again. I started running, and I found her right here," he pointed. "This monster was lying on top of her. But by the time I got to her, she wasn't screaming any more. She was just lying there. I thought she had, you know, given up. Well, I saw who it was. That groundsman I see around campus. And I see his boy, standing at the top of her head like he had been holding her arms or something. When he saw me, he ran off through the woods.

"I didn't know what to do about the groundsman, so I looked around and saw those bricks lying all over the place. I grabbed one. I ran toward him as fast as I could. He didn't even mind me. He kept doing what he was doing. It was dark, so he didn't see I had that brick in my hand."

Walter stopped. He looked at his hands and choked up, as if he was reliving the horror of the moment."

"Keep going, son," Officer Andrew said to him.

"So I . . . I swung that brick as hard as I could. I hit him right in the head. But I swear abbot, I swear I didn't mean to kill him. I was just so afraid. I didn't think. I just wanted to save Catherine. He fell. I didn't even look at him after that. I sat Catherine up and held her in my arms. She had been violated so terribly. She was all beat up like you see here. Her pretty face had been beaten in. Her, her clothes all torn . . . and she wasn't breathing.

"I didn't know what to do, so I ran to the student center. I knew we just put that new telephone in there. I picked up the receiver and asked the operator for the police."

"We got three officers looking for the boy," Officer Andrew said. "What's his name, abbot?"

The abbot hesitated, trying to process the moment. "I . . . I don't know. It's . . . it's hard enough remembering the students' names." The abbot turned to Matthias. "You don't know his name, do you?"

Matthias thought for a moment, seeing the abbot looking wide-eyed at him.

"I don't know his real name. I've heard him called other things."

"Like?" asked Officer Andrew.

"Like 'Son' and 'Boy,' and maybe there's some other names like that."

"Well that doesn't help much," replied Officer Andrew. "They live in Stumptown with the other niggers?"

"I believe so," answered the abbot.

The officer paused, looked around, and hollered. "We have an accomplice on the loose. Spread out and start searching the grounds. I'll call in a search party to scour every last inch of Stumptown if necessary."

The abbot's eyes locked in on Walter. The young man's face had changed. There was the slightest look of pride, of victory. "Be a shame if a guilty man got away scot-free," he said to the young abbot.

The abbot nodded, looked at Percy's body, at Catherine's body, and back up at Walter.

"One may escape the justice of man, but one will never escape the justice of God."

Chapter 3

The Hermitage

With his arm around Hack's shoulders, Brother Bruno walked him through the long, dark halls of the monastery. Portraits of Benedictine saints stared down at Hack, giving a mixed feeling of comfort and intimidation. The lineage of the old order gave an uneducated outsider like Hack a sense of protection. But he also felt small, foolish, and in the way.

They saw Father Roth standing erect in the hall with arms crossed.

"Where is the abbot?" he demanded of Brother Bruno.

"He went with Officer Andrew."

Father Roth looked down at Hack. "And where are you taking him?"

"To the hermitage."

He huffed through his long, thin nose, closed his eyes, and walked away.

"Don't mind him," Bruno said to the scared boy in his care. "He doesn't like anyone . . . and no one likes him."

At the end of the long hall, they turned left and entered through two great wooden doors that led to the rear of the abbey church. The wooden floors sang out with every step—an impediment to any young monk with an inkling to sneak around under the cover of dark. They passed the sacristy on their left, golden vessels for Mass left out on countertops beside rags and polish, a cleaning job left incomplete. When the bell rang for prayer, a monk dropped what he was doing: whether a spade in the garden, a hoe in the field, a polishing cloth in the sacristy, a pen at one's desk, a book in the library, a knife in the kitchen, an ax at the wood pile, or a conversation in the hall (especially those with an undignified bent).

Straight ahead was the split-entrance behind the high altar, leading to the choir stalls. The wave of monks entering the sanctuary from this direction would part like the Red Sea, some going to their right, others to their left, depending on the location of their stalls. Hack noticed multiple peepholes on the wall between the two entrances, never imagining they were for monks to know when the liturgy had come.

Brother Bruno gave him a tug around the elbow as he passed the choir entrance and turned left again toward a narrow staircase. Bruno paused.

"*Scheisse!*"

Hack gathered this was a curse word in the brother's native language, uttered because of the complete darkness that stared back at them from the first step. Bruno turned quickly and looked around. He found matches, coals, and incense on the stand from which a thurible dangled, but no candle.

"Damn it."

He spun around, his habit spinning through the air with him. The Great Bavarian looked on every shelf and in every cabinet.

"Ha! There you are, you dirty Bolshevik."

Hack had heard of cartridge and votive candles from unloading boxes with his Pa, but he had never heard of a Bolshevik candle.

Brother Bruno struck the match, lit the Bolshevik candle, and down he went into the darkness. Hack followed obediently, though not without fear. At the bottom, they came into an exceedingly long room filled with boxes and crates and fabrics and every sort of miscellaneous item imaginable. Bruno kept leading him through the mess but paused as something caught his eye. He grabbed a dusty lantern made of metal and glass and put the candle in it, throwing more light into the darkness.

At the end of the room was a door flanked by a narrow hallway that led to an exterior door with a small window. A small sense of comfort came to Hack knowing that, if all else failed, he could run down that hall, burst through the door, and be somewhere outside.

But Brother Bruno pulled his attention back to the old wooden door that lay before them. He slowly pushed it open and held the lantern out in front, lighting a small room.

"The hermitage . . ." Brother Bruno said.

Ever since Christ's retreat into the desert for forty days, Christians have been fleeing the world in order to get closer to God. In fourth-century Egypt, tens of thousands of zealous young men and women withdrew from the external noise of Alexandria only to find the internal noise of a restless mind; they fled the fleshy temptations of Alexandria only to find the sharp temptations of the spirit; they hoped to escape the difficulties of the world only to find the more testing toils of the desert; and many thought they left the devil behind in the bars and brothels of urban life only to find the most egregious diabolical assaults known to man in the solitude of a hermitage.

If the lives of the great desert fathers and mothers teach us nothing else, they teach us that the real battle is not fought in the world but in the soul. Paul of Thebes (the first hermit) spent one hundred and seven years alone in the desert trying to conquer the simple flesh that hung on his bones. Anthony of the Desert was plagued by the devil in the form of wild beasts and was beaten so badly by demons that he was believed dead. Saint Jerome, who undertook rather important work, such as translating the entirety of scripture into the Latin Vulgate, was continually distracted by visions of beautiful women dancing around him lustfully. And then there was Mary of Egypt, who dispensed her sexual favors free of charge throughout Alexandra and Jerusalem due to her "insatiable and irrepressible passion" but later fled to the desert as penance and was eventually found naked and so emaciated that she was, according to Saint Zosimas, unrecognizably human. These lives, though extreme, show that hermits shall not find ease in solitude. Peace perhaps, but never ease.

Huts with roofs overhead or caves carved into the side of cliffs could be considered extravagant; the more austere monks might do like Simeon the Stylite (fifth century modern day Syria) who, in an attempt to escape the less disciplined monks in his monastery, dug a hole in the corner of the monastery garden, jumped in it, and stayed there for two years. And yet he was annoyed with the constant interruptions to his prayers. He decided to separate himself further from man so he could be alone with

God, fully exposed to the elements as a way to defeat the longings of the flesh. He built a pillar sixty feet high off the ground, climbed up, and stayed there for forty years.

Other hermits convinced friends and family to wall them up in solitary confinement—sometimes right in the middle of town—to escape the chaos of city life and to be alone with God.

Theologians, philosophers, and doctors will spend the rest of time speculating as to whether these men and women were crazy or holy, or both . . . or if it is even possible to be both. But it seems clear, as the Church has developed through the ages, such austerities have been largely abandoned. Yet, the truth still found in the darkness of these hermits' cells is that solitude—to some extent—is a glorious thing for those called to it. And so, there continues today many partial-hermits—those who live in a monastic community but remain more secluded than the rest. Often, they participate in communal prayer but are spared from the drudgery of common work and are permitted instead to engage in the drudgery of greater solitude, silence, and contemplative prayer.

Such was the case in Good Shepherd Abbey. When the first abbot arrived with five young brothers in 1874, the twenty-five-year-old Brother Gregory, of Americus, Georgia, was among them. Brother Gregory was deemed the architect by process of elimination, merely due to having the most experience working on a farm—as if that had anything to do with constructing a building. The young Gregory read all the books available to him on the subject and learned on the job. He was so successful that, to his chagrin, he was elected abbot in 1881 at a mere thirty-two years of age. Thus, he spent the next forty years saying, "If the damn bell tower would have caved in on us, I would have been spared the torturous eight-year term." For though he was appointed abbot for life, he did the unthinkable and resigned at the age of forty. There was a unanimous voice to deny his resignation. "But I became a monk to be a monk, not an architect, and not an abbot," he continually declared. The monks smiled at his humility but pushed harder still. In what became the stuff of legend, Gregory picked up a walking stick and began swinging it at the electors as they approached him like a mob demanding he continue on. Ancient tradition holds that a disgruntled monk poisoned Saint Benedict's wine due to his continued leadership; rumor holds that a disgruntled monk, out of pure bitterness, poisoned Abbot Gregory's wine due to his resignation.

Nonetheless, when the young Brother Gregory began drawing up the plans for the abbey, he envisioned a small room beneath the choir stalls with the ancient hermitic custom in mind. They had no hermits in those days, nor would one have been permitted; every spare hand was required to quarry the stones forming the foundation and shaping the red North Carolina clay into bricks for the great bell towers. Brother Gregory was indeed a visionary all those years ago, and still was at seventy-six years old.

In the fifty-year history of Good Shepherd, there had never been a permanent hermit, though many monks did temporarily withdraw for forty-day retreats in imitation of our Lord's own forty days spent in the desert. During such forty days, some would go through the long room outside the door, up the circular staircase, and join the community in the choir stalls for the Hours. Others would halt just outside the back wall of the sanctuary and look through the peephole to see their fraters. And still others would stand at the bottom of the circular staircase with a more faint but audible sound traveling down its way. It was said, however, that if one stood close to the stone wall in the hermitage, he could ever so faintly hear the hum of the brothers.

As all brothers thought, there was something beautiful yet eerie about the small cell. And although little Hack could have never known all of this history, he experienced the same sensation as the brothers.

The small room glowed with a yellow hue as Brother Bruno held the lantern out across the threshold. It was not much bigger than a prison cell. The walls, floor, and ceiling were cold gray stone, whatever stones the first monks could cut from the quarry. The back wall was lined with a bookshelf from floor to ceiling and held only a smattering of old leather books. A mattress lay on the floor next to the right wall. There were no blankets or pillow. A wooden stand rested at one end of the mattress with a washing basin, water pitcher, and towel. And a small wooden table with a single chair sat on a rug, a large, black leather book lying at the center, along with a pencil.

Brother Bruno entered first and sat the lantern on the table, but Hack stood quietly at the threshold.

"Come, come, come," Bruno said, waving his hand gently.

Hack entered. He scanned the room and walked over to the wall. He rubbed his hand against the cool stone, feeling the mortar that held them together, feeling the roughness as if the stones had just been cut from the Earth. He walked to the bookshelf and swept his fingers gently across the leather spines, curious as to what was held within. And then he returned to the table in the center of the room. He reached out and touched the large book resting on the table.

"What is this?" he asked Bruno.

"This is where the monks have written about their time in the hermitage."

A sense of wonder distracted Hack from the agonizing feeling of his father's death.

"What's it say?"

"Don't know. You don't get to read it unless you're on a forty-day retreat here. Forty days of silence and Brother Bruno don't go together."

"Why forty days?"

Bruno looked at him with a little smile. "You know the Bible. What took forty days?"

Hack thought back to all those Bible stories his Pa had told him.

"It rained on Noah for forty days. And Moses sat up on that mountain with the Commandments for forty days. Goliath messed with Saul's army for forty days, till little David cut off his head."

"Well, that's more than I knew, but you missed the big one. In the Gospel?"

"Jesus fought the devil in the desert for forty days."

"I'll be darned, Hack. You know your Bible better than most of the monks tucked into bed upstairs and better than any Bavarian ever did."

"Pa told me all the stories," he said, looking away, tearing up, and beginning to breathe heavily.

Bruno pulled the chair out, grabbed Hack by the arm, and sat him down.

"It's okay, Hack. We'll figure something out."

With tears now streaming down his soft black cheeks, Hack said, "He ain't never coming back. Momma ain't never coming back. I gots no one."

And as he did in the abbot's parlor, the Great Bavarian did all he knew to do: he squeezed the boy into his shoulder so tight an onlooker might think Hack would suffocate.

"Hack, that isn't true. You have me. You have Abbot Ambrose. You have Matthias."

Hack pushed back, wiped his face, and said, "Yous gonna keep me here with you?"

Bruno took a deep breath and his eyes opened wide. His cheeks burst out like a man about to explode with uncertainty.

"I don't know. But I can tell you this," and with a humorous tough-guy face, he curled his fist up toward his chest flexing his bicep, "any son-of-a-bitch who tries to hurt you is gonna get every ounce of this German's muscle pounding him senseless."

Hack giggled a little as Bruno began flexing both his arms.

Brother Bruno went over to the mattress on the floor, plopped down, and leaned up against the wall.

"Well, I guess we wait now."

"Brother?"

"Yes?"

"Why are we here?"

And then it hit Bruno: Hack didn't understand the danger he was in.

"For now, ah . . . for now we need to keep you a secret."

"Why?"

Bruno was not sure how to answer. It pained him to not tell Hack the truth. But how could he tell this young boy that he was not hiding from Walter but from the police? How could the truth be so twisted as to turn the victim into the accused? It angered Bruno to no end. And he was desperately curious as to how the conversation was going with the police. He said nothing to Hack's question.

"Brother?"

"Yes?"

"How long am I staying here?"

Chapter 4

Render Unto Caesar

May 22, 1924

One of the most unknown ascetic practices of holy men and women through the ages is far more austere and (some would argue) even more effective than celibacy, fasting, or even self-flagellation: and that is sleep deprivation, extreme forms of which have been a means of torture as long as evil men have been capturing their enemies. But if moderated properly, it can be just enough to calm the body. In one sense, going without sleep has the opposite effect of taking a cold bath; in another, they both cool the passions.

Abbot Ambrose had found that just the right amount of fasting, just the right amount of cold water down one's back in the early morning, and just the right amount of physical fatigue kept one calm during frustrating times—one of many spiritual insights the abbot gleaned from Aristotle's golden mean between extremes.

For Abbot Ambrose, such moderation in sleep was found in rising very early for prayer or fighting his heavy eyes in the evening while he toiled through his correspondence duties. But missing an entire night's sleep? It was, for his temperament and station in life, an extreme. And it brought out the worst in him.

How could any decent man see the bodies of Percy and Catherine and then tuck himself in? How could any man of justice stare into the eyes of Walter Brooks and then close his own and drift into a dreamland? How could any Benedictine abbot have a twelve-year-old boy stowed away in his basement and fluff his own pillow for a good night's sleep?

Of course, the abbot and Mathias returned from the murder scene and visited Hack. Neither of them found much to say other than, "Let's talk in the morning. You need some sleep." And without having to ask him, Brother Bruno insisted on remaining all night in that small wooden chair at that small wooden table so Hack could sleep on the mattress. He asked Matthias for a few books from his cell and a few more candles for the lantern. Matthias retrieved them along with some blankets and a pillow and made Hack's bed for him. They left Brother Bruno and Hack for the night, while the abbot sat in his own cell and kept vigil.

It was now the next morning and Abbot Ambrose knew what must come first. But a paper was handed to him. It was the story of the murders—Walter Brooks' version, that is. The journalist made it a point to call Walter "a hero." And for the sake of all who would read it, Walter lamented, "Just wish I could have done something earlier." The paper emphasized that the police were still looking for the colored boy. They expected that he would be hiding in Stumptown, and they would search every home until he was found.

He put the paper down and continued with his initial plan for the morning. He headed to the abbey and into the choir. As expected, the retired Abbot Gregory sat perfectly still in his stall. Ambrose sat next to him and, as expected, the old man gave no reaction. His eyes remained closed, his breathing faint, neither of which meant he was not prepared to listen.

Ambrose began in a whisper. He told the story as succinctly as he could. On occasion, the old abbot looked over at Ambrose, not so much with astonishment, but with sadness—a sadness for the victims, for Hack, for the unthinkable situation in which Ambrose found himself. Mostly, however, Gregory bowed his head and raised his folded hands to his mouth, praying harder and harder as the story unfolded.

". . . and now, he sits in the hermitage with Bruno, some food, and a checkerboard."

Silence. Then, with the shaky voice of an old man who had said all he ever wished to say on this Earth, Abbot Gregory said, "Follow the system."

"System? What system?"

"The system God has given you."

Ambrose sat quietly, confused.

"The system that every abbot must follow. Call your senior council. Understand their thoughts and concerns. Make sure you fully understand not necessarily what they say," he held up one finger with a chuckle, "but what they are *trying* to say. Then, study the Rule. Make sure you understand what it says and what it is trying to say. And then . . ."

He paused, cleared his throat, tapped Ambrose on the knee, "and then follow the Gospel unapologetically with a healthy disregard for the Rule, for the words of your senior council, and especially my own."

"A healthy disregard? But shouldn't God's message to me come through the Rule and those he places around me?"

"Of course, it should. But it doesn't. And that, my young abbot, is why this," and he waved his hand around the abbey, "is not a democracy. There is one abbot. And it is God's will that you make your own decision."

Ambrose stirred in his seat. "Will you come meet him?"

"Not yet. My role is to pray for you and for him. We will meet soon enough. For now, he needs you to be with him and me to pray for him."

Brother Bruno and Brother Matthias made it a point not to leave Hack alone for even a moment—a dozen games of checkers, a few card games, a lesson in solitaire (an appropriate game to learn for the future).

"What do you like to do?" Matthias asked him, trying to carry on a conversation.

"Don't know. Everything I ever done has been with Pa. I like to go fishing with him. I like to hear his Bible stories. I like to listen to his cowboy flute playing at night."

"Cowboy flute?"

"Harmonica. Pa called it a cowboy flute."

"Ha! I have one of those. Let me go get it."

He stood up, headed for the door, but stopped. He turned and looked at Hack.

"I'm okay."

"I'll hurry," Matthias said excitedly, jogging away, his footsteps ascending the circular staircase.

For the first time, Hack sat alone in the hermitage. He was not afraid, but it was palpable. He had been in plenty of small rooms in his life, sheds and outhouses mostly. But this was different. He looked back at the bookshelf. The black leather journal that originally rested on the table sat squarely in the middle of the top row; it had to make way for the black and red checkerboard and card games. He wondered if he was even capable of reading it. But before he entertained the idea, Brother Matthias returned, smiling and out of breath.

"I like all things musical," he said as he polished the harmonica on his sleeve.

"You play?" Hack asked.

"Well, I've just been learning. I grew up playing piano; then I took up the violin in my novitiate. I've dabbled with a few other instruments. But then," he laughed at himself, "I start thinking that drawing is a higher form of art, so I throw myself into that. And then I see a painting and think *that is drawing at its highest form*, and so I become obsessed with that. And then I realize that words are the most incarnational of all forms of art—just as Christ was the *word* of God—so I wander off into the woods and write as much poetry as I can. And then I realize they are no good . . . and return to the piano." He sighed deeply. "Then, I repeat the cycle all over again."

"What's incarn . . . incarneee"

"Incarnational? Oh. Well. It's when something becomes a body. *Carne* means flesh."

"So how are words incarnaaa . . ."

"I don't rightly know. In one sense, a picture's worth a thousand words. But in another way, words are surged with meaning. You know what Mark Twain says?"

"Who's that?"

"Oh, goodness," Brother Matthias said, shaking his head. "We are gonna fix that. Mark Twain was an author who wrote great books for boys your age. Anyhow, he said, 'The difference between the right word and the almost right word is the difference between lightning and a lightning bug.' Picking just the right word at just the right time is something better than choosing just the right color on a canvas or hitting just the right note on this here harmonica."

He took a breath and began playing "When the saints go marching in."

The sound seemed to take Hack right back to his little house in Stumptown where his Pa would play late into the night. It soothed him like a lullaby does a baby, but he also had to fight back tears.

"Can you play?" Matthias asked, holding it out to Hack.

Hack didn't answer right away but was rather awestruck that a white man was about to share a harmonica with a negro. A child of Jim Crow, Hack had never used a white man's bathroom (until last evening when Bruno took him down the hall to the basement bathroom), never drank from a white man's fountain, never used a white man's anything. He certainly never would have believed that a white man would swap spit on a piece of metal with him.

"You want me to put my mouth on that?" Hack asked sincerely.

"Oh, sorry about that . . ." and wiped it down on his habit sleeve. "That should be better for you."

Before he could give it a single blow, Abbot Ambrose slowly pushed open the door.

"Anybody home?" he said with a smile.

"Is this my new home?" Hack asked innocently.

The abbot's face confessed to his regret for using such a phrase.

"How are you holding up, Hack?"

Hack thought for a moment. "You gonna bury my Pa?"

The question hit the small cell like a thunderbolt. The look that the abbot gave to Matthias bemoaned the fact he had not even considered the subject. And yet, he answered immediately upon gathering himself.

"In the most sacred ground we have."

On most occasions, Brother Bruno would jump at the chance to drive the newly purchased Model-TT truck for the farming operation. He seemed to be the only monk at Good Shepherd who Abbot Ambrose trusted to not wreck the community's newest addition.

But this trip to the police station was not one he looked forward to. It had been less than twenty-four hours since the police embraced Walter Brooks as a hero and cast the most disparaging accusations on one of the kindest men Bruno had ever met this side of the Atlantic.

The unusual silence of Brother Bruno and Abbot Ambrose was impossible to ignore as the thin tires of the top-heavy truck bumped along the dirt road. The abbot looked through the back window at the wooden rails lining the bed of the truck, swaying left and right with every pothole. Blades of straw were flying to and fro, and the smell of the recent pigs unloaded at the abbey farm hung in the air.

"Percy was a real gem," Brother Bruno finally said.

"Indeed. And I can only assume Catherine was too. I'm sure her parents will do her justice. But we must do so unto Percy."

"You know I don't like coming here," Bruno added.

"It's been a few months." A small smile crept on the abbot's face. "I'm sure things have settled."

Brother Bruno let out a grunt.

Upon arriving, the two monks conspicuously entered the police station with a dozen or so pairs of eyes locked upon them.

"The lion's den," snarled Bruno.

"Behave. I mean it," the abbot said with an all-too-serious tone.

In many respects, Bruno's analogy was right. The police station was a den, not of lions, but of Klansmen. And in that year of 1924, the Klan had reached a fever pitch of aggression against negros, Jews, and Catholics. Early in the year, the political stardom of New York's governor, Al Smith—a Roman Catholic—as the potential Democratic presidential candidate, was met by the Ku Klux Klan with a nationwide protest and threats of violence. The ripple effect for southern Catholics was palpable. It was not a good year to be Catholic living in a hotbed of Klansmen. Prudence dictated, therefore, that the abbot tread lightly across the threshold of the police station.

The abbot stepped toward the receptionist and politely asked to see Officer Andrew.

"Brother Bruno," she said with a tilt of the head. "Fancy seeing you again. Third time this year?"

He said nothing but gazed off into the distance as if he couldn't hear her. She chuckled to herself, stood, and walked away, returning a moment later with Officer Andrew.

"Good afternoon, Abbot . . . Bruno . . ." He shook both their hands. "Back so soon?" the officer said patting Bruno on the back with a hard smack. Bruno grunted.

"He hasn't been to the pub in months," the abbot said. "And he is learning to control that temper like a good little monk."

"Little!" the officer burst out with laughter. "The poor bastard he threw through the window was little. He," he said pointing to Bruno, "ain't little."

"And the name-calling bastard wasn't that little either," Bruno defensively added as a matter of honor. "If he was an anti-Catholic shrimp, I wouldn't have wasted my time. But he was stocky. He had some meat on him. Fair fight."

Officer Andrew glared at him. "If you gonna fight every anti-Catholic in this town, you gonna be fighting a long time."

Bruno exhaled through his nose so hard that the papers slightly blew up from the officer's desk.

"Officer," the abbot said before the conversation went off the tracks, "we are here for an important matter."

"Found the boy?" the officer asked, leaning in toward them with a level of excitement.

The abbot shook his head with sufficient ambiguity to ease his conscience. "We would like to request Percy's body for Christian burial."

The officer squinted with near disgust. "You can't be serious."

"Dead serious," Bruno shot out.

The abbot raised his hand to keep the Great Bavarian quiet.

"I repeat: We would like to request Percy's body for Christian burial."

Officer Andrew shook his head and tapped his pencil on his desk.

"Don't know why you'd want to pollute your holy ground with a raping nigger."

And the abbot's hand again arose, but this time at Officer Andrew.

"Please, the language. And please . . . the body?"

A long silence followed as the officer considered the request. He shook his head in disgust and took a deep breath. "Fine." He made a note on a pad with his pencil. "You can have it. I'll have the morgue send it over."

The abbot stood up and extended his hand across the desk. "We'll get out of your hair now. Thank you, Officer Andrew."

"Wait a minute," Officer Andrew said. "Take this." He pulled a small plastic bag out of his desk drawer and threw it on the table. Inside, a harmonica.

"Personal belongings. Get that nigger saliva out of my office."

The abbot took the bag. "Thank you," he said, and left the station as quickly as possible.

Immediately following Vespers, the senior council convened. The prior, Father Vincent Roth, choleric by nature, would crack the whip without a moment's notice. Father Roth had worked hard and succeeded at getting his protégé, Father Henry, as his sub-prior: two taskmasters of the same temperament, which meant that all was well when they were of a harmonious mind, but a blood bath might ensue if disharmony arose. The melancholic artist, Brother Matthias, was perfect in the porter's position, for though he was often lost in dramatic thought, he was intellectually curious about every visitor, which in turn creates a rather intriguing conversationalist—an important skill for he who deals with various guests coming to and from the abbey. The sanguine Father John was novice master, perhaps too friendly for such a job. In keeping with his temperament, he could befriend a newcomer faster than anyone, but far too easily drifted from his duties, leaving novices ill-formed. And to balance the group, Abbot Ambrose presided with phlegmatic personality.

Most people, however, would be surprised to call the abbot phlegmatic. After all, he carried such gravitas with him everywhere he went. As a child, as a novice, and even as a young fully professed monk, he went largely unnoticed. His performance on any assigned task would be exemplary, but given that he never touted his accomplishment, others barely knew his name. His ability to focus on a problem surpassed all others. And his natural ability to let the words and actions of others roll off his shoulder was in large part due to this God-given natural disposition. It was, in fact, this quiet introversion, coupled with spiritual zeal for God's will, that enabled him to do what many choleric, melancholic, and sanguine personalities are surprisingly unable to do: he spoke directly with truth and charity. A phlegmatic leader, to the unbelief of many, can be a superb leader. The choleric too often relies on his brute force, the sanguine on his people skills, and the melancholic on his deep-seated inner passion and brilliance. The phlegmatic, however, relies on simple and direct truths without bluster, drama, or overthinking.

Perhaps more than anywhere, a Benedictine community is the perfect environment for this particular temperament to flourish. The phlegmatic, after all, is seen as the most *monkish*. And yet every coin has two sides. One of the many negative aspects of this God-given temperament is that the cholerics in the room tend to see the phlegmatic as easy prey.

Ambrose had not been in the abbot's seat long. And the community was already murmuring (which is strictly prohibited by the Rule) about whether the prior would ever *let* the abbot be the abbot. Thus, while Abbot Ambrose valued Father Roth's experience, he kept his guard up and his eyes open—yet again, an ability uniquely present in the soul of a phlegmatic.

"What's he doing here?" Father Roth asked of Brother Bruno, as if he wasn't within ear shot.

"I have asked Brother Bruno to join us as Hack's temporary caretaker. What we say here concerns him more than any of us."

Father Roth's face showed disapproval, but he saved his energy for more notable battles.

The abbot began: "We all know the story. I see no need to repeat the heinous events of last night. But a pressing matter is upon us. Brother Bruno and Brother Matthias's report is in direct conflict with the incredible story Walter Brooks has told to all who would listen. It is a story spewed forth directly from the Father of Lies. It condemns the memory of a fine man, contaminates the truth of Catherine's death, and puts Hack's life in jeopardy. The police are looking for him right this minute all through Stumptown.

"His word would be nothing against that of a Brooks. Hack's best scenario would be life in jail despite being a minor. But we also know that he would most likely never get to a trial. I wouldn't put it past the Klan to beat him, even kill him. They're holding more rallies than ever, especially with Al Smith in the running. Sometimes I think they are just bored and want to take it out on someone. In short, the justice system isn't *just* in such matters. How could we, in good faith, hand him over?"

"But what option do we have?" asked Father Henry.

"We could keep him here for a while. And then get him out of Dodge to a safe location."

"You can't be serious!" exclaimed Father Henry. "This is no place for a boy. And we Catholics in a Protestant town are in no place to defy civic law."

The room was quiet for a moment.

"We shall rely on the Rule, shall we not, Abbot?" Father Roth shrewdly asked.

"Most likely," replied the abbot.

Another headshake from the prior.

"First off, the Rule calls in Chapter 3 for the abbot to call his brothers in for counsel, which I am doing now."

"Yes, yes, and good for you." Father Roth's patronizing tone was not lost on anyone. "But rather than any kind of analysis of the Rule, you must recognize the *a priori* fact that the Rule is for monks, not for negro boys in the basement. The Rule is made to protect our community from disruption within and without these walls. Granting asylum to this child is a perilous disruption to our way of life . . . to our very security."

"Father Roth," the abbot replied, "Chapters 30 and 37 are dedicated to dealing with children in the community. And 59 is specifically about receiving children into the monastery. This would not be the first time a monastery welcomed in the young, particularly those in distress."

"Isn't the issue even more basic?" asked Brother Bruno. "Chapter 53: *Let all guests who come to the Monastery be welcomed like Christ Himself.*"

"And the same chapter says," Father Roth interjected, "that *by no means let anyone mix with or speak to the guest.* The reason is obvious: the abbot must preserve the community, even if that means turning away a guest. Guests are only permitted to the extent they do not disturb our sacred way of life."

"Chapter 5: *unhesitating obedience* to whatever the abbot decides," Brother Bruno spat across the room.

"The spirit of that passage adds *in all things lawful!*" the prior yelled. "For as Saint Augustine rightly said, *An unjust law is no law at all.* We aren't Germans; we do not follow the barbarian commander blindly."

The room stirred for a moment. How much of that was directed at the Great Bavarian or at the abbot himself?

Father Roth calmed himself, but the tension he spread through the room was palpable. He whispered through his clenched teeth: "This Rule has worked for nearly fifteen hundred years. Why? Because we shut out the evils of the world. Just as our forefathers escaped to the desert, we must escape behind these walls. The Rule is the path to peace, and we break it at our peril."

"Charity is the path to peace," Abbot Ambrose said calmly, directly.

Father Roth slid down in his chair, looked up, and shook his head at the ceiling with a small laugh. "What a nice sentiment, my young Abbot. You see, experience will teach you that throwing that word *charity* around like a ragdoll gives a sense of comfort to the one who uses it. And yet, it does little practical good. The father of a family can say the word *Charity! Charity! Charity!* But does it put bread on the table for his hungry children? A missionary can learn the word for charity in every backward jungle that the heathens populate, but does it teach them how to give up their evil ways? And an abbot can preach charity from the pulpit every day, but does it keep the wheels turning so this great legacy of the Church continues on?"

"What about Christ?" asked Brother Bruno. "If we are supposed to welcome all as Christ, why would we not welcome Hack? Hack will be locked in prison or perhaps killed. Would you allow that to happen to Christ?"

"An unfair comparison!" spat Father Henry. "We're talking about a negro boy."

"And why don't you explain why being a negro matters in this situation?" Bruno asked Henry, leaning forward. "We all know your opinion of them."

Father Henry looked away, shook his head, and changed the subject. "He could be guilty, you know."

"How on Earth could a twelve-year-old be guilty in this situation?" said Abbot Ambrose with disbelief.

"He could have held her down, just as Walter reported," Henry replied.

"Well, he didn't!" the abbot demanded.

"Forgive me, Abbot. But how do you know? Why would you take the word of a negro over that of respected young man who will be a great leader of this town and, I might add, a great patron of this monastery one day."

"I just know it. I know it like I know the sun set last night. And I know it because Bruno and Matthias saw the crime scene before Walter altered it for his own benefit. Percy and Hack are the heroes; Walter is the monster."

The young sub-prior had seen that he pushed his luck with the abbot and reluctantly withdrew his case. But the prior, with his age and experience fueling his audacity, continued on: "You have been abbot a few short months. Divine inspiration usually takes longer to descend upon the holiest of men. You should claim certitude sparingly, my young Abbot, lest the community opine that your head has grown too big for your miter."

Abbot Ambrose gave him a long stare, recognizing the veiled threat from the prior's words. No one said anything, but it was apparent in the abbot's eyes that his mind had not yet changed.

"Perhaps," Father Roth continued, "we should ask the boy if he would like the right to defend his father's honor?"

"That's bullshit and you know it!" Brother Bruno yelled.

"You know that isn't fair, Father," Brother Matthias calmly added.

"Of course he would opt for that," said the abbot. "But that's the whole point: I want to protect him because he has no way to protect himself. He's too young, too helpless, has neither family nor friends, nor ability to maneuver through this impossible situation."

Father Roth gave a sly smile, shrugged his shoulders, and asked, "Why not vote on it in general assembly?"

"You know what the results of that will be," replied Abbot Ambrose.

"And doesn't that tell us something?" asked Father Henry.

"More importantly," said Father Roth, "does not the Holy Spirit work through our collective mind?"

"Excuse me," said Brother Matthias, "but doesn't the Rule indicate that most decisions are too complex for the entire community and therefore must be reserved for the abbot alone?"

Father Roth sneered at the young brother.

"Unhesitating obedience . . ." repeated Brother Bruno.

"In only that which is lawful," said Father Roth.

"Are you saying, Father Roth, that if I were to protect this young boy behind our walls from a racist and violent society that I would be acting unlawfully? As we said earlier, Chapter 59 talks directly about taking boys into the monastery," said Abbot Ambrose.

"Not in direct defiance of civil law," replied Father Roth.

"You yourself have emphasized that an unjust law is no law at all."

"There is nothing unjust in questioning a boy who was present at a murder. The state has the right to do so."

"But more importantly than the civil law or the Rule is . . ."

"I'm sorry Abbot: Did you just say more important than the Rule?"

"Yes, Father. I did. More important than the Rule are the words of Jesus Himself: *What you do to the least of these, you do unto Me.*"

"If you want to use the words of our Lord as an excuse to escape your duties, then you ought to cogitate on another of His teachings."

"Which is?"

"*Render unto Caesar what is Caesar's, and unto God what is God's.*" Father Roth sat up and leaned toward his abbot. "A Christian ought to never dismiss the power of the state. Even Christ said to Pilate that his Roman authority was given to him from above. He did not say his authority came from below. Yes, that is right: God the Father gave Pontius Pilate the power to crucify His Son. It was not the devil who gave this power. And it was not the devil who made Caesar emperor who in turn gave Pilate his authority. It was the Father of Jesus Christ. And thus, throughout all the ages and all of Christendom, the Divine Right of Kings has been a doctrine of Holy Mother Church.

"Let us not forget, my brothers, that if it were not for strong state authority, Constantine would have been unable to legalize Christianity, and we would still be celebrating Mass in the catacombs. And what was the turning point in our two-thousand-year history? Was it something a lonely bishop did? Was it some great saint being charitable here and there? No! It was when Constantine called the Council of Nicaea. It was a layman—an emperor in fact—who put our Church on the path to greatness. It was this statesman who knew that the Church was on the brink of at least division and perhaps collapse. The holy saints of the time could not even agree on whether Christ was fully human and divine! *Homoousia* or *Homoiousia* . . . Ha! We'd still be putting people to death over the one *iota*. St. Athanasius of Alexandria may have been right; he may have been a great saint, but he was a great saint who was losing terribly. The tide had turned completely against him. The vast majority of Christians were no longer Christians but Arians. Does this not teach us a simple truth? Being right and being holy are not enough. You must be strong.

"We would all be Arians rather than Christians if not for the strong hand of a mighty ruler. God used the power of the state to settle the issue once and for all. Imagine if the bishops pushed Constantine aside and said, 'Charity will solve all issues. All we must do is follow the Gospel.' If it were that simple, Athanasius would have never needed Constantine.

"And what about the Nicene Creed? We might well call it the Creed of Constantine, for without that great man, we would be nothing but desert monks bickering over one proposition of dogma over another. Or we would still be treating Clement of Rome's Letters as part of Sacred Canon. We churchmen could not even get the Bible together! We required the strong hand of the state.

"My brothers, this is not merely due to clerical squabble. It is due to God's divine providence wishing to harmonize the Church and state. If you ever desire for the kingdom of God to return to this Earth, as it was here with King David, as it was here with the Holy Roman emperors, if you desire to ever see again the holy pontiff place the crown on an emperor's head, then you must begin by seeing the state as a vessel of God's justice rather than an enemy to keep at bay.

"It is for all these reasons, my brothers, that Christ said, 'Render unto Caesar what is Caesar's.' It is so that God will once again build his heavenly kingdom on Earth. And if a few injustices must be suffered as a means to this end, so be it."

A deafening silence filled the room. Eyes darted back and forth, waiting for reaction from others.

After Father Roth allowed his words to sink in, he added a final point, as if settling the issue once and for all. "Do not trouble yourself anymore with this issue, my brothers. Hand the boy over to those who God has appointed as the head of state and return back to work in God's great vineyard. The negro boy, my brothers, belongs to Caesar."

Father Roth leaned back in his chair and folded his hands as if he were a great litigator who just rested his case. And the jury seemed to be out; everyone sat perfectly still and quiet, for everyone knew the next word belonged to one man and one man only.

Abbot Ambrose took a deep breath and said with a calm resolution, one that made it clear to everyone that the issue was over: "Not today, he doesn't. And I remind all of you: this abbey is not a democracy."

He stood to indicate the council was over but added one last thing. "I command each of you to holy obedience: you will not breathe a word about Hack's presence to anyone who does not already know. If you do, I solemnly swear to you: you will impinge your own soul with your own tongue."

As he walked out of the room, he remembered something that Abbot Gregory told him upon his appointment: *True abbots are not elected: they are self-made out of necessity.*

It was then that Abbot Ambrose realized he was truly abbot.

Father Roth's Journal

May 22, 1924

I hope the community is seeing the colossal mistake they made with Ambrose. So idealistic. Totally naive. Lying to the authorities; hiding a negro boy in the basement; dismissing the Rule as if it's nothing more than a book of suggestions by a man who has been dead for 1,500 years.

If I had been elected . . . well . . . what's the point now?

But when the Lord closes a door, He opens a window.

There is still Henry. He has the pedigree. He has the temperament. And he actually takes stock in my advice. A true monk. A true Benedictine.

The Lord is merciful indeed. His plan may well be for Ambrose's sanctimonious hubris to be a teaching moment for the entire community. If the authorities discover the boy, they might well hold Ambrose responsible. A vote of no-confidence and removal from office would be expected, whether or not Ambrose is locked up.

The Lord works in mysterious ways.

Father Henry's Journal

May 22, 1924

I can appreciate the abbot's motives, but this is just not worth it. Actually, the more I consider them, the more I question them.

The world has dividing lines . . . and for good reasons. The rich do not usually mingle with the poor; religious do not usually mingle with non-religious; whites do not mingle with negros.

The more I think of it, the more I see it as the God-given natural order of things: you don't find lions sharing dens with bears or whales swimming in schools with sharks. Or what would the abbot think of sharing our monastery with Mohammadans, Jews, Buddhists? Nonsense.

People should not have to apologize for sticking with their own kind. It is the way God made the cosmos.

Furthermore, why do people take such offense at the notion that God has graced different races with different capacities? Archeologists are showing that modern man is much taller than ancient man. Are both myself and Abraham sons of God even though I am a good deal taller? And our African brethren? God has given them gifts he has not given to us. They have been graced with those physical abilities to survive the wildness of Africa. This is a gift from Almighty God. They can run and jump and carry a heavy load. Even their skin is God-made natural protection against the sun.

It is not uncharitable to say that they lack our mental capacity. It is, on the contrary, uncharitable to hold them to our standards! Every day there are fewer and fewer people willing to discuss the obvious truths. And if I utter one word . . . Bigot!

Even monks are giving up intellectual honesty for the sake of faux charity. Make no mistake about it: it is this false sense of altruism—a false sense of being compassionate—that hides the boy in the basement.

I will do my duties. I will obey the direct orders of my abbot—whomever that may be—but I will not indulge this nonsense, even if it reflects poorly upon myself before the eyes of the community.

Chapter 5

Jesus Wept

May 23, 1924

Nearly every night since his election, Abbot Ambrose walked the floors. He followed no particular order or pattern; rather, he meandered about like the fresh breath of God blowing where it wills. It was not only his favorite time but also, he believed, his most productive.

During these long walks, the abbot routinely reflected on a peculiar truth: that the external appearance of order often veiled the inner reality of disorder. Certain people, for example, who placed order and structure above other virtues were often compensating for certain disorders. Said another way, those whose souls were adrift—aimlessly searching for peace and security—all too often govern their external world with a relentless demand of cleanliness, organization, routine. It is as if these sad souls have nothing permanent to grasp and, therefore, grasp only the most fleeting of things, like chores and schedules and a certitude of what comes next.

And in the first few months of the abbot's governance, he noticed the inverse to be true on more than one occasion. Those monks whom the prior would admonish for being unkempt, tardy, lax, or in his words, *wayward*, were often the most kind, pleasant, empathetic, and passionate of all. Was not the same dynamic seen with Mary and Martha? It was the productive woman who was admonished by Christ. (And yet, it was a favorite saying of old Abbot Gregory's, with tongue in cheek, to say *The Gospel might have read differently if Jesus had been hungry.*)

Was it the case, the abbot wondered, that those inclined toward the spiritual world were not as concerned with the material world? Or was it the other way around? Was it that those who lacked a certain worldly proficiency gravitated by default to those things which were not so easily judged by a twelve-inch ruler? The abbot remembered as a schoolboy, noticing how the less popular kids were the nicest of the bunch. He noticed that those who struggled to fit into society were more inclined to a religious vocation. Who then, he asked himself, would ever want their son or daughter to be the life of the party? On the other hand, is there any moral merit in embracing God only after being shunned by the world? And does the most merit go to he or she who embraces God despite the world lifting them up on a pedestal? Which came first: the chicken or the egg?

The abbot's meandering may have been physically aimless, but it was not spiritually so. Rather, there was a great and specific purpose to it. The pressures of the day were gone. The chaos and conflict had been laid to rest. But more importantly, the silence and solitude reminded him that despite whatever problems had occurred, a fine day of work had been accomplished in the name of the Lord. The workers in the vineyard had done their best, and they would try even harder in the morning.

He thought better at this time of night, particularly as he strolled down the hall with his hands crossed behind his back. Only the sound of his own footfall could be heard. In the silence and tranquility of the halls, he could sense the presence of God filling every crack and crevice of the brick walls and stone floors, as if divinity was the very mortar that held everything together.

During these strolls, he would pass by the cells of his brothers, brothers of differing ages and differing duties and differing styles of piety. Some would be reading, some would be writing letters, some would be praying, and some would already be entering a dream. He would sometimes pause and give a sweeping motion with his two fingers and thumb, like a father who makes the smallest sign of the cross on his sleeping baby's forehead. (The monks knew, however, that someone—presumably the abbot—routinely stopped before their door. Not only could one hear everything in this abbey, but the abbot's shadow would break the subtle light that came beneath the door.)

The abbot prayed for wholesome dreams to descend upon his monks. He knew that the deepest regions of the mind, with any of its unresolved attachments to the world, could percolate up to the gray area between the conscious and unconscious during the night. The abbot also knew that God had used dreams throughout all of salvation history to deliver a message, to communicate His will, and to move the waking man away from evil and toward the good.

Just as God impressed chastity on the sleeping mind of Abimelech, warning him not to sleep with Abraham's wife, the abbot prayed for the Lord to bring a chaste mind to his monks; just as God showed Jacob a ladder to heaven, the abbot prayed for the Lord to reveal the ascetic life as rungs unto paradise; just as God gave the young Joseph a glimpse of his great destiny under the guise of eleven sheaf bowing before one, the abbot asked the Lord to reveal His providence to each monk; just as Solomon asked for wisdom before all else during his encounter with God in the depths of sleep, the abbot prayed that his monks would be so wise as to ask God for wisdom; and just as an Angel told Joseph to take Mary as his wife during the most important dream in all of human history, the abbot asked the Lord to send His heavenly messengers down upon the abbey, giving comfort and hope to all those who desired to do His will.

But not all dreams were pleasant.

Just as Pilate's wife had a nightmare about Jesus's trial, the abbot asked the Lord to communicate grave truths to his monks even if through dark and foreboding dreams.

So many different monks—seventy-three in all. From the newest novices to those at the threshold of death, from the most deviant to the most obedient, from Father Roth to Abbot Gregory, every last one was in his charge. And now, so too was a young boy in the hermitage below.

Thus, tonight's stroll through the lonely halls of Good Shepherd was not to bless each monk or to pray for wholesome dreams, nor was the abbot alone—thank God. Tonight, Abbot Ambrose, accompanied by

Brother Matthias, made his way through the monastery, down the spiral staircase, and through the long dark hall to the hermitage.

Brother Matthias reached out to turn the knob, but Abbot Ambrose stopped him with the lifting of his finger. Instead, out of respect for their new resident, Abbot Ambrose gave a gentle tap on the door.

"Come in," the young voice said.

The abbot entered first, followed by Brother Matthias. They found Hack sitting at the table alone, playing solitaire with his deck of cards. He looked up at the approaching monks but said nothing.

"Good evening, Hack," the abbot began. "I'm sorry it's so late."

"It's all right. Brother Bruno just left. We've played as much checkers and cards as he can stand."

The abbot sat at the second chair that Brother Bruno had at some point in the day placed at the table. Brother Matthias gladly stood next to the wall, giving preference to the abbot's lead in the conversation. As the abbot sat down, he noticed the harmonica on the corner of the table.

"You play?" the abbot asked.

"Not much. Brother Matthias let me borrow it."

Both Hack and the abbot looked up at Brother Matthias with appreciation.

"The cowboy flute, as Hack calls it. And he's getting there," Matthias said. "In no time at all he'll be filling these halls with joyful song."

"Well, maybe he should practice with this one instead." The abbot pulled out Percy's harmonica and handed it to Hack.

"It's Pa's!" Hack said with wide, excited eyes.

"It's yours now, son."

"How'd you get it?" Hack asked as he reverently took it into his hands.

"It was recovered . . . from his pocket."

It was a difficult thing to say, a difficult thing to hear, but a beautiful gift for Hack to receive. If there was one thing that reminded Hack of his Pa more than anything else, it was his cowboy flute.

As Hack looked down affectionately at the harmonica, the abbot said, "Hack, the senior council has just approved you staying here until we find a nice place for you to go."

Hack looked disconcertedly at the abbot. "Aren't you the boss?"

"The boss? Well, yes, I suppose so."

"Then why's it matter a hill of beans what some council says?"

"Well, Hack, a monastery is a community. And the abbot, the boss, should take advice from certain monks to make the best decision."

"What if they're wrong?" The question lacked any pretense. In fact, its innocence rang out through the air like the echo of a church bell.

The abbot leaned forward as if with a contrived measure of strength: "Then the boss makes the right call, no matter what they say."

Hack nodded, as if granting his approval to the words of Saint Benedict himself.

"Guess you wouldn't be the boss no ways if you can't tell them to pound sand."

The abbot looked to his side at the young porter, arms crossed, trying to rub the smile off his face.

"Look here, Hack," the abbot said, getting back on track. "Do you have some family around here?"

"Ma died from that flu from Spain. I ain't got no grandma or grandpa. It's just . . . or it was just me and Pa." He looked away, as if the stone walls had something to tell him.

"You see, Hack . . ." The abbot paused and regrouped. "You see . . . the police are looking for you."

Hack looked up excitedly. "Did they catch Walter?"

The question nearly knocked the wind out of the abbot. He turned to Brother Matthias and saw a tear welling up.

"No, son," the abbot said. "You see, Walter told them a horrible lie. He told them that he found your Pa hurting the girl. He told them that he tried to fight your Pa off of her. And that he killed your Pa while trying to save her."

"That ain't true!" Hack stood up so fast that the wooden chair behind him flipped over. He slammed his fist down upon the table. "I saw it, Abbot. Pa tried to save that girl. He was gentle with her, like he was with everyone. He threw that boy off like he was nothing, and the boy grabbed a brick and hit him for nothing. And then he choked that girl hard and she died . . . I saws it all. And then he chase me and . . ."

The abbot put up his hands, calming him. "Hack. Hack. I know, son. I know." He waved him down back into his chair. "I know Walter is lying."

"Then why the coppers want me?"

It was a fair question.

"Because, son, Walter says that you were helping your Pa hurt that girl."

Hack slid down in his chair. His eyes drifted down as if a little bit of his innocence had been stripped from him right then and there. His mind turned, trying to put together the crude idea that others already had in theirs.

The abbot continued: "He said that he found you holding down her arms."

Hack didn't say a word. He looked like a child being asked to think through a long equation. It was not only the offensive notion that struck him but also the complexity of the idea that was nearly too much for him to fathom. But slowly, reality returned to him. He realized why he had been hiding away in the hermitage.

"This whole time, I been thinking I was hiding from Walter."

"I know, son. I'm sorry."

"If they get me," Hack said with a degree of confidence, "they gonna hurt me. The way the Klan hurts some coloreds."

"Maybe, son. I don't know. But we are going to keep you safe."

Hack nodded with a look of resignation.

"Look, Hack, we are going to find you a great place to live. I promise."

"Why?"

"Because you can't live here in a monastery."

"Why?"

"This is no place for a boy."

"Why not?"

"Why do you ask so many questions?" the abbot said with a little smile, welcoming any moment to lighten the mood.

"Because you ain't giving me a real answer."

The abbot was astonished yet again at the boy's ability to speak directly without a hint of offense or impropriety. He wished his monks were capable of such communication.

"This is a monastery. We don't have what it takes to raise a child."

"What's it take to raise a child?"

The abbot looked again at Brother Matthias, who shrugged his shoulders. They were both stumped.

"Well, I'm not exactly sure . . . which, come to think of it, is exactly the point."

Hack remained silent, but somewhat accepting of the abbot's logic. It appeared to the abbot as if the subject could be changed. He looked around the room.

"Can I get you anything?"

"I don't know," Hack replied.

"What did you do at home, for fun?"

"Listened to Pa play harmonica. Play checkers and cards. He'd read the Bible to me."

"What parts of the Bible?"

"The Psalms mostly. The book of Job . . . said it was his favorite book. The Gospels . . ."

"Did you do school?"

"He made me memorize some of the Psalms. Is that school?"

"Of sorts. Of a rather important sort. Did you learn to read?"

"A little. Not smart-like."

"Brother," the abbot said, turning back to Matthias, "I want you to hunt up some children's books, ones with lots of pictures. Get them down here first thing."

"Yes, Abbot," Matthias replied.

Hack's eyes lit up a little as he leaned forward.

"Can you teach me?" he asked the abbot.

"Me? Oh, well. I can get someone to teach you."

"Who's that?"

After saying goodnight to both Hack and Brother Matthias, the abbot began one of his late-night meanderings through the halls. He had much more on his mind than the sweet dreams of his brothers. *Who will I get to teach him to read? Surely, Bruno or Matthias.* But just as those names came to mind, he found that his aimless wanderings had brought him to a cell with the light still breaking forth into the hall from beneath the door. Whoever it was, he was most certainly awake, for stirring of sorts could be heard. The abbot looked about to get his bearings, saw what hall he was on and what door he was standing beside. It was Father Henry's. *Of course*, the abbot thought. The Shakespearian scholar? The most literate man in the abbey? The sub-prior? An ideal candidate, except for the glaring fact that Father Henry was known as the most inhospitable to those of color.

This was not the first time that the abbot found himself standing before something that seemed to make no sense. He felt drawn to knock, nonetheless. The abbot was not the sort to divinize every whimsical act that nature took through the day. When the kettle sang, it was not *per se* from divine intervention; rather, God made the laws of physics and made sure that the laws of physics pertained to that particular kettle and that particular water at that particular time. When the Spanish flu of '18 swept through town, the abbot did not see it *per se* as a curse from the Lord for the sin of infidelity; rather, he saw a virus spread as they were designed to spread and lack of sanitization reaping its own nasty reward. Perhaps he had just happened to meander up to Father Henry's door, and perhaps Father Henry just happened to be fiddling around in his cell long past the time everyone else had retired.

Or, perhaps the Lord knew years ago that Abbot Ambrose would at that particular moment wander aimlessly through that particular hall and stop at that particular door, and thus made sure to have the prior assign the then-young Brother Henry to that particular room. And perhaps the Lord conditioned Henry's workload as sub-prior to ensure that this particular night he would have to stay up and organize his papers or straighten out his books, or whatever he was doing to cause the noise which communicated *Do not hesitate to knock, for I am awake.*

Whether by chance or by a magnificently devised divine algorithm, Abbot Ambrose concluded that it was suitable to knock on the door.

"Enter," a surprised voice rang out.

"Abbot!"

Father Henry leapt off the floor where he was organizing files.

"Please, stay where you are. May I have a minute?"

"Of course. Please, have a seat." He pulled his chair out for his abbot and sat on the edge of his bed.

"Excuse my mess, Abbot . . . I was . . ."

"Oh no, Father. Excuse my intrusion at this hour. But I do have a question for you."

"By all means."

"Weren't you a schoolteacher?"

"Why, yes. When I was a very young man, right out of college."

"And how did you like it? You know . . . teaching children. I know you are rather used to college students these days."

Henry thought back. "The good students, I enjoyed. But the jokesters or those slow ones, not so much. Why do you ask?"

The abbot cleared his throat.

"I was thinking that until we find a good home for Hack, you might, if you have the time, of course, teach him each day, help him with his reading, whatever you are able to pass along."

Father Henry's eyes went lifeless. "You can't be serious."

"I'm very serious. The boy is so bored down there. Bruno and Matthias are doing all they can, but . . ."

"Then why can't they teach him if they like him so much?"

"Perhaps they could. But I'm sure your experience would expedite the process. After all, we might not have much time. Maybe just a few weeks or so."

Henry looked away with frustration, gathered himself, and spoke directly to his abbot.

"Excuse me, Abbot, but as I just said, I did not take great enjoyment in teaching the slow children."

"He seems quite witty to me. His mind is sharp, Father. Don't kid yourself."

"But really, Abbot, what potential do they have? Why not use the time to teach him something useful for his type. Perhaps blacksmithing . . . carpentry . . . farming . . ."

"If you were a blacksmith or carpenter or farmer, would you like to read on the side?"

"Of course I would, but . . ."

"And we shall do unto others as we wish them to do unto us?"

Henry stared, having a sense that he would lose this battle to his abbot, no matter the logical argument set forth.

"I will not order you to do this. I ask you, not as your abbot, but as your friend."

Henry sighed, nodded. "For you . . . but with little or no hope in the outcome. Besides, he won't be here long. Right?"

"I will do everything in my power to find him the perfect home. I give you my word."

Father Henry's Journal

May 23, 1924

A PhD in Shakespeare, and now you are teaching a negro in the basement how to read. . . . What ever became of you?

May 24, 1924

With the perfect silence of his cell, the monks' early morning chant descended through the ceiling, down the wall, and came to rest right next to his head lying peacefully on the mattress. While the stone wall was cold, the chant seemed to radiate heat coming forth as God's supernatural method of awakening one from slumber. Even the greatest kings throughout all of history would not have imagined having seventy monks stand outside the royal sleeping chamber, chanting along with the rising sun.

It was, however, in perfect keeping with divine preference: Moses with a stammer was chosen as the mouthpiece of God to bring down the pride of pharaoh; a shepherd boy was chosen to bring down the great Goliath; a meaningless little girl in a meaningless little town was chosen to become the living Tabernacle of the God-Man; and now a meaningless little boy was awoken in more beautiful a fashion than any royalty could envision for his regal self. Truly, God shall humble the proud in their conceit and lift up the lowly.

Hack's eyes fluttered open with comfort and ease: the third day of God's new creation in his young life. He arose, lit a few lanterns, straightened up his blankets and pillows, drank some water, splashed his face over the basin, and put on the clean pair of clothes that Bruno had somehow found for him the day before.

Familiar footsteps approached. Hack was already learning the difference.

"Morning, Brother Matthias," he said before the door was knocked upon.

"How'd you know it was me?" the young brother asked as he pushed the door open.

"Everyone's feet are different."

With one hand, Matthias slightly pulled up his habit and took a peek at the black sandals he wore and shrugged his shoulders. In his other, he held a stack of books, which he placed on the table.

"I come bearing housewarming gifts."

Hack grabbed one off the top and gazed at the cover.

"Mc . . . Guffey's . . . Reader."

"I found it early this morning in the library. These are primers, which means they help you learn to read. That one in your hand there, it's called a primer." He pointed to the cover.

Hack was already thumbing through.

Matthias tapped the second volume. "This might be your level. If you could read the cover of the primer, you might be beyond it."

Hack made no reply but continued to gaze at the first volume in wonder.

Matthias sat quietly for a minute, watching Hack's lips move silently as he flipped to random pages, testing himself.

"Well, I guess I'll excuse myself and let you enjoy your new companions."

Hack didn't look up.

"I will come back before lunch to visit."

Still, he didn't look up.

And so, he headed for the door and passed through it. But just before he closed it, he heard a small voice mumble, "Thank you so much, Brother. So much . . ."

Not long after, Brother Bruno made his morning visit and found Hack poring through the McGuffey Readers. And after failing to elicit any meaningful response with his deck of cards, Bruno said, "I'm not going to sit and watch you read. You want to play cards or not?"

"Sorry, Brother." Hack finally set the book down.

Halfway through their first game of Gin Rummy, Brother Bruno looked strangely at Hack. "What is that?"

"What's what?"

Bruno reached across the table and pulled a piece of candy from his ear. Hack unwrapped it and ate it instantly. He fell for it every time.

Before he had swallowed, Hack looked up at the door.

"What is it?" Bruno asked. And then he finally heard footsteps making their way toward the cell. "No problem, Hack, just someone coming down here."

"Someone new."

"New? What do you mean?"

"Those feet ain't been here before."

The door was then pushed open rather forcefully without a knock. Bruno spun around in his chair. "*Was zum Teufel!*"

Father Henry stood straight and proud with a stern look, like a drill sergeant before his newest recruits.

He glared at Hack. "I was instructed to teach you how to read." His displeasure could not be more evident.

"I'm sorry," Hack replied apologetically.

It caught the sub-prior off guard. He opened his mouth a little, closed it, and cleared a discomfort from his throat.

Brother Bruno stood up, shaking his head at his superior. He had always hated bullies. With hands on his hips, as if rank meant very little in this cell, the Great Bavarian decided to put Father Henry in his place. He leaned in closely with squinted eyes, examining Father Henry's stern face with a look of concern. Looking down at him, Bruno asked, "Father, are you all right?"

"Yes. I'm fine," he replied, leaning his head back to gain a little space from the giant before him.

"What on Earth?" Bruno said.

"What? What is it?"

Bruno slowly moved his right hand up toward Father Henry's face. "Excuse me, Father . . . just please . . . allow me . . ."

"What? What is it?" Father Henry said with greater alarm.

And with a quick sleight of hand, the Great Bavarian pulled a small piece of chocolate candy from the Shakespearean scholar's ear. Bruno held it before him, smiling.

Father Henry swatted Brother Bruno's hand with an "Aaahhh, get out of here, you big oaf!"

Hack covered his mouth but could not control his laughter, and a rather undignified flatulence sound came forth from his hand, ringing out between the stone walls. Father Henry's sharp eye tried to stop the boy in his tracks, but to no avail.

Brother Bruno smacked Father Henry on the shoulder, turned back toward Hack, and flipped him the chocolate.

"See you after lunch," he said and made his grand exit, leaving Hack still giggling and Father Henry still standing awkwardly in his rattled indignation.

Father Henry gathered himself, took a deep breath, and sat at the table across from Hack. Silence followed, until he asked coldly, "What is your educational background?"

"Read the Good Book with Pa some."

Father Henry nodded. "And I see you have McGuffey here." He grabbed the second volume. "Let's see how good you are." He flipped through the pages with a great sigh.

"Why don't you like me?"

A spear thrown from the hands of Achilles could not have hit Father Henry harder and with more surprise. He simply looked up from the book and blinked profusely.

"It's okay," Hack said. "I don't much like you either . . . yet."

"Yet?" the distinguished professor asked.

"Pa would say you're like broccoli."

"Broccoli?"

"You're stiff. If someone ate you, you'd be tough to chew."

Still taken aback by the original question, Father Henry felt he should lighten the mood. "I would prefer not to be eaten at all, whether soft or stiff."

"But you can get soft."

"Really?"

"Pa said broccoli people just need to be cooked a long time, so they get soft."

"Really?"

"And Pa said if you can learn to eat broccoli, you can learn to like broccoli people. So, I might like you one day."

"I see."

"And maybe you'll learn to like me too."

There he was again. Father Henry, backed into a corner by the young, uneducated negro boy. Father Henry nodded. "And if you were a vegetable, you'd be a hot pepper, for you have burned me within seconds of coming in contact."

"See!" Hack blurted out. "We already becomin' friends."

Father Henry tried to conceal a smile. "Let's focus on a reading lesson. Shall we?"

"Why do you say *shall?*"

"Why do you say *ain't?*"

"Ain't *ain't* right?"

"No. It ain't."

"Why'd you just use it then?"

"I was just . . ." he sighed and rolled his eyes. "I was poking fun. The word is not proper."

"What makes *shall* right?"

"Grammar books make *shall* right and *ain't* wrong."

"But didn't they have words before books?"

"Yes. But now we have grammar books, and we shall follow them and we *ain't* going to rely on the local vernacular."

"What's vernacular?"

"It's how ordinary people speak."

"Why you want me to speak weird?"

"Weird? What?"

"Ain't weird the opposite of ordinary?"

"No. Not here. Here, ordinary is weird."

"That don't make no sense to me."

Henry's face conveyed how equally confused he was. "Look here. Read this page to me," and he tapped the top of a page while sliding the volume across the table.

May 25, 1924

The stars had disappeared. Dense clouds slowly drifted overhead, hiding the beauty of their glimmer from the world below. It was dark as coal, save the last quarter moon. Tomorrow, it would be a waning crescent, and the next day, it would wane some more, and the next and the next until the greatest of all nocturnal illuminations was all but extinguished. It was as if the majesty of the cosmos, with billions upon billions of stars, all withdrew in their remorse, as if they could not bear to look down upon that lonely young boy standing next to a large pile of red clay, under the cover of night, burying his father.

Hack looked at the pile of dirt: a cold chill shot through his body as he remembered the pile of dirt that lay next to his mother's grave. The only reason it looked smaller this time was because he was taller.

The wooden coffin rested in the ground as Abbot Ambrose sprinkled water on it and rattled off prayers the boy could not understand. Brother Matthias followed him round, holding a lantern up near the little book from which the abbot read. Brother Bruno occasionally put his hand on Hack's shoulder. Father Henry stood at a comfortable distance.

It was almost midnight. And it was the darkness, with all its gloom, that provided Hack the protection he required.

But man is not meant to be buried at night. There is something dismally unnatural about it. Even a man who dies in prison enjoys a burial in the freeness of open sunlight, with birds chirping, or flowers blooming, or snow falling, always with something you can see moving freely. Even if man's life is a secret to conceal, his death should never be so. Being buried before all to see is the final redemption of any man's life, no matter how great or horrific it may have been. Man should not be buried in the dark. It is a final insult to the dignity of his life, his meaning, his purpose.

Yet this was happening so that Hack could attend his own father's funeral. He knew it. And he resented himself for it. His Pa deserved better.

Standing there, with Bruno's large hand resting on his shoulder, he stared at the wooden coffin, knowing the mound of red clay laid still next to him. He was overwhelmed with the anxiety of imminent finality: the murder was not the end; placing the body in the coffin was not the end; the lowering of the coffin in the grave was not the end. Maybe the doctors made a mistake; maybe they would hear him bang on the lid any moment. Maybe Pa would rise. Was Jesus weeping? Was Hack's faith the size of a mustard seed, he asked himself.

Hack leaned over the great hole in the ground, looked at the lid, looked at the sides of the lid, at each corner of the lid. Was there any movement? Hack's chest raised up and down, and he looked back and forth between the mound of red clay and the wooden lid of the coffin. *Please. No.* It wasn't over yet. Not yet . . .

After the Latin rattling stopped, the abbot handed him a small shovel, as tradition dictated.

Hack grasped the handle. He looked up at Bruno, back at the coffin, and back at the mound. He couldn't. He couldn't bury his own Pa. He couldn't bring this to completion. He handed it back over to Bruno, dropped his face into his hands, and wept.

Bruno said nothing but gently removed his hand, stepped over to the mound, and thrust the shovel in. Hack grabbed his arm. "No, wait!" He pulled the shovel from the mound, took the few short steps to the grave, and stopped.

His Pa's face and smile and laughter . . . the way he tilted his head and looked away for a verse . . . the strength of his hands. . . the same hands that poured the golden syrup over the pancakes on their last day together . . . the voice . . . the voice which, at that same breakfast, had told Hack to live every day as if it were his last; it all came rushing through his mind. And then another image came: His Pa holding a shovel, tossing dirt on his mother's coffin. He remembered watching his Pa's face so intently at that moment; his mouth was moving constantly with a soft hum coming forth—surely a verse being repeated over and over and over, like a madman fixed on convincing himself of something. And his Pa didn't get anyone's help with that mound of dirt. He insisted on throwing each and every speck of dirt on his beloved, as if he owed it to her.

Hack extended that shovel over the coffin in the ground and slowly turned his wrist.

The red clay that had made bricks for the monk's abbey, standing tall behind them, was now splattering over the lid of his Pa's coffin. Even though a large mound remained to be shoveled, at the turn of his wrist, it was finished.

Brother Bruno grabbed a shovel off the ground.

"No!" Hack said. And he kept shoveling faster and faster.

Brother Bruno looked at the abbot, who in turn raised his hand, telling him to leave the boy alone.

After a few minutes, Father Henry slowly returned to his cell.

The abbot, Brother Bruno, and Brother Matthias all watched carefully. Finally, the abbot said, "Hack, allow us . . ."

"No!" Hack screamed, frantically shoveling still faster.

"Hack. Hack!" the abbot said, grabbing his shoulders. "You suffer; we all suffer. You shovel; we all shovel. We are one."

Hack slowly nodded.

The three monks rolled up their sleeves and went to work with Hack. Thirty minutes later, Hack and the three monks stood around the grave, catching their breath, trying to show one last sign of respect.

"Are you ready, Hack?" the abbot asked, knowing it was time to retire for the night.

Hack did not answer but shook his head slowly, not as an answer to the question, but out of confusion at some inner thought occupying his mind.

"God protected Noah because he was good. . . . Pa was as good as Noah."

The monks exchanged glances.

"And Jesus wept. Pa said it was the shortest verse in the Bible. *Jesus wept.* He wept for his friend, Lazarus." He looked up across the grave at the abbot. "Is Jesus weeping now?"

"Yes, Son. He most certainly is."

"Then why don't Pa rise from this grave like Lazarus walked out from behind the stone?"

"I don't know."

"And Pa said we gonna rise on the last day."

"Indeed. We will, Hack."

"Well, when is it?" Hack demanded. "Dern it! When's the last day. When I gonna see my Ma and Pa again. Why I get left behind?"

"I don't know. I wish I did."

"Don't you monks get some answers from God. I got no answers. You ain't giving me answers neither."

"Hack, we monks don't have any special knowledge of the ways of God. But we look upon life and death with the eyes of faith."

"Ain't my faith bigger than a mustard seed?" Hack yelled. I believe every word Pa taught me from the Bible. That's faith. Then why can't I move mountains. Huh? Why not? All I can move is a pile of dirt on my Pa's coffin."

The monks dared not interrupt him. It was his time to vent. It was his time to say anything and everything he wished.

"Forgiveness. Pa always told me about it. I ain't forgiving Walter Brooks, though. Know why? He ain't asking forgiveness. He ain't wanting forgiveness. That's easy for me." Hack stabbed his shovel into the ground between his feet. "But I don't know this one: Should I forgive God?"

"God did not take your father, Hack," Brother Bruno answered.

"Ain't saying that. That's just stupid. I ain't stupid. I mean: do I gots to forgive God for giving Walter Brooks free will? That seem to me a stupid thing to do. A mean thing to do. I gots to forgive God for that?"

The abbot walked around the small mound that lay on top of the grave. He grabbed both shoulders and looked him deep in the eyes.

"If I answer you, it will not suffice. God must answer you. But you must ask Him. You must ask Him over and over and over again until He does answer you. Knock, and the door will be opened. But you must knock and knock and knock until your knuckles are bleeding and you can't knock any more. God will answer that question. I promise you that. But you got to keep knocking and you got to look at everything and listen to everything to get your answer. But Hack, as God is my witness, He will answer you."

The anger in Hack's face slowly receded. His eyes looked one last time at the grave. He pulled the shovel from the ground, tossed it to the side, and slowly walked back to the hermitage.

Chapter 6

The Shadow of Death

The soothing chant of monks had stirred him awake for the past two weeks. He would roll off the little mattress next to the wall, his bare feet stepping softly across the stone floor through the door and down the long hall toward the circular staircase where he would take a few steps up, turn around, and sit down. Half asleep, his head would bob up and down or rest on the railings or in the palm of his hands. But the chant was sweeter than early morning sleep.

While the individuality of the monks burst through his door every day with the flamboyance of a Bruno or the sternness of a Henry, during the chant there was but one communal voice echoing throughout the abbey. There was no bickering between the voices, as was expected anytime more than one monk gathered; rather, there was perfect harmony. There was no rank or privilege to hold over another's head, as the prior and sub-prior did at every opportunity; rather, there was perfect equality.

If there was a virtue to ascribe to this one voice, it was humility. Even the cantor who intoned all others seemed to be a single note that momentarily stepped out of the melody but would meekly come back into the fold as soon as his job was done. Indeed, if that cantor had been the greatest tenor on Earth, he would have harnessed his power back to a mere whisper not much louder than the echo that would follow. It was in choir that the monks were monks first and men second. It was in choir that resentments and factions and squabbles were conspicuously absent, as if left outside with the muddy boots.

The melodic chant gave Hack a peaceful sense of belonging. He felt perfectly safe, perfectly at home, even though he was secluded in the basement. In fact, the only negative aspect to the morning ritual was that he had a growing desire to walk up those stairs, pass through the sacristy, and assume the choir stall closest to the back wall. He wondered if anyone would even notice if they were as lost in prayer as they sounded. Perhaps someday, he told himself. Perhaps someday.

This newly loved morning ritual was not the only part of his daily routine. If there is one thing in a monastery you can count on, it is routine. Despite the fact that monasteries have every sort of person within, from Saint Teresas who levitated off the ground, to villains who corrupt all those around them, the routine is paramount and seems rather resilient in the face of extreme personalities. It is as if a *Rule of Life*, as the spiritual directors called it, is the surest path to perseverance in the face of adversity, for nothing on Earth seems to bring the great Benedictine Order to a halt. The routine continues to turn and turn as if intricately bound with the turning of the Earth day-by-day, spinning round the sun year-by-year. While every abbey has its springs of new life, summers of long droughts, autumns of harvests, and winters of death, the sacred rhythm of their daily life keeps all things moving to the next season. Indeed, it is not entering the anguish of a blistering summer or the sorrow of a bitter winter that is to be feared; it is stopping the cycle that is the real problem.

And thus, it is of paramount importance in a community that things just keep moving, no matter who leaves, no matter who enters. It does not take long, therefore, for a new resident in a monastery to fall squarely into the daily rhythm. As it takes a killifish a mere two weeks to grow to full maturity, it took about the same for Hack to become warmly accustomed to the rhythm of his new life.

First, he would rise at 5:00 a.m. for Lauds, hearing the voices of the monks, making his way up in the dark staircase. Then, returning to the hermitage, he would eat some fruit and bread left the night before by Brother Bruno, while simultaneously diving into one of the books given to him by Father Henry. Midmorning, Brother Bruno would join him without fail. They played checkers and cards and read articles about the Big Leagues, which Hack had introduced to the Great Bavarian. Hack would also ask Bruno to find articles on the Negro Leagues, reported sporadically in the papers. A talk of a Colored World Series was spreading throughout the media. The previous few years had failed to produce such a contest due to interleague conflict. But this year, Hack hoped, was the year. His Pa had passed down to him a love of the Kansas City Monarchs. The season had yet to begin, but Hack wanted to review every paper just to make sure. Truth be told, rummaging through the daily paper helped his reading as much as the more refined pedagogical material given him by Father Henry.

Late morning was the time for Father Henry. There was little dialogue. It was a matter-of-fact instruction. Hack would read aloud, and Father Henry would make corrections. He would stop him at mistakes and insert a phonetic lesson as needed. It was productive but cold, like a textile mill in the dead of winter.

Brother Matthias would bring him lunch after the hour of Sext. Hack would eat and Brother Matthias would practice his newest instrument: the recorder. There was little that Hack enjoyed more than to nibble at an apple while Matthias practiced chords with his fingers pressing against the little holes. There was something oddly elegant about the sound coming forth from that small instrument. While the harmonica was enjoyable with a sharp sound, the recorder was so gentle, so innocent. "If there was one instrument before the Fall," Brother Matthias said, "it was the recorder."

An image was thus placed firmly in young Hack's imagination: Adam sitting on the bank of a river, feet dangling in the mini rapids, playing a recorder carved from a small limb that fell from the Tree of Life. And as he played, he gazed upon Eve downstream, who rested peacefully in the cool of the day. All was perfect. No other instruments were needed, just one small bit of wood with little holes carved therein. The little creatures in the trees and those burrowed in holes and tucked beneath bushes poked their heads out, unafraid, as the human played his music. They were enraptured at this ability of man. Hack wondered if, before the Fall, the animals were conscious of this striking difference between themselves and he who was made in the image of God. Perhaps the sin of man brought on a darkness of intellect to all animals as well so that they no longer understood their own limitations. And perhaps it was the sin of man that robbed him of his ability to pick up a thin piece of wood and play intuitively. Forever after, man has had to toil by the sweat of his brow and the blistering of his fingers to play an instrument, one of the darkest of consequences of a fallen world.

During the mid-afternoon, Hack was alone. He would read the McGuffey Readers and any other material given him by Father Henry. He would play his harmonica. He would even play checkers against himself and had recently asked about a game called chess he had heard about once before. When he needed a break from the mental concentration, he would try to do the one-handed pushups and one-legged squats with which Brother Bruno had challenged him. Despite his best efforts, his skinny limbs couldn't handle it yet.

Around Nones, 3:00 p.m., Hack began taking naps, most certainly not out of laziness, but out of fatigue. And Brother Bruno would do the same.

At 6:00 p.m., Hack would make his way to the bottom of the staircase for Vespers. He was just beginning to recognize oft-repeated words, speculating at their meaning. After Compline at 7:00 p.m., Abbot Ambrose would come for his daily visit.

They did not try one-legged squats or play poker or play the harmonica and recorder. Instead, they would discuss a predetermined subject. The agenda gave the abbot a great sense of ease. During his first few visits to the hermitage, the abbot learned that while Hack was perfectly comfortable to stare at him without talking, he most certainly was not comfortable staring back. So, each day would end with, "What do you want to talk about tomorrow?" Hack would think for a moment and come up with something terrifically interesting, such as *Words that sound funny* or *What kind of animal certain people would be* or *Things that come in pairs of three*. Without fail, however, such random subjects would evolve into a theological discussion; the abbot would often spend the rest of the evening trying to trace how *Father Henry would be a honey badger* ended up at the *Hypostatic Union*. (The good abbot did not want to know what he thought Father Roth would be.)

Such conversations were the perfect way for both of them to ready themselves for sleep. Hack, however, invariably slept only for a few hours.

Around 11:00 p.m., when the abbey grounds were completely void of any college students (for in those days, the strictest curfews where in place), Brother Bruno would take Hack into the large courtyard outside the external door off his hallway—the very door that Hack had noticed as his escape route on his arrival.

The courtyard was a perfect square, measuring thirty yards in length and width. The wall around it was eight feet tall. It would have been perfectly secluded from the outside world if not for the large wrought iron gates in each of the three walls. While no visitors were ever permitted in this cloistered courtyard, any person walking past could easily sneak a peek through one of the gates and have a view of all that the walls enclosed.

Within these walls grew a rather pathetic garden begging for some tender care, a few statues of unrecognizable saints of the Benedictine Order, a fountain with a few goldfish fed by fat old monks, and a long stretch of green grass running the entire back portion from wall to wall. It was the perfect place to throw a baseball, especially with those stone saints to play outfield. But there were numerous obstacles: first, while Brother Bruno would fight anything other than a circular saw, he was afraid of a small baseball coming at his head; second, Hack never recovered his tattered glove from his house, nor any other personal item, after that fatal night; and third, the light of moon and stars was all the lighting they had. Hack, however, patiently believed that if God could part the Red Sea and make manna fall from the heavens in the desert, he could miraculously make two gloves, a ball, and sunlight appear in the not-too-distant future. Brother Bruno would be forced to make a leap of faith to play catch, just as Peter stepped from the boat on rocking waters.

Until that miracle occurred, Hack and Brother Bruno would walk the perimeter of the courtyard and discuss all sorts of things, including the interesting discussions Hack had had with the abbot just hours before. They would do pushups and squats. They would do wheelbarrows (in which Bruno would hold his feet and Hack would walk around on his hands). And they would play checkers or cards by the light of a lantern.

Brother Bruno did all he could to get Hack outside, but he grew frustrated with his limitations and planned on taking action in the very near future.

Father Henry's Journal

June 10, 1924

I have been surprised, as any reasonable man would be, at the progress the boy has made. He must have jumped two grade levels within a mere two weeks. And while I would like to take credit as a stellar teacher, I must admit that it seems an inborn capacity. It would be interesting to see what full capacity is for a colored. I give him due credit: If he had the opportunity, he would reach that ceiling, wherever it may be. But would his kind ever be able to partake in the greatest pleasures of the intellectual life? Homer and Virgil? Dante and Shakespeare? While I wish it were possible, I just don't see it given the history of his race.

And yet, we will never know. He will be shipped out of here soon . . . if the abbot would get his act together. I do have, however, a sense of satisfaction that the negro will take from my instructions some worthy tools for whatever trade he engages down the road, if the law does not toss him in prison. I pray he will be better for his time here.

But the time has passed.

"All right Hack," Father Henry said, sitting down at the little desk for another lesson. "How did the assigned chapter go?"

"I read the book," Hack said dispassionately.

"The chapter, you mean?" Father Henry asked confusedly.

"No. The book."

Henry took the fourth volume from the McGuffey set into his hands. Hack had begun at the second volume a few weeks ago. But Henry had decided to give him a challenge that would defeat him. He wanted a little failure, not out of cruelty *per se*, but out of a desire to test his limitations.

"You mean to tell me, Hack, that you read the entire fifth volume . . . last night?"

"Sorry." Hack shrugged his shoulders.

"Did you sleep?"

"Not much. Brother Bruno didn't come down last night. I'm used to working out at that time, so I had lots of energy. I just read and kept on reading. The book just gots easier the further I read. And then I sorta gots this idea that I could read the whole dern thing. And it was like a game against myself, like when I spin the checkerboard round and round playing myself."

Father Henry thumbed through the book in disbelief.

"Very well. Let's move on to writing. Let me see your sentences."

It was his writing that really needed work, which set Father Henry more at ease. While he read like an advanced middle schooler, he wrote like a small child. His Pa had never put a pencil in his hand.

Father Henry had given Hack a black leather book, the sort that all the monks used for journaling during their forty-day retreats in the hermitage. And now Hack had his very own. Father Henry had not anticipated the joy with which Hack would receive the small gift. In fact, Henry did not see it as a gift at all, but an assignment. Surely a gift is all in one's perspective.

For the past two weeks, Hack had begun the most basic of copy work. He began by copying the letters of the alphabets and basic words taken from McGuffey assignments. Yesterday, however, Father Henry's assignment was to write his own complete sentences, whatever came to mind.

"Let's see what you came up with. Give it here." Father Henry took the book in his hand. The handwriting needed work, but it was still legible. He cleared his throat and began to read it aloud.

"Pa is a . . ."

He paused. His cold heart sank.

"Pa is a hero. He is brave. People lie about him."

Henry put the book down and gently closed it. He looked at the boy sitting across the table.

"Very good, Hack. Very good."

And Hack noticed for the first time a tenderness in his voice.

"Hack, I have some memory work for you."

He spun Hack's book around, grabbed the pencil, and swirled his fingers across the page with such speed Hack could scarcely believe it.

"Here, read this and memorize it."

Hack took the book in hand. "*A coward dies a thous . . . a thousand times before his death, but the val . . . val-i-ant taste of death but once.*"

"That's right. Memorize it. And bring it to your mind many times throughout your life."

"What does val-i-ant mean?"

"It means brave."

"Is this from the Good Book?"

"No. But from the next best thing: Shakespeare."

Having the certitudes of the mind directly challenged by others all too often emboldens a man's opinion, causes him to dig his heels in, causes him to search every nook and cranny of God's green Earth to find justification for his position; for a single act of humble surrender can be the most laborious task known to man. But when he stumbles upon his own error in the solitude of his own mind—freed from the humiliation of public repentance—the sensation is rather different. Whereas the former causes him to grind his teeth, the latter causes him to merely bite his lip in uncertainty. He can also, then, retain his dignity by telling himself that it was keenness of mind that found the error. He can be humble and take the credit at the same time.

In the case of Father Henry, he was beginning to question his views on Hack's ability. With his logic intact, he likewise began to question his view on the negro race—at least in terms of academic capacity. Henry had clear memories of many students Hack's age over the years and struggled to recall one so sharp and so quick, and perhaps most importantly, so witty.

And so, he sat in his room later that evening, biting his lip.

A knock on the door.

"Come in."

Father Roth stuck his head in.

"Father Henry, may I intrude on your solitude?"

"Of course, Father. Please . . ." and he spun his chair around for Father Roth. Father Roth closed the door and took a seat.

"How are your lessons going with the boy?"

"Surprisingly well. He is—how should I say—inquisitive and hard-working. He has a solid work ethic, to say the least."

"His kind are made to work. It will serve him well one day when he lands in whatever field or factory is waiting for him."

Father Henry bit his lip again.

"He might . . . just might . . . be capable of more than that." He surprised himself saying it out loud, especially to Father Roth.

"Perhaps. Easy for me to believe. And you might . . . just might . . . have been a good farmer. But God's holy will ordered things differently. He places everyone in the hierarchy of the cosmos for a divine reason that you and I may or may not understand. Hack has his role to play. And so do you, as a Shakespearean scholar ought to appreciate."

"I do," said Father Henry, bowing his head.

"And is not every role necessary for a beautiful performance?"

"Indeed."

"And is it for the actors to choose their own roles?"

"Certainly not."

"And what is your role, Father Henry?"

"Sub-prior, I suppose."

"For now, yes. But what happens—in a play that is—if the lead actor becomes unavailable?"

"Unavailable?"

"It happens all the time."

"Yes, but . . ."

"Is it the case that the second lead actor takes his place? Or is that role critically important as well?"

"True. Most often it will be a third role that leapfrogs to the lead role to preserve the integrity of the second. And usually the right actor for the second role is the wrong actor for the first."

"And why is that?"

"Well, usually there is contrast: one might be young and the other old; one might be a hero and the other a villain. It is the contrast that makes for a great story."

"You have said it better than I could myself."

"Your point, Father?"

Father Roth adjusted in his seat.

"You see, Henry, it is my job, as the second role, to be a contrast to our young abbot. I must watch carefully on the horizon for what might befall this community. I am at times like a scout that goes out over the ridgeline to see the dangers that approach. And then I report such dangers to the abbot. But in this particular case, our good abbot—God bless him—is the danger himself. Yes, yes . . . with the purest intentions. Pure intentions, however, do not excuse a cold hard fact that you and I must contend with."

"Which is?"

"Which is that Abbot Ambrose is breaking the civil law in no small way. He is an enemy of the state. Unfortunately for him and the rest of us, his compassion, giving the boy the benefit of the doubt, has slowed his departure. Every passing day causes greater risk to us that the authorities will learn about the boy's presence. And therefore, every passing day the abbot increases his own risk of criminal charges for aiding and abetting a fugitive."

Father Henry sighed.

"The best-case scenario, I hate to admit, is that the authorities would forgive the abbot—let him off the hook—but that our community would lose all faith in his ability to lead. Unfortunately, the abbot has forced us into a consequentialist position: if this plan of his works out, the monks will have faith in him; if it does not, they will lose faith in him. God does not judge our actions based on their consequences, and neither should we. Yet, this is the very situation unfolding before our eyes.

"As the scout out on the hill, I can clearly see a massive disruption to our community on the horizon. And as the second lead, as prior, I know that the community would be unlikely to place me in the abbot's chair. I have been typecast, if you will. The community is used to me in this role.

So be it. But you, my young friend, are the third role: sub-prior. You have not been typecast . . . *yet.* You have the pedigree. And with my support, I believe you would be seen as the logical choice for the lead role."

Father Henry was just a few years older than the abbot himself. Before the previous election, he was certain that Father Roth would be elected. He was wrong—and shocked by that fact. Since then, he was doubly sure that if anything happened to the abbot, Father Roth would be the only choice.

Upon listening to Father Roth, he followed the logic. It was, of course, flattering. Henry had seen himself as abbot one day, but he assumed it was twenty years in the future. To Henry's mind, one must prove himself a reliable monk, then a competent sub-prior, then an outstanding prior before even being considered for the abbot's chair. Thus, the very reason for his disapproval of the election of Ambrose, who had never served in either position. Competent, yes. Reliable, yes. But he had not earned his stripes. Father Henry, however, was in the ideal process of doing so.

He was quiet for a long minute. Father Roth sat back in his chair, crossed his legs with a small grin creeping onto his face, and watched the idea seep into his protégé.

Father Henry said the only thing that would not come across as unappreciative of the vote of confidence or as vain by a too easy acceptance of it.

"But really, what are the chances that police will find out about Hack?"

Father Roth took a deep breath.

"All it would take is the slightest hint leaking to Officer Andrew."

Another long moment of silence. Father Henry could envision Abbot Ambrose being taken in for questioning, the monks losing confidence in their abbot, even a new election being called. And then it hit him: the abbot would not be the only one taken in. Hack would go as well. And what would become of him? Were the abbot's fears justified? Would the boy be tried? Would he be lynched? Would it truly be his word versus Walter's?

There was so much uncertainty. Too much to continue this conversation.

"Much to think about Father Roth."

With that, Father Henry patted his knees and leaned forward as if politely announcing it was time to stand.

Father Roth complied.

"Good night, Father Henry. I enjoyed our chat."

"Good night, Father."

Father Henry closed the door behind the prior and sat back on his bed.

And he bit his lip.

Abbot Ambrose's Journal

June 11, 1924

I believe I have the right place, the right family. But this is taking longer than expected. There are many factors as to whether Hack would be a good fit.

Too many know . . .

Who am I kidding? There is a good chance every single brother knows at this point. It only takes one bad apple. When you cannot avoid something, you must confront it. There is simply no other path.

This is God's will for now, and I should not hide it from the brothers.

A General Assembly it is . . .

Thy will be done.

Speculation, rumors, anxiety, gossip are all more contagious and can spread faster than the Spanish Flu. They can be more deadly as well; that is, if one considers the soul to be something capable of dying. To guess at the inner workings of a man's mind, in particular his motives, is to turn him into clay and turn oneself into the divine artist that shapes man into his own image and likeness. Looked at this way, speculation as to another's motives is the least creative thing of all, for we are simply looking in the mirror and pretending we figured something out.

The creative approach to another, Abbot Ambrose had learned, was to refrain from speculation as to another's inner workings. Rather, the abbot found humility to be more creative: if we do not pretend to know others, we in fact see and list out more possibilities. But when we think we know another person—like a book—we remove the dynamism that comes with humanity and free will and the unpredictable variables that derive unpredictable outcomes. The humble man is never shocked, never crushed by disappointment, never angered by missed expectations, for he knows he does not know, and thus anything is possible.

The abbot was rather young for such a mature perspective. His God-given temperament, that of the phlegmatic, contributed greatly to this rare attribute. The cholerics were often wrong but never in doubt; the sanguines jumped to and fro without thinking much at all; and the melancholics would either drown in despair or experience paralysis by analysis.

At Good Shepherd Monastery, the more than seventy monks were a great melting pot of all four temperaments, three of the four of which gravitated toward certitude of opinion. The good abbot called a General Assembly to discuss an important matter. And thus, whispers of this certitude echoed through the halls throughout the day.

For a man who had been punctual his entire life, the abbot was uncharacteristically late. What the monks did not know, however, was that he had been in his private office praying for guidance and wisdom like never before.

As he walked before his brothers, the young abbot looked resigned to accept whatever came from his announcement. He also looked resolved to make his point, stand by his decision, and to make demands upon his flock. Calmness and strength: usually the two do not stand together. But when they do, they are nearly indestructible.

"Brothers, thank you for setting aside your duties for the evening. I do not know how many of you know what I am about to say. But I believe all of you deserve to know.

"I regret I must do the following. Nonetheless, it must be done. Everything you hear this evening must be held in the strictest confidence. As your abbot, I give each of you the commandment of total silence as to the contents of this subject. You are forbidden from discussing this issue with anyone outside this room. That, my brothers, is a thick black line. Do not cross it."

The monks stole looks at each other.

"Now, each of you know that Percy was killed along with the young girl, Catherine. I have every reason to believe that Walter Brooks's story is a lie. A cold, hard lie. I will not go through all those details, for I do not wish to debate it with anyone. Suffice it to say I am personally convinced that he, in fact, was in the process of raping Catherine, that Percy tried to save her, and that Walter killed Percy for it."

Gasps filled the room. Mumbles grew and grew until the abbot raised his hand calling for order.

"Walter then turned and killed the girl who had just witnessed the murder. He arranged the scene to look as if Percy was the rapist and that he, Walter, tried to save her, unintentionally killing Percy in the process."

A few trusting monks covered their faces in horror. But a greater percentage shook their heads in disbelief. One or two even said, "No!" as if the abbot's story was simply not believable.

A smile crept onto Father Roth's face as he sat back perfectly still and quiet, watching it unfold before his eyes.

"It's true, damn it!" yelled Brother Bruno at the room.

"Silence, Bruno!" demanded the abbot. The Great Bavarian breathed through the nose like a bull about to charge through the room.

"You have all read the papers. Percy had a son, and the police are looking for him. You may remember him working the grounds with Percy. Well, Walter says the boy was holding the girl down while Percy violated her. But the boy took off as Walter approached. They are just now beginning to think he escaped town and are calling off their efforts."

The abbot took a deep breath, but then his eyes fell upon Abbot Gregory sitting quietly in the back of the room. He was the only one with a smile on his face, other than Father Roth. So often, Abbot Ambrose thought, did people do the exact same thing for the exact opposite reason. Abbot Gregory was beaming, as if he did not understand what on Earth was being said. And yet, Abbot Ambrose thought to himself, Abbot Gregory is probably the only one in the room who does understand what is being said. What were the chances that one of the oldest and holiest men in the abbey was clueless as to the severity of the situation? Abbot Gregory nodded his head at Ambrose, as if telling him, *keep going*.

"What some of you do not know is that on the night of the murders, the boy took refuge here, in our monastery."

Moans of disbelief shot through the room.

"And what is more!" the abbot yelled above the room. "What is more, he has been living ever since in the hermitage."

"Outrageous!" a voice cried. "Sacrilege!" cried another. And the negative feedback grew rapidly, even with a few hand slaps on the tables. But with equal or greater force, another wave of voices rang out against them: "Shut your mouth! The only sacrilege is your lack of charity!" one monk screamed at another.

The room had erupted into utter chaos, the very worst kind a Benedictine abbey could imagine.

Abbot Ambrose's heart sank. He was lost. And yet, Abbot Gregory was still smiling at him. He indeed looked like a man out of his wits, smiling and nodding his head at the young abbot while the fifty-year-old community began to crumble before their very eyes.

Father Roth continued to sit in silence with a grin of satisfaction.

"Brothers! Brothers! Please!" the abbot hollered over the noise. Eventually, they settled down enough for him to continue.

"Listen, please. I have almost found a permanent home for him; he is leaving shortly. But please understand: if I were to have handed him over, he would be found guilty despite his innocence, despite Percy's innocence. I would not put a lynching past the Klan. Would you?"

He looked around the room. No one said a word.

"My brothers, if I am wrong for this, it is my own soul at risk, not yours. I have reviewed the facts and I have prayed; I've prayed harder than I have ever prayed. Perhaps I am so filled with self-righteousness, so narcissistic, so blinded by the pride of this office that I'm incapable of seeing the obvious. I readily admit that, for I am a sinful man with the most limited intellect to discern the will of God. I sought counsel from trusted advisors, many of whom are staunchly against my approach. And yet every fiber of my being seemed to command me to save the boy. Know, my brothers, that I would have preferred to shirk my duties as your leader so that someone wiser could make these decisions. For some unknown reasons, to my chagrin, it was you, brothers, who put me in this chair. And if I sit in this chair, I will make the decisions as best as I know how.

"This I promise you, brothers: if every single one of you prayerfully advises me to do one thing, but my own prayer tells me to do another, I will do, every time, that which my own prayer instructs. Is this because I do not trust your judgment? Of course not. You are wise, especially as a collective whole. But God has not appointed you abbot of this monastery. He has appointed me and me alone, not because of my greatness, but because of my lowliness. He has chosen the weakest of His vessels from time immemorial to lead His people. Thus, I am not surprised that I, of all people, am your leader for this limited time.

"Therefore, brothers, I ask you to forgive me if I am wrong. I ask for your prayers. But I command your obedience until the day and time I am no longer your abbot. If that is in eight years, so be it. If it is this very night, so be it. I have little attachment to this life. I have only attachment to the will of God as I understand it."

The room was perfectly still. Every monk in the room clearly saw the sincerity of the man they recently elected. They could see his humility and his zeal in equal measure. While many disagreed with his decision, their head-nods seemed to express a level of respect.

"Brother Bruno," the abbot said. "Please go get Hack."

A sea of monk heads turned anxiously. Abbot Ambrose stood perfectly still with head down, as if in prayer. The room remained silent.

A few minutes later, Brother Bruno entered the room with young Hack following behind. He looked so small, so skinny beside the Great Bavarian. He was nervous. He looked somewhat frantically to the abbot, toward Bruno, and he searched the room for the other familiar faces: Brother Matthias, Father Henry.

"Brothers," Abbot Ambrose said, "meet our guest, and welcome him as Christ."

Nearly seventy faces Hack did not know by name gazed upon him as if he was a caged animal in a zoo. They scanned him up and down.

Some smiled. Some shook their heads and rolled their eyes. Father Roth scowled, and Abbot Gregory nodded at Hack with affirmation.

An awkward moment followed. Evidently, the young abbot had not thought through this part. What was supposed to happen now? Was Hack supposed to shake all of their hands? Were the monks supposed to ask him questions? If he did not know, surely Hack did not know.

A rather foolish question came to him: "Is there anything you'd like to say, Hack?"

Hack stood there scanning the faces—mixed emotions on some, raw emotions on others. Fear struck him deep. All that came to his mind was what his Pa used to tell him when he had nightmares. Without a conscious decision, his eyes closed, his lips began moving, and his words became more audible the more they came out.

"The LORD is my shepherd; I shall not want. He maketh me to lie down in green pastures: He leadeth me beside the still waters. He restoreth my soul: He leadeth me in the paths of righteousness for His name's sake. Yea, though I walk through the valley of the shadow of death, I will fear no evil: for Thou art with me; thy rod and thy staff they comfort me."

He stopped. He opened his eyes to see if the monks were still there; part of him wondered if they had gotten up and left, for he had never experienced such silence in a room full of people.

Brother Matthias sat crying; Father Henry rubbing his eyes with his hands, as if trying to figure out something complex . . . or perhaps so simple it seemed complex. Father Roth was rolling his eyes. Brother Bruno was looking around the room at the response. And Abbot Ambrose had his hands folded at his mouth with his own eyes shut, as if he prayed the twenty-third Psalm along with him.

Then, the sound of a cane tapping the floor from the back of the room. Abbot Gregory made his way through the crowd. Everyone's attention turned, watching as the old man hobbled to the front of the room and approached Hack slowly. The smile on his face remained. He put his hand on Hack's shoulder, bent down and kissed him on the top of his head, then left the room.

Another monk, a young one this time, walked to the front of the room, patted Hack on the shoulder, and proceeded. Another monk did the same. And another. And another.

Father Roth stood up and walked out another door in disgust.

Chapter 7
The American

Late June

Under the cover of early morning, Brother Bruno loaded Hack up in the Model TT Truck, the windshield fogged by the predawn humidity. The anxiety could be seen on Bruno's face, but he knew beyond doubt that the boy had to get a break from the monastery walls. It had taken all of his persuasive powers to convince the abbot. Thus, Bruno felt the weight of Hack's very life in his hands.

He instructed Hack to drop his head down at a moment's notice in the event they came upon someone in downtown Capstone, though unlikely at 4:30 a.m.

Hack's heart pumped as the warm air blew in through the windows and the land breezed past at unknown speeds. It was his first time in an automobile.

It had been over a month since Hack had taken refuge in Good Shepherd. Bruno, who had spent his childhood running and playing in the Great Bavarian black forests, felt that the most unnatural place in the world for a boy was the basement of an abbey. He was thinking about what he was doing at Hack's age: building forts, hiking to the tallest peaks of the mountains, getting lost, swimming in the cold rivers and streams winding through the hills. And then a question came to mind:

"When is your birthday Hack?"

"Don't know."

"No, I said when is your *birthday?*" assuming Hack didn't hear him right.

"Don't know."

"What do you mean you don't know?"

"I remember Ma baking a cake for me every year, in the summer. And Ma and Pa would sing to me and give a little gift. But after Ma died, it was like Pa didn't know. He just gave me gifts any chance he got and made pancakes all the time. That's as close as we gots to a birthday."

"Did you not ask him when your birthday was?"

"Nope."

"Why not?"

"Because I figures he forgot it or something. Didn't want to make him feel bad."

"But you are twelve, right?"

"Somewheres round there."

"And you remember having a party in the summer?"

"Think so."

"So, you could be thirteen?"

"I reckon."

It was tough for Brother Bruno to fathom. But nothing Hack said or did was typical. It was as if the boy was unaffected by the regular doings of regular people maneuvering through the world, for there was a purity and innocence permeating his every move.

"Have you ever been hiking?" Bruno asked.

"Not up a mountain."

"Well, you're in for a treat. I grew up hiking every mountain I could find. And I found a small mountain called Crowders right on the Carolina line. Should be there about 6:30. You know how much convincing of the abbot I had to do to get the automobile?"

"How much?"

"Lots. Lots and lots. If it was for a monk or any other personal reason, there's no way he would have agreed to an all-day trip. But for you . . ."

Hack nodded his head in gratitude.

"'You get a scratch on that thing,' the abbot told me, 'and you'll be shoveling horse shit in the stable for a month.'"

"That don't sound like the abbot I know."

"Well, he said it a little tongue-in-cheek. After all, he isn't just in charge of prayer. He's in charge of the financial well-being of the institution. And this here," he tapped the steering wheel, "is the largest investment Good Shepherd Farms has made in recent years."

As dawn spread rose-colored rays across the state line, as if the fingertips of a Greek goddess blessed the morning, Brother Bruno pulled off the side of the road to look over his map. He mumbled a few things in German, which told Hack that something was not exactly right. Bruno dropped the map on the seat, looked out his window, and said, "Well, there it is," and pointed to a rocky apex of a small mountain that appeared out of nowhere. It was as if this peak just burst forth from the core of the Earth unexpectedly, for there were no other mountains for miles around.

"How'd that mountain get there?" Hack asked.

"I guess God thought it looked like a good place for a mountain. But I wish he'd tell me where the damn public entrance is."

He kept on driving until it seemed like they were doing a circle around the mountain.

Up on the right, a small building came into view, a filling station. An automobile was parked out front alongside a few horses and wagons. A large sign on the edge of the road read "Breakfast Served."

"Perfect!" Bruno announced. "Directions and food. Better than the apples in our bag. And far enough from town."

Three men sat on a bench and rocking chairs outside the storefront smoking cigarettes and drinking coffee. Bruno, donning layman's clothes, climbed out of the Model TT.

"Fine looking truck there, Mister," one of the men said between puffs on his cigarette. "That's the Model TT," he said to the other men.

And then Hack got out.

The men's pleasant demeanor changed instantly.

"Take him round back," the third man said.

Only the grace of God allowed Bruno to swallow his rage. "We just want some breakfast and directions."

"Is that a German accent I hear?" the second man said.

"It is," Bruno said proudly.

"Look at what we've got here, boys," said the first of the men. "We gots ourselves a colored and a Kraut. I wonders if this here's the Kraut that killed my brother in the war."

Just as Bruno felt his patience coming to its end, he felt a tug on his elbow. Hack pulled him toward the Colored sign pointing around back. Bruno reluctantly followed, grabbing a newspaper off a wooden stand on his way.

Around back, a single picnic table rested just outside the backdoor to the kitchen, beside the garbage cans. Trash had piled up, leaving a rank odor.

"Some sausage will be a step up from our apples," said Bruno.

They both sat down. Bruno began reading the front page of the paper.

"*The Perfect Crime*," he read aloud from the headlines.

"Coffee?" a most unwelcoming voice hollered from the kitchen door. A fat man in a white apron showed himself a few seconds later.

Bruno looked up from the paper. "Coffee. Black. And orange juice for my friend here."

A grunt in reply as he disappeared back into the kitchen.

Bruno returned to the paper, unusually interested in its contents.

"What's so interesting?" asked Hack.

"I've been following this story."

He spun the paper around and showed a picture of two young men sitting shoulder to shoulder, both with slicked hair, legs crossed, looking dapper, one in a bow tie and the other in a double-breasted suit. One of them had a smile on his face and the other a darker grin.

"Loeb and Leopold. Memorable names; an even more memorable crime. They were indicted just a few weeks ago. Awaiting trial. Probably will get the death penalty."

"What'd they do?"

"The facts are a little sketchy right now; it will all become clear in the trial. But the papers have been getting more and more of the facts from the indictment. Allegedly, they murdered a fourteen-year-old boy named Bobby Franks. Horrible thing. But there are lots of murders . . ." Bruno paused due to the obvious discomfort of the topic. ". . . as we know too well."

After a pause, Hack said, "Go on. I ain't squeamish."

"Okay. Well, the interesting thing about this case is that it was a philosophical murder."

"Philosophical murder?"

"That's right. You see, these two young men went to the University of Chicago. They studied Nietzsche, as I did as a young man in Germany. A dangerous philosopher, to say the least. And here we see it play out in the lives of these college kids in Chicago. Fascinating."

"Why's he dangerous?"

"Lots of reasons. But the one that influenced these boys was *Übermensch*—the Overman . . . the Superman. Nietzsche taught that creatures continue to evolve from worms to higher beings, then apes, and then to man, and finally to an Overman. And just like men do not have to follow the rules of apes, the Overman does not have to follow the rule of man. The Overman is intellectually superior to the average man and has thus been liberated from the moral necessity to follow the laws.

"So these two guys decided they were Overmen. As the story has been unfolding in the papers, it seems that they began testing their theory of being superior to the rest of men and to the law by committing little crimes of theft here and there. But they decided to commit *the Perfect Crime* of murder, as they called it. It would be perfect because they were smarter than the cops and would never get caught. Plus, they were not morally guilty of anything, since the laws did not apply to them.

"Apparently, they planned for months ahead of time. They planned the abduction, the murder weapon, and they wanted to collect a ransom despite having completed the murder. They came up with elaborate schemes to collect the money without being traced. And then it came to selecting their victim . . ."

The coffee and orange juice arrived.

"What you wanna eat?" a fat and grumpy cook said to Bruno while wiping his hands on a filthy white apron.

"You have sausage?" asked Bruno.

"Yeah."

"I'll have two orders of sausage. Not sure what one order is, but I'll take two."

Bruno gave Hack a look. "Pancakes please."

The cook turned and went back into the kitchen.

"Anyhow, the victim: they chose a boy, Bobby Franks. They lured him into a car. Leopold drove the car," Bruno pointed to the one in the double-breasted suit with rather unattractive conjoined eyebrows, "while Loeb," pointing to the other, "stabbed Franks in the head with a chisel over and over again. Loeb then dragged him in the back seat of the car and gagged him until he died. They dumped him in a predetermined spot and disfigured his body, trying to cover up the boy's identity. Then they proceeded to enact their ransom plan and contacted the boy's parents.

"But it wasn't long until the body was found, and a pair of eyeglasses were found next to the body. Eyeglasses are common, of course, but this pair had a unique hinge on it. The authorities were able to determine that this sort of hinge had only been sold three times in the area.

"So there you have it: the geniuses left their eyeglasses with the body. You'd think some humility would set in after being so stupid."

"Will they hang?"

"I suspect so."

"You think they should be hanged?"

"You're damn right. Well, I mean, perhaps . . . but you know, maybe not. Maybe they need more time to repent. Only God has the right to kill, perhaps . . . Ah hell, hang them. They deserve it. Or maybe not. Hell if I know. Don't ask me such tough questions."

Hack smiled. "Thanks for clearing that up."

"The point, Hack, is that ideas have consequences. I'm afraid my great country is taking the words of Neitzsche to heart, and it will result in its downfall."

"Ideas have consequences." Hack repeated, not as a question, but as a reflection.

"Damn right."

Bruno shook the paper a little and returned to reading the most up-to-date account while waiting for his breakfast. When it came, it was a good breakfast, despite the rudeness of the establishment's owner.

As they were paying, Brother Bruno addressed the owner: "We're going on a hike at Crowders Mountain. Can you tell me where the public entrance is? I see it on the map, but it doesn't really make clear the last few turns."

The owner explained matter-of-factly that they missed the turn just a few miles back and that there was a large parking lot just at the entrance of the trail. Bruno thanked the man and, along with Hack, made his way back to the Model TT. The same three men were admiring the automobile up close. When they saw the Great Bavarian walking with his intimidating limp toward them, they backed away. One of them spit his tobacco juice right at the tire. "How'd a Kraut and nigger get a fine piece of machinery like this?"

"None of your damn business; that's how!" Bruno said.

They both jumped in the truck and double backed as fast as they could go.

"Schmutzige bastarde . . ."

Hack held back his smile.

The public entrance was found, the truck was parked, the canteens were slung over shoulders, and the trail was taken. The morning twilight had passed, and the sun was climbing the sky much faster than they would climb the mountain. The sun was still low enough to shimmer through the green foliage surrounding them, like a million little dancers made of light springing above and below every leaf. While inclined to gaze upon the wonder of the morning sun, Hack had to keep his eyes downcast to avoid the hefty roots protruding from the dark dirt beneath every step, not unlike how the humble must travel through life.

The heat of the day could be sensed before its arrival, but in the interim, it was as glorious a morning as one could imagine. Hack figured his wonder at daybreak was simply due to being cooped up in a hermitage for the past month. But perhaps not. The day was a glorious masterpiece, one that no human could replicate with a paintbrush; no stained-glass window could allow light to break through in such a majestic manner; no poet could choose words surged with enough meaning to adequately explain the divinely made canopy overhead.

But Brother Bruno did not seem so enthralled. Rather, he seemed to be looking for an answer lying beneath the roots he avoided with every step.

"Penny," Hack said.

"What?"

"Penny for your thoughts."

"Oh . . . I guess I'm thinking about Loeb and Leopold, about the thrill of doing evil. Even St. Augustine in his *Confessions* admits stealing a pear not for the sake of eating it but for the sake of feeling the thrill of stealing it."

Hack said nothing, allowing him to continue at his own pace.

"When I was a kid, I stole a pie, right off the windowsill of a nearby farmhouse. But I wasn't like St. Augustine: I ate every last bite of that pie myself."

"Did you steal it for the fun of it or for the pie?" Hack asked.

"Pretty sure just the pie. I felt guilty, but the pie was good . . . really good."

"If you gonna steal a pie, seems like an insult to the baker if you don't enjoy it."

"Hmm," Bruno said. "You know, I've felt bad about it all these years. But now I think I feel a little better about it."

"You're welcome," Hack volunteered. Bruno chuckled.

The talking faded as the breathing increased. The trail grew in elevation the farther they went. They reached a place where large boulders laid scattered about. The trail essentially came to an end, forcing them to climb a little here and a little there, trusting the trail would pick back up on the other side of the rock formation.

"Looks like the mountain threw up," said Hack.

"A creative mind, Hack. To say the least"

An hour into the hike, they came to a momentarily flat part of the trail.

"Let's take a breather," said Bruno, plopping down on a boulder and drinking from his canteen.

"You think them boys, Loeb and Leopold, are goin' to hell?"

Bruno almost choked on his water as it poured down his throat.

"Hack, you should give someone warning before asking such a question."

"Well, are they?"

"Hell if I know. That's a question for one of the educated monks."

"But if they killed that boy for fun, seems like they'd rather be in hell than in heaven. And God ain't gonna force someone to enjoy heaven."

"Why do you think they'd rather be in hell?"

Hack looked up at the sun and squinted his eyes.

"Just like my eyes hurt when I see at the sun, their souls hurt when they see God. Pa said some people like darkness 'cause they can't stand the light. Them boys like darkness."

"If that's hell, Hack, then what's heaven?"

"Pa told me that heaven was like this," and he pointed around at the beautiful forest enrapturing them.

"A forest? I hope so. I grew up in the Black Forest of Bavaria. And I'd love to go back for all eternity."

"Not a forest, but a new Earth. That's what Pa said: Jesus would make a new Heaven and a new Earth. He gonna make all things new. And we'll see everything 'cause a bright light will shine on it all."

After a few more minutes of peace and quiet, they continued on.

Another hour went by with little conversation. When they reached the top, the sun was still off to the east, warm enough to enjoy but not so overhead as to bake you like a pie in an oven. That would come later.

With the clear sky, they could see until the trees disappeared over the curve of the Earth. The plateau was a solid rock surface. A few pine trees somehow survived up there, growing from the slightest cracks between rocks. And a hundred-foot drop lay before them. They could look down directly on to the tops of trees far below. Death was certain if one went over; thus the Great Bavarian grabbed hold of Hack's arm as he peeked over the cliff.

"Let's dangle our feet," said Hack, excitedly.

Bruno sat himself down and insisted on keeping right next to Hack as he dropped his feet over the side. Hack leaned over ever so slightly, looking down. Something in him conjured up the image of falling into a deep abyss, not onto the top of the trees, but into blackness, completely helpless, totally dependent on someone else to save him. He had a sense of helplessness as he looked over the precipice.

"Once upon a time," Bruno began abruptly, "there was a rock climber. He was a staunch atheist, never having faith in God. But on one particular climb, his grip gave way, and he began to fall. Just in the nick of time, he grabbed hold of a small branch sticking out of the rock. His whole body dangled, just as our feet dangle now. Setting aside his atheistic beliefs, he said a prayer: 'Is anybody up there?' And to his astonishment, he heard a reply: 'Yes.' He asked, 'God? Is that you?' The voice said, 'It is I.' 'Will you please save me?' he begged. 'Yes, I will. All you must do is let go.' The man thought for a moment and said, 'Is there anybody else up there?'"

Hack burst into laughter.

"Hack," Bruno continued after laughing himself, "sometimes you just have to let go. Then, only then, can God work miracles."

Hack nodded, not knowing exactly how, or even if, this applied to him. It was a truth, however, that he recognized, and he took it to heart.

They both laid back and enjoyed the morning sun for over an hour. They spoke of many things; Bruno asked Hack about the rules of baseball; Hack asked Bruno about German food; Bruno asked about Hack's Pa; Hack asked about Bruno's Pa.

"My Pa and I did not get on very well, which is why I was happy to go off to war. I thought it was the answer to all my problems: no more abusive father, no more cranky mother, no more school."

He swatted the memories away as if a fly was bothering him. "Ah, you don't want to hear about all that."

"You mean you don't want to talk about all that?"

Bruno sighed. "Not really."

"How'd you end up in America?"

Another sigh. "It's a long story."

"Is it a good one?"

"Depending on your perspective."

"What's your perspective?"

"It's a sad story, but it has a happy ending, I suppose."

"How's it end?"

"Right now, I guess it ends laying on Crowders Mountain looking up at the blue sky with you."

"Sounds like a happy ending to me."

Hack waited patiently, but nothing more came. "If this is the end, what's the beginning?"

"Tough question. When you get older, Hack, you realize that every second of your life is another beginning of the rest of your life. The philosophers speak about cause and effect: I've asked myself many times if the effect was landing in a monastery, then what was the cause? I don't remember much of Aristotle, but you pick up a lot living in a monastery. He has four causes I think, but hell . . . I can't keep that stuff straight." He paused, then said, "I often wonder whether God or Hank was the cause of coming to America . . ."

"Who's Hank?"

Bruno took a deep breath, as if realizing that the story was now beginning.

"Sargent Jameson Henry Baugham. The man I took into the woods to execute."

"The Battle of Verdun: 1916. The longest battle of the Great War. Lasted 302 days. We counted every day—some of us with tick marks in journals, some of us in our heads. Everyone tried to count the days, but many times we lost track of what was day and night or whether we had just taken a thirty-minute nap or had slept all night. At certain points of exhaustion, however, you don't really care if you slept six hours or six minutes. In fact, you stop caring about whether you live or die. You just become a walking shell of a man who follows orders subconsciously, like a slave who has had free will beaten out of him. I became that man, even though I swore I never would.

"I was in the Fifth German Army. By the end, we lost over 300,000 men. And the French lost more. All for the sake of a strategic position in a city that, if captured, would crush the morale of the French people. After months of being there, the absurdity of the plan was apparent. Worse yet, the soldiers, on both sides I later learned, understood that the point of this battle was to be a meat grinder: the goal was to slaughter as many Frenchmen as possible, no matter how many Germans it took. Erich von Falkenhayn, our Chief of General Staff, even wrote in his Christmas memo, which I saw much later, that the purpose was not to take territory but to take lives: to cause the French army to 'bleed to death.'

"Toward the very end of the battle, in December of '16, we captured a downed pilot. An American of all things. It confused us because America hadn't entered the war yet. But there was a group of American pilots called the *Lafayette Escadrille*, or the *Lafayette Flying Corps*. It was named *Lafayette* because of Marquis de La Fayette's help in your Revolutionary War. And although America had not entered the war, a bunch of American boys joined a flying corps and fought for France. Imagine that: using an airplane in battle. It blew my mind and still does.

"We kept this pilot as a prisoner of war for a few days. I had only seen him from a distance until my commanding officer called me over and said, 'We don't need the baggage of a prisoner: take him across that tree line into the woods, execute him, and leave the body behind.'

"As I said, I was a shell of a man at this point. I didn't salute; I didn't say *yes sir* . . . I just pointed my rifle at the prisoner and yelled at him in German, *Gehan! Gehan!* I didn't speak much English at the time and didn't have the energy to try. He looked at me with cold eyes, and then at the tree line, and back at me again. He understood exactly what was about to happen. And he was one of the only men around as big as me. I've wondered if this is why my officer chose me; maybe I came to mind when he looked at him. The pilot had large and manly features, which was unusual to see after being surrounded with exhausted and tattered men more emaciated than ever. He had a broad chin with a big dimple, high cheekbones, with a large nose, but everything was proportional. His neck was as thick as most men's legs, and his shoulders were so broad that one wondered how on Earth he fit into the cockpit of an airplane. And his hair: it was so thick that it still was in its perfect place after crashing an airplane and being a prisoner for two days. He must have had a haircut recently; again, something that a man without a haircut for over many months notices. The sides of his hair were trimmed neatly, the part in his hair was sharp, and the thickness of his hair looked as if the wind from his flying left a permanent wave. He was as sharp looking a soldier as you were going to find. And it was my job to kill him.

"He walked as directed. In fact, he puffed his chest out at me and nodded his head. I could tell he was resigned to die like a man; he was going to look me in the eye the entire time with dignity and daring. But how I wished he would whimper and cry and display less honor. I didn't want to kill an honorable man. A coward on the other hand . . .

"Anyhow, we walked a hundred yards or so to the tree line and into the forest. After moving about twenty yards or so deep into the forest, I told him to stop. He immediately spun around to look at me. *Dreh dich um!* I told him, nudging him with the rifle. Surprisingly, he complied and turned around, fearlessly.

"But then he spoke for the first time, something under his breath. It was not English. It was neither German nor French. But I recognized it from my childhood: *Ave Maria, gratia plena, dominus tecum. Benedicta tu in mulieribus, et benedictus fructus ventris tui, Iesus.*"

"Sounds like the language you guys speak during prayer," Hack said.

"Latin. The mother tongue. In fact, English is the child of German and Latin."

"Which one is Ma and which one is Pa?" Hack asked.

Bruno became almost frustrated at the interruption at such an important part of his story, nor did he know the answer to such an odd question. He ignored it altogether.

"How could I shoot a man praying, especially in Latin? I felt like I'd be shooting the Church herself! And yet it was a direct order. If there was one thing in life I understood, it was to not disobey a direct order given by a German commanding officer. But what if the order conflicted with a divine commanding officer?

"I had no problem shooting people. I'd shot more than I could count, at least from a distance. But at this moment, we weren't battling. He wasn't attacking me. He was my prisoner, yes. Both human and divine laws, however, prohibited me from killing him as he stood before me defenseless. Everything in me said not to shoot him.

"So, the decision I then made changed everything in my life. This decision was one of the main causes of everything that was to come. I think lawyers call it a *proximate* cause, or something like that. Aristotle would call it one of his four causes, but I never paid much attention in philosophy. My point is that it just simply changed everything. There is no way I'd be here right now, sitting on a mountaintop in North Carolina with you, if I had made the other decision.

"I pointed my rifle at the back of his head, put my finger on the trigger and, strangely enough, I was so fearful of the consequences of my action that I closed my eyes before pushing the gun ever so slightly to the right and pulling the trigger.

"An echo rang throughout the forest, scattering the cawing crows. But the man still stood before me. He gently flinched, no doubt from the deafening sound ringing in his right ear."

"You didn't shoot him?"

"No. I didn't. Sometimes in life the decision not to act is far more impactful than the decision to act. Had I killed him, my life would have continued on pretty much the same trajectory. I might have died that night in the trenches, or I might have gone on to a career in the military. But I had now disobeyed a direct order. And all I had to show for it was a man staring at me in shock.

"As he turned toward me, I waved him off with the rifle whispering, *Lauf*! *Lauf!* or *Run! Run!* My plan was to walk right back to my unit and continue with life as usual, but with a slightly improved conscience. The man nodded at me with his broad chin. He gave me a small smile and then took off without a moment's hesitation, running and leaping over brush like a buck in springtime.

"I turned back, feeling rather good about myself, but off in the distance, standing up on a small ridge, a German soldier was staring at me. Maybe it was this moment, rather, that was the biggest turning point. I don't know. But he pointed his finger right at me and yelled a solitary word that rattled me more than any French artillery had to date. *Verräter!*"

"What's that mean?"

"*Traitor.*"

Hack nodded.

"I knew I would be dead by dinner, if not within minutes. But I wasn't ready to die. I wanted to live. I wanted to do so much more than stand in a trench and pull triggers. I had no Earthly idea where I could go at that very moment. It was as if my options closed in on me faster than gunfire would rain down upon you during a bombardment.

"I spun in a circle looking for where I could go. Off in the distance I saw the American running in a certain direction. I thought to myself, *maybe he knows where he is going*, so I took off after him. And then the thought came to me: if I was caught chasing after him, I would have an excuse. I would say that I had stumbled just before pulling the trigger, missed him, he then took off, my rifle jammed, and I was in pursuit to finish the job. Therefore, I concluded rather quickly, the absolute best thing I could do at that moment was to chase after him as fast as possible. If caught, I had a story. If not caught, well, in that case, I had no idea what would happen next. So, I ran. I ran as fast as I had ever run. The man on the ridge pursued me. I could tell he had gotten word to the rest of my company; it would only be a matter of minutes until they would be bearing down on me. The Germans would go to great lengths to capture a deserter.

"A deserter . . . I couldn't believe it. I had witnessed a few in my time. To me, they were disgusting excuses for men, cowards, betrayers of our Motherland, traitors to their countrymen willing to stay the course and suffer in the trenches. I had never felt the slightest remorse for an executed deserter. They had no honor. And this was one of the worst insults a man could give another. *You have no honor.* For a man can be a coward but still have a remnant of honor; a man can be a liar but have a remnant of honor, but if you have no honor, it is because you are both a coward and a liar. If you have no honor, you have nothing else, and nothingness should not roam the Earth, taking up our space, breathing our air.

"But how could shooting an unarmed POW be honorable, especially one who stood tall and proud and brave, who stood with honor himself! It was right of me to spare his life; I knew that. But was it right to run in shame? Was it right to avoid the consequences of my decision? Would it have been more honorable to stand my ground, look at my commanding officer in the face, and say, *Your order was without honor?* Then, I could have died that day, a young man, with more honor than most fools ever possess in their long lives. But no; I ran fast and furious through the forest, like a crazy man who cared more for his own life than anything else.

"The American eventually looked back and saw me following. He looked past me and saw the German soldier in pursuit of me, or in pursuit of us. I could see him processing the situation. He kept running, but something in me said he was running slower for the sake of letting me catch up. It was hard to believe.

"When you're running for your life, it is hard to calculate the distance. For one, you are in fact running faster than you ever would otherwise; the adrenaline catapults you forward with a force that cannot be conjured up by brute force. If man could tap into adrenaline on demand, he would become a super-soldier, undefeatable in most circumstances. But for some reason, the human mind just knows the difference, knows if survival is really on the line or not. So, your normal sprinting pace in boots while carrying a rifle might be one speed, but with adrenaline, it is another.

"At the same time, you have tunnel vision: you can't see anything to your left or right, above or below; you can't think about five minutes ago or five minutes from then; you can't even feel pain. Everything is focused on the goal of escaping. And in my tunnel vision was the American. He had no rifle and was probably faster than me anyway. Yet, I ran faster than I had ever run before. How long we ran, I don't know. It may have been twenty minutes or forty. We left the German soldiers chasing us far in the rear. He was out of sight. But I had a fear that any minute a band of half-a-dozen Germans, my own countrymen, would be firing at us from a distance.

"I had gained ground on the American. I was just a few feet behind him as we came upon a small creek. He stopped and, with a motion of his hand, told me to wait. He looked around as if trying to gain his bearings. He looked up and down the creek. He then slid his boots through the ground as hard as he could, heading away from the river, making footprints as visible as possible. He patted his pockets, looking for any belongings, but he had nothing after everything was confiscated upon his capture. He looked at me, and I understood. I patted my pockets down. I found a handkerchief and a few cigarettes. I held them before me. He grabbed them quickly with a nod, ran back to the decoy path he was creating, went another ten yards or so and softly dropped the handkerchief. He trenched his boots further and further. He dropped a cigarette and threw another one a few feet away. He then carefully tiptoed back to me, trying not to disturb the tracks he had made.

"He then jumped in the creek, up to his knees. I followed. The water was freezing, absolutely freezing. I dreaded the thought of wet socks for the foreseeable future. But in fact, the freezing water was actually a good deterrent against any German soldier who happened to have a lazy streak in him. At its deepest, the water was up to our waist. I held my rifle overhead to keep it dry. We would have to get our clothes off before long to avoid hypothermia.

"On the other side, the American took no rest, but darted off again, looking back and waving me onward. He knew he was faster, but never left me all together. The only choice I had was to continue on. I kept up with him, but only by pushing myself to the very limits of endurance.

"There are two types of physical exhaustion in a long run like that. First, there are the times when you feel your heart and lungs would detonate at any moment, but those are only when darting up a muddy hill or something of the sort. Intensity of movement is what could give you a heart attack, even in your early twenties. But there are also the times when you have physical fatigue from constant movement. Your feet feel like they are made of porcelain, like they would shatter with the very next fall to the ground; your legs throb and cramp and ache without ceasing; your back develops a certain misery, sometimes in one spot with a shooting pain, others with a general scream of agony with every step.

"I for one prefer the former over the latter: the short-term pain of having your internal organs explode from intensity over the long suffering of general exhaustion. And as my life has unfolded, I still feel that way. If there is one thing I now know about the Christian life, Hack, it is that suffering is necessary. There is no escaping it."

"Why?" Hack asked.

"I'm not sure I know. It has something to do with detaching from the kingdom of man so that we become residents of the kingdom of God; something to do with uniting with Christ's sufferings; something to do with a test of faith; something to do with purification of our sins and those of others. . . . Frankly, it's a big mess in my head. And I have less worry when I tell myself: *You don't need to know, Bruno. You just need to believe.* When I do that, I feel a hell of a lot better. I'll leave the know-how to the theologians, the thoroughbreds of the Church."

"The what of the Church?"

"Thoroughbreds. You know the racehorse?"

Hack shook his head.

"Anyway, the theologians are like the racehorses that get all the glory. But God made Bruno dumb and strong for a reason: he needs a pack mule. And you know what? When you are on a long journey, you usually aren't racing; you are usually going nice and slow and carrying lots of important things with you. You need a good pack mule. Maybe the pack mule is carrying someone important. After all, a mule carried Mary to Bethlehem, and a mule carried Jesus into Jerusalem. That isn't too shabby."

"I'd rather be a pack mule," Hack said.

"I think you are going to be both, Hack."

"But I don't care if I understand suffering; I just want to be strong enough to deal with it, like my Pa."

"Precisely what I mean. You're already proving you can deal with it. But you will one day understand it as good as any theologian."

"But the abbot's gonna send me away. And I bets any schooling is gonna stop right then and there."

"And I thought my life was gonna stop right then and there when I was running from that German soldier. My ending was God's beginning. Same will be true for you."

Hack accepted this with a nod. "So what happened when you crossed the creek?"

Bruno looked up at the sky. "I wonder how long we've been up here?"

"Why's it matter?"

"I promised to be home by Vespers. And we have a two-hour hike down and a two-hour ride home."

"If it was two hours to get up here, it can't be two hours down."

"Oh, you'd be surprised. On steep climbs, especially with boulders to maneuver around, it can take as long or longer to go down safely. Going up, you are fighting against gravity, which keeps you keenly focused on every footfall. But when you are going down, you can easily go too fast, thinking gravity is your friend, when in reality, it is your enemy. I learned this very lesson not long after crossing the creek."

Hack waited anxiously for Bruno to continue. Instead, Bruno stood up, slung his bag on his shoulder, and said, "Time to start our descent."

Disappointed, Hack stood up and looked around at the majestic scenery one last time. He took a small step toward the cliff and peered over it into the dark abyss lined with the sharp tops of pine trees. There was something ever so enthralling about the abyss. Just as he knew something was beneath the treetops, he knew there was something embedded deep in his heart, but did not know what. After living with the monks for a month, the feeling, the longing, had come closer to the surface. Just as the abyss had been brightened by the sun, so had life at Good Shepherd begun to shed light on the deepest longings of his heart. It was a curious sensation, like having the name of something on the tip of your tongue but failing to bring to mind. He knew he longed for something hiding in the abyss of his soul, but it had no face; it had no name.

All this came flooding through Hack's mind as he said goodbye to the rockface beneath his feet, the blue-sky overhead, and the hazy horizon that stretched out until the curve of the Earth stole it away.

Then, he felt a hand on his shoulder.

"Time to go, Hack."

Bruno was right. The descent was trickier than Hack had expected. Bruno, who walked as aggressively as he spoke, who frightened people just entering a room (except Hack), descended like an old man. He carefully placed each foot in front of the other, as if landmines were hidden beneath every root and stone.

"So, what happened?" asked Hack after silence lasted too long.

"What happened when?"

"When you crossed the creek?"

Bruno kept walking and took a deep breath to jump back into his story.

"Not long after the creek crossing, a steep hill appeared. The American seemed to have endless endurance. Up the hill he went. I followed as best as I could, hoping and praying—yes, praying—that the decoys we left behind would lead the Germans astray. We had no clue if they were in pursuit, but when life or death are the only options available, you leave nothing to chance.

"Halfway up that hill, I fell the first time. I began to wonder how much longer I would be able to move. I had decided, definitively, that my feet would keep moving. Period. By pure strength of will, I swore to myself that I would not stop picking up one foot and placing it in front of the next. And so, without a second thought, I climbed back to my feet and kept them moving. But as the hill seemed to never end, I confronted a problem much greater than my will power to move my feet: and that was passing out. My heart and lungs were pumping so hard; I was gasping for air. It felt like I was breathing through a straw. No matter how hard I breathed in, I could not get enough oxygen. But my feet kept moving. I fell a second a time and slid back down a few feet. I fought the temptation to lay there and rest. I climbed to my feet yet again and pushed on. The American in front of me became hazy. I wondered whether he would wait with me when I passed out. In many respects, I hoped he would not. I had saved his life once; I did not want to be the cause of losing his life now.

"Just toward the crest of the hill, the energy was all but gone. The incline increased to such an extent that I fell a third time. I tried to get back on my feet, but could not. I began to crawl on hands and knees. The rifle was in the way and slowed my crawl. The American came back and grabbed the rifle, a rather disconcerting experience. Any other time, I would have never allowed an enemy to take my firearm, despite the strange bond we had developed. But my exhaustion was on the verge of killing me. In fact, it occurred to me that a bullet from the American would be much more welcome than a bullet from the Germans. I did not want to be shot as a traitor. But as an enemy combatant . . . there is honor in that.

"When he took the rifle, I looked up at him, heaving for air. He held the rifle out with one hand and with the other reached out to take mine. My right arm went up with the little bit of energy left in my body. He grabbed my forearm without saying a word and yanked me to my feet. He then threw my arm around his neck and wrapped his hand around my waist. He all but carried me to the crest of the hill.

"How many times since then, during the Fifth Station of the Cross, have I seen his face in my mind's eye? I was no Christ, but he was surely a Simon.

"We reached the crest and looked down the other side. While I was so thankful the uphill was over, I also saw it was essentially a mudslide to the bottom. The last place we wanted to remain was on the crest of the hill, in plain view to anyone around. We started down immediately with one step after another. I had gathered myself a bit and no longer needed him to hold on, or so I thought.

"With every step, the Earth would slide a foot or two. Every step was a controlled crash. The American wisely began sliding on his backside, inching down. For some reason, I thought a long stride would get me down faster.

"In one of these strides, my foot became lodged in something—a rock, a root, I do not know—beneath the mud. Gravity propelling my body down, but my foot remained jammed and my knee became locked.

"A pain shot through my knee. I have never been hit by a bullet, but I imagine it would have felt similar. My falling body eventually pulled my foot free, I hit the ground and rolled sideways all the way down the hill. The pain in the knee so consumed me that I hardly noticed the tossing of my body and the countless bumps and cuts I incurred on stones and limbs all the way down. When I reached the bottom, I was covered from head to toe in mud, freezing from the creek, and holding my leg. It would no longer bend.

"Without thinking, I screamed out in pain. The American reached me shortly thereafter and was shushing me as politely as a man could in such a situation. He eventually covered my mouth with one hand and raised a finger to his mouth. He looked around frantically, wondering if there was anybody around, wondering if there was anywhere to hide. He felt my knee with his hands. It was clear my kneecap was dislocated."

"Is that why you walk funny?" asked Hack.

"That is why I walk funny."

Bruno's steps downhill slowed even further as the painful memory occupied his mind. He said nothing for some time.

"What'd you do after that?" Hack asked.

"The American told me with his hands to stay put, as if I could have gone anywhere if I wanted to. And he ran off. It was a lonely moment. I felt fairly confident that he was looking for shelter, but I wasn't certain. He did return, and probably much quicker than it seemed.

"He looped his forearms under the pits of mine and dragged me along the bottom of the hill. I tried my best to keep from screaming out in pain as my leg bumped along. It was agony . . . agony.

"Finally, we reached the side of the hill. Thick oak trees had fallen across one another, creating an almost tent-like structure against the side of the hill. And the earth of the hill looked as if it had been dug out a little—certainly not by a man, but perhaps by a bear or wolf or something that made the hovel a little home. The American ducked beneath the oaks and pulled me into the hovel. He laid me flat on the ground and knelt next to me. Sweat dripped from his face on to me. The warmth of his breath in the cold air looked as if he was smoking a thick cigar in a night club. He looked around—at my leg, at our shelter, at the rain that had just begun to fall, from which we were partially covered.

"Then he spoke. It was the first word I heard him say, other than the Ave Maria. And it was the perfect word, a word that summed up everything that had happened the past few hours: his fear of being killed, my fear of being ordered to kill; his fear of running from his enemy and my fear of running from my own countrymen; our fear of exhaustion and of injury; our fear of being lost with someone with whom you could not communicate.

When Bruno didn't go on, Hack said, "Well, what'd he say? What was the word?"

"Shit."

Hack put his hand to his mouth, smiling.

"Of all the words in all the languages, it was the perfect word. It was one of the only English words I knew. And I replied, 'Shit.' He looked at me and slowly began to laugh harder and harder until he fell over to his side. Finally, the American was catching his breath.

"There we were, lying next to each other with our heads under shelter, our feet getting rained on, no idea what to do next. Nothing was said for a few minutes. We both looked at each other a few times to see if the other had slipped into a coma or had fallen asleep. But the wet clothes had to be taken care of. The sun was setting, and our body temperatures were dropping from wading through the creek.

"The American took off his shoes, socks, and pants and laid them out to dry. He then turned his attention to my leg. He pulled up my pant leg over the knee. We could both see the kneecap shifted to the outside of my leg. The look of it made the pain increase. He motioned for me to take my pants off. While it was awkward, I did not want to freeze to death. And it was the easiest way for him to work on my knee anyway. I unfastened my pants and he slowly tugged at my pant legs. He carefully removed my socks as well.

"The American spoke, but of course I couldn't understand. Seeing he needed to try another form of communication, he went down to my foot and motioned with his hand that he must pull with all his might, hoping the cap would slide back into place. I knew there was no other option. I had learned in battle that bone breaks and dislocations could cause circulation problems, resulting in amputations. I nodded my head in consent.

"He grabbed a stick lying nearby, broke it into a smaller piece, and demonstrated that it was for me to bite down on, for the pain. He handed it to me, and I immediately pushed it to the back of my teeth.

"He gave me a nod. I nodded back. He pulled my ankle as hard as he could. I bit down on that stick so hard but still couldn't help screaming out in pain. My head fell back as the shooting pain somehow covered my entire leg. But I did not know if it had worked. When I gathered my senses, I sat up on my elbows and looked at my leg. Both the American's face and my leg showed a look of defeat. The kneecap had not budged. He looked closely at the leg. He touched it gently, feeling exactly where the cap was and what tendons and ligaments were in its place.

"He felt my pulse in my ankle and shook his head in concern. He moved to the outside of my leg and showed me his next plan: he put his two hands in the air and moved both thumbs up, indicating that he must push the cap in place with his thumbs. My head dropped back in disbelief. I didn't know if I could take any more.

"What he did next surprised me: he leaned over the top of me and smacked me right across the face. And hard. Then he backhanded me across the other side of the face. What the hell was he doing? Here I was in agony and he's hitting me? *Son-of-a-* . . . , I thought to myself. I sat back up on my elbows and considered hitting him back. But before I could, he smacked me even harder with his open hand. And just as I prepared myself to grab the devil and pound him with my fist, he grabbed my leg with both hands, one just below my knee and the other just above, placed his thumbs at the bottom of the cap on the side of the leg, and squeezed that cap up the side of the leg and pushed it back into place. I flung my head back on to the ground. I had no stick, but bit down on my own arm as hard as I could and screamed. It was over. The cap was back in place.

"The American fell back in relief. He exhaled as if he had gone through the pain himself. He then crawled back down to my foot. He took my pulse again just above my ankle. He sat quietly for a few seconds, patiently waiting to feel something. I heard him say under his breath, *Please*. Another word I understood. And then, his eyes went wide and his jaw dropped. His mouth broke into a smile with a little laugh. He sat back again with a look of satisfaction."

It was time for a short break. Bruno found a large boulder on which to sit, and Hack followed suit. The sun was right overhead, but the brown branches and green leaves reaching out overhead kept the temperature bearable. They drank from their canteens.

Hack saw a fatigue on Brother Bruno's face he had not seen before. It was due not to the hike but to the story. Recounting this event sapped his energy, and Hack understood why. He, too, would be exhausted if he had to recount the events of his father's murder.

Bruno's eyes wandered. He gazed into the forest and up into the sky and down at the ground. Something was moving fast in his mind, something that he had laid aside for many years that he did not wish to revisit on a regular basis.

"You don't have to tell it all," Hack said.

Bruno nodded. "It's one of those things, Hack: you don't want to go there, but once you do, you must finish."

"Why? Why not just stop if it hurts to tell?"

"Because my friend's story deserves to be told. If it is begun, it should be finished."

They sat quietly for some time, until finally, Bruno stood up, put the water away, and continued on. They walked for a long time and nothing was said. Hack had no need to prod him along as he had been doing, for Bruno had already committed to finishing. He would speak when he was ready.

It seemed to Hack that a good listener does not listen out of mere curiosity but out of compassion. Most people, it seemed to him, listened for themselves. But a good listener listens for the sake of the one who is speaking. And once the ear's use has come to an end, it should turn away and never pry again. He wanted to be this kind of listener and felt a sense of remorse for his previous curiosity that had thrown Bruno into the state of having to tell the entire story.

After they cleared a large section of boulders, which required a modest amount of climbing, Bruno said, "Where was I?"

"Your kneecap was set."

"Right. My kneecap was set. The American took two thick sticks and broke them into similar sizes. He took the arm strap off my rifle. He looked around for something else he could tie. He saw my pants that had been removed, took out his knife, and cut the pant leg off. He placed the two sticks on the side of my leg and wrapped the upper part with the arm strap and the lower part with my pant leg. It was as good a splint as we could have at the moment.

"He motioned to the rifle, and I could tell he was asking me how much ammo we had. I patted down my pockets and found three rounds. We dumped those on to the ground and looked at them not knowing what good they would do.

"As the sun set and the cold gripped us, I said, *Feuer*, which he rightly understood. He waved his hand above his head in a swirling fashion and said, *Smoke*, which I rightly understood with his signing. And the point was clear: Smoke would easily give away our location. What then was there to do? If a giant buck came walking by and dared us to shoot and eat him, we would have wasted the ammo. First, the gunfire would draw attention to us; second, we needed a fire to cook the meat, and that too would bring attention to us. There was but one thing we could do: wait. And we both knew it. The condition of my leg could be further investigated in the morning.

"But there was one more important thing to do. I looked at him, tapped my chest, and said, 'Stefan.' He tapped his chest and said, 'Hank.' He reached out to shake my hand. I squeezed it hard. *Danke*, I said. And he replied, *Thank you*. We both had much to be grateful for."

"Your real name is Stefan?" asked Hack.

"No. My real name is Brother Bruno. My birth name was Stefan."

Hack pulled his chin back, furrowed his brow, but wisely decided to let the story continue.

"I laid back, closed my eyes, and slept surprisingly hard despite being cold and wet. The few times I arose was because I heard Hank moving to look around, as if he heard something. He kept the rifle next to his side. And I was grateful."

The descent became easier with every passing step. The decline eased down to the bottom of the mountain and over the course of the next thirty minutes, became the long flat walk back to where they had parked. Hack was sad to see the adventure coming to an end. And while he wanted the story to continue, he could tell that Bruno needed another break. Besides, there was a solid two-hour drive home with no roots and no stones to watch out for. There would be nothing to do except talk and listen.

"You know, Hack," Brother Bruno began again as they approached the beginning of the trail, "when you've been through pain and suffering, when you have been to hell and back, you learn that the small inconveniences in life are but annoyances. When I was younger, I had such a temper. I would explode at the drop of a hat. After surviving the war, I found a certain amount of peace. But it wasn't until I joined the Benedictines that I found true peace. The rigor of war time calms the passions; you exert your energy to such an extent that there is little left to aim at the small things in life. And the rigors of religious life have tempered my passions to an even greater extent."

"I got bad news for you, Brother," Hack said.

"What?"

"You ain't known around Good Shepherd as calm, nor around town."

"That's because I'm misunderstood." People often confuse passion for anger. Passion is a gift from God. Anger is misapplied passion. Passion enables you to get stuff done. Anger prevents you from getting stuff done. I'm at peace in a way I have never been. True, I've gotten in a few fights at the pub . . . but alcohol was involved . . . and you obviously can't judge a man for what he does when drunk. But when I'm sober, things roll off me in a way they never did before. And I thank Saint Benedict and God for that."

Hack nodded in order to be agreeable.

"Never forget, Hack, that passion is a gift from God."

Up ahead, they could see a clearing in the trees that led back to the automobile. The clearing came closer and closer, but something seemed out of sorts. Finally, they reached the opening. The automobile was not there.

Bruno spun around as if looking for a different parking location.

"Wait! Wait!" he yelled, as if someone was trying to move. "Is this where we parked?"

"Yep."

"Are you sure?"

"Yep."

Bruno slowly walked to the middle of the cleared area and spun around one more time, as if double checking that he had not missed the automobile. He looked around his feet in case it had shrunk to the size of gravel. He even looked into the air in case it had grown wings and flown away. Hack began to walk toward him, but then saw his face and slowly backed away.

Bruno squatted to the ground for a moment, then stood up violently, slung both hands out to the side as if he were a wild Bavarian brown bear standing on two legs, growling at his prey. He belted out a scream like none Hack had ever heard.

"Gottverdammt! Ihr dreckigen rassistischen Bastarde!"

Hack backed away further. And then it came to him. "Those men at the filling station . . . ," he said to himself, but out loud nonetheless.

Bruno looked and yelled, "Yes! Who else except those sons-of-bitches eyeing the truck this morning?"

Bruno paced back and forth a minute with his hand on his mouth. Apparently, no good plan came to mind. During this pacing, he found himself near the entrance to the trail, grabbed a large branch off the ground, and swung it like a homerun hitter at the large and unforgiving oak tree. *"Wenn ich dich finde, werde ich dir den Kopf abreißen und dir in den Nacken scheißen!"*

Hack not only took another step back but turned around, squeezed his mouth as hard as he could, knowing full-well that the worst thing he could do was show Bruno his smile.

Bruno plopped down on the ground, elbows on his knees, hands on the back of his head. "The abbot is going to kill me."

Hack finally walked closer to Bruno, who looked up and caught a smile.

"What are you smiling at?" Bruno demanded.

Hack shrugged. "Passion is a gift from God."

Chapter 8

Eve and Her Garden

When one does not know what to do, it is only logical to sit tight. But when a Great Bavarian sits perfectly still and stews for more than ten minutes, the onlooker could get rather concerned. That ten minutes can feel like a lifetime.

Hack was more comfortable with Brother Bruno cussing up a German storm and smashing large branches across oak trees than he was with him sitting still and silent.

Every few minutes, however, Bruno would say under his breath, "The abbot is going to kill me," as if he was stuck in a loop.

"What about Father Roth?" Hack asked.

"Oh, I enjoy pissing him off but never the abbot. No sir. Not the abbot."

After a moment, Hack said, "Brother?"

"Yes?"

"What are we doing?"

"I don't know."

"But you have to make a decision at some point, right?"

"Right."

"Well, can you do me a favor and make the decision? You ain't gonna know anything new in another ten minutes."

Bruno nodded. "Let's go."

The two of them started walking back to the filling station. Bruno hoped to find the men there, but he doubted it. Still, it was the only place anywhere around, and if they were lucky, the owner would be able to let them make a telephone call to the abbey. Brother Bruno estimated that the station was about a half-hour walk away.

A mere ten minutes into the walk, however, fortunes seemed to change as an automobile came barreling down the road. Bruno waved it down. The driver slowed and took a close look at them. His eyes came into focus on Hack. He sped up and passed by without ever looking back.

"Bastard," Bruno said.

Hack shrugged his shoulders. "It's okay, Brother. I'm liking our adventure."

"Adventure, huh?"

"Brother?"

"Yes?"

"What happened after Hank set your kneecap."

"Oh, yes. You want more of that old story?"

"Well, you can't just leave it where you left it."

"Fair enough."

Bruno gathered his thoughts.

"The next morning, we tried to communicate about the fact that I couldn't walk anywhere. Hank made some hand motions, and I realized that he was saying he had to go get help from the French. I understood why, but it was a rather disconcerting thought. Was it better than returning to the Germans? At this point, no doubt. And so we agreed in our own broken way of communicating that he would go in search of French help and that he would return. He also explained that if he was captured by the Germans, he would tell them of my locattion. The thought was not comforting, but I figured it was better than starving to death.

"After we had a plan, he sat next to me, took my hand, and squeezed it hard. I knew it was a sign that he would, at all costs, return and bring me to safety. I believed in him. I insisted that he take the rifle along with the three rounds left. If he was attacked by Germans, it would give him a fighting chance. But he said that I might need the gun for wild animals. I won the argument and waved him onward.

"As I saw him disappear into the distance, I remember having the loneliest feeling I had ever felt. It was as if my only lifeline had vanished. I remember saying a prayer. It was short and to the point, but it was sincere."

"What'd you say?"

"I don't know. It was something like, 'It's up to you now, God. Not me. And I guess it always was. I'm yours to do with what you want.'"

"Sounds like a dern good prayer to me."

"If I didn't say those exact words, I definitely felt the sentiment. I was helpless, surrounded by the wet and cold, by wild animals. . . . I was a completely broken man, internally and externally. It taught me, Hack, that the feeling of helplessness, of complete defeat, is a good thing for a man to feel at one time or another, or else he may live his entire life thinking he's actually in charge.

"So I laid there all day. I did nothing except look around my surroundings over and over again. Toward the evening, I decided to test my leg, more out of boredom than curiosity. I managed to stand, but I couldn't put the slightest weight on my injured leg. So I spent the next few hours making a crutch as best I could out of a thick branch."

"Like that branch you attacked the oak with?" Hack asked with a smile.

"Yes, Mr. Smarty Pants. Like that one. But I couldn't get anything to work. It hurt too much to bend my knee. And moving over the thick brush and stomping through the mud required a bendable knee. I estimated it would be a day or two before I could limp out of there . . . if I had not weakened too much from lack of food and water.

"That night was horrible. I slept very little. I heard every step in the forest. Every squirrel or night creature sounds like a bear or coyote or a German soldier. Abandoning yourself to the moment is the only remedy for total fear. Acceptance of misery and death is the only way to properly handle it.

"The next day was even worse. I began to wonder if Hank would ever return. Had he been shot? Captured? Was he wounded? The uncertainty was hard to bear.

"As night approached, I heard a sound in the distance, a sound unlike those of the animals I had been hearing. It was human footsteps, multiple men. But was it German or French? I almost chuckled at how badly I wanted those to be French footsteps. I had killed countless Frenchmen in Verdun, and now I saw them as my saviors. I had proudly fought for Germany and saw them as the enemy. My life had changed forever. I was not only a man lying in the woods, beaten and broken, but I was a man without a home, without a nation to call home.

"I then saw a man dart from the group toward me. As he came into view, I couldn't believe my eyes: it was Hank! He came right to me with a huge smile and grasped my hand. He said something in English which I didn't understand, but I imagined it was *I came back for you, my friend. I came back.*

"He handed me a canteen and helped me sit up while I drank. Two other men stood behind him, one with the emblem of the Red Cross on his uniform. The other carried a stretcher. He knelt down next to me, inspected my knee, and removed the handmade splint.

"He took a bandage from his med kit and wrapped my leg tightly. They laid the stretcher next to me and allowed me to scoot myself on to it. The other soldier gave me a good pat down, found the knife on my side, confiscated it, and found I carried no other weapons. The medic and the other soldier took the first shift of carrying me while Hank walked alongside us. Hank made sure to swap with them at the first sign of their fatigue.

"After about a two-hour walk, we came to a clearing in the woods. A horse-drawn wagon was waiting for us as the driver petted the horse and smoked a cigarette. A large red cross was painted across the wagon. It was a beautiful sight."

Bruno paused as if he was seeing the horse and wagon in his mind's eye.

The story was so vivid for Hack that he thought he could hear the clap of a horse's hooves on the road behind. Then he turned and realized there really was a horse and wagon coming up behind them.

The chances of such a coincidence were not unrealistic. In that rural part of the state, horses were just as common as automobiles, if not more.

They stepped to the side of the road and watched the driver come into view: a beautiful lady with long blonde hair blowing in the wind, her elbows on her knees as she controlled the reins with assertiveness and grace. Despite her beauty, she wore overalls—unbecoming of a lady in most settings. She did, however, have a delicate white blouse underneath the overalls with small red flowers on it, adding a feminine twist to the rugged look.

The wagon slowed to a stop. "You boys don't know where you going, do ya?"

Her blonde hair and striking blue eyes reminded Bruno of the quintessential German beauty.

He smiled a little and said, "What makes you say that?"

The lady sighed, shook her head, and looked straight ahead over her horse. "German, huh?"

"Yes, ma'am. Yes, I am." And he turned to Hack and said loud enough for the lady to hear, "I've got to get rid of this accent and you've got to get rid of that skin."

"I didn't say that," the woman said. "But I'll ask you again. You don't know where you boys are going, do you?"

"We're going to the filling station up the road."

"It's closed. You gonna sleep there?"

"Our automobile was stolen."

She nodded and thought for a moment.

"You planning on camping on the side of the road?"

"We gots no plan, ma'am," Hack said.

She sighed again. "Oh dear Lord . . . Well, come on, get in."

Hack gave Bruno the biggest smile of the day and jumped in without a second to waste. He climbed into the back while Bruno took the seat next to the lady. They did not ask where they were going but knew it was better than walking along the road.

"Joyriders took your car I bet," she said. "I reckon they ain't bringing it back neither. Probably drive to Charlotte or Atlanta and sell it. Where you headed?"

"Capstone."

"That's about seventy miles or so. Two hours by automobile. Eight hours by buggy."

Bruno nodded.

"Well, I guess you have to stay at my house tonight—only tonight, you hear?"

"Thank you kindly, ma'am. Do you have a telephone by chance?"

"Shoot no. Just me, the farm, and this here horse. Can't afford no fancy anything. Who you need to call?"

"Ah, no one really."

The horses naturally took a dirt road without any coaxing from their driver. A small house and barn were nestled at the end of the road, with a large field spanning out both left and right from the house. The setting sun did its miraculous work on the clouds behind the house, turning them a most spectacular orange and yellow and pink, all merging and folding and bending together in an ocean of color, or a canvas filled with the brush strokes of an angelic painter, or perhaps they were a mere playful thought of a divine artist.

The house had a front porch wrapping around one side. Empty flower baskets swayed in the wind as they hung from the ceiling. Two lonely rocking chairs stood motionless.

The field was separated into different crops, all in different states of growth, some looking as if the summer heat had killed them off. A small pigpen was next to the barn with a handful of pigs doing what pigs do, more fascinated with the brown mud beneath their hooves than the majestic sky above their heads. And while the house was kept up nicely, the barn was in a state of disrepair—the screen door leaning off to one side, a shutter missing, the rooster weathervane bent to where it no longer rotated with the wind or pointed toward the bursting colors of the west but depressingly fixated on the dusty road beneath it, not unlike the pigs' snouts.

"Is your husband home?" Bruno asked after seeing that such a place was far too much for a young lady to keep up herself.

"Nope. He was killed by Germans in the war. He's lying in some trench over there. Got a letter. No details. Just a few weeks from coming home."

Bruno's head followed that of the pigs and metal rooster, dropping to the ground. No wonder his accent had stung upon their meeting.

After dismounting the wagon, Bruno and Hack stood awkwardly as she unhitched and unbridled the horse. She spoke to him with a gentleness and affection they had yet to hear, like a mother tucking in her small child.

"Hey, Gus!" she hollered over her shoulder at the pigpen, then turning to Bruno and Hack, "That big one there's my favorite pig." She then made her way to the kitchen door on the side of the house, waving the man and boy along with her. As they entered the kitchen, they saw a small table for two with a white tablecloth and tea set sitting ready, as if guests were expected.

"Sit down. I'll feed you."

Bruno and Hack did as ordered. The lady busied herself in the pantry, lit the stove, and set the table.

"We married only a few months before he shipped off in '17. He inherited the farm from his dad a few years before."

She paused for a moment.

"I was eighteen. He was twenty-three. Not exactly the way a young girl plans to start her married life."

"No. It's not," Bruno replied somberly.

She continued moving about the kitchen.

"By the way, I oughta know the names of the boys sleeping in my house."

Bruno looked quickly at Hack with an unnatural hesitation to such a simple question. Hack returned the look in similar fashion. When they didn't answer, she said, "My name's Evelyn."

"Nice to meet you, Evelyn," Bruno said. "We're very appreciative of your hospitality."

After a pause, she said, "You boys wanted by the law or somethin'? Or you forget your names?"

"Ma'am, we ain't commit no crime," Hack said, "but we live in secret."

"Why?"

"That's what makes it a secret: we can't say. But I'm speaking truth, even if it's just a kernel of truth rather than the whole thing. Are you all right with a kernel of truth so long as there ain't no lies choking it?"

Evelyn thought a moment.

"I suspect I am. But I'm calling you something. Gus and Russ." She giggled. "My biggest pig and smallest pig."

For both Bruno and Hack, seeing a woman smile was more refreshing than cool water on a summer day.

After a modest dinner, Evelyn left the kitchen to prepare both the guest room for Bruno and the couch for Hack. They stared at each other the moment they were alone.

"I like being near a woman," Hack said.

Bruno knew of the multiple connotations but replied with equal innocence, "Me too."

Evelyn returned after a while and made some coffee. As the hot water heated in the kettle, Hack asked permission to explore the barn and pigpen. He went to talk to the pigs and easily found Gus and Russ. He found a horse brush next to the horse's stall, slid the door to the side, and entered. The beauty of the black animal was impressive. The muscles twitched every time a fly landed on its thick coat. The mane was perfectly groomed; Evelyn must have taken great pride in caring for her horse, which was consistent with the motherly tone she used before.

Hack couldn't help wondering, so he bent over and looked underneath: a gelding. He was glad to see a male, even if castrated, was around to take care of the lady of the house.

Although Hack usually stayed up much later than sundown, it had been an unusually long day. He told the two adults he wished to go to bed and, after thanking his host again, found his way to the couch in the living room. The windows, of course, were open all day and every night in the dead heat of summer. And while he did not intend to eavesdrop on their conversation, Hack could hear everything Bruno and Evelyn said.

"So why'd you come to America?" she eventually asked.

Bruno cleared his throat.

"Can't tell me that either, huh?"

"It isn't that. It's just a long story."

"You can't summarize?"

"In short, I am, I was, a deserter of the German Army. But not intentionally. By accident, really."

"How'd you accidentally become a deserter?"

"That's what makes the story long. I spared an American's life when I was supposed to execute him. But I got caught. We fled together. I spent two years in a French POW camp, then made my way over to America."

She nodded. "That's not what I expected to hear."

"Life is stranger than fiction."

"Tell me about it, I have a German deserter and negro boy both living a secret life staying at my house. Don't get much stranger than that."

"No, it doesn't."

"You're taking care of him, aren't ya?"

"And he's taking care of me," Bruno said. "We all like to give a little help, but we all need help too."

"That sure is true, but I didn't used to think it. I thought if I just took care of the pigs and crops that I would never need someone again, like I needed Logan."

"Your husband?"

"Yes."

There was a long moment of silence. Hack almost felt his eyes getting heavy until Bruno spoke up again.

"God knew the garden and the animals were not enough for Adam."

"Yeah, but in that story, they remained together the rest of their days, even through sin and darkness. In *this* story, He took my Adam away, leaving me alone in my garden."

"A bullet took your Adam."

"I've sat on this porch a hundred times, sipping on coffee, and thought about that very thing. God allowed it. Same damn thing for Logan. Same damn thing for me."

"God allowed it because He loved that Kraut who shot Logan so much that He gave him the free will to pull the trigger or not. Otherwise, that Kraut would be a slave to a divine tyrant."

"You sound like a preacher."

"I'm not."

"But a man of God?"

"I hope so."

"What about you? You have an Eve?"

Bruno looked down at his plain clothes, a contrast to his normal habit. In the silence, Hack wondered if they were staring at each other or looking uncomfortably away.

"Not exactly," Bruno finally said.

"Another mystery surrounding you."

"Trust me, it is indeed a mystery of the highest form."

Although the metal rooster on the barn could not do his job on account of its bend, a rooster perched on a picket fence most certainly did his. Hack was amazed how late he had slept given that his routine at the monastery had him up much earlier.

Evelyn was the first one up and had baked fresh biscuits and laid out fruit and coffee and juice. It seemed a feast fit for kings considering they had seemed doomed to sleep on the side of the road until the damsel came to them in their distress.

As they ate, she explained that she had a friend she hoped could help them get home, a friend with an automobile. So they loaded up the wagon and left her farm. The thirty-minute ride was a long and quiet one. It was as if Bruno and Evelyn were too embarrassed to talk to each other. But the cool morning air made the ride most enjoyable for Hack, even though he was disappointed at not hearing her voice along the journey.

Off in the distance, a small general store came into view.

"Y'all ever hear of the Holiness Movement?" Evelyn asked.

"I've heard a little," Bruno said, "but don't know anything about it."

Evelyn smiled. "Well, hope you ain't afraid of the Holy Spirit, 'cause you're about to get a boat load full of Him."

A wiry old man was sweeping dust and dirt from his front door. His gaunt frame and slumped posture belied his flamboyance, which became apparent the moment he saw Evelyn. He grabbed her shoulders and pulled her in, as if they hadn't seen each other in a while. They spoke as if the two strangers were not sitting in the wagon. Finally, she pointed to them. The old man listened carefully, nodding his head. A moment later, he walked inside and returned with a wide-brimmed hat. He closed his front door and flipped the Open sign over to Closed.

"Let's go boys," he hollered, waving his hand toward the Model T parked beside the building.

Bruno and Hack hopped out. Hack extended his hand toward Evelyn and thanked her again. He found himself holding her hand longer than was appropriate.

"Best of luck to ya," she said. "Not sure what's going on with you, but you seem good stock to me."

Hack smiled but then took a step back, making room for Bruno.

Bruno and Evelyn exchanged a silent look for what seemed to be a long time. "I'm so grateful, ma'am."

"Evelyn," she corrected him.

"Evelyn."

Hack felt something funny turn in his stomach while he watched Bruno rub the back of his neck, searching for the right words.

Evelyn said, "Hope you boys work through your secrets."

"And I hope God sends another Adam into your garden."

Evelyn smiled softly. "Go on, now," she said, her voice choking a bit.

They loaded up in the old man's car, finally heading home.

"Herbert's the name," the old man announced. "And apparently you boys have to use the name of Ms. Evelyn's pigs 'cause you gots lots of secrets."

They didn't know what to say.

"Capstone, right?" he asked.

"Yes, sir. And thank you very much," Bruno replied.

"Now, boys, I'm good with secrets because to the Lord there ain't no secrets. And I'm happy with colored folk or German folk or any kind of folk, all I care about is if you're baptized Christians."

"Yes, sir. We are baptized," Bruno assured him.

"Then we are Christian brothers. That's all I need to know to help a fella in need."

Hack was curious if this meant he would *not* help a non-baptized fella in need.

"Hey, boy," Herbert said over his shoulder. "You know who the Holy Spirit is?"

Hack thought for a second.

"My Pa said the Spirit blows into our lives like the wind, and we don't know which-a-way it's coming and which-a-way it's going."

"Oh, how right your Pa is! The way you talkin' 'bout him has me assumin' he's moved on to paradise?"

Bruno looked back at Hack. The boy was looking out the window. "I guess the Spirit blows like the wind," Hack said.

"Oh, how right you are, my boy. How right you are. How about you, my German brother? You know the Spirit?"

"Yes, sir."

"You believe in the gifts of the Spirit? Gifts given to the Apostles?"

"Yes."

"What church you go to?"

Bruno took a deep breath. "I'm Catholic."

"Catholic! My good word . . . she didn't say nothing 'bout . . ."

"Well then pull the damn automobile over if this Christian seat is too clean for this dirty papist."

"Now, I didn't say that. It just caught me by surprise, that's all. After all, you said you was baptized Christians."

"Well, we are!" Bruno said.

"I mean full Christians. Bible Christians."

"Am I half Christian? One-third Christian?"

"Maybe you got Jesus, but maybe you also got some idols, like that pope of yours, or Mary."

"Listen, buddy: I got Pope Pius XI the same way Paul had Peter, and I got Mary the same way John had her at the foot of the cross."

The old man grunted.

"What about you, boy? You Catholic?"

"I don't rightly know," Hack said.

"What you mean?"

Hack said nothing. But it dawned on Bruno: Hack was not actually Catholic.

Herbert decided not to pry but turned his attention back to Bruno.

"You go to that big monastery for church?"

"Yes," replied Bruno with a smile.

"What's it like with all those boys in black robes? I hear they chant like zombies."

"They chant the Psalms like David did with his lyre," Bruno said.

Herbert nodded. "You speak Latin?"

"A little."

"You know Jesus didn't speak Latin. Don't make no sense why your church does."

"You know Jesus didn't speak English. Not sure why your church does."

Herbert bit his lip and grunted again. "Well, I guess we got more in common than we do different."

Bruno smiled. "Amen to that."

Herbert began humming softly. But as time went on, he hummed louder and louder, until Hack asked, "What you humming?"

The old man cleared his throat and belted out as if standing before a congregation:

On a hill far away, stood an old rugged Cross
The emblem of suff'ring and shame
And I love that old Cross where the dearest and best
For a world of lost sinners was slain

So I'll cherish the old rugged Cross
Till my trophies at last I lay down
I will cling to the old rugged Cross
And exchange it some day for a crown.

"Can you teach it to me?" Hack asked.

"I sure can. For the Lord wants it in your heart. Guess I gotta put it in your mind first."

Herbert began slowly, line by line, and Hack would repeat it. They went through three verses. It was not only a beautiful song but a beautiful way to pass the time and to put their differences aside.

The two-hour trip passed in a flash for Hack. As they approached the boundaries of Capstone, Bruno realized it was not safe for Hack to be seen. It was midday, the busiest possible time in town. And Capstone was so small that a visitor like Herbert might stick out, drawing attention to Hack in the back seat.

Bruno had no other choice but to tell Hack to lay down flat in the back seat.

"Ah," Herbert said. "I understand. You protect the boy."

Bruno made no reply but began giving directions to an old horse road running behind the abbey grounds. It was far enough away from town that Bruno doubted anyone would see them, but it was likewise far enough away from the abbey that Herbert would never guess the final destination.

When they climbed out, Bruno thanked Herbert profusely. Herbert replied with a blessing. He placed his hands upon their heads and called the Holy Spirit to descend upon them and remain with them always. It felt like an apostolic blessing from an archbishop decked out in miter and crosier.

"Thank you, my Christian brother," said Bruno, closing the door.

"I hope the Spirit blows your way," added Hack.

"Oh . . . He will. He will indeed."

As Herbert drove off, you could hear him break into song louder than ever:

So I'll cherish the old rugged Cross
Till my trophies at last I lay down
I will cling to the old rugged Cross
And exchange it some day for a crown.

Chapter 9

Comings and Goings

The adventure was not over. They had a good hour walk through the thick of the woods before reaching the abbey. And the Great Bavarian worried every step of the way that Hack would be seen.

"Brother?" asked Hack.

"Yes."

"You left your story off at getting loaded up in the Red Cross wagon."

"Ah. So I did."

"I heard you say last night you were a POW for two years? What's a POW?"

"You were listening?"

"No. But the windows were open. I can't close my ears."

Bruno smiled. "A POW is a 'prisoner of war.'"

"You was a prisoner?"

"Well, technically, yes. The Americans took me to a French camp, and since I came from the German army, their enemy, I had to be treated accordingly. They took some personal information while Hank told them the story. The medic said my leg would have to heal from thereon by itself. It was set and that was all there was to it.

"The new fear, however, was the true story getting out to my fellow German prisoners. If they learned I was a deserter, they would kill me on the spot. My story was simple: I was chasing after the escaped pilot when I dislocated my knee. He grabbed my gun, left me in the woods, and they came and picked me up. Easy. I must have told that story a hundred times over the next few years.

"I heard Hank tell the commanding officer to take extra good care of me because I had saved his life. And they did. As my leg healed, I was given only the most modest physical labor."

"What'd you do there for two years?"

"It was not unlike the monastic life. We had a set time to wake up and eat and work. We had down time during the day. We were stuck with the same people over a long period of time. And you went to bed at the same time every night. There were no communal prayers, but it was community life, with all the goods and bads that come with it.

"I could talk about my time in that camp all day, about the men who came in and out of the camp, about the fights and murders that happened before my eyes, about the chaplains who were permitted to minister on the rare occasion, about learning French and English, about generous guards and viciously evil guards . . . but let's try to finish this story."

"Sounds good."

"After being admitted into the camp, I didn't expect to ever see Hank again. But he kept coming back to visit me until the war was over. At that time, the guards handed us a new pair of clothes and two envelopes—one with cash and the other with a certified letter stating in French that I was a released POW. As I walked from the gates, I had no clue where I would go. I couldn't go to Germany in case there was a record on me as a deserter. And I doubted that the French people would take kindly to a huge Bavarian applying for a job around town. And so I walked out of the gates and, to my amazement, saw Hank standing right there waiting for me. He asked where I was headed, and I admitted I didn't know. Then he said something that would change my life forever."

"What?" Hack asked. "What'd he say?"

"He told me he'd found a civilian ship headed to Wilmington, North Carolina, and that I could come to America with him. I had never heard of Wilmington, but it sounded good to me. He said he could set me up with some farmers for a job. I accepted the offer and used a good chunk of the cash in the envelope just handed to me to purchase the ticket.

"The ride over is a whole other story. Our friendship grew. My English improved. But about halfway across the Atlantic, Hank began looking sick. Within a few days, he was stuck in bed with a horrific fever. In fact, there was an outbreak on the ship. Over half of the people on board became deathly ill. About one-third of the poor souls on board died within a few days of reaching North Carolina. The German's couldn't kill Hank, but the Spanish Flu could. And it did."

Hack looked up at him. "My Ma died from that."

"I know, Hack. It was a terrible thing. So many people in such a short period of time . . ."

In the distance, they could start to see the peak of the monastery's highest bell tower.

"I walked off the boat and started down the street. It was not too long before I saw the steeples of a Catholic church, not unlike how we see the abbey's bell towers right there," he said pointing through the trees. "But the steeples were different. They were twin towers with domed cupolas and little crosses on top, with a huge copper dome between them. The red brick seemed very bright amidst the green pines surrounding it. It was a beautiful sight to see after coming off a boat with as much death as a trench in Verdun.

"It dawned on me: if there was anyone in town likely to help a German POW, it would be the Church. I didn't want to leave my chances up to just any anti-German American. So I went in the front door.

"I had never felt so at peace in a church. It was as if the sanctuary was truly my sanctuary from the horrors of the war, from the POW camp, from the Spanish Flu . . . and from my own uncertainties. The interior was constructed with a unique blend of brick and tile that made the church look like a thousand-year-old cathedral from the East. I would come to learn, however, that the church was but a few years old. The arches throughout the building were masterful, holding enormous weight through the purest rules of geometry rather than the brute force of rafters and beams. I couldn't find a nail or piece of wood in the entire church. It was as if the most esteemed Greek and Roman architects had risen from the dead and convened in Wilmington, North Carolina, for the sake of rising this basilica in defiance of gravity.

"There were small stained-glass windows lining the back of the dome over the high altar. The marble floors looked perfectly polished and cool to the touch. The tabernacle was small but looked as if a master-craftsman had spent a lifetime edging every centimeter of the gold and silver with precision.

"I plopped myself down in the front pew and noticed two things that have forever given me peace and comfort. The first was the sanctuary lamp with the dim glow through its red glass. It was a Christian symbol borrowed from our Jewish elder brothers that signifies the Lord dwells within this house. It seemed to me an eternal flame, an eternal light, standing forever vigil before the tabernacle in which the Most Blessed Sacrament was reposed. Every time I walk into our sanctuary and see the red light, I think how the Lord is with us when we are most alone, most in need . . . most abandoned by the world around us.

"Secondly, I noticed that I heard nothing. I had been surrounded by noise for so many years. First, it was deafening shells and gunfire and agonizing screams of war, then it was the constant drumbeat of grumbling POWs, then the moans of people dying of the Spanish Flu. And now . . . only a beautiful silence. I could hear my head ringing from years of constant noise. I felt that if I sat in silence long enough, the ringing would dissipate into the past and make room for God alone to speak. As I reflect back on it, it must have been this moment that God put the first seedling of desire in my heart for the monastic life.

"I do not know how long I sat there, but I had not been that alone for that amount of time since I was injured in the woods, waiting for Hank to return with my captors.

"A moment later, I heard footsteps behind me. It was a priest with thick black hair and bottle-cap glasses. He walked with a certain confidence, as if this was his home, and indeed it was. He had a serious but kind look on his face. It was the face of an intellectual, but not a snob. He wore a large white collar around his neck and suit jacket, unlike many priests who wear cassocks. His curly hair looked as if his fingers had been stuffed through it for the past hour while reading over a book at a desk.

"He asked if he could help me, and when I said 'I hope so,' he immediately noticed my accent. Noting my bag at my feet, he pursed his lips, genuflected toward the tabernacle, and sat next to me. He introduced himself as Father Christopher Dennen, pastor of Saint Mary's Church. He asked me if I was fresh off the boat. He asked if I was from Germany. He asked if I had been a soldier. I was amazed at his ability to read my situation with such precision, which enabled me to open up to him with clarity and sincerity. I gave him a condensed version of my story, of the death of my friend on the boat . . . and before I could tell him I was needing to find work, he interrupted me."

"What was your friend's name?" he asked me.

"Hank . . . or Sargent Jameson Henry Baugham," I replied.

"He slowly lowered his head and made the sign of the cross. He had known the Baugham's for many years. He had known Hank—or Henry as he had called him—since Hank was a child, serving Mass in the older church just down the street. And that's when I told him the details of how Hank's *Ave Maria* had spared his life, for I could not shoot a man praying to Mary in Latin. He grabbed my shoulder and said that I may have saved Hank's life but that I saved my own soul.

"I eventually got around to asking about finding work and lodgings. He told me that he had no work for me, but I could stay in the rectory with him for the night, which I gladly accepted. He then told me about Good Shepherd Benedictine Monastery a day's train ride from Wilmington. He said how he had spent time there as a young priest and that he stayed in touch with Abbot Lawrence, God rest his soul.

"That night while I ate a huge meal at his table, he wrote a lengthy letter to Abbot Lawrence on my behalf, asking the abbot in friendship to consider all possible employment for me as a farmhand on the abbey grounds. The next morning, he took me to the train station, paid for my ticket, stuffed my pocket full of money, and carefully placed the letter in my jacket pocket. He blessed me, told me to stay in touch, and waved as the train slowly moved from the platform. And we have been friends ever since.

"Any how, to make a long story short . . ."

"Please don't," Hack said.

"Don't what?"

"Make the long story short. I like the long stories."

Bruno laughed. "Don't you think this story over the past two days has been long enough?"

"No."

"Well, I'm bored telling it. So . . . to make a long story short, Abbot Lawrence put me to work in the fields and allowed me to stay in the monastery until I saved enough money for my own lodgings. I started attending communal prayer, and a year later, I entered the novitiate.

"And that, Hack, is the story of how I went from trench warfare in Verdun to praying Vespers at Good Shepherd Abbey."

Hack nodded, thanked Brother Bruno for the story, and looked up through the trees as they approached the back of the monastery, happy to be home.

"Thank God you're all right," said the abbot, standing from his chair and grasping Bruno's arm as he walked into the office. "Now, where the hell have you been? Is Hack okay?"

Brother Bruno, despite his stature, hung his head like a puppy about to be scolded. He launched into the long story, beginning first with the incident at the filling station.

"You know, Abbot, I kept my cool. You would have been proud. It is a great shame to see the evil in men's hearts."

"Indeed, Brother. But again, where have you been?"

"One day soon, Abbot, I believe that the prejudice against negros will begin to wane. And I think that as we get further from the Great War, Germans will be more warmly welcomed in this country too."

"Yes. Yes. But where have you been?"

"Well, you see, Abbot, it was a beautiful hike . . ." and Bruno continued with details that he would normally never volunteer.

"I get it, Brother. It was a beautiful hike. Did you just camp up there or something?"

"Well, you see, Abbot, we got ourselves into a little bind . . . but we were met by a young lady whose generosity was that of a true Christian. Unlike those men at the filling station, she had no prejudice in her, and she welcomed us into her home. Her husband had died in the war, and she took over the . . ."

"Did you sleep at her house?" the abbot exclaimed in shock, with a tinge of premature anger.

"Well, yes, but it isn't what it sounds like."

"One of my monks, and Hack, decided to spend the night with a young widow?"

"She was very kind. She cooked us dinner and . . ."

"You were hungry, huh? So, you met some filly on your hike, and she offered to feed you boys, and your Bavarian belly just couldn't resist?"

"No. That's not it, Abbot, I swear."

"What else could it be? You have a brand spanking new automobile to drive home in, but you instead decide to lodge up with a total stranger, a young widow of all people!"

"Well, that's the thing, Abbot. . . . You see, the automobile . . ."

"I told you to take the extra gasoline canister. You ran out of gas, just as I had worried about."

"No, Abbot. No. It's worse than that."

"Oh, dear Lord," the abbot dropped his head to hands. "You wrecked the damn thing. How bad is the damage?"

Bruno paused.

"Abbot?"

"Yes?"

"It's worse than that?"

"How could it be worse than that?"

"You remember I told you about those racist bastards at the filling station?"

"Yes."

"Well, I also got directions to the hiking site from the store owner."

"Yes . . ."

"And, well, when we came down from our hike hours later . . ."

"Yes . . ."

"The automobile . . ."

"Yes . . ."

". . . was gone."

A man of virtue does not lack emotion. Rather, he has, according to Aristotle, merely habituated his emotions to work in tandem with his reason. The man of virtue often acts like the rest of us in small situations—with a quick burst of temper or sign of frustration—for he knows that such reactions are not terribly destructive to himself or others. But where he differs from the bulk of humanity is in the more challenging situations.

He has the wisdom to know when an eye roll is acceptable and when it would pierce another's heart; he knows when raising his voice at a subordinate is the equitable method and when yelling would crush his spirit like a boulder dropped from a mountaintop. Indeed, he may growl at the small imperfections of another but, ironically, laugh off the most egregious transgression as the mere tragedy of human frailty—never to take sin lightly, but as an act of compassion for the sinner in us all.

All this is to say that when Brother Bruno finally dropped the bombshell, the abbot's frustration vanished into thin air. It was as if a father saw a wounded child and all he cared about was expressing his fatherly love. Besides, the abbot could not see how Bruno had done anything wrong in the first place.

In fact, the good abbot spent a good deal of time lifting Bruno's spirits.

"But the money, Abbot. The money . . ."

"Brother, don't you know that money grows on trees in heaven? God can pick it and send it our way anytime He wants."

Departing from Bruno, assuring him again everything would be all right, the abbot made his way down to visit Hack, rather concerned for the boy's state of mind. Being subjected to more racism, being abandoned on the side of the road, having to stay in a stranger's house, driving home with yet another stranger. Could Hack take much more uncertainty in his life?

"It was the greatest trip in my whole life! Well, the only trip in my life. But the greatest!"

"It was?" the abbot asked.

"Oh, Abbot, riding in an automobile with the wind blowing in the window . . . and the hike and beautiful trees and sky, and the drop off. Did you know that if I fell I'd be dead?"

"No. I didn't know that."

"Sure would. And Brother Bruno told me his war story. The whole thing. Do you know his story?"

"Yes, he has told . . ."

"Isn't it amazing?"

"Yes, it . . ."

"And then I thought we was gonna sleep on the side of the road! And then the lady, Evelyn . . . Did ya know her name?"

"Brother Bruno didn't mention . . ."

"We didn't give her our real names, ya see, so she named us after her pigs. And she had this great big black horse. And I went in its stall. And I slept on the couch. And in the morning, we had the biggest biscuits your eyes ever seen and your stomach ever held. And then the old man who drove us home, he didn't like Catholics much . . . oh, and by the ways . . . am I Catholic?"

The abbot struggled to keep up. "Ah . . . no. I don't believe you are. Would you like to be?"

"If you and Brother Bruno are, it's good enough for me."

"Well, we'll need a better reason than that."

"Was Jesus Catholic?"

"That's a tricky question."

"I bet He was. I mean, He wasn't Baptist or Methodist or anything like that. I guess He was Jewish and Catholic. Can you be both? I'd be both if I could be. Anyhow . . . the old man taught me this great song called 'That Old Rugged Cross.' Do you know that song?"

Apparently, the abbot's worries were unfounded. Hack was more alive than ever before. This produced two seemingly contrary thoughts in the mind of Abbot Ambrose: first, it showed that a boy his age must be out in the world, experiencing life, meeting good and bad people, taking risks, hiking mountains, walking along the sides of roads, and even wondering where he might sleep the night—all fabrics that weave together to make the adventure of life; second, it showed that the monks could provide such an experience, even if some of the details were less than ordinary. But he quickly shook off the second of these thoughts, knowing that the boy would not be staying much longer.

"What's wrong?" Hack asked.

The abbot realized his face must have given a window into his emotions. "Oh, nothing, Hack. Nothing. But," the abbot continued as he rose from the chair, "I must return to my duties upstairs. It was nice visiting. And I'm glad you are ho . . ." He caught himself. ". . . you are safe."

"Abbot?" Hack said.

"Yes."

"The Spirit blows where it wills."

The abbot paused, considered it for a moment, nodded his head in affirmation, and closed the door behind him. As he walked down the hall, he could hear Hack singing:

So I'll cherish the old rugged Cross
Till my trophies at last I lay down
I will cling to the old rugged Cross
And exchange it some day for a crown.

On his way back up to his office, Abbot Ambrose saw Father Roth loitering around his door.

"Can I help you, Father Roth?"

"I hear Bruno and the boy lost our automobile?"

"It was stolen, but yes."

"Well, Abbot, what would you have me do? Buy another one? We don't have that kind of cash lying around."

"I know. I know."

"Well then . . . ?"

"Just give it some time, Father. Just give it time." He patted the crusty prior on the shoulder, trying to move him aside so he could escape into his office, but the prior persisted. Father Roth despised any attitude toward him that even whiffed of paternalism, especially from a younger monk, abbot or not.

The abbot was trying to escape into his office, but the prior persisted.

"How is your search going?" he asked.

The abbot sighed, turned partially back toward the prior, recognizing the uncomfortable fact that he owed him an answer.

"I have found the right family. They are in Jefferson, North Carolina. Tucked away in the mountains."

"Excellent. Now, when shall he depart?"

"I haven't decided yet."

"You mean you haven't decided to *let go* yet?"

The abbot hated hearing it from the prior, but knew he was right.

"Perhaps."

"Not perhaps. Most certainly. This is no place for a boy. And the longer you drag your feet, my dear Abbot, the deeper the boy implants his feet in the abbey's soil. You are doing him no favors."

Abbot Ambrose was wise enough to know that the ulterior motives of Father Roth did not negate the truth he spoke. In his humility, the abbot agreed with the prior, thanked him for his words, and entered his office. He sat at his desk, stared at the letter from the family in Jefferson that welcomed Hack under all the facts and circumstances, and he prayed.

The beautiful, melodic, comforting, peace-bearing routine of Hack's life at Good Shepherd returned the very next morning, which all began with the gentle chant of the monks above. Later that day, Father Henry came down for the reading lesson just minutes after Abbot Ambrose informed him of the family in Jefferson.

"Father Henry, why you acting differently today?"

"Am I?"

"Yep. That's all right. You don't have to tell me. But you looking sad."

"Am I?"

"Yep. But that's all right. We all allowed to be sad sometimes."

Father Henry proceeded with the reading lesson as usual, but an angst set into his heart. The purity of Hack's mind would be missed by all, including Father Henry. And it was in this moment that Father Henry became grateful for the short time he had spent with Hack.

It was a long walk for Abbot Ambrose down to the hermitage. He would have rather faced King Darius's den of lions or Nebuchandnezzar's fiery furnace than the boy living in the Good Shepherd basement. At times in life, however, there is little else to do than say kindly and directly what must be said. The abbot, with his gloriously phlegmatic personality, had often reflected on the odd fact that men tried to get to the truth by saying everything other than the truth, a result of original sin, no doubt.

Traditionally, it was believed there were three results of the Fall: darkness of the intellect, weakness of the will, and proneness to evil. *Which of the three led to convoluted communication,* the abbot often wondered as he watched men twist and turn and finesse to the point of near psychological abuse of those around them. He often considered the miraculous improvements awaiting communities, families, enterprises, the sacrament of confession, the training of novices . . . yes, miraculous improvements awaiting everyone if a simple prayer could be learned: To ask the Holy Spirit for the gift of simplicity in thought and speech. Such a gift was not listed among the conventional seven gifts of the Spirit: wisdom, knowledge, understanding, counsel, fortitude, piety, and fear of the Lord. *Simplicity of thought and speech,* he had concluded, was like a penumbra emanating from these enumerated gifts of the Spirit. If one's thought, for example, was filled with wisdom and piety, it would surely avoid the layers upon layers of convolution brought on by a haughty mind. If one's heart was filled with understanding and fear of the Lord, one's speech would surely set aside all the silly craftiness of rhetoric, as if our words give life to the world.

While Abbot Ambrose' temperament helped him in that regard, he always remembered to invoke the Holy Spirit for this gift. And thus, he was one of the clearest thinking and speaking people you would ever meet. None of this, however, made his job any easier with Hack. He would rather face the jaws of lions or the heat of flames than tell him what must be done. But during this long walk, he prayed and prepared himself for the discomfort about to be incurred.

"I have found a family for you, Hack. The Tanners."

"But this is my family."

"You deserve a real family."

Hack hesitated, then asked, "What makes a real family?"

"A mother and father . . . maybe siblings."

"Pa and I was a real family. And we ain't have a Ma or siblings."

"True. That is very true. But you deserve a real family again. You should be with a negro family, with a mother and father to love you every single day. They're in Jefferson, a small town up in the mountains. They work the land of a man sympathetic toward the plight of negros. His name is Mr. Grey. And I hear he treats Mr. and Mrs. Tanner . . . well, like family. And much of the area up there is Republican and has been since the Civil War. If you are going to be safe anywhere, Hack, it's up there with people like that."

Hack thought for a moment.

"Why can't this be my family?"

The abbot took a deep breath. "Because it isn't right for you. This is no place for a child. And it certainly is no place for you while the authorities still have you on their minds."

"Isn't love the most important thing about family?"

"Yes. But . . ."

"I've seen more love here than anywhere else in the whole dern world. That's more important than being with negros or being able to run around outside or being around Republics, whatever they are."

The abbot could not disagree with such simplicity in thought and speech. His duty, however, was to bring this to an end in a charitable fashion. He did not want unnecessary bantering to make it even harder for the boy.

"Hack, you leave tomorrow, not because I don't love you, but because I do love you."

Hack looked down at his hands, rubbing them together nervously. Looking back up, he asked, "What about Brother Bruno?"

"What about him?"

"How's he gonna handle me leaving?"

"With difficulty, I'm sure. I know you've become friends."

"More than that, Abbot. He ain't himself if he ain't taking care of someone."

"Brother Bruno is a resilient man. He will miss you dearly. But he is a better monk now because of you. And I will ensure that he writes you regularly."

"Will you?"

"Yes, Hack. I will write too. I will write you all the time. I promise."

The abbot stood to leave.

"Abbot?"

"Yes?"

"I understand why you doing this. But I gots some bad news for you."

"What's that?"

"You wrong about me needing to leave here. Really wrong. I know it like I know the sun is gonna rise on Jefferson tomorrow."

Part Two

Chapter 1

Lily

Early July 1924

Humility is the primary virtue. It is the prerequisite for all others. One cannot be patient without humility—or merciful, or charitable, or even prudent. It is the first virtue to go when one starts down the road to perdition: a speck of self-righteousness sneaks in with flattery from others; a hint of hubris slivers into one's diligence in performing duties; or better yet, one conjures up a petty ruse for sympathy from loved ones. Humility has many definitions, all with differing intensities of theological overtones. But suffice it to say that Abbot Ambrose was a humble man.

Such quality was demonstrated this particular morning in many respects. First, the abbot never considered any other option than personally delivering Hack to Jefferson. It did require, however, Brother Bruno to drive them to the train station in the next town over in the early morning (in the much older and unreliable automobile). The abbot was still not comfortable with Hack being seen in the town of Capstone.

Brother Bruno joined them on the platform as they approached the train. He looked not like a Great Bavarian black bear but a wounded bear cub. He made no issue of showing his emotion. He hugged Hack as tight as he had that first night of refuge in the monastery. Hack had seemed to grow so much in the short time at Good Shepherd that it was he who gave comfort to Bruno.

"The more I learn to write, the more I will prove it to you," he said to Bruno.

"That sounds nice."

"Do me a favor, Brother."

"What's that?"

"Stay out of jail. Let the anti-papists say what they want."

Bruno nodded at the sound advice and even smiled a little as he wiped his eyes.

"And you, Hack, enjoy the mountains. I grew up in the mountains, you know. Different land, different language, but mountains are majestic in any part of the world."

Abbot Ambrose loaded up with Hack on the colored car of the train. His lay clothes helped to disguise his true identity—certainly not out of embarrassment, but out of prudence and concern for Hack's safety. This did not keep people from eyeing him though.

"Why you sitting with me?" Hack asked.

"Why not? We're traveling together, aren't we?"

"Yeah, but . . ."

"A true Christian, Hack, places little importance on rank and class."

"But they gawking at ya?" he said, leaning over and whispering in his ear.

"It's good for one's humility to be the odd man out from time to time."

"Pa would say you was humble."

"He would, huh? That's fine praise for anyone. But no need to fill me up with pride. He didn't know what a lousy person I can be." The abbot chuckled.

"Pa said humility was not thinking less of yourself but thinking of yourself less often. And you don't seem to care one bit about where you sit. I'd say that was thinking of yourself less often." He paused for a moment and looked off to the side. "Yep, I'm sure of it now. He'd of said you was full of humility."

"Ha! Full of humility. Never heard it said like that. Full of pride? Yes. Full of garbage? Yes. But we usually think of humility going along with emptiness."

"How can it be good to be empty? Don't you want God to fill you up?"

"Yes, but don't you have to empty yourself first so that God can fill you up?"

"Empty yourself?" Hack asked.

"Sure."

"Sounds kinda prideful to me."

"What do you mean?"

"Why would someone not want credit for being filled up but want credit for being drained empty?"

The abbot felt his mind getting a bit tangled. "Well, I guess that makes sense."

"Seems like God has to make you empty first, like He parted the Red Sea. Seems like if we emptied ourselves, we would get all prideful and fill ourselves back up just as fast as we bailed our pride out, like a man bailing water in a leaky boat."

"Where do you come up with this stuff, Hack?"

Hack stared out the window, remembering how his Pa would ask him similar questions. He didn't have an answer then and he didn't have one now.

The train sighed and lurched forward. The trip was underway. It would be a long ride with a few train changes. The closer they got to West Jefferson, the more anxious Hack became. He could not help but wonder what the new family was like.

As he looked out the window, trees and cows and the infrequent building flew by. It made him think of how fast his time at Good Shepherd had gone. He wondered if life in Jefferson would pass just as quickly. He worried not. And if life was not flying by, he thought to himself, it wasn't much of a life.

In a manner of speaking, death is the most objective reality of this world. It is all around us. There is no escaping it. Yet in another manner, there are highly subjective perspectives that bring about as many experiences as there are personal subjects. A man of philosophy, such as Socrates, welcomes death as a freeing from the sensual nature of the body, the necessary path to seeing unencumbered truth, goodness, and beauty. A man of faith welcomes death as the new life which he has been seeking through suffering and sacrificing. Other men, of course, sadly fight death with their every breath, raging against the darkness enveloping them, cursing the unknown, resenting the little time they had to prepare for the profound moment.

And so it is with little moments of death that hit us throughout our time on this mortal coil: we either welcome them with an abandonment to providence or rail against them with an unhealthy dose of self-determination.

As Hack watched the mountain landscape come into view, he pondered how his life was about to be altered against his will. He prepared himself to say goodbye, yet again, to one of the only people in his life that he had loved and that had loved him in return.

The trees towering out of the hillcrests and brush growing up and down the mountainside called to mind his Pa's tale of the oak and the reed. The oak stood mighty and proud in the wind, mocking the little reeds that bent with every gust of wind. But when a great storm arose, the oak was pulled up by the roots and came crashing down. It was the humility of the reeds, willing to bend down low and gently, that enabled them to survive even the most violent of storms.

In one respect, Hack wanted to stand tall and mighty and rage against the unwanted storm of change; in another, he felt his Pa would want him to bow humbly before the wisdom of the abbot. As the train pulled into the West Jefferson station, he gazed upon the reeds lining the tracks yielding to the oncoming train, as if genuflecting before the divine providence of the sacred moment.

A negro couple stood arm in arm on the platform as the train rolled in. The man was of medium height and wore work overalls with a brown newsboy cap. The lady on his arm was short and stocky but elegant in a yellow country dress. She wore a wide-brimmed hat that one might wear to church on Sunday, but tall black boots that betrayed the physical labor of her station in life. A nervous smile occupied both faces.

After stepping off the train, the abbot wasted no time extending his hand first to the man and then the lady, introducing himself. "And this is Hack," he said, patting him on the shoulder with the slightest nudge forward.

"Haskell," said Hack, looking up at the abbot.

The abbot was taken by surprise.

"I'm sorry?"

"My real name is Haskell."

The abbot looked back and forth between the couple and Hack. "I'm sorry, Haskell, I never knew that."

The moment was awkward enough for everyone to wonder, even Hack himself, why he had waited until this moment to tell the abbot his real name. But the possibility that Hack was already placing a formal barrier between himself and his new family did not escape the three adults standing around, waiting for the next move.

"Nice to meet you," Hack said.

"My name is Dox," the man said. "Dox Tanner." He stuck out his hand, but Hack didn't shake it.

"And I'm Mamie," said the lady, filling the silence. "We're awfully excited for you to come home with us. And we can't wait for you to meet Mr. Grey. He's a good man. You'll like him. He's . . ."

Dox held up his hand, cutting off her nervous rambling. Hack offered her a slight nod and a half-smile.

The abbot turned to the boy. "I guess this is it, Hack," he said, his voice choking. "You may not understand this, but you have given us more than we have given you. The best I can give you, Hack, is a family."

Hack tried to be a reed rather than an oak. "You promised to write," he reminded the abbot.

"And I keep my promises."

"Will you make sure Brother Bruno writes?"

"I won't have to, but yes, I will."

He turned to Dox and pulled an envelope from his jacket pocket.

"What's this, sir?" Dox asked.

"It's a little something to help you. There could be some unexpected expenses. You never know."

Dox peeked inside the envelope at a wad of cash. "Oh Lord, no sir! We can't take your money."

"I insist."

"I'm ever so grateful, sir, but please, my pride just won't let me."

The abbot smiled, nodded. He stuffed the envelope back into his pocket.

There was but one last thing left to do. Abbot Ambrose pulled Hack to his chest and squeezed tight.

It was yet another death in the short life of Haskell, and they both felt it keenly. But they did not rage against it. Rather, they bowed like reeds in the face of stormy winds.

An old wagon behind a slow, brown mare carried them up through the mountains. Dox carried the conversation mostly by himself, explaining the glories of the mountains and the river and the streams. Countless species of trees spanned as far as the eye could see: red maple, yellow birch, white ash. Though it would be a few months before the majestic shades of the autumn leaves would unfold, summer bloom in the mountain climate provided a kaleidoscope of colors among the flowers: the white purity of the Alleghany blackberry, the striking violet of the bellflower, and the odd but mesmerizing Carolina lily with its brilliant red-orange petals, punctuated with brown spots. It was a feast for the eyes. The soil from which it all grew looked so rich and pure that you could just eat it rather than wait for the harvest.

The landscape gave Hack some solace despite his mood. He took it all in, and was tempted to point out everything he saw but still not in the mood to talk. Though he did not see an abbey church built by the hands of monks, he did see a cathedral of nature giving glory to God. The jagged mountain peaks in the distance were His steeples; the long narrow valley the nave; the light flickering off the New River like the morning sun coming through stained-glass windows; a lonesome crane perched on a branch hanging over a small rapid like a saint statue tucked away in a niche, blessing every pilgrim passing beneath; an eagle soaring overhead, wings motionless, like a mosaic fixed to the dome ceiling for all to gaze upon.

And the sounds of this great cathedral were just as sublime. The gentle and steady sound of the river provided a background hum for all other sounds to build upon; the rolling of wooden wheels on dirt and gravel; the songs of the Carolina chickadee and Carolina wren, the whistle of the wind; the ruffling of oak leaves . . . each and every sound of nature came together in a harmonious chant glorifying God.

"They say the New River is one of the oldest in the world," Dox said.

Hack hesitated, as if determining whether or not he would finally speak to them. He couldn't keep his curiosity at bay. "Who's they?"

Dox brightened a bit, happy to hear the boy's voice. "Everyone who's ever been 'round here, I guess."

"How would they know how old it was if no one was around when it started?"

"Well, I don't rightly know. But I do knows something else," Dox said, regaining a little pep in his tone. "This here river flows north. Don't need no scientist to tell you that. You can just look. I ain't never seen another river that flows north. I hears the Nile in Egypt does, but that's about it. Seems awful special to me. What about you, Mamie?"

"Awful special," she said smiling as the wagon bounced along.

"Some things in life are just awful special," Dox added. "And this here river running through this here valley, giving life to all 'round it in so many ways . . . awful special."

Hack was always interested when two contrary words were stuck together for greater effect. His Pa was the master of the mental-twister, and a few memories flowed through his mind like the New River rapids flowed through the little boulders scattered throughout: *We's just alone together . . . I sure is clearly confused . . . You sure are busy doing nothing . . . Your mama was painfully perty. . . .* Hack made a mental note to add *awful special* to the list.

"See that fat mountain over yonder," Dox said to Hack, pointing past a few small hills. "That's Jefferson Mountain, or some calls it Panther Mountain."

"Why's it got two names?"

"It used to be called Panther Mountain 'cause a big old black panther ate up a small child long ago. And the locals, maybe even the Cherokee, started calling it that. But recently, people been calling it Jefferson Mountain, named after Thomas Jefferson and his daddy who came down through Virginia and surveyed our land."

Hack considered asking who Thomas Jefferson was but then figured he'd just call it Panther Mountain.

"You know, Haskell," Dox went on, "that there mountain was an underground railroad."

"A train goes under it?"

"No, no. When we was slaves, you see, the path to freedom in the North was called the underground railroad. Jefferson Mountain was a natural spot because it's got caves at the bottom, though I ain't never seen any caves. But I sure like to think about runaway slaves taking refuge in our mountain. . . . Yes, sir."

"Why?"

"I don't know. I guess it gives me a sense of pride. What you say, Mamie?"

"Gives me pride, I reckon," she said softly.

"And maybe that underground railroad is why this area has always been a little friendly to our kind. Ain't no place perfect. No, sir. You can have some troubles in town. But the country folk have cared about our kind since the war between the states. You know, Haskell, a good chunk of the men here fought for the North. That's right . . . And that's why stories are told about brothers fighting brothers on the battlefield. Can you imagine? Fighting your brother on the battlefield?"

"No. I don't have a brother."

Except for all seventy of them at Good Shepherd, he thought.

A little white house with a wraparound porch came into view, a steep hill rising behind it like a ramp to heaven. For about an acre or two, a pasture ran before it and continued over the road toward the river, picking back up beyond the opposite bank. That pasture looked like the most serene farmland imaginable. Another picturesque pasture lay on the far side of the river, glistening, calling one to wade the river and run through the field with all the speed one could muster.

"That your home?" Hack asked, pointing.

Dox smiled. "Everything your eyes can see is our home, son. The fields, the rivers, the hills . . . it's all yours now. But no, that ain't our house. That's Mr. Grey's house. Our house is tucked behind it. And we get to live there for free because we work with Mr. Grey."

Hack noticed how Dox used the word *with* rather than *for*.

As they pulled around the white house, Hack saw a red barn built into the side of the hill, as if the hill had spit it out. Behind the barn, a small log cabin sat nestled before the trees, a brick chimney rising from the roof.

"Home, sweet home, Hack," Dox said as he pulled directly into the barn. The simplicity of the barn and cabin was of no concern to Hack. But living in someone else's backyard gave him pause.

Just as he unloaded himself from the wagon, he heard the slam of a screen door. A young lady leapt down the steps from the door. She was a number of years older than Hack, but he wasn't quite sure he'd call her an adult. She moved with childlike spirit but had the beauty of a woman in her prime. She had the whitest skin he ever saw, like a Greek goddess carved from ivory. Her hair was smooth and dark and flopped behind her as she trotted toward him. She wore a white dress that gave her a prim and proper look, but her energy betrayed her garments: her dress held her back from conquering the world like a warrior princess of ancient lore.

And then . . . her eyes: the rarest and most enchanting green eyes he could imagine. It was as if her green irises trapped every flickering of green light from the New River Valley. They were so striking that she appeared to be looking at you even when she was not. Hack wondered if the Blue Jays ever mistook her eyes for food to be foraged, or if mad pirates sailing up the New River (if they ever did so) mistook them for Blackbeard's lost treasure, or if trout ever mistook them for an oasis pond as she walked along the banks. If he had been small enough, Hack thought to himself, he would have fallen into those eyes and happily lived there forever.

She was smiling before she ever reached him, as if she had been waiting anxiously for his arrival. And that smile; it was a smile that would light up a dark room . . . or a dark soul. There was purity in her face.

Hack wondered if those green eyes had ever shed a tear. Had her face ever shown a furrowed brow? Had her white teeth ever been ground together in anger? It was a face undisturbed by human frailty and complexity. It was a face preserved in the New River Valley, as Eve's face was preserved in the Garden of Eden.

In a word: Lily was *painfully perty.*

"Hey there, Hack. I'm Lily."

She kept smiling as she introduced herself. Hack couldn't believe such a warmness from a young white lady was directed at him. Perhaps these mountain folks, he considered, never learned to be racist . . . or maybe they unlearned before everyone else.

Hack stared back at her, stumped for words. Dox stepped in. "Actually, Ms. Lily, it's Haskell. We just learned it ourselves."

Hack smiled awkwardly and waved his hand. He took a little step toward her: "Call me Hack, ma'am."

She put her hands on her hips: "Now let's get one thing straight, young man. If me and you are gonna be friends, you better not call me 'ma'am.' Ya hear?"

"Okay . . . yes Ma' . . . yes, Lily."

"Excellent! Now, how do you like my mountains?" She put her hands out and swirled around. *My mountains,* he thought. It wasn't arrogant, but intimate. It was as if she grew right out of the ground; it was as if she was one with all that formed millions of years.

"I like them."

"Come on," she grabbed his hand, her touch softer than anything Hack had ever felt. "Let's show you your new house."

Lily walked him to the front door of the log cabin. Flowers brightened the threshold and front window sills. "My daddy was born in this house. He built our house when he and momma married. His parents stayed here until they died. And then five years ago when momma got sick, daddy looked for a maid and cook so I could go to school in town.

But he ended up with the best farmhand these mountains ever seen." She smiled at Dox.

"Come on now, Ms. Grey. You flatter me."

"And see that window right there," she pointed to the second floor of the white house, just over the kitchen door. "I was born in that room."

"How long ago?" Hack asked.

"Now Mr. Haskell, didn't anyone ever teach you never to ask a lady her age?" She smiled when Hack hung his head. "Just teasing ya. Seventeen years ago. I hear you're twelve?"

"I think I'm thirteen now," Hack said, kicking the dirt beneath his foot.

"You think?"

"I don't know my birthday."

"Wow!" she squealed. "So you get to pick your own birthday!"

Hack looked up from the ground and tilted his head ever so slightly to the side.

"You could pick Christmas!" she said, but then immediately dropped her shoulders. "No, that's a terrible idea. You oughta spread it out so you get more than one big celebration a year.

"And I don't like the idea of stealing Jesus's birthday," Hack added.

"Ha! I didn't think about that. He likes to share, but you have a good point. Why not put it in the summer so you have a special day every six months?"

"Pretty sure it *is* in the summer, actually, somewhere. Let's just say I'm thirteen now."

"Works for me. Now, do you see that garden over there?" she pointed to a white picket fence between the cabin and the house. "I help Mamie grow and prune everything in there, don't I, Mamie?"

"Sure do," Mamie said from behind them.

"You garden, Hack?" Lily asked.

"No, but I want to."

"Well, we'll teach you everything. Won't we, Mamie?"

"Certainly will," she replied, walking toward the cabin. "We're harvesting lots of good stuff right now: watermelon and cantaloupe; zucchini and green beans; and every size and shape of tomato you can imagine. And we'll be fall planting before too long. You'll love it."

Hack followed Mamie to the cabin door, but Lily stopped. "Well, I'll let you get settled."

"Thank you, Ms. Lily," said Mamie. "I'm gonna get Haskell washed up, fed, and then we'll introduce him to Mr. and Mrs. Grey this evening."

"See ya soon," Lily said as she walked away waving over her shoulder.

Hack watched her walk away until she disappeared into the house.

Mamie showed him his room in a polite but matter of fact way. It was about the size of the hermitage at Good Shepherd. No books or bookshelf, but it did have a window which looked out at the back of the white house.

Hack began to unpack. He placed his Pa's harmonica on the pillow and took out the McGuffey Readers Father Henry had given him and placed them on the dresser. A few changes of clothes the monks had given him were slipped into the small dresser. And that was it. It was all he had from his previous life.

The log walls of the room were nice and smooth, but the mortar oozed down onto them. It reminded Hack of the thick mortar of the stone walls in the abbey basement. He wondered which was older: the abbey or the log cabin. He rubbed his hand across the smooth logs and oozing mortar, as if feeling his way into a new home.

"Welcome to our home."

Hack spun around. There in the doorway, Dox stood with his arm around Mamie. They were both smiling, as if the process of bringing Hack home was now complete. He was finally in their home, in his new room, and the seedlings of a family were trying to take root in this log cabin, hand-hewn from the timbers of the rolling hills.

As Dox squeezed Mamie a little closer into his side, Hack finally understood: They wanted a child. He had not considered it until now. He thought the Tanners were a couple willing to take on the burden of an orphan, that they were the gift to him; now he understood that he was just as much a gift to them.

"Thank you," he said.

"Let's have a seat," said Dox, waving him to their table in the center room. When they all sat down, Dox said, "We understand you's been all alone because your momma and daddy died."

"Ma died," Hack interrupted. "But Pa was . . ." his words trailed off.

"We knows it all, son. Mr. Grey told us everything. We awful sorry about all that."

The word *son* aggravated Hack. "I wasn't alone. I had the monks."

"But Abbot Ambrose is right. You need a momma." He squeezed Mamie's arm. "And this here woman will be a goooood momma. And he was right that you need a daddy, and I'll do my best to be a good daddy. We alls need a family."

Hack wanted to argue, not with whether one needs a family, but with the implication that the monks were not family. He felt obliged, however, to accept their generosity.

"Do you have questions for us?" Mamie asked.

"Since you're farmers, does that mean I'm a farmer?"

"You look like a strong boy," Dox said. "I think you'll like working with us. I can teach you a lot. How's that sound?"

"Can I go to school?"

Dox shook his head. "I'm sorry, but there ain't no colored school."

"Can you . . ." but he caught himself. He knew the answer and did not want to offend.

"I knows where your mind is going," Dox said. "We never learned to read and write. But Mr. Grey has all kinds of books. Maybe we can borrow them from time to time."

Hack nodded.

Dox and Mamie moved to the kitchen to prepare dinner. Hack sat awkwardly for a while, then went back to his bedroom. He sat on the edge of the bed and allowed his mind to travel back on the train, back to Capstone, back to Good Shepherd. He thought of Brother Bruno and the checker games and his cursing in German; he picked up the harmonica and thought of Brother Matthias's kindness and desire to find beauty everywhere he went; he looked at his readers and was saddened by not having a reading lesson with Father Henry tomorrow, and although it had only been a few hours since he had seen Abbot Ambrose, he felt that it had been a year of total absence. And then it hit him: he was miles and miles away from his Pa's grave. A pain in the stomach came on suddenly and tears followed. He missed his Pa now more than he had ever missed him.

Hack stared out the window. As the wind shook the leaves, he saw Lily slip by the kitchen window, and it felt like the fresh mountain air blew away some of the pain and sorrow.

In the evening Dox and Mamie escorted Hack to the back of the main house, through the kitchen, and into the main dining room. The interior of the house was simple, with bright white drapes on each window giving contrast to polished dark wooden furniture. The windows were open, allowing the drapes to dance a woodland waltz with the gentle breeze. It was this movement, Hack noticed, that seemed to make the rest of the house serenely calm.

A rifle hung over the unusually low front door, within arms reach of any average height adult. Hack wondered if it was used more for bears or deer or bandits drifting drunkenly down the river.

In the living room, tall bookcases were filled with leather spines, hubbed and rough and tattered, which meant craftsmanship and wisdom and love. A couch and two high-backed chairs gave order to the small room. In one of these high-backed chairs sat a thin man with long skinny legs, one crossed over the other, holding a book on his knee. He had a white beard hanging down to his chest, which he stroked with his free hand. A picture of a proud and stiff civil war soldier with a rifle and bayonet sat on a small table next to him. The dark blue uniform pegged him as a Union Soldier.

The bearded man in the chair was immersed in the book on his knee and seemingly did not notice the creaking floors beneath their feet.

"Mr. Grey, is this a good time, sir?" Dox said apologetically.

The man began to move his head but kept his eyes on the sentence, struggling to pull himself away.

Finally, he closed the book and looked up, waving them in. "Yes, yes. Of course. Come in." He placed the book on the table beside him. "Mary Lou, come on down," he hollered up the stairs, smiling at Hack. "We have a visitor."

Hack's attention drifted to the book set down in front of that soldier. He tilted his head to read the spine like a dog inquisitively looking at a human.

"Now go on and introduce yourself," Dox said with a friendly nudge in the back. Hack pulled his eyes away from the spine.

"I'm Haskell, sir."

Just then, Lily came into the room. She almost said hello but stopped when she saw her father was about to speak. Mr. Grey rubbed his bearded chin for a moment and stretched out his hand and spoke with a dignity and formality Hack was unaccustomed to.

"I'm Mr. Grey, and it is a distinct pleasure to make your acquaintance. But I must say, I expected a certain Hack."

"Haskell's my real name, sir."

"Ah . . . well, I hear Lily is calling you Hack . . . which is fitting. Nevertheless, welcome to our home," and he made a small sweeping motion with his hands.

Hack's eyes ventured back over to the spine of the book.

"Are you a reader?" Mr. Grey asked.

"Yes, sir. At least a little."

Mr. Grey smiled and picked up the book.

"This paragraph . . ." as he opened it back up to the place he left off, "it was quite beautiful. I was rereading it for a third time when you came in." He flipped the book around toward Hack and handed it to him. He tapped the page. "Can you read this paragraph here?"

Hack looked at the book and then around the room to Lily and Dox and Mamie. It was not like Hack to be nervous about anything. He struggled over a few words, but Mr. Grey helped him without even looking at the page:

"I frequently sat down to meat with thankfulness, and admired the hand of God's providence, which had thus spread my table in the wilderness. I learned

to look more upon the bright side of my condition, and less upon the dark side, and to consider what I enjoyed rather than what I wanted; and this gave me sometimes such secret comforts, that I cannot express them; and which I take notice of here, to put those discontented people in mind of it, who cannot enjoy comfortably what God has given them, because they see and covet something that He has not given them. All our discontents about what we want appeared to me to spring from the want of thankfulness for what we have."

"Bravo! Bravo!" Lily clapped.

"And you said you read just a little?" said Mr. Grey.

Dox and Mamie looked at each other with a small smile followed by a hint of insecurity.

"I've only had a few lessons, sir. But I fiddled with lots of books at the abbey."

"Fiddled indeed. Can you read the title?"

"*Robinson Cru-soe. Daniel DeFoe.*"

"Ever heard of it?"

"No, sir."

"It's about a man shipwrecked on an island. He must survive despite the loneliness and hardships, and learns a lot about life and himself in the process. But it is a little tougher than some other books on this shelf." He stood and wandered over to the wall, reaching nearly all the way to the ceiling.

"And it just so happens I have a gift for you, a welcoming gift." He pulled one down.

"Have you heard of Jules Verne?"

"No, sir."

"See if you like this."

Hack took the book from him, looking at the cover. *Journey to the Center of the Earth*, he read to himself.

"If you like it, just swap this out for another as soon as you turn over that last page. No better feeling on Earth than turning over the last page and running to get a new first page."

Hack's heart filled with joy as he ran his fingers smoothly over the leather cover.

He held the book like a pirate would have picked up a lost treasure, or how Achilles held the shield forged by the hands of Hephaestus, or how Helena held a beam of the cross. It was sacred to the touch.

"Thank you, sir."

"I love Jules Verne. He takes you on adventures like no other. I've been to a mysterious island with him, and to the depths of the oceans, and once I even went with him to the center of the Earth, which is where you are headed soon."

Hack held the book, resisting the urge to break it open and begin reading. He peeked over at Lily. She walked over to him and whispered in his ear, "Maybe today really is your birthday."

Mr. Grey looked toward the stairs. "Well, I suspect Mrs. Grey won't be coming down right now. But I'm sure you'll meet her soon enough."

Dox shuffled up behind Hack, placing his hands on his shoulders. "Thank you, Mr. Grey. We'll be getting on out of your hair now. But we'll be seeing you bright and early."

"Bright and early," repeated Mr. Grey. He reached out his hand. "Pleasure meeting you, Haskell."

Hack looked up from his book, shook his hand, and made solid eye contact for the first time. "Thank you, sir. Pleasure meeting you. Thank you for Jules Verne."

"He's an old friend," Mr. Grey said as he returned to his seat. "Please give him my regards."

And with that, Dox led Hack out of the room, through the kitchen, and back to their house. Before the door closed behind them, he heard Lily holler, "See you tomorrow, Hack!"

"Do you have a lantern?" Hack asked Dox the moment his foot landed outside the house.

"Sure thing. I'll dig one up out of the barn."

After a small but pleasant dinner, Hack dismissed himself early to bed, acting more tired than he really was. He just wanted to meet Mr. Verne.

He read until the sun was down and then lit the lantern, huddling next to it as he worked through the pages. Every paragraph or so, there was a word he didn't know, but it was rare enough to where he could still enjoy the story. As his eyes and mind tired after an extraordinarily long day, he became distracted by thoughts of Brother Bruno and Brother Matthias, one of whom would have been visiting him in his cell about now. He wondered if Father Henry had ever read Mr. Verne. *Of course he had,* he answered himself. *Father Henry has read everything.*

Upon closing the book, he thought about the paragraph Mr. Grey had him read. He remembered the last sentence near perfectly: *All our discontents about what we want spring from the want of thankfulness for what we have.* It made him consider the kindness shown by Dox and Mamie and the warm welcome by Mr. Grey. He should be more grateful than he was. But it was hard to be grateful when all he desired was to be at Good Shepherd.

There was, however, one thing that Hack felt an overwhelming sense of gratitude for: the angelic presence that enraptured every word and move of Lily Grey.

Perhaps he could live in the New River Valley after all. Perhaps he could be shipwrecked on a deserted island. Perhaps he could dwell at the depths of the oceans or at the center of the Earth. Perhaps he could live anywhere . . . so long as she was with him.

The Lauds of the morning dew chanted praise to the coming autumn; the Sext sun no longer burned like hellfire; the Vespers of the mountain breeze grew a little crisper, preparing for the night in a way a summer evening never could. And the world was settling into its own Vespers, bringing the year to a close as the little lamps of light spanning the heavens began to gleam earlier every evening.

An array of colors showed themselves on deciduous trees. Plants scattered their seeds on the mountain breeze. Flocks of migratory birds formed and looked for their flyways. All of nature yawned as the woodchucks, chipmunks, and black bears meandered, looking for a hermitage for the next few months.

Hack could breathe deeply.

Lily must have told him it was her favorite season every time they ventured out on one of their long walks. And it was on these long walks that Hack learned what it meant to love. Through the rest of his life, he would find many forms of love, as does anyone who pays attention.

There is familial love that naturally arises between parent and child. Given how natural it is, there wasn't much merit to it, he thought. He could see it in every mother duck leading her chicks from one pond to the next. And yet, if it were not glorious, why did the mother duck grieve at the loss of a chick?

There was love between friends, which was beautiful in part because it was unnecessary. The world's population could continue, fields could be plowed, and meals could be set on the table without a single friendship, though it would be hell on Earth. It was by free will that one gives oneself to another in friendship, as the monks of Good Shepherd had given themselves to Hack, and as Lily had as well.

It was on these long walks that Hack felt they were the only two people on Earth. Lily did most of the talking and Hack did most of the listening. But he was a good listener, a proactive listener, a listener who was never looking to insert himself but trying to embrace the other with his mind.

The purity of heart Hack sensed from Lily was the most attractive attribute imaginable. And on the rare occasion that he was able to touch her, his world shifted to a greater degree than the tectonic plates had shifted to raise the mountains around him.

They would reach a narrow part of the river and decide to cross. They would take off their shoes, tie the laces together and throw them over their shoulders. Lily would take one hand, hike up her dress above her knees, and extend her other toward him. He would pause awkwardly, feel his stomach churn, then place his hand in hers. The river would be cold, but her skin was warm enough to warm him from head to toe. And she would lead him to the other side.

It was here that Hack brushed up against the other kind of love: romantic love (for want of a better word). It was not vile. It was not selfish. Nor was it directed at any woman walking by, but at a singular individual, and no other woman would do. The perfect event for him would be holding hands for an hour, or perhaps a hug for a minute, or perhaps he could, with the palm of his hand, touch her face for a second. That was as far as his imagination could go at this stage of life. Yet even this he knew was too far for his conscience. He would feel guilty with such thoughts.

He loved her like the sister he never had. He knew, however, that a romantic love was present. It was not an intruder, *per se*, for its purity was not dampening the friendship. But it was a distraction that he tried to keep at bay. At times, he wondered what would happen if this romantic love increased. Would he run away from her and never come back? Would he ask if he could touch her face? Would he burst into ash like a volcanic eruption, forming a thick atmospheric blanket, blocking the sunlight from all living things, driving all of God's creatures into extinction except for the smallest rodents and insects that thrive in the cold and darkness?

Years later, however, looking back on that time, he would wonder whether it was a more mature love than most men ever experience, for it sprang from innocence and humility and freedom.

Chapter 2

The Bible Salesman

Hack sat beneath the largest ash tree he had ever seen on the bank of the river. The trunk was so thick that it would take two Brother Brunos to wrap arms all the way around it. The wind rustled the tall grass like a million little dancers moving obediently to the breath of God sweeping through the valley.

He was reading Jules Verne's *The Mysterious Island* and thought of this valley as the mysterious valley. It was like an island unto itself. He had almost reached the end of his third book by Jules Verne in the past few months, among other authors pulled from Mr. Grey's bookshelves.

He wondered if Capstone felt the same cool breeze or if wind even blew that far. He pulled a letter from his pocket, carefully unfolding it to read for the fifth time:

Dear Hack,

All is well here. We are rather busy right now with the tenant farmers preparing for fall harvests. The brothers are doing fine. Brother Bruno is surviving without you, though barely. I must find him a new project or he is bound to murder someone.

Brother Mathias has thrown himself into his music these past few months like never before. I do wonder if this is the way he grieves.

Father Henry stays very busy with his daily duties.

We have just admitted two new novices. The first's name is Brother Adrian. He comes from a long line of farmers. Seems to know everything about everything that grows, including livestock. He should be helpful around here. His father just died, his older brother inherited the farm, and so he has decided to give religious life a try. Not necessarily the best of reasons, but such vocations have come to monasteries since Benedict built Monte Casino.

The other is Brother Dominic. He has a doctorate in Philosophy. A rather brilliant mind and a kind soul.

Perhaps someday you will meet them both.

I am very glad to hear about Jules Verne—and to answer your question . . . yes, I have read him, but only 20,000 Leagues Under the Sea. *Get lost in the story, Hack. Fiction is the closest man gets to becoming a creator. But remember this: one who loves fiction too much, especially if he can write it well, is one who may be unhappy with the reality around him. The greatest stories are those before your eyes. Look up and see.*

God Bless You,
Abbot Ambrose

Hack put the letter up and gazed out at nature's autumn afternoon. A strange feeling came over him. It was as if the picture before him was but a thin film, a cover, a mask hiding a deeper reality beneath it. He saw beauty with his eyes but knew it was merely the surface of true beauty. It was wrong to call it an illusion, but it was not the truest reality either.

He felt he could reach out and slash away the veil before him to see what lay beneath. He wondered: Was the reality he sought beneath or behind or beyond what he saw? The water, the million little dancers of the field, the shifting clouds over head . . . something was trying to burst forth from it. Something wanted to reveal itself to Hack. Something wanted to give him its name so that he wouldn't call it trees or grass or water or sky. And this name, it was like a word stuck on the tip of his tongue, a word he knew but could not seem to remember. It was a feeling of excitement, but also frustration, for he knew he could not reach that which he was certain existed.

Just then he heard his name. It was Dox asking him to return to work. And Dox was right: Hack was not acting like a very good farmhand. *Oh well,* he thought. *I'll have to find that name some other time.* He closed his book, hopped up, and returned to Dox.

"Looks like you were dozing," Dox said.

"Just thinking."

"What about?"

Hack paused and considered telling him. Dox was a spiritual man. But for some reason, perhaps unfairly to Dox, Hack didn't want to go into it. He felt guilty about this, for it had become evident that Hack kept Dox and Mamie at a distance. He did not know exactly why. They could not have been better to him. Perhaps he was trying to not get too attached. He wouldn't dare run the risk of growing close to someone new only to have them taken away, too. He couldn't bear that again.

Dox finally spoke up with a grin. "You know Saint Paul said whoever ain't working ain't eating. So you best start working 'cause I know what Mamie is cooking up right now."

As they strolled in from the field, Hack saw Lily sitting on the porch. He noticed in an instant, however, that she lacked her usual vibrance. After promising Dox to come in momentarily, he asked Lily what was wrong.

"I have the worst tooth ache," she said as she rubbed her check. "I'm going to the dentist tomorrow. Daddy's gonna take me when he conducts business in town. Hey, why don't you come with me?"

"To town?"

"Yes, to town. I'll ask Daddy."

To take a trip in town with Dox was one thing. But with Lily was quite another.

"You think he'll say yes?"

"His little princess is wounded. How's he gonna say no? Somebody has to keep my mind off the pain during that long, bumpy wagon ride."

The ride into town was indeed a long and bumpy one. Poor Lily, Hack thought the whole ride there. He had never seen her in pain; in fact, he had never seen her not bounding with joy. He wished he could take it and give it to himself.

Mr. Grey dropped her at the front steps of the dentist office. "We'll be back in about an hour. And if you aren't out, Darling, then I'll come up to get you."

"But Hack has to stay with me," she said.

"What? No, no. It could cause problems."

"I'll handle it," she said with an unusual sternness.

Her father took a deep breath. He looked like a man who knew he would regret what he was about to say, but who also knew he could never say no to his princess. "Very well."

Hack took a seat in the waiting room as Lily checked in at the receptionist desk. He sat across from the only other person waiting. It was a young man, perhaps a few years older than Lily. He wore a three-piece suit with a large white handkerchief in the breast pocket and had a stripped blue tie running down his torso. He held a thick black bag on his lap under both hands, a posture that bespoke of trying to protect its contents. Lily came to her seat next to Hack. The young man smiled at her, revealing a chipped front tooth.

"Morning, ma'am," he said.

"I don't think one can have a good morning at the dentist," she replied.

The man smiled again, but this time with a bit more gazing than mere looking. Their eyes locked for just a second until she forced herself to look away. Hack noticed she was turning red beneath her jaw line faster than a stove when ignited. The scarlet ran all the way down, disappearing beneath her collar. She began to fiddle with her collar like a person in need of more air.

The receptionist leaned through her little window.

"Ms. Grey, just one moment please," motioning her to come forward. Lily complied. Hack saw the receptionist say something beneath her breath to Lily in private.

"No, ma'am!" Lily suddenly yelled, spinning on her heels. She marched back to her seat and plopped down in a fashion unbecoming of a lady.

The tooth must be really hurting her, Hack thought to himself.

"You all right, ma'am?" the young man asked.

"Fine," she said with a tone that betrayed her words.

The receptionist came out and approached Lily. "Young lady, please don't make this more difficult than it needs to be."

"It isn't difficult. You are difficult. Now leave me be. My tooth is just throbbing, and I don't have the patience to deal with your . . . well your . . . well, I just don't have the patience."

Hack had never heard her like this before. He was confused, even a bit scared. And yet, there was something awful entertaining about seeing her riled up. He peeked up at the receptionist and saw she was looking right at him.

He now understood.

"We don't want to make the other patients uncomfortable," she said.

"Uncomfortable?" Lily barked. "The discomfort in this room is stuck squarely inside my tooth. But I'd rather be uncomfortable with this tooth than send my friend outside." She shot her eyes over to the young man and beamed into his eyes with furrowed brow, like a Union soldier sticking the bayonet right between his eyes. "Are you uncomfortable with my friend here?"

Caught off his guard, his mouth opened and closed a few times without sound, and his eyes darted back and forth between all three people looking at him. But he quickly came to his senses, realizing there was only one person in the room whom he wished to please. "Ahh . . . no, ma'am. I'm quite comfortable. Thank you."

"There. Ya see? My friend will sit in this chair until my appointment is over or my appointment will never begin."

Lily stared the receptionist down like a cowboy in a duel, ready to draw a pistol at any moment. Knowing what was good for her, the receptionist slowly retreated to her window, making more grunts of dissatisfaction the further away from her opponent she went.

Hack felt he had just seen the final battle of the Civil War, won by a seventeen-year-old girl with a toothache. It was beautiful. It was glorious. It was arresting and stirring.

The young man gazed on her in amazement until his gazing became gawking.

"It isn't polite to stare you know," Lily said with the slightest smile.

"I'm sorry," he said, shaking his head. "But that was somethin' else."

"That chipped tooth must have hurt when it happened," Lily said, happy to change the subject.

"Oh, this?" he pointed to his tooth. "I'm not here for this," uncouthly raising his front lip and pointing at his front tooth. "I'm here to sell the dentist the Good Book."

He delicately removed a large Bible from his bag and spun it around in presentation fashion for her.

"You're a Bible salesman?"

"Yes, ma'am. Just going to Charlotte from Tennessee. Sleeping here a few nights, so figured I'd walk up and down Main Street to see who needs a Bible." They locked eyes for a moment. "May I show you?"

"Of course," she said, showing the man a little of the usual Lily that Hack had come to love.

He was tall when he stood up, and lanky. The suit hung off him like a father's suit hangs off a son. But he still looked sharp and quick and agile. He slowly lowered his 6′3″ body into the chair by Lily. She turned her eyes to him, giving Hack a clear view of her neckline: it was now as red as a fiery furnace.

"The highest quality binding you're ever gonna find," he said, beginning his sales pitch. "It will last for generations to come." He turned to the family registry page. "Imagine your wedding date right here. And your children's names and birthdates, and one day far off, your grandchildren's names and birthdates."

Just what was he really selling, Hack thought to himself.

"I see," she would say every few seconds.

The tension in the room had become so thick that the dentist couldn't cut it with his scalpel. The salesman continued with his pitch, and Lily nodded with words of affirmation. Hack's leg touched the sides of her dress every now and then, but despite the closeness, he felt as if he was in the next county over. Lily and the Bible salesman were more alone than Adam and Eve in the garden. But a disruption broke into their paradise no less violently than the serpent did himself in the first few pages of the salesman's product.

"Miss Grey. Dr. Smith will now see you."

Lily rose from the chair. The young man stood as well. "Miss Grey?"

"Yes, that's right. Lily Grey."

"Lily Grey," he repeated slowly. "Edward O'Connell," he said, extending his hand. "But my friends call me Ed."

She ever so gently shook his hand.

"Well, Mr. O'Connell. Thank you for showing me your beautiful Bible." She turned toward the receptionist.

Despite his smooth presentation of God's word, Edward O'Connell couldn't seem to find his own. He could speak about the words of Christ in red as symbolic of the sanctifying blood of Christ, or the gilded pages in honor of the majesty of the Divine King, but he couldn't find words to stop the young lady from walking out of his life forever. All he could manage was her name. "Lily."

She turned quickly. "Yes?"

He continued searching.

"How might I . . . I mean . . . would you like to . . ." But that lanky Bible salesman just stood there like a man on his very first sales call, more stumped than a hundred-year-old oak tree cut to the ground. As he dropped his eyes in despair, they landed on the Good Book. And whether it was grace arising from the Bible itself or his God-given salesmanship coming to fruition, he had his answer. He looked up with confidence. "Miss Lily, might your family be in need of a magnificent Bible such as this? Perhaps I should come to your house and present this sacred book to your father?"

Lily smiled and looked toward the ground. She began to sway her hips just enough to show she was up to something. "I think he would love such a Bible." She asked the receptionist for paper and pencil and wrote down instructions to her house.

"But on one condition," she said as she walked slowly toward him, holding the note between two fingers in front of his face.

"Name it."

"Since your name is Edward, and your friends call you Ed . . ." she slipped the note in the front jacket pocket, right on top of the handkerchief, and whispered in his ear, "I get to call you Eddie." She spun around like a dancer in the Royal Ballet and walked past the receptionist, disappearing through the door as it closed behind her.

Hack sat quietly and watched the Bible salesman stand frozen, his Bible in hand, the note sticking out the top of his pocket. He slowly stepped back, more falling into his chair than sitting. Stunned by a heavenly apparition, a celestial branding iron left an indelible mark upon his soul. Staring straight ahead, he hardly blinked. Hack thought his eyes would dry up and fall out.

After a minute lost in thought, Eddie slipped the Bible back into his bag and stood up to leave.

"Aren't you gonna sell a Bible to the dentist?" Hack asked.

"Nope. No need to," he said dismissively. He straightened his tie, put on his fedora, tilted it to the side, and said, "Because I'm gonna sell a million of them for her." And he was gone.

Lily was loopy on her way out. Hack considered how glad she must have been that Eddie was gone, sparing her from the rather undignified episode.

"Please direct me to your outhouse," she said slowly and intentionally to the receptionist.

"We have indoor plumbing. The restroom is right down this hall."

Gasping aloud, Lily said, "Doing your business indoors?"

The receptionist gave her a little push in the right direction, happy to have her, and Hack, out of their office.

"How barbaric!" Lily said when they reached the hallway, using a much louder voice than she probably intended to. Hack was not sure if she spoke of the treatment received by the dentist, the receptionist, or the use of a toilet indoors. "Are they gonna start chopping wood inside next? Or will they keep a compost heap in the kitchen? Or let's just feed the pigs off the dining room table! My word! I'd rather explode than do my business inside."

Hack shushed her. "Now quiet down, Lily. You don't wanna make a fool of yourself."

"What's it matter? Everyone around here makes a fool of themselves by relieving inside!"

"Lily, please. Quiet!" Hack looked down the hall to see if anyone was coming. He saw a sign of discomfort come over her loopy face, that universal cringe that strikes the face of every human on every continent throughout all of history when nature calls. Hack pushed her right through the restroom door and pulled the door shut.

"Hack! What on Earth are you doing?" she screeched as she banged on the inside of the door.

"I'll stand guard so no one disturbs you. Do your business and let's get out of here." A growl came from inside. For a moment, Hack worried that she was just standing in there with her arms crossed in defiance. But then he heard the sound of a sharp stream piercing through water.

When she clambered out from that lair of barbarism with as much dignity as she could muster, she closed the door behind her, cleared her throat, patted her hair as if she had just been through a wrestling match, and glared at Hack, who, despite his best efforts, could not help but let a smile slip through his countenance.

She punched him in the arm with the strength of a lumberjack. "Stop."

"What? What I do?"

She grabbed his arm and pulled him from the building and out onto Main Street. And there they stood: a loopy white young lady and a negro boy who couldn't stop laughing.

That afternoon before supper, Eddie showed up as early as etiquette allowed. Hack snuck in through the kitchen in the back of the house and settled in close to the swinging door leading to the dining room so he could listen to the salesman make his pitch.

A formality ensued, with no mention whatsoever of Lily, who stood in the living room watching and listening to the two men go through a song and dance for her sake. It was a crisp presentation, one that was worthy of the Good Book. But as it came to a close, Mr. Grey, a dignified and self-educated man, finally steered the conversation to the issue at hand.

"Before we get to the reason you are here, young man, might I ask which church you attend? After all, many denominations appreciate this here King James translation you are presenting."

"I'm Catholic, sir."

"A Catholic? Ya don't say? And how is it that a Catholic came to be selling this here King James Bible?"

"Well, sir, our Bible is the same, it's just a little thicker."

"I see. I see." Mr. Grey considered where to take the conversation next. "Why do I sense you're after more than a sale?"

"Oh, no sir. I'm only after a sale."

Hack could not see Lily but was most certain a strange look had come over her face.

"What I mean to say," Eddie continued, "is that everything in life is sales."

"*Everything?*" Mr. Grey asked. "Even sacred religion?"

"Especially sacred religion, sir. Didn't our Lord become flesh and blood to sell us on the idea of the kingdom of God? Sales. To live the Beatitudes? Sales. To take up a cross so that our bodies could resurrect on the last day? Sales. Didn't he say *if you give me your whole heart, soul, strength, and mind then I will give you paradise?* Mr. Grey, if that isn't a deal to be struck, if that isn't negotiation of eternal significance, if that isn't the ultimate sales pitch, then I don't know what is."

"Interesting. Very interesting," Mr. Grey said. "All right then, why do I get the sense that you're trying to sell me on more than the quality of this Bible?"

"I can tell you're a biblical man, so I want to respectfully make a friendly amendment to your statement."

"A friendly amendment?" inquired Mr. Grey.

"Yes, sir. I would never try to sell you just a Bible. I would also sell you those principles within it."

Mr. Grey sighed. "Can we come to the point? You're running at the mouth like the New River on a rainy day. You're on the verge of violating a provision of both Sacred Scripture and the code of salesmanship."

Eddie's silence proved he did not know what was coming.

"Scriptures saith, *Let your yes mean yes and your no mean no*. And doesn't sales material say, *Never be afraid to close the sale?*"

Eddie smiled. "Sir, you are as wise as your daughter is beautiful and strong-willed. And while the former is enough to capture any man's attention, it is the latter that kept mine and drove me along the New River to your front door. I suppose I'd be lying if I didn't admit there was never more of a sale I wished to make then to obtain your blessing to come calling on your daughter."

Mr. Grey smiled, his suspicions confirmed. "Well, let's see how you overcome objections."

"Daddy!" Lily hollered at him. "Leave him alone."

He ignored his daughter. "What if I said you must choose between your Catholicism, which I do not like one bit, mind you, and my daughter?"

"Well, now, that's a false dilemma," Eddie said without missing a beat.

"A false dilemma?"

"That's right. A *logical fallacy*, as my philosophy professor would call it."

"How so?"

"I would not have to choose between my religion and your daughter. Only between my religion and *your blessing* at the current moment."

"Are you saying you'd take my daughter without my blessing?" Grey asked.

"I'm saying, sir, that the Good Book says *a man must leave his mother and father and cling to his wife*. And I'm sure that it means a woman must do the same. And our Lord said, *Let no man separate what God hast joined.*"

"But the Lord has not joined you, young man."

"But the Lord has in fact joined us in two ways. First, it was by providence in that dentist office, and I will not be convinced otherwise that it was not written by the higher hand. And secondly, is not God outside of time? And if in God's eternity, we are already joined, then no man shall separate us, even prior to our joining within this limited perception of what we call *time*. And so, I repeat, sir, let no man separate what God has joined."

Grey cleared his throat. "Look here, I'm no philosopher, but it sure sounds like a lot of fancy words held together with loose logic that would not withstand the critique of a more qualified logician. Frankly, son, it sounds more like a sales pitch than a sound biblical argument."

"Everything is sales, sir."

Mr. Grey laughed.

Seeing he had the upper hand, Eddie went for the close. "Thus, in furtherance of closing the deal, as you so astutely pointed out as a tenet of good salesmanship, I ask you directly: May I call on your daughter? Oh, and may I remind you, sir, of the wise axiom you shared with me a moment ago: *Let your yes mean yes, and your no mean no.*"

Lily laughed. "He's got you now, Daddy."

At that, Mr. Grey knew he must surrender. He gave a verbal affirmative under his breath. But he also saved the best for last, for this self-educated man of dignity and tradition was going to have the last word: "You may call on Lily. But let me remind you of one thing: I might enjoy sparring with you using biblical passages and logic as weaponry. But my weapon of choice is hanging over your head."

Eddie turned to see the M1903 Springfield Rifle hanging above the front door.

Listening from outside the room, Hack could not resist. He cracked the kitchen door and saw Eddie looking at the rifle just as he expected.

Eddie turned back. "Your message is received loud and clear." He handed the Bible to Mr. Grey. Grey couldn't help but smile.

Lily skipped over to her father and kissed him on the cheek, then stepping past him, grabbed Eddie's arm and pulled him onto the front porch.

"Wait a minute," Mr. Grey said. "You never gave me a price for the bible?"

"That's because it never had a price tag for you, sir." And they walked down the front steps and strolled down the gravel road.

Hack, meanwhile, ran around the back of the house, watching the young couple walk down the gravel road away from the house. Hack felt Lily was walking to the other side of the harvest moon.

A few hours later, as Hack was cleaning out the horse stalls for Dox, Lily and Eddie approached with smiles on their faces. "Hack, Eddie's got something to tell you."

Hack glared at him.

"I went to Good Shepherd."

The young boy's face softened. "You did?"

"I told him that the monks helped you," Lily said, "but that was in the strictest confidence. And that's all he knows for now." She looked at Eddie with a look of seriousness, and he replied with a look of seriousness, showing he understood.

Wanting to move on from the discomfort of the moment, Eddie asked, "Do you know Abbot Ambrose?"

"Sure. He was very kind to me. I received a letter from him just the other day." Hack pulled it from his pocket, looked at it for a moment without unfolding it, and slipped it back.

"And the prior? Father Vincent Roth?"

Hack nodded with a look that lacked a fondness of memory.

Eddie sensed it and waved his hand. "Ah, no one ever liked him. Don't worry about it."

Hack smiled.

"And what about Father Henry, sub-prior?"

"He taught me to read."

"No one ever really liked him either."

"He's broccoli: you only like it after you have a lot of it."

"I'll take your word for it. Who else did you spend time with while you were there?"

"Brother Mathias and me played music together," and he pulled his harmonica from the other pocket.

"Can you play?"

"Learning. Can you?"

"Nah. Too busy working to learn fun stuff like that. Maybe someday when I'm old and gray you can teach me."

Hack thought for a minute. "All right. If I knows you when you're old and gray, I'll make sure you learn."

Lily and Eddie laughed, but Hack didn't.

"Okay Hack," Eddie said, "here's a tough question. Who's your favorite?"

"That ain't tough. Brother Bruno."

"The big German with a limp? Sure, I remember him. He came in just as I was leaving. Hell of a story, I hear, though I don't know it."

"You heard right. But it's a story that's more heavenly than hellish. You just gots to look past the hellish to see it."

"Well, maybe someday you'll help me do that."

"Do what?"

"Look past something hellish to see something heavenly."

Hack nodded again. "All right, I'll do just that. But that's two things I'm supposed to do for you now. You ain't doing nothing for me yet, so not sure that's fair."

"What can I do for you then Hack?"

Hack wanted to say *leave and never come back*. But he knew better. Rather, he said, "I don't rightly know. But I'll ask when I need it."

Eddie looked lovingly over at Lily. "Just as I told you: everything is sales." And he stuck his hand out to Hack: "You've got yourself a deal."

Eddie stayed two weeks but had to leave town, having sold a Bible to all possible prospects, including the dentist. He came by the house every other day and walked Lily up and down the dirt road. He promised to return in a few months. She would be eighteen and old enough to marry, at least according to Mr. Grey's standards.

She received a letter two weeks after he left. Hack saw her read it over and over while she swayed on the front porch swing. Her girlish personality had changed. She was more somber and distant. She did not bounce as she walked but swayed, as if dancing with Eddie in her heart. It was so peculiar to Hack: she was happier than ever before, yet sadness seemed to weigh on her.

It was as if she knew her womanhood was upon her and that she would be leaving the family of her youth. She would be leaving the paradise of the New River Valley. She was preparing herself, and trying to prepare those around her.

Her time with her father changed, especially since Mrs. Grey remained upstairs virtually all day with her ailments. Lily cared for him almost like a wife rather than buttering him up as his little princess. She went on long walks alone in the fields, not always inviting Hack to come along like she used to. She was saying a long goodbye to everyone and everything, including the river and fields and rolling hills that had given her a majestic childhood. She was thanking them, and Hack had the most compelling feeling that they were thanking her.

Mr. Grey changed as well. He knew what was coming. He looked older. He looked tired. He spoke less and touched her more: an arm around her on the front porch swing, a long hug goodnight, holding her hand while he joined her on a few of those long walks along the riverbank. By the time they returned, her arm was wrapped around the inside of his elbow.

And then one day as Hack cleaned the fireplace and Mr. Grey sat enjoying a book in the living room, Lily walked into the room. Her face said it all: her head tilted to one side, her smile ever so slight, her eyebrows bending down in sorrow. It was a look that only a little girl can give her daddy. And in her hands were two fishing rods, reminders of something this daddy and daughter had once upon a time done so frequently. But with the onslaught of adulthood, their time together on the fishing bank had slowly and sadly waned.

The old man froze. His chest stopped moving up and down with breath. His eyes fixed on her face and slowly moved to one of the rods. He slowly lowered the book to his lap, tears welled up, and his bottom lip quivered. His entire world crumbled before him while memories of paradise rushed through his mind like rapids. He stood up, letting the book crash to the ground, extended his arms, took a few steps, and embraced her. He finally breathed. He sounded like a man coming up for air after a deep dive into a black abyss. He squeezed her hard and long, never wanting to let go. She dropped the fishing rods and held him close, as if one hug was the only way she could say *goodbye*, and the way she could say *thank you* for a glorious childhood. He pulled back, wiped his eyes, and apologized profusely to her. She said nothing but picked up both rods and placed one in his trembling hand. She wrapped her arm around his elbow, led him out the front door, and straight across the field to the river.

Hack sat on the floor. It was the most beautiful thing he had ever seen. And yet, the soot of the fireplace covered his hands and face. He was alone again.

And his heart broke.

Chapter 3

Homer Jones

The fateful day came. She was leaving. The family attended a justice of the peace ceremony. And then Lily and Eddie took the long drive alone to Good Shepherd for the sacrament of Holy Matrimony. It was a private ceremony, followed by a short honeymoon.

Shortly thereafter, Lily returned home to collect a few last belongings and to say her goodbyes. She invited Hack on one last walk along the riverbank. He accepted but wouldn't talk.

"I'll miss you, too," she said, reading through the silence.

"Why does everyone I love have to leave me?"

Lily stopped and looked at him. He was staring at the ground, his hands deep in his pockets.

"You have a wonderful family here, Hack. They love you. You should try to love them more. And besides, I will always love you. I will always write you. And I will always visit you. And someday soon, you'll visit me."

"Ain't the same."

"No, it's not," she admitted. She grabbed the back of his head and pulled him in for a hug. He wished he could stay there forever. If something was so perfect, why did it ever have to change?

"I'm so tired of hurting, Lily."

With both hands on his shoulders, she pushed him back and looked deep into his eyes.

"Listen here, Hack. This is important. Only those who love really suffer. Others might have aches and pains, but real suffering is the child of love. And if there's one thing I've learned about you, it's that you know how to love in a way most people don't. But this means you're gonna keep suffering throughout your life in a way most people don't. It's the lot God gave you. It's what you're made for. And it's why I love you, in a special way, more than anyone else in the world."

"More than Eddie?"

"In a special way . . . yes, more than Eddie. And I always will. You can count on it more than you can count on the sun falling tonight or the river flowing tomorrow."

They walked along for a bit longer. She asked him to look after her daddy. She also asked him to let Dox and Mamie into his heart.

He said nothing.

The house was not the same after she left. Worse, it was clear it would never be the same. Even Dox and Mamie were silent. All one could hear was the New River in the distance, the grandfather clock ticking, and Mr. Grey turning pages he wasn't reading.

As winter covered the valley, the Tanners slowly returned to their usual selves. But Mr. Grey did not. The gloom of his wife's sickness settled in like a snowstorm that would never leave, silencing the beautiful autumn chirping of the magnolia warbler and the hooting of the saw-whet owl. It was a cold and still winter. Hack survived it not unlike the hibernating black bears of the Blue Ridge Mountains. Despite Lily's request to open his heart to Dox and Mamie, Hack found a nice comfy spot for his soul to climb into, removed from all human affections and dependence. His soul slept with all those creatures hiding beneath the frost and ice and snow. Just like the bear who would find no nourishment scavenging around until spring, Hack had no reason for his soul to surface. The deeper, the longer it slept, he thought to himself, the safer it would be, the less hungry it would be. Looking for belonging is like looking for food: the longer one looks the more one needs.

What he failed to consider, however, was that bears wither away in hibernation. A male bear loses 30 percent of its body weight; a lactating mother, 40 percent. Hack did not consider he would become a shell of himself. Sure, he was fed. But his face lost its vibrancy; his shoulders slouched; his eyes no longer looked around in wonder. He withered in not only his grief but in his defiance. He refused to come out of his cave, despite a loving family waiting for him in that small cabin behind the white house.

I ain't doin' this no longer, he told himself over and over again. And as he began to notice his own decline and his own injustice to those who loved him, he was pleased. He was pleased, for he knew he should no longer continue to treat the Tanners in such a manner. He now felt a moral duty to resolve the issue.

I ain't doin' this no longer.

One early spring morning, Dox found a note on the kitchen table. A note he couldn't read. He quickly looked in Hack's room. All of the boy's possessions were gone. Sitting patiently until Mr. Grey awoke was difficult. Mamie was already in the white house preparing breakfast. He had no reason to break the news to her until he got the truth of the letter from Mr. Grey.

An hour later, Dox saw Mr. Grey stirring in his living room.

"I'm sorry to bother you so early, Mr. Grey, but I found this here on my table. And it seems Hack is gone."

Mr. Grey read it.

Dox,

You and Mamie are kind and loving. Thank you for trying to make me into your son. I love this place, the river, and all the good things and all the good people. But I am meant for something else. I am going home.

If you love me, you will let me go.

Hack

Mr. Grey put his hand on Dox's shoulder. There was nothing to be said. The house was becoming used to loss.

Dox looked up at Mr. Grey.

"Let him go?"

"Let him go."

At the earliest stage of dusk, when the mere haze of the sun's rose-colored fingertips climbed over the farthest edge of the horizon, Hack had been walking three hours. He had not been to the West Jefferson train station since his arrival nine months ago. It was a cold April morning. An hour ago, he could see his breath in the moonlight. He wanted a rest, but there was no time to spare. He feared Mr. Grey's wagon with Dox at the reins would come barreling down the dirt road at any minute.

He had little to say for his plan. He had no money. He had no idea how to sneak on a train. Even if he did, he did not know which train would be headed to Capstone.

He did know, however, that his hibernation was over. And he knew that Lily was no longer in the mountains.

Reaching the train station, he listened to passengers discussing their destination, trying to figure out where they were going.

"Hey, boy, what you doing here?"

Hack turned around. The station master stood over him.

"Morning, sir. When is a train leaving for Capstone?"

"You ain't getting on this train, boy. Even the negro cabin requires an adult."

The truth, Hack thought to himself, *use the truth . . . or at least part of it.*

"I live with Mr. Grey."

The station master nodded his head. "Fine man. Give him my regards when you get outta here. Now go."

"But Mister, Mr. Grey sent me down here to get the schedule. He's got business in Capstone."

"Oh, well then . . ." the man waved him toward the glass ticket sales window. He grabbed a small piece of paper that folded out into three sections. A map of the railways spanned across the entire back of the paper. On the front side were listings of different schedules from different stations.

"Hand this to him."

Hack looked up. "Thank you, sir. Have a nice day." He slipped around the corner of the platform, sat Indian style against a wall, and studied the map and schedules. In less than an hour, the *Virginia Creeper* would depart in the direction of Capstone.

All he had to do now was figure a way on to the train, and the next, and the next. And the answer provided itself as a mixed freight and passenger train slowly crept into the station.

One of the sliding doors to a freight car in the train's rear was slightly ajar. He considered bolting through the platform and jumping through the crack but knew that he must strategically jump on at the last moment to avoid apprehension. A handful of passengers disembarked; a handful climbed on. He waited patiently until the train slowly began its departure. He stood up and walked back around the corner to the main area of the platform.

"You again?" said the station master. "What else do you need?"

Hack slipped his small brown one-strapped bag, possessing everything he owned, over his head.

"Sorry, Mister," he said, moving toward the train. "I forgot something."

As the *Virginia Creeper* exited the platform and gained speed, so did Hack.

"Hey!" the man yelled. "No stowaways, God-dammit!" He chased after him.

It was now or never. Hack jumped from the platform onto the tracks and took off. It was not a question of whether he would catch the freight car, running alongside the train, but whether the man in pursuit would catch him. Metal hand bars jutted out right next to the cracked sliding door and a metal rung as a step would make for an easy boost into the compartment.

He grabbed the hand bar, flung himself onto the metal rung with one foot, twisted back, and watched the station master run to the end of the platform, down a small flight of stairs, and take off down the tracks. He ran for a few seconds, but age and weight won the day over anger. Shaking his fist in the air, he yelled, "You God-damn pickaninny!"

Hack smiled, gave him a little wave, and climbed in.

Now that the train was picking up steam, there was no reason to slide the door shut. In fact, it provided light and a draft, something Hack thought would be nice for his lonesome trip to the next station. He would then have to finagle a strategic disembarkment followed by a strategic embarkment on the next train without being caught.

But now, it was time to relax. The compartment was used for the staff's inventory and passengers' personal items. It was filled with luggage, mostly in the form of large chests. A handful of round boxes, evidently for ladies' hats, were stacked in different areas. Wooden crates were filled with eggs and vegetables. The rattle of silverware could be heard but not seen.

"What the hell is that?"

Hack turned toward a voice in the back of the cart. A man in his early twenties rested beside a stack of crates. His clothes were tattered, his hair long beneath the newsboy cap, his beard ratty. The sole of one of his boots was flopping off at the toe. He had a bottle of white lightning resting on his chest between his suspenders, jostling with every bump of the train. He lay on a thick blanket against a wall. A handful of boxes and chests had been left open next to him.

"Sorry . . . I was . . ." Hack couldn't find the words.

"You're a stowaway, like me, you idiot."

He sat up and leaned toward Hack. He squinted like a man blinded by light or in desperate need of spectacles. The top row of his teeth were brown with thick black lines along his gum, and one of his front teeth was missing.

"A nigger. Son-of-a-bitch. I ain't stowing away with no mosshead today. Get out."

Hack looked at him but said nothing.

The man's eyes dropped, as if sleep was on the verge of overcoming him. "I said get out!"

"I can't. No place to go."

The man flopped to his side, his face buried in the blanket. Slightly above a whisper and muffled by the blanket smashed against his face, he said, "No place to go . . ." and fell quiet for some time.

Hack took a seat against the wall, while the man clutched his bottle to his chest, guarding it with what little strength he had left.

It had been a long morning. Hack sighed and dropped his head against the wall behind him. He felt sleep coming on but fought the urge, needing to keep an open eye on his fellow stowaway.

An hour passed before the man stirred from his slumber. He wiped his face of drool and rubbed the crust from his eyes. He looked over at Hack, at first surprised, then the foggy memory returning to him.

"I told you to get out."

"And I told you I ain't got no place to go."

"Yeah. I know you did."

He stretched hard, trying to bring oxygen back into his muscles.

"What's a nigger doing taking up my space?"

"It don't look like your space. You look as lonesome as me, catching a ride somewhere far away."

"Let me guess," the man said. "Your daddy done beat the tar out of you. And you hit the road instead of hitting him back."

"What? No . . . My Pa's dead anyhow."

"Lucky bastard," the man said, followed by a short moment that looked like reflection. But then, as if an anger burst forth from within, like molten lava from the core of the Earth, he looked at Hack: "Then I bet your momma's a whore and you gettin' away from the bitch."

The anger within the man lived not only in his voice but seemed to give his face a distinctive look of perpetual wrath and misery. Hack was afraid of him like he had never been afraid before.

"Ma's dead, too."

The man wiped his mouth with his sleeve. "Doubly lucky bastard . . ." He scooted back on his blanket to lean against the wall, agitated by how uncomfortable he was.

Hack sat quietly, watching for his next move. Without thinking, he said, "I'm sorry."

"Sorry for what?" the man replied while staring up at the ceiling, fiddling with the cork on the top of his bottle.

"Sorry your daddy beat the tar out of you and your momma is a whore."

The man slowly lowered his eyes towards Hack. They opened wide in fury. "What'd you say to me?"

"I said I'm sorry your daddy beat you and your momma's a whore."

"That's what I thought you said." The man reached behind his back and pulled out a revolver.

Hack backed up against the wall but had nowhere else to go. "Mister, I ain't mean anything by it. I really am sorry for you."

"You really are sorry? What you mean?"

"What you mean what do I mean? Don't you know what sorry is?"

"You ain't picking on my momma and daddy?"

"No, sir," Hack said, trying anything to show respect. "I means it. I'm awful sorry for you."

He lowered the gun and put it on the blanket next to him. "I'd shoot you dead if it didn't give me away to the conductor. We don't need any more niggers on God's green Earth anyhow. Maybe I'll kill you when I'm getting off."

Hack knew silence was the best course of action, but his nerves wouldn't allow it. He tended to talk when he was nervous.

"How long you been stowing away?"

The man shook his head. "This train . . . since yesterday sometime. Started up in Virginia. Other trains . . . I've been stowing since I was fifteen. Over seven years now. Shit, seven is supposed to be biblical. Ha! Coming to an end though."

"What's coming to an end?"

"Stowing away."

"Why?"

"'Cause I'm gonna die soon." He rubbed his head as if a headache overcame him.

"From what?"

The man held up the revolver.

"How's that gonna kill you?"

"Like this . . ." and he put the barrel in his mouth, held it there for a moment, and jerked his head back, imitating the explosion.

"Why you gonna do that?"

The man looked back at him. "Why you ask so many questions? Why don't you just shut your mouth before I shut it for you?"

Hack sat there quietly watching him.

Without warning, the man jumped from the blanket, took one step toward Hack, and kicked him as hard as he could. Hack covered his head and fell into a ball on the floor as he began to kick him in the ribs. Hack moaned and grunted.

"I'd smash your nasty face in, but I don't wanna get my hands dirty on nigger skin." He stumbled back to his blanket and collapsed down.

Hack managed to sit back up, rubbing his ribs, keeping a careful eye on the man who had the bottle in one hand and the revolver in the other. "Thank you, boy. That felt good."

Unfazed, Hack asked, "Why?"

"Why what?"

"Why'd kicking me feel good?"

"Better you than me."

"But I ain't kicking you."

"Nope. You ain't. Don't matter. Others have. And you are others."

Another long spell of silence fell on them, and Hack found himself with a question he felt compelled to ask.

"If you are gonna kill yourself, why haven't you already done it?"

"I gotta do it in Charleston."

"Why?"

"I already kicked you for asking me questions. You want me to do you worse?"

Hack shrugged.

After a few minutes, the man said, "I hate Charleston. I want my brain matter to flow across the fishing pier. Maybe some will seep through the cracks and give the sea creatures a tasty meal. That's what I want."

Hack considered the image for a moment. "What'd Charleston do to you?"

"You know, you probably too stupid to get this . . . but one of the worst things you can give a boy is a memory. The kind of memory you can't shake. The kind of memory that's so real, that's so fresh no matter how far removed you get, it can drive a man crazy."

Hack nodded. "I got some bad memories too."

"Shit, I ain't talking about bad memories. I got tons of those. Those don't bother me. I can fight them with my anger and this here bottle. It's the memory in Charleston that don't fit. It's the memory that I can't fight . . . that I can't . . . I can't understand." He rubbed his eyes and mumbled every curse word in the book, one after the other, a litany of hatred.

"If it ain't a bad memory, then is it a . . ."

"You got it! You dumb shit. A good memory." He glared at Hack again and began to chuckle. "Speaking of shit, what's the difference in a nigger and a bucket of shit?"

Hack waited.

"The bucket!" He dropped his head back, popped open the cork, and took a swig. "Ah shit, kid, I'm just teasing you. You know . . . I got some colored folks in my family tree from way back. Sure do . . . and they all still hanging there!" He laughed at himself.

"Your daddy teach you those?" Hack asked.

The bottle froze at the man's lips. He slowly lowered it, pushed the cork back in, and pushed himself off the blanket, revolver in hand. He knelt down in front of Hack, grabbed the back of his hair, pulling his head back. The fury possessed his face: wide eyes, clenched teeth, trembling edges of his mouth. He slowly slipped the barrel in Hack's mouth.

Hack began to shake. He made the decision, however, to keep his eyes open and aimed right into his attacker. He calmed himself and watched the man slowly calm himself as well, making his way back to the blanket without saying a word. Hack breathed heavily and dared not utter a word again.

He looked at the door, leading to the car in front of the caboose. Knowing it was better to get busted for stowing away than to remain hidden with this vicious vagabond, he started to rise.

"Sit!" said the man, waving his gun.

Hack complied but was dead set on figuring a way out of this mess. He watched the man carefully. He would steal the revolver if the booze knocked him out again. Unfortunately, he seemed rather awake at this point, gazing out the open door as trees flew by, lost in thought.

"A good memory," the man said calmly. "The damndest thing . . . Why would a good memory hurt so much? Hell if I know. . . . I wasn't much older than ten, I reckon. Daddy had business on the road. Momma was shacking up, or so he told me over and over again. Hated her for it . . . not for shacking up, but for leaving me behind with that filthy bastard. So I was stuck on the longest road trip I ever imagined. At times, he got drunk and beat me up, even in public. The embarrassment hurt worse than the knuckles.

"But the next day, as he sold blankets and pots and pans door-to-door, I would stand back and watch him become a different person right before my eyes. The man who knocked on those doors wasn't the son-of-a-bitch that I knew. He was charming. A sweet talker. He'd pat the little kids on the head standing next to the lady of the house. He pulled a coin out of a few ears . . . son-of-a . . . anyhow, he wasn't the same man I knew, that's for damn sure.

"When we got to Charleston, he decided to take some time off. He took me to this fishing pier, rented a few rods and a cup full of shrimp. And we stood on the edge of that pier for two days. For some reason I'll never know, he wasn't mean. There was no cussing. He didn't blame me for nothing. I didn't say anything stupid or move the wrong way. He didn't even drink liquor, just some cold beers, that made him happy.

"And would you believe it? I caught a blowfish and a damn squid. It wasn't no beautiful blue marlin, but it was prettier than anything I'd ever seen. He called other fellas over to see what his son had caught, and we laughed and just looked at that squid. It was a perfect two days. I remember every minute . . . every minute haunts me."

He took a swig.

"So why am I gonna blow my brains out on that pier? Because it has caused me more pain than any of his backhands. Ever since then, I knew what life could have been . . . I knew what other kids got from their daddies. I think the bastard, you know, gave me those two days just to torture me the rest of my life. And the minute we left that pier, and he got back into working mode, I started saying the wrong things and stepping the wrong places and looking with the wrong face. The beating picked up where it left off.

"I must have cried myself to sleep a hundred times wishing for that pier to return. But it never did. Wish I would've burned it to the ground years ago. But I got a better idea now."

Hack thought back to the fishing trips he took with his Pa, especially the one right before the murder. He couldn't remember his Pa ever raising a hand at him. His heart nearly broke just thinking about the possibility of it. His life would have crumbled had his Pa took his anger out on him, or if his Pa slandered his mother's dignity. He remembered Lily standing in the living room, holding two fishing poles in her hands, as her father melted in grief. Perhaps there was something about fishing.

And then he realized something while looking at the slobbering, filthy, vile creature across from him that seemed to ooze gluttony and wrath: that this broken man probably had more gumption, backbone, and grit than he had. The drunken man had made it all these years with an unthinkable pain stoking his anger, scourging his self-identity, siphoning off any remnant of humanity.

The man became human again in Hack's eyes. And so, the courage to ask another question came to him, the only appropriate question when one realizes that the villain is still human.

"My name's Hack. What's yours?"

"Homer Jones," he said after a long pause.

Hack watched him gaze out of the window, lost in the memory, not knowing how to deal with that irreconcilable snapshot of fatherly love. Homer was as disconcerted by the memory of a loving father for two days as Hack would have been with the memory of an abusive father for two days. Hack understood, but in the reverse.

Man takes in the world around him—sights, sounds, tastes, feelings, touch—and then constructs the only worldview he can. If hatred is foreign to this world, then revenge provides no reward. If lust is foreign, it is not exciting. If gluttony is foreign, it is not filling. And yet, if tenderness is foreign, then—for some unfortunate souls—it is not comforting but threatening, for it threatens the fabric woven by a million threads of cruelty and savagery and sadism. Man (especially when he is a boy) grows used to the clothes woven by his father's strength and weakness, presence and absence, love and hatred.

It was apparent to Hack that Homer was one who had grown comfortable with evil, like one who has grown comfortable with the dark. Any sense of charity was like a blinding light—painful to the eyes that had lived in darkness. And this memory of a tender father on the fishing pier radiated through his memory like that blinding light amidst the darkness of his everyday reality and every memory of his past. The revolver was meant to extinguish the light—forever.

Killing himself at the site of the good memory was a way to kill the place at the same time, like a man who burns a picture of the woman he used to love so that she would no longer look at him. Homer wanted not only to extinguish his memory but revenge on the location that gave birth to it. He would have burned the pier to the ground if it was not too merciful on the pier; he would have killed his own father if it was not too merciful on him. He wanted his father to forever suffer the guilt for his son's actions. He wanted the pier to be forever stained with his blood.

"Is there anything I can say, Homer, that won't make you mad?"

"Yes."

"Name it."

"Say, I hope you feel the bullet. Say, I hope you feel unimaginable pain for minutes before you slip into nothingness. Say, I hope your mother and father feel so much guilt that they try to kill themselves but fail over and over again and then are locked up in straitjackets, never allowed to put themselves out of their misery. I won't get mad at that. I might even offer you a drink."

Hack dropped his head. He considered what Lily would say. He considered what Brother Bruno and Abbot Ambrose would say. He considered what his Pa would say. Nothing came to mind. Homer was lost in a world that Hack did not know. But his sympathy for him was bursting.

"No one should have to live like you live," he finally said.

"That's why I'm ending it. Just a few more days . . ."

"Is there any other way?"

Homer shrugged. "I used to wonder that. But now . . ." he smiled, "I don't want there to be. If I could change it, I wouldn't."

"Why?"

"Because all I have is me. I have my hatred, and it has become me. Here's the thing . . . I ain't really killing myself."

"What do you mean?"

He took another drink.

"You can't kill what's already dead. I'm dead. I even see dead things. Guess I'm part ghost or something. Used to scare me. Not anymore. Living people scare me. You scare me."

"I do?"

"I know I can kick your ass and all, but you look alive, like all them people on the train," he wagged his revolver near the passenger cars. "With their smiles and laughs. Like my memory—terrifying. When I was a boy, you know, I was scared of the dark. Hollered out for Pa until he gave me a bloody nose in bed. Then whipped me with his belt for pissing my bed. Afterwhile, I wasn't scared of the dark, but of the rising sun. I ain't scared of the dark, but I am of the light. And despite you being a nigger, you remind me of the rising sun. That's why I oughta kill you dead. But it'd give me away. I gotta get to Charleston and put out the light once and for all."

He sat still for a moment, started to breathe a little faster, until he popped his cork and chugged every last drop. He coughed once it was all gone, then slowly lowered his head and passed out again.

Hack sat looking at him for the remainder of the trip, knowing that he would have to switch trains soon. He stared at the revolver, still in his grip.

After an hour, the train reached its stop. It was time to leave, but he couldn't get his mind off that revolver. Homer looked hopelessly unconscious. Hack concluded it was safe to take the revolver and throw it in the nearest woods. He asked himself why he should bother. Homer would just find another way. He had no answer but knew he must.

As the train slowed into the station, Hack stood up. As he did, he felt in his own pocket, his Pa's harmonica, reminding him of his father's sweet melodies, easing him to peaceful sleep. He took it out of his pocket. It was the only possession he had of his father's; it was the most tangible connection he had with him, he thought to himself. *No!* he then thought. It was not. It was a piece of metal, filled with dried saliva and tender memories. And those memories would never leave him, no matter if he lived a thousand years, no matter if he blew on the same metal that his Pa had during those long nights after his Ma's death, no matter if he could hold it at night like he was holding his Pa's hand. It was the memories that were the most tangible connection with his Pa. And he then realized that he needed nothing else of his Pa; he already had everything of value a father can give a son.

Hack slowly slipped the revolver from Homer's grip and put the harmonica in its place.

Before jumping from the train, he turned back and looked at the broken man living in darkness, holding Pa's harmonica rather than a revolver.

"Goodbye Homer," he whispered. And then in the silence of his mind, he shot something up to heaven that one may call a prayer if he so chooses: *Look after him, Pa. Somehow. Someway. Look after him.*

A faint whisper in the dark . . .

"Brother Bruno . . ."

No response.

He gently nudged his shoulder.

"Brother Bruno . . ."

"*Was zum Teufel!*"

"Shhhh . . . it's just me."

"*Der Hurensohn!*"

"It's just me."

"Who the hell is *me?*"

"Hack."

"Hack?"

"Hack."

"Turn on the damn light."

"There."

"Hack?"

"Ain't no dream."

"You ran away from home?"

"I ran away *to* home."

Chapter 4

Return Home

Bruno's heart was pounding, feeling the anxiety of the moment.

"It's good to see you, Hack, but this is no place for a runaway colored boy."

"It ain't no place for a German deserter either."

Bruno hated it when Hack took him in mental loops like that. He just dropped his shoulders, not knowing exactly what to say. He rubbed his eyes awake, trying to collect his thoughts. "You didn't like the Tanners?"

"Liked them fine."

"Didn't like the mountains?"

"Loved the mountains. Beautiful. Open. Cool. A good place for a monastery."

"The abbot is not going to like this."

"That's okay. He doesn't have to."

"He's the abbot. Of course he has to."

"He's holy."

"And yet . . . still the abbot. He gets what he wants."

"He's holy. Means he gets less of what he wants. Right?"

Bruno scratched his head. "It doesn't feel like a time to do this with you. What time is it?"

"About 2:00 a.m."

"You know that girl was just married here."

"I know. Lily was like my sister."

He looked away, then turning back, "You know Father Roth is going to explode."

Hack let a little smile edge onto his face.

"I see that smile," Bruno said, pointing at him.

"Sorry."

Bruno replied with his own smile. "Seeing him explode is kind of funny, isn't it?"

Hack nodded.

"Time for you to go to your cell. I'll break the news to the abbot in the morning."

Hack stood up and turned for the door.

"Hack?"

"Yes?"

Bruno stood up and hugged him. "Good to see you."

"Will I stay this time?"

"Good night, Hack."

"Good night."

Immediately following Lauds, the abbot discreetly made his way down to the hermitage. Hack was drifting in and out of a peaceful sleep, weary from his long journey.

The door was pushed open slowly, stirring Hack to an upright position.

The abbot shut the door behind him, gave Hack a long eye of disapproval, then stretched his arms out, smiling. Hack leapt from his cot and quickly embraced him. The abbot squeezed his head to his chest.

"What a surprise. Did you get my letters?"

"Read them many times." Hack pulled them from his pocket.

"Hack, why are you here?"

"I had to come home."

"We found you a home."

"You found a wonderful family to live with, in a beautiful place to live. But you didn't find me a home."

"How did the Tanners treat you?"

"Couldn't have been nicer."

"And the Greys?"

"Couldn't be better."

"Then what's the problem?"

"I told you that ain't my home. I had this pain in my stomach every day, even though Lily made it mostly better from time to time. I thought if I got back into this abbey, it would go away. And it did."

"You can't stay."

"But I can. I can because God wants me to."

"And how do you know that?"

"How do you know He doesn't want me here?"

"That's not how it works."

Hack thought for a moment. He remembered Eddie's words to Mr. Grey: *Everything is sales.*

"Abbot, if you pray hard and God tells you to make me leave, then I will leave and not come back. I promise."

The abbot eyed him suspiciously.

"Do we have a deal?" Hack asked.

"Where did you learn to bargain?"

"Eddie."

"Ah. Of course."

"Abbot, let your yes mean yes and your no mean no."

"Well, sometimes, Hack, the honest answer is, *I don't know*. And . . . I don't know. But for now, we'll say you came to visit, and I will consider the options going forward."

The day was filled with numerous visits from his old friends: Brother Bruno, Brother Mathias, even Father Henry came to exchange some pleasantries and inquired as to his advancement in reading.

But then another knock on the door came.

"Come in."

A young monk poked his head in. He had thick black hair nicely parted to one side, a long nose, and arched eyebrows.

"Excuse me," he said. "May I come in?"

"Sure thing," Hack said, waving him and standing.

"My name is Brother Dominic."

"Nice to meet you. I'm Hack. The abbot told me about you."

"Did he?"

"In a letter, while I was away."

"Ah. Well, I've heard about you as well. You're a legend here."

Hack squinted his face. He was not flattered by the comment in the least. In fact, there was something disconcerting about it.

"I . . . I mean that in a good way, of course."

"I don't wanna be no legend."

"But it's endearing, nonetheless."

"Nope."

Brother Dominic was already beginning to see why he was a legend. No conversation was normal.

"Sorry, Hack. I didn't mean anything by it."

"I don't wanna be a legend. I just wanna be real. I want the monks to think of me as real."

"Ah, I see. Legends may or may not be real."

"Either way, aren't they just in your head?"

"What do you mean?"

"Like . . . ideas?"

"I suspect so."

"Not sure how being an idea is endearing. Sounds like a low blow. The lowest blow possible."

"Very interesting. Why do you think that?"

Hack thought a moment. "I gots an idea of my Pa. But he ain't really here. When I was in Jefferson, I had ideas of coming back here, but it wasn't real until it was. The horse manure was more real than most of the ideas in my head. Ideas were painful because they weren't real. Call me horse manure, but don't call me a legend."

"I see your point. But do you like ideas?"

"Ideas that aren't fake people? Sure do. They're fun to play with."

"I like ideas, too."

"Abbot said you're a philosopher. Not sure I know what that is though."

"I wonder the same thing sometimes. The word means *lover of wisdom. Philia* means 'love,' and *sophia* means 'wisdom.' I guess that makes me a lover of wisdom," he said, smiled.

Hack went wide-eyed and leaned forward.

"Then my Pa was a philosopher. He loved wisdom." Hack looked off to the side in imitation of his Pa, "'*Teach us to number our days, so that we'll have a heart of wisdom.*' Somewheres in the Psalms."

"Indeed."

"And he said all the time, '*With humility comes wisdom.*' Somewheres in Proverbs."

"Your Pa sounds like he was a wise man."

"So philosophers study Psalms and Proverbs, looking all 'round for wisdom?"

"Not exactly. We look for it in philosophers outside of the Bible, like Plato and Aristotle."

"You can't find enough wisdom in the Good Book?"

Dominic opened his mouth to reply, then closed it, then smiled, nodding. "It's a good question. But God gave philosophers some wisdom apart from the revelation He gave to prophets."

"Why study something apart from God?"

"Well, it's not really *apart* from God, but it's . . ."

"That's what you said."

"Yes. I did. But I didn't really mean that."

"What'd you mean?"

Dominic looked around and rubbed his forehead. "Let's start over."

"Where?"

"Where what?"

"You mean you wanna walk in the room again?"

"No. I mean let's start with philosophy again."

Hack waited as Dominic repositioned himself in his seat.

"God revealed His truth to the Jewish people in the Old Testament, right?"

"Sounds like Pa."

"Good. But what about people in a different part of the world? Like the ancient Greeks?"

"What about them?"

"God didn't give them a burning bush. He didn't give them the Ten Commandments. He didn't have prophets in Athens or Sparta."

"Where's that?"

"Greece."

"Oh."

"So He didn't give the Greeks truths through revelation. But do you think He taught them in other ways?"

"Pa used to say God wrote common sense on the heart."

"Exactly!" Dominic hollered, nearly jumping out of his seat. "And your Pa was a wise man for saying that! Philosophy, as most of us use the word, is a search for the law that God wrote on the heart rather than the law God wrote on the Ten Commandments or on the parchments of prophets and evangelists."

Hack liked the sound of this. "Philosophy. The love of the law written on the heart?" he said softly, considering the import of the words. "Can you teach me these laws?"

"One does not usually study philosophy until much older, Hack. It's rather hard stuff."

"If it's written on the heart, it ought to be easy. I gots a heart beating right now. Why not just tell me the stuff written on it?"

"It doesn't exactly work like that."

"Sounds like it should be the first thing you teach to people. Not one of the last."

Dominic was stumped again. He rubbed his face. "Look, why don't I just give you some things to read and we can talk about it?"

"Can you go get them right now?"

"Well. Okay." Dominic awkwardly arose and made his way out of the hermitage while Hack sat waiting for his return, thinking about laws written on his heart. He tried to remain still and feel anything that seemed like a law. He knew that the letters making the words and the words that made the laws were not etched in stone or marble or even ink. They must be spiritual words written on a spiritual heart. He still tried to feel them. After all, he considered, one can feel memories, like Homer Jones felt memories. Why couldn't one feel the law written by the finger of God?

As he sat in silence, his eyes slowly closed. His mind drifted away from Homer Jones, away from his Pa, away from Brother Dominic. His mind created a picture of the heavenly Father's finger, slowly coming forth from the unseen world that lay behind the seen world. And this finger, outstretched, came to his heart, and like a conductor's baton before an orchestra, began swiping this way and that, in looping motions and strikes and gentle swooshes, writing the most elegant script imaginable. Hack felt it in his chest but did not know what it said.

A knock on the door broke his train of thought.

"Come in."

Dominic carried a small, thin blue book with gold letters on the spine. "I know no better place to start than with the death of Socrates."

"Who's Socrates?"

"He was a great man who lived in Athens, ancient Greece, in the 400s BC. He is considered the father of philosophy. It's said that all philosophy is a mere footnote to his thought."

"What made him so good?"

"Great question. He's famous for . . . wait . . . what was the Proverb you quoted?"

"*With humility comes wisdom.*"

"Yes. And Socrates is famous for the humility of knowing that he was not wise . . . which helped him become wise."

Hack smiled. "I like brain flips."

"Me too. There's a great story: Socrates's friend, Chaerephon, went to the Oracle of Delphi, which was like a prophet in ancient Greece, and asked if anyone was wiser than Socrates. The Oracle said *No! Socrates is the wisest of all.* But when Chaerephon told him this, Socrates couldn't believe his ears. He thought this was crazy; he knew he was not wise. So Socrates went on a quest to find a man wiser than himself. He spoke to different experts in different fields. And he found that their knowledge in one area made them think they were knowledgeable in other areas. After a long search, Socrates reluctantly concluded that the oracle was right in one sense: he was the wisest because he knew he wasn't wise. He was aware of his own ignorance. He was humble. And as your Pa's Proverb says, '*With humility comes wisdom.*'"

After a moment of silence, Hack said, "More. Give me more."

Dominic smiled. "Socrates will give you more. Here. Read this first."

He slid the small blue book across the table.

"*The Trial and Death of Socrates*," Hack read aloud.

"Read the *Apology* first. It's the second dialogue in here."

"Dialogue?"

"Plato wrote in dialogues, like you and I are talking right now. He believed it was a better way to find truth rather than one person just bloviating on paper."

"Plato?"

"Sorry. The stories of Socrates were written down by his student, Plato."

"Why's Socrates saying sorry in here?"

"Saying sorry?"

"You said start with the apology."

"Sorry again. I should have explained. An *apology* in ancient times was a defense. The *Apology* in this book is Socrates's defense."

"Defense against what?"

"Some bad guys accused him of corrupting the youth and worshiping false gods. Anyhow, you'll see if you jump into it."

"But why we reading about his death first?"

"Because you can learn a lot about a man by the way he dies."

Hack hung his head.

"Oh, dear. I'm sorry, Hack. I know . . ."

"It's all right."

Dominic smiled. "When you begin a journey, do you not begin with the end in mind?"

"My journey yesterday began with Good Shepherd in mind. Lots of walking and lots of stowing away."

"Exactly. So you can see, the best beginning is the end."

"Makes sense."

"To begin a search for wisdom, then, one can begin with death, which waits for us all. If we want to learn how to live, we must first learn how to die."

Hack thought for a moment. "How will you die?"

Brother Dominic pursed his lips. "What an interesting question. That's something I'll have to go think about. Enjoy that book, Hack." He stood up and headed for the door but stopped and turned back. Hack was already thumbing through the thin blue book.

"Now I understand," said the young priest.

Hack looked up. "Understand what?"

"Why everyone missed you so much."

Hack looked at him with an innocence, a confusion, a wonder of what he meant. Just as Socrates was wise for knowing he was not, Hack had been missed precisely because he was one who never considered whether he would be missed. He just knew he missed them. And that was that.

"But we were better off with him and worse without him!" Brother Bruno yelled across the table at Father Roth.

"Your opinion is as vapid as your German breath is foul. I shan't dignify you with a response," Father Vincent Roth snarled as he looked at Father Henry sitting next to him, as if expecting some kind of visual affirmation.

"Bruno!" the abbot demanded. "Sit civilly and speak civilly or leave this room."

Brother Bruno lowered himself down while glaring at the prior across from him. He eventually looked away, exhaled, and humbly said, "Yes, Abbot."

"And Father Roth, please sheathe your sword and unsheathe your charity."

Father Roth grunted.

"Abbot, if I may . . ." interjected Brother Matthias. "As we have stated in the past, the Rule has a section on young boys. And if we were in 1224 or 1524 or 1724 or even 1824, admitting a thirteen-year-old would not be unique. Our sister abbeys in Europe do such things now, at least those abbeys preserved from the modern era. Our American and modern perspective is a bit limiting."

"Who is to say the old way is the right way?" said Father Henry.

"Exactly," replied Father Roth. "And why do you think modernity, in the most powerful nation in the world, has put an end to such a practice?

In fact, I often hear within these walls a disdain for modernity. But let me tell you something," he said looking around the room. "This world is evolving. It is progressing toward greatness. America is not the most powerful nation on Earth because it has held on to ancient values but because it has embraced progress. And if we are to give Christ's Kingdom a home on Earth, we must evolve with it. The seeds were planted millennia ago, yes. But the Church has become a magnificent tree, far greater than the mere seeds planted. There are complexities and efficiencies that neither the early Christians nor the medieval monks could have fathomed. They are called the dark ages for a reason. We are enlightened in ways they can never understand, both by the light hanging over our heads and by the progression in the theological and spiritual sciences.

"Truly, I say to you: your nostalgia is of the devil. You live in the past and pretend it has the answers. And what you don't understand is that we don't even have the same questions anymore. The old questions have been answered. Lay them to rest. The new questions will have to be answered by an enlightened Church. The Church of tomorrow is not the Church of yesterday. She has grown and set silly things aside. And thus, the monastery today is not the monastery of yesterday. Please, for heaven's sake, no more appeals to the old way of doing things. It does nothing to build up the Kingdom on Earth. In short, the boy must go. It is not the way of modern times, and for good reason."

A deep cough bellowed from the end of the table. Everyone looked at Abbot Gregory.

"Are you all right, Abbot?" Abbot Ambrose asked.

"I think I have done my part here," and he stood up slowly and began walking out of the room.

After the door was shut behind him, Father Roth said under his breath, "He didn't do anything. As usual ..."

Abbot Ambrose cleared his throat.

"There is no decision to be made here. I am not trying to act like a medieval monastery. And I am not trying to usher in a new Benedictine era of progressiveness. I just want to do the right thing. And for now, there is nothing to do other than welcome him as a guest. I will prayerfully consider other options. I ask you to do the same."

Abbot Ambrose went immediately to Gregory's cell after the meeting. He was welcomed with a warm smile and a wave of the hand. Something told Abbot Ambrose that Gregory expected him.

"Why will you not speak in counsel?" Ambrose asked.

"I was speaking the entire time."

"You know what I mean."

"You don't think speaking to God counts?"

"But I could use your help."

"I helped you more with my mouth shut and my heart open than the other way around. I prayed for you to have wisdom, perseverance, and peace of heart."

"Will you talk to me now? Directly?"

"I can try."

They stared at each other.

"Well . . ." Abbot Ambrose said with his hands lifted in anticipation. "Tell me: What am I supposed to do?"

The old man pursed his lips and squinted, as if looking for the simplest way possible to speak the truth: "There are but two rules: Love God with your whole mind, heart, and strength, and love neighbor as self. The Rule of Holy Father Benedict is nothing more than a poor, frail, human attempt to live out these two rules of our Lord."

"Yes. But I am the abbot bound by an oath to lead these monks according to this Rule. And it is a beautiful Rule that I love."

"No more textual torture!" the old man said with more spunk than usual. "No more academic gymnastics. You know the Rule just fine. Simply follow the Gospel and go to a peaceful sleep."

"I can't be at peace with all these uncertainties."

"Now that is complete nonsense, my young and foolish abbot. If you abandon yourself to God's divine providence in this very moment, if you use your mind and free will to detach from every possible concern in this world, if you desire nothing but total and complete unity with God in this particular moment, if you see this moment as eternity breaking into your life and heaven laid before you, then you will understand that no matter the facts surrounding you, no matter the bickering, no matter the lack of control of those around you, you will understand that your life is perfect. It is perfect even if you were to be burned in the coliseum and fed to lions before cheering spectators. You don't need certainty! You don't need clarity! Remember, Ambrose, Lucifer was the angel of light. He had great clarity. You need nothing of the sort for peace of heart. The only certainty you need, my son, is the certainty that you have no attachment to anything on this Earth except God's will, total certainty that the desire to do God's will, will tell you what to say, what to do, what to eat, and when to sleep. And when the desire to do God's will directs you to lay your head down on either a soft pillow or a wooden board, whatever God's will dictates, then you will drift away into the sweetest sleep imaginable, that is, until His will is for you to suffer vigils and other nightly torments. And even then, you will be able to endure it with peace of heart."

Abbot Ambrose nodded as he considered the counsel. "Is it fair to say that if Hack stays this time, he is here forever?"

"Who can say? Let providence dictate that. You are too focused on planning out this life. It is passing. Pay no attention to the nonsense espoused by your prior. The kingdom of God is not of this world. He is inverted. And worse, he lacks the very peace of heart I was just mentioning. Plan for what is forever, which is heaven or hell."

Ambrose sighed, looking away.

Gregory smiled. "I do understand your question, Ambrose, despite all my words of wisdom seeming as though I am trying to avoid answering it. Here is a little advice. He is thirteen. He must reach eighteen before this community can officially welcome him anyway, at least according to our more recent standards. Do not think 'forever'. Think about loving your neighbor, Hack, one day at a time. Constantly judge his happiness. Do not worry about what is normal. Worry about what makes him happy, or better yet, joyful."

"What's the difference?"

"Oh, I'm not terribly sure. I think about it all the time. But when I see joy, I recognize it. When I think of happiness, I think of Aristotle's *Eudaemonia,* a fulfillment. But there is something dreadfully dull in that. It sounds like Roth, actually. But joy! Joy is dynamic. It is passionate. It is in love with all that is lovable. Joy is filled with the beautiful gift of God called laughter. And laughter is something monks need to do more often. It is something that those who are stuck in the Middle Ages never do and something that those obsessed with progress never do."

The old abbot chuckled at the very mention of laughter. But then his reflection took him back to a more serious thought.

"I was joyful as a child, and the war between the states robbed me of it. I regained it building this abbey by laying bricks and praying the office while standing around a furnace and sleeping in a tent. Then the abbot's chair robbed me of it again. I have spent every day since then detaching myself from this world, as an old man must do, in search of an unquenchable joy. And here we are! Full circle. Joy comes from a knowledge that God's will is one's only desire."

He smiled and laughed a little, content with the reflection.

The young abbot still looked distressed but would not persist.

"Go. It is time for me to lay my head down and enjoy that peaceful sleep I mentioned. I will pray, as I drift off, that you will be blessed with the same."

Abbot Ambrose's Journal

May 1, 1925

Initially, it was my zeal and adrenaline that kept him with us, like running in front of an oncoming train to save a helpless boy. But now a decision must be made.

I found him a home, a place he was safe. He started a new life, a life he deserved. But our hearts sank when he left us. And our hearts rejoiced when he returned, for the hand of God is on this child like none I have ever seen. He is like young David, anointed by the prophet, far too early for people to understand.

Must prudence win the day? Something tells me that the insidious nature of Walter's crime will not die an easy death. It may lie fallow for decades and return with a vengeance if little Hack—or big Hack upon that predestined day—is discovered.

And yet, Hack pleads to stay. The natural reasons are clear: fear, uncertainty, loneliness. But I have prayed so hard, dear Lord, I have prayed on this harder than anything in my life. Despite being no place for a child, despite violating Holy Father Benedict's Rule, despite God-given common sense.... That still, small voice seems to whisper that something supernatural is at hand.

Prudence. Does God call us to practice practical prudence? How shall we know when to control the circumstances so the circumstances do not control us? How shall we know when to accept the unthinkable as only thinkable due to God's holy will?

Did not mud and spittle give sight to the blind? Did not one loaf and two fish feed five thousand men? Did You not die in order to defeat death? The paradoxes of this faith are at times too much to fathom. The paradox of this colored boy in my basement is too much to fathom.

Lord, I know not how to lead this young man, a giant among men, a saint among sinners, a stranger among even those who love him.

Kyrie Eleison. I know not when a miracle is at hand. I know not the difference in your holy will and my unholy pride. I would not know, dearest Lord, a burning bush, even if it spoke to me.

Kyrie Eleison. Christe Eleison. Kyrie Eleison.

Hack's Journal

May 21, 1925

Pa has been in heaven for a year. I miss Pa. I miss Lily.

I am happy and sad at the same time. I have friends. Brother Bruno is my best friend. He is big and strong and funny, like Pa.

I know Pa can see me. He can hear me. But I cannot see him. Or hear him. Abbot says Pa is happy in heaven with God. Brother Dominic says Pa has reached something called a final end.

Before I left for the mountains, Father Henry made me memorize, "Cowards die many times before their deaths; The valiant never taste of death but once." That means my Pa was brave. I hope to be brave one day. Lily is brave. Homer Jones is brave. I hope he did not kill himself. I hope Pa took care of him.

Brother Mathias says I should write a song to Pa on my new harmonica because David wrote songs for God on a lyre. Maybe I will.

I love the monks. I can hear them chant. It is like the sound comes from inside me. I love it. I do not want to ever leave. Abbot thinks I should leave someday.

I think the monks need me.

The most obvious but disconcerting reality of Christianity is that many (if not most) of those who wear the label do not follow the Way. The only thing more obvious is the fact that such a reality should not be legitimate fodder for the sceptics to feed upon, and yet they feast at their leisure with smug superiority. One might consider it an act of humility to willfully join a religion of hypocrites and readily admit that hypocrisy is indeed one's greatest daily struggle. A freedom is found in such resignation, while the skeptic stews in obstinance, alone in his moral-laden ivory tower.

What the skeptic fails to see is that those rare acts of true Christianity are so fertile that they cover a multitude of sins; true acts of charity are humble and so pass beneath his stiff nose stuck in the air. The glory of Christianity is found in the grotesque—the epitome of which paradox is found in our chosen symbol to represent truth and goodness . . . and beauty.

But nonetheless, the Catholic Church is made up of sinners, and we will never escape this unfortunate situation. We will continue to make fools of ourselves, as we always have. In the earliest generations of Christians, apocryphal gospels were written for fanfare, including fanciful tales of the Child Jesus threatening to strike Joseph dead if he did not comply with his wishes; in the Middle Ages, popes purchased Peter's Chair and on occasion, shared a bedchamber or two with ladies of Magdalen's profession; monasteries throughout Christendom were susceptible to becoming fiefdoms of bondage for the disposable peasant; and clerics have relied on intimidation in no more clever a manner than the ancient Pharisees did to perpetuate their rank and privilege.

In fact, it seems a natural temptation of clerics to fall back on intimidation when the face of charity and the apparent authority of logic fail to produce their desired outcome. It was no different in Good Shepherd, despite the unflinching charity of so many monks.

Father Vincent Roth was running out of options. His arguments were falling on deaf ears. Being second-in-command as prior was as useless as being a negro groundskeeper in his mind, at least when a young abbot thought he knew better. And many of the monks around him had, so he thought, blindly followed their abbot, as sheep will follow each other right off a cliff. It was time, he concluded, to use intimidation on the most vulnerable of the bunch, and it was his own virtue of charity, he was certain, that kept him from using this option until the end.

One night, after everyone had retired, Father Roth made his way down to Hack's hermitage. He did not knock.

"Father Roth!" Hack said, standing.

Father Roth shut the door behind him and took a seat. He did not make immediate eye contact with Hack. He stared at the table in front of him, waiting for Hack to take his own seat. He did so.

"Do you know what sin is?" Father Roth asked.

Hack nodded confidently first, then shrugged sheepishly.

"Well, boy, which one? Yes or no?"

"Both."

"Don't be difficult. Do you know what sin is or not?"

"I know what sin is in the big stuff. But sometimes I don't know what it is in the small stuff, like my own thoughts or feelings. Do you know God's law in the little stuff?"

"Yes, of course I do. But that's not my point. The point is . . ."

"Can you teach it to me?" Hack asked excitedly.

"Teach what?"

"How to know God's law in my own thoughts and feelings?"

Father Roth shook his head. "Just be quiet and listen. I came here for a reason. You need to know something that the abbot isn't willing to tell you. Leaving the Tanners was a sin, all right Hack? Coming here was a sin. Staying here is a sin. You must tell the abbot that you want to go back to the Tanners at once."

"Why are those things sins?"

"Is it not obvious? Because you belong there and not here."

"Why do I belong there and not here?"

Father Roth squirmed in his chair. "You're too young to understand, and you're too young to be in a monastery. It's just that simple."

"But I want to be here."

"That has nothing to do with it. Absolutely nothing. And you can't seem to see that your desire means nothing. It is time for you to leave, and for good."

Hack looked down at the floor for a moment, then back up. "Why did you become a monk?"

"Excuse me?"

"Why did you become a monk?" the boy repeated.

"I'm not sure how that's relevant, but because I was called by Almighty God, that's why. Unlike you."

"How'd he call you?"

"I have no desire to go through my story with you. This meeting is about . . ."

"Please? Just a little of it."

The prior sighed. "Very well. If you must know . . . I had a pure and unadulterated calling. I was sitting in Mass and heard the Gospel: *Amen I say to you, there is no man who hath left house or brethren or sisters or father or mother or children or lands, for my sake and for the gospel, who shall not receive a hundred times as much, now in this time.* I knew then that my kingdom awaited me. No more poverty or hunger or backbreaking labor for no benefit. Jesus promised me a return hundreds of times what I was willing to walk away from." His bottom lip jutted out as he shook his head like a man who was showing no doubt or remorse for his actions. "I went home, packed my bag, and walked out. And the rest is history."

"What'd your Pa say?"

"He was dead. He said nothing."

"Your Ma?"

The prior looked away and huffed with the hint of a smile.

"She tried to stop me. She grabbed my arm, my bag. She pleaded with me to explain what I was doing. I told her I was called by God to something higher than a hovel with a leaky roof."

"You just walked out on your Ma?"

The prior glared across the table. "Did the Apostles not drop their nets and follow Christ? Did He not say that we must hate our father and mother to follow Him? Did Jesus not say He brought a sword? You have the same problem as most people: you think the Kingdom is filled with hugs and kisses. It isn't. It is filled with truth. And truth hurts. It hurt my mother . . . so be it. It hurts . . ."

"Did it hurt you when you were walking away from her?"

"What? What kind of silly question is that?"

"I don't know. I loved my Ma so much . . . figure I'd hurt more than her if I walked away from her. Father Roth, did you love God so much that it didn't hurt you to walk away?"

Father Roth seemed to drift away in his memory. "Well . . ." he said in a softer tone than Hack had ever heard him use. "I remember her yelling *please* over and over again as I walked down the street. I remember thinking how the neighbors must have thought she was going mad. I remember thinking that I would never see her again, and that felt good and bad at the same time."

He shook his head and turned back toward Hack. "Never mind that. You must go. And it is a sin for you to stay."

"Did you think of her lots at night when you was going to bed? That's when I think of my Ma."

Father Roth's face went soft for a second, but he straightened up and returned to his usual intensity not a second later. "She was dead to me. I gave myself to God. Period. I knew I had to be reborn. And I was."

"But when my Ma was dead to me, it hurt more than anything in the world."

"Yes, well, that was a different kind of dead. And besides, you were a mere child."

"How old were you when you walked away."

"Seventeen."

"Well dern, Father! That's only four years older than me." Hack looked at him suspiciously. "There ain't no way a seventeen-year-old don't miss his Ma."

"That's not the point, Hack."

"But why you telling me fibs, Father? I know you miss her awful when you was walking down that road. And I bet you thought about her most nights your head hit the pillow, just like I did for the longest time."

"Don't you accuse me of telling fibs!" Father Roth demanded, wagging his finger.

"Okay, I won't," Hack said reluctantly. "But I gots another question. Might as well ask you since you're already mad at me."

"Make it quick."

"Why you hate me?"

Father Roth pulled his chin back and furrowed his brows.

"I do not hate you."

"Then why do I scare you?"

"What on Earth . . . ? How dare you! Why would you say such a stupid thing?"

"'Cause I was with this nasty hobo named Homer Jones. And he called me nasty names and kicked me and put a gun in my mouth and said he was gonna kill me."

"What? When did this happen?"

"And then he said he was scared of me because I was so different from him. You ain't ever been anything but mean to me. So I figures you think we're so different, like Homer did . . . and that you're scared of me, like Homer was."

Father Roth gasped. "How, how dare you, you little bastard you."

Hack looked at him quizzically. "Why are you so mad?"

"Because you are an outrage!" He stood up and placed both hands on the table to lean forward. "You are a plague on this community. And you can't fool me, Hack; you're filled with a devilish pride beneath that calm demeanor. You, a colored orphan, dare to challenge me, the prior of this abbey! Pride, I tell you! It is the slyest thing in this world, just as you are, you little snake. I don't know if you have filled yourself with the lie that you are worthy of being here or if you are too stupid to see how much pride has infested your little black soul. But it disgusts me. And I have no need to sit and listen to your depraved accusations. . . . Ha! Scared of you . . . I've never been so insulted in all my God-fearing life.

"And what is it now?" Father Roth continued. "What is that nasty look you are insulting me with again?"

"I don't rightly know why you are being so mean. I thought living with God would help you love. Pa always quoted the Good Book saying, '*Charity suffereth long, and is kind.*' But I ain't sure where it says that. Do you know?"

"I know the scriptures boy," the prior barked. "Again, you dare to accuse me of lacking charity. It is charity for my community that compels me to put you in your place, and then expel you from here once and for all."

"So, you think you're bein' charitable?"

Father Roth's upper lip quivered in fury. "God-damn you . . ." he said with clenched teeth.

"Pa said God made that commandment the second one and for good reason. Almost as bad, you know, as worshiping Baal, whoever that is. Father, who is Baal?"

"You bastard!"

Hack dibbed and dapped his head in thought.

"Take one for the Lord."

It was such a random statement that even in his rage, Father Roth had to ask. "What?"

"When Pa was called names, like *nigger,* he would look down at me and say, 'Take one for the Lord.' And *bastard* ain't near as bad as *nigger,* so I guess I should be happy if saying it keeps you from breaking the second commandment."

Father Roth blinked. He spun around in a rather feminine fashion, threw open the door, and walked as loudly as he could down the long hall and up the winding staircase.

Hack sat at his table, for some reason feeling more at home than ever before. He was happy to *take one for the Lord* if it helped Father Roth in even the slightest way.

Father Vincent Roth's Journal

April 5, 1925

Who is this stranger among us, distracting us from the Rule, bringing disorder to our community, contaminating our proper view of all things of the highest importance, infecting the abbot with altruistic nonsense? The boy will destroy our way of life if we let him.

He must leave. Somehow . . . someway. It is my duty to protect this abbey from all enemies, whether from without or within.

God writes straight in crooked lines, and these lines, over time, become the thread of the Master Weaver. All the while, we think we are skillfully stitching our own tapestry. But at some point in our lives, usually when age has the better part of us, we step back from our alleged masterpiece, look upon it, and have the stark realization that the picture is utterly different than what we ever intended and more beautiful than we could have ever imagined on our own.

Brother Adrian, the young farmer who entered the novitiate with Brother Dominic during Hack's stay in Jefferson, decided that religious life was not his calling. The community was sad to see him leave. He was kind, gentle, and possessed a work ethic only reared on a farm. Saint Benedict would have gladly taken him himself had the Lord not had other plans.

Adrian left but did not know where to go. He had no intention of returning to his home farm inherited by his older brother. He was in search of a farm job, suitable to his trade and temperament.

Brother Bruno informed Hack that Adrian would be leaving. It was Hack who looked off in the distance, thought for moment, and then said to the Bruno, "Eve needs an Adam for her garden?"

"What?" asked Brother Bruno.

"Evelyn. You know. Evelyn. I heard you say that you'd pray for God to send an Adam to her garden."

Brother Bruno's eyes wandered off along with his mind. He stood up quickly and ran out of the room.

Adrian knocked.

Evelyn opened the door but remained behind the screen.

Bruno said nothing about her being beautiful, he thought.

"Can I help you?"

"I'm hoping I can help you."

"Don't get smart with me. You some kinda a salesman?"

"No, Ma'am. I'm sorry. Two friends of mine said you might need a farmhand."

"And who was that?"

"A big German and a negro boy. You know them as Gus and Russ."

Evelyn's eyes opened wide. She said nothing for a moment. Neither did Adrian. The next word belonged to her. A gentleness came across her face. She patted her hair, wondering just how disheveled she looked.

"Would you like some coffee?" she asked, pushing the screen door open.

"I'd love some. Thank you kindly."

Part Three

Chapter 1

The Ku Klux Klan

October 1928

It is a known tragedy of old age to regret the squandering of youth. Some regret not catching the great love of their life; others not having climbed mountains while both heart and sinew are in their prime. Some regret not treating education as the glorious adventure that it is. Older men of a reflective disposition often mourn how many wonders are wasted on youth's inability to appreciate it: the ability to jump and run without fear of pulling a muscle, the smooth skin of one's first love, the absence of a calendar or watch. But many of these men also mourn their failure in youth to appreciate a certain glorious leisure only found in reading great books.

Not so with seventeen-year-old Haskell. (At some point early in his stay, the abbot concluded that it was better to use his birth name, which no one had ever heard, just in case anyone tried to connect the dots to the murders of Percy and Catherine.) Whether it was due to gratitude flowing from his humble upbringing or a natural propensity, the monks never knew. Nonetheless, Haskell's desire for education was insatiable, and it grew with age.

His retention of the words on the page was unparalleled. Haskell's unique attribute was his ability to read the meaning of the words simply and directly, without bias, without presupposition and postulation, without falsely accusing the text of saying what he wanted it to say. It is often said that classical works are easier to read than their countless commentaries, which is precisely what makes them classics. And yet, the self-centeredness of man cannot help but project his own partiality (even his casteism) on the work.

Despite the academic's inability to comprehend it, humility truly is the foremost virtue of the scholar. This in turn explains why the greatest scholars of the Church have been men and women of irreproachable character and, accordingly, have had such low opinions of themselves. It was Saint Augustine, the man to whom most of Catholic theology is indebted, who said, "If you should ask me what are the ways of God, I would tell you that the first is humility, the second is humility, and the third is still humility." It was Thomas Aquinas, the Angelic Doctor, who said, "All I have written seems like straw to me." It was yet another Doctor of the Church, Teresa of Avila, who called herself repeatedly a "worm" and "very stupid" and "wretched" and even one who was "not worthy to live." Though radical (as the greatest saints often are), it was their humility that allowed God to shed light on the text brighter than any kerosene lamp lighting a monk's cell. And Haskell's pure soul allowed God's light to shine right through and on to the text.

And yet there was another unique aspect to Haskell's education, one that was unintentional and unorthodox, despite his instructors' efforts to the contrary. And that was their utter failure to educate him in the typical structured and bifurcated manner with one subject here and another there with strategic progression. Every school in history has had curricula with a certain scope and sequence. But Haskell's inquisitiveness and creative mind repeatedly prevented this from happening. His mind was like the wind, blowing where it willed. It made no sense to Haskell to have divided subjects. There was but one big, beautiful subject with three principal aspects: truth, goodness, and beauty. There was just reading books, solving equations, debating, learning languages, and playing music, all in pursuit of those three aspects. Through his questions and detours and bursts of interest, the instructor could never seem to get through a subject without colliding with another.

Father Henry taught Shakespeare, Virgil, Homer, and Dante, but Haskell would force him into the Song of Songs, the Psalms, and Job. Abbot Ambrose taught him the joy of Scriptures, but before long, they would be flirting with the dark mind of Raskolnikov in *Crime and Punishment*. Brother Dominic went through the works of Plato, Aristotle, and of course Aquinas, but Haskell would have him straining over Raphael's *School of Athens* or even Michelangelo's *Last Judgment* to see the obvious hidden in plain view. Brother Matthias trained him in the violin and painting, but before a score was completed or a canvas filled, they would find themselves in the garden gazing at the evidential power of beauty in a snow pea.

And perhaps best of all, at least from Haskell's standpoint, was his time with Abbot Gregory, which could barely be called a class, despite Abbot Ambrose's insistence to call it such. Abbot Gregory would assign a topic to be contemplated, read, written about, and prayed over, followed by a meandering walk throughout the courtyard together rich with discussion.

As time went on and as time allowed, Abbot Ambrose would join these discussions, even if he did not prepare for them over the previous days. These topics spanned the gamut. More often than not, however, they would dwell on a few words from Scripture or prayer. *Jesus wept,* was a favorite of the old abbot's. So was *My kingdom is not of this world. Be perfect* was one that often troubled Haskell but made Abbot Gregory giggle. *As we* from the Lord's Prayer was a source of interest for Haskell but an oddly discomforting source for the holy old man.

But again, the subjects varied and were not limited to Scripture. Human frailty was a frequent subject, one that engendered compassion and mercy for the stupidity of man, for when one looks at a single vicious act in the spectrum of humanity, one sees that man "gets it honestly."

On the North and South Carolina border in 1928, one could not spend much time talking about the frailties of man without bumping up against the ever-increasing and ever-threatening presence of a group which did not like Catholics much more (though more) than they did the Jews, whom they did not like much more (though more) than the negros. And that was the Ku Klux Klan.

On this particular cool October afternoon, the leaves were losing their radiant color and were beginning to take flight on the gentle breeze traveling through Good Shepherd's courtyard. Haskell missed the chirping of summer birds but took pleasure in the rhythmic clunk of Abbot Gregory's cane against the stone path wrapping the courtyard. A handful of Good Shepherd college students could be heard talking in the distance beyond the tall brick enclosure, which always seemed to be the slightest annoyance to Abbot Ambrose. He believed (and rightly so) that they were monks first and educators second, and thus, the students were guests in their home and, by golly, ought to act like it, no matter where they were on campus. Haskell had come to believe the attitude was the natural consequence of a monk who was like a fish out of water as chancellor of an academic institution. This same monk-turned-abbot loved education but preferred meandering through the courtyard rather than a stuffy classroom filled with hungover eyes looking at you, fighting to stay open.

"This was a terrible topic to cogitate on," said Abbot Ambrose. "I'd rather be teaching those hooligans on the other side of that wall than talking about this. Whose crazy idea was it?"

"Yours, my young Abbot," replied Abbot Gregory.

"I don't think that's true."

"You brought up the question in passing, perhaps even rhetorically. I just formalized it as our topic, knowing that it should not be rhetorical."

"Very well. Can either of you remind me of the exact wording?"

"How could I forget it," said Haskell, smiling. "*Can a good man join the Klan?*"

Silence followed.

"I say we just go in for an early dinner," said Ambrose, half-jokingly.

"You've had over forty-eight hours, Abbot," instructed Abbot Gregory. "What say you?"

"Haskell, you realize this is uncomfortable for me, especially with you," said Ambrose, looking over and up at Haskell who, by this age, towered over both abbots and took up as much horizontal width as the two of them combined.

"I do."

"It is tough to answer. But I must say, yes. I read once that there were a staggering four-plus million Klan members nationwide. It is hard to conclude that they are all evil, just as it is hard to conclude that all Aztecans were evil who sacrificed children to the gods, or that all Roman soldiers who persecuted the Jews were evil, or all southern slave owners were evil. History is filled with black marks on every culture, in one form or another. If we deem all such people evil, very few of us will ever escape that designation in the eyes of our progeny."

Hack nodded affirmatively but said nothing.

"Very true, Abbot. Very true," said Abbot Gregory. "But will not the Aztecan mother face the same burning flame, at least a purgative one, that she willingly allowed the priest to throw her child in? Will not the Roman soldier feel the puncture of the very sword he held at the necks of God's chosen people? And will not the slave owner be bound by the very chains he used to dehumanize Haskell's ancestors?"

"I think so," Abbot Ambrose agreed. "God's justice will not be skirted around. He will have the final word."

"But then the question remains: *Can a good man join the Klan?* Or one might ask: *Can a good Aztecan woman sacrifice her baby to a demonic god?* Or: *Could a good farmer buy a slave to plough his fields?*"

"On the one hand," said Abbot Ambrose, "I say good people have done such stupid things throughout all of history and that they deserve and will receive their punishment. But on the other hand, I believe no punishment is due unless culpability is present. It seems that only an unjust God would punish a man or woman who has no culpability. And yet, the soul must be made right before beholding the beatific vision, whether he intended to partake in evil or not. For evil makes a lasting impact, independent of the motives of one partaking therein."

"True again. Very true," said the old Abbot. "But what about you, Hack? Is this a topic too close to home?"

"No, Abbot. Not at all," Haskell said. "My home is right here. I feel for my negro brethren, of course. I know that vile racism killed my father. I know it slandered his name for the rest of time and then cast me into a dark basement. The older I get, the angrier I can feel about it. Anyhow . . .

"The last two days, as I meditated on this rather disconcerting subject, I received very little from my own thinking. My gut was telling me, *No, a good man cannot join the Klan.* For God has written His law on our hearts. A man may not be thinking clearly when he puts on the white garb and follows around the Great Wizard, or whatever they call him, but I do know one thing: a thousand little decisions were made throughout his life up to that point conditioning him to stifle the natural law that God placed on his heart. Sure, he has original sin that has darkened his intellect. But children, as far as I can imagine, are not racist. And I imagine that even though they are nearly brainwashed by their elders, they are, of their own accord, making little decisions to join them. An act of the will is present, even if subtly. I cannot see invincible ignorance removing culpability. And perhaps that small act of the will is due to their pride, wanting to be accepted. Perhaps it is due to envy, wanting to have the reputation of the leaders in their group. Perhaps it is due to cowardice, fearing the punishment or rejection that will ensue. Whatever it is, they've made a thousand little acts of the will, moral decisions, culminating in the dawning of that pointy white hat.

"And so," Haskell continued after taking a deep breath, "I concluded that they have culpability for doing so, not directly from a decision then and there, but from the habituation, as Aristotle would say, they formed over years of allowing their passions to overcome their reason.

"This is beside the obvious fact that many men reject their upbringing in such circles. Not every Aztecan mother handed her baby over to the temple priest. I'm sure many ran away and suffered immeasurable difficulties in the wilderness, alone and afraid. I'm sure a handful . . . at least a handful of Roman guards were killed on the spot, or scourged, or crucified because of an unwillingness to carry out a ruthless order. I'm sure a good many slaveholders freed his slaves despite the inevitable financial ruin.

"So, it was for these reasons that I concluded that a good man cannot join the Klan. I was ready to make my case with you two today, however poorly formed that case may be.

"And then, as I was walking out of my cell this morning, I did what I always do. I looked upon the crucifix. I usually look at it for ten, maybe twenty seconds, as you, Abbot Gregory, told me to. This time, however, all I could hear was a voice in my head saying, *Forgive them Father, for they know not what they do . . . they know not what they do . . . they know not what they do.* For the rest of the day, all I could think about is our silly little words, *good man*. Can a *good man* join the Klan?

"Abbot, all I know now is that for me to conclude they are not good is foolish of me. God has showered me with innumerable blessings, education, friendships. Who am I to conclude that those three million people are evil? I can with zeal and certitude condemn their doctrines and actions. But it is for God and God alone to condemn them. And that is my final answer to the question."

Abbot Gregory chuckled.

"What's so funny, Abbot?" asked Abbot Ambrose.

"Seventeen," he said, and he swung his cane and smacked Haskell in the belly. "He's seventeen. How can that not make you laugh?"

Shortly after their discussion in the courtyard, they attended Vespers, followed by dinner, followed by free time. The two abbots went about their own business, but Haskell looked forward to an hour in the recreation room with the monks. He could usually find someone to take him up on a card game or chess match or, at the very least, a hearty conversation.

Haskell was already bigger than every monk, save for Bruno, who sat across a small table from him staring down at his cards with the intensity of a German soldier in the trenches at Verdun. Brother Matthias was relaxed as always, barely looking at his own cards, lost in a thought somewhere else. Haskell sat in the chair backwards, a difficult posture for a monk in his habit. Haskell still enjoyed wearing lay clothes, even though he lived a complete and full life as a monk.

"*Das Glück ist heute Abend auf deiner Seite,*" Haskell said with a near perfect accent.

"I don't believe in luck," replied Brother Bruno.

"Well then . . . *Hast du ein Ass im Ärmel?*"

"I don't cheat! I'm just more patient than you."

"*Geduldig! Du?*" Hack showed his playful disbelief.

"Why must you speak in German?" asked Brother Matthias. "How do I know you aren't conspiring against me?"

"Skat is a German game. I feel obliged," replied Haskell with a smile.

He looked at Brother Bruno and said, "I wouldn't do that," which sent Bruno into a flurry of concentration, and a few curse words in German under his breath. Haskell looked at Brother Matthias and winked.

Bruno grunted as he concentrated earnestly on his cards, hoping to pull off a rare victory against his former pupil.

As some of the other monks made their way in for recreation, they went immediately to the corner of the room and examined the newest addition to the monastery.

"What do you think?" Brother Matthias asked.

"It's small," said a brother with a thick French accent. "And completely black."

Bruno looked up at Haskell: "Like you were when you got here," and laughed at his own joke while turning his attention back to his game.

Haskell looked over at it again. "It looks like a black banana to me."

"I do not care," said the French brother, as he stroked the handset gently with a rather romantic touch. "Black banana or not, she is beautiful. And because she is a French Telephone, one must only speak French to her."

Haskell stood up and made his way to the French telephone. He picked up the handset for the first time, looked at it funny, not exactly knowing what to do with an all-in-one speaking and listening device (though he never used the candlestick design with a detached speaking device, he saw it used countless times). After concluding roughly where to place the handset against his face, he said, "*Excusez-moi parlez-vous anglais?*"

The room chuckled.

He listened carefully.

"She said *Oui*," Haskell said to the French monk. "But then she asked that you do not stroke her so. She said it was *inapproprié pour un homme de Dieu*."

The room erupted into laughter. Haskell put down the receiver and grabbed the French monk's arm and gave it an affectionate squeeze and pat. He did not want to push his luck too much with his French tutor.

"You still sound like a German speaking French," the Frenchman said.

"You can blame Bruno for that."

"I'm glad he learned German first," interjected Bruno. "Better to sound like a German speaking French than a Frenchman speaking German. But tell your student in French to sit down and finish the damn game."

Haskell looked at his tutor and said, "Damn?"

"*Zut*."

"*Zut*," repeated Bruno. "Even I can remember that."

And while on this particular evening the new French telephone provided a source for jokes and poking fun, in just twenty-four short hours, it would be used to communicate a message darker than its own blackness.

The year of 1928 was a pivotal point in our nation's history in more ways than one. While the infamous Black Thursday was not until the latter days of the following year, the weight of collapse began to be felt. The roaring twenties were coming to a screeching halt, like the needle of a record player coming to the end of a long Duke Ellington album.

Economic growth had more than slowed: it had stopped for the working class. Investment bankers of the North and textile tycoons of the South rode out the decade in style, enjoying long nights in jazz clubs and speakeasies, with their lady flappers in one hand and their bootlegged liquor in the other, while police officers were slipped a twenty to look the other way. But during the day, both the investment banker and the textile tycoon saw the trends shifting. Overproduction since the Great War had caught up to them, and the only means to keep their top hats stiff was to squeeze more out of those who lined the shop floors for less, and if it took a few children with mauled hands and knocked-knees, well, at least they were eating.

While the decade roared in both production and revelry, like a national voice of rejoicing at the close of the War, another war was ensuing. It was, in fact, another civil war: a war for America's soul. But this was not a war between North and South. It was, however, a war over the rights of man, no matter his color, creed, or country of origin. America was experiencing the rebirth of its first nation-wide terrorist organization: the Ku Klux Klan.

Before trying to steal the soul of America, they stole a great word, and countless symbols along with it. κύκλος (*kuklos*) was a word of beauty to the ancient Greeks meaning "circle" (the Latin derivative being *cyclus*, and the English derivative being *cycle*). A circle (Kuklux) for the Klan was a union of brethren for the suppression of those of another kind, which in reality was a circle of hate. But for the Greeks, it meant just the opposite.

Kuklos was the perfect shape, a symbol of divine symmetry, giving both beauty and motion to the cosmos. For Aristotle, all the cosmos was one great spinning sphere, a cycle eternally in motion. And all the heavenly bodies were a series of celestial orbs nested concentrically inside one another. There were stars at the outer rim, and moving inwards, the sun and planets, and then the moon. A smaller ring of fire was next, followed by an even smaller ring of air. And like a Russian nesting doll, a tiny, beautiful sphere called Earth rested at the center of this divine machination. Working backwards, the movement on our little planet was caused by that ring of air, which was moved by the ring of fire, which was moved by the moon, which was moved by the sun and planets, which were in turn moved by the farthest most stars of the cosmos. And finally, beyond this celestial realm, beyond this most beautiful array of *kuklos*, resided the Prime Mover who put all things in motion.

If Aristotle had risen from the dead and visited the South in 1928, he would have pleaded with the Klan to use a square, a triangle (perhaps to match their pointy hats), an octagon. But for heaven's sake, not the circle.

It will come as no surprise when members of the Klan are judged by Almighty God for sin against neighbor. But it will be a surprise when an additional sentence is passed for sin against shape, for a circle is a spectacularly beautiful masterpiece of an infinitely loving Geometrist.

No doubt, a man has more value than all the circles ever drawn, for he is made in the image and likeness of God. And through the Klan's history, they have proven they care not a whit for this dignity. Historians have codified the Klan's stain on this great nation into three eras, and it continues on. The First Klan was formed by six former officers of the Confederate army in 1865, largely due to boredom. Those first members enjoyed the intrigue of holding secret meetings at night, though they had no particular agenda at first. But as nighttime fun and games progressed, they began dressing up like the ghosts of dead confederate soldiers and lying in wait to tantalize any negro passing by.

Shortly thereafter, they solicited and elected the Confederate general Nathan Bedford Forrest as the first Grand Wizard—*wizard* stemming from Forest being known as *The Wizard of the Saddle* during the war. Forrest had a more serious agenda: to stop Radical Reconstruction in the South. The war-beaten South was still raw with anger at Sherman's fires. Many native Southerners could not digest the notion that a former slave would have equal rights to them. They also loathed Carpetbaggers: those opportunistic Northerners migrating to the south in order to profit from Reconstruction—the embryonic beginning of the Klan's resistance to any form of immigration.

Over time, the notion of white supremacy became an official tenet of their fraternity. They targeted freedmen and their allies with threats and violence and, on occasion, murder. But other targets included those with political influence, including those white politicians, north or south of the Mason Dixon Line, who fought for equal rights. Thus, it was not only the freed black man who had to watch his back but also the white Reconstructionist trying to help him find a job. Due to internal disorder and lack of control over its sadistic members throughout the land, the First Klan deteriorated into a small band of thugs by the end of the decade. Nathan Bedford Forrest officially disbanded the Klan in August of 1869, with his ego intact, by conveniently claiming the objective of disrupting Reconstruction was accomplished.

There remained, however, a fascination with the Klan in the American mind. In 1905, a novel by Thomas Dixon Jr. entitled *The Clansmen* captured America's attention. Dixon's preface reads in part:

> The Clansman develops the true story of the Ku Klux Klan Conspiracy, which overturned the Reconstruction Regime. . . . In the darkest hour of the life of the South, when her wounded people lay helpless amid rags and ashes under the beak and talon of the Vulture, suddenly from the mists of the mountains appeared a white cloud the size of a man's hand. It grew until its mantle of mystery enfolded the stricken Earth and sky. An "Invisible Empire" had risen from the field of Death and challenged the Visible to mortal combat.
>
> How the young South, led by the reincarnated souls of the Clansmen of Old Scotland, went forth under this cover and against overwhelming odds, daring exile, imprisonment, and a felon's death, and saved the life of a people, forms one of the most dramatic chapters in the history of the Aryan race.

The American imagination was rekindled from the ashes. But it was not for another decade that the power of the burgeoning film industry would enable one lunatic's vision to infect a nation with prurient interest.

In 1915, D. W. Griffith adapted the *The Clansmen* into a film, originally with the same title. But upon seeing the epic nature of his production, he retitled it *The Birth of a Nation*. This infamous silent epic drama, this first film with numerous close ups and panoramic battle scenes with countless extras, this first film played in the White House, came to be known as the most controversial film ever made in the United States. At an unprecedented three hours long, it began with the assassination of President Lincoln and featured a pro-union family and pro-confederacy family and their differing perspectives on the issue of slavery. It depicted blacks as unintelligent and sexually aggressive toward white women and presented the Klan as a heroic force. It had a significant impact on many of its viewers, including protestors and those who tried to ban its public viewing. The movie was egged in New York, and violent protests broke out in

Boston. The president of Harvard, Charles Elliot, condemned it, and the Massachusetts legislature nearly banned it. Booker T. Washington called it inflammatory, which seems an understatement to say the least. Its sensation, nonetheless, was largely due to the unofficial endorsement by the president of the United States, Woodrow Wilson: "It is like writing history with lightning . . . and my only regret is that it is all so terribly true." The film grossed eighteen million dollars.

It also had a life-changing impact on a man in convalescence after being struck by an automobile. The man's name was William Joseph Simmons. And after being so moved by the power of a mere film, featuring men with white pointy face masks and long white garments draped around their horses—like so many knights from King Arthur's court—Simmons gave rise to the Second Klan on the evening of Thanksgiving in 1915 atop Stone Mountain in Georgia.

Relying on literature from the First Klan and the living memory of a few original members, Simmons constructed an enhanced creed, decked out with the white costumes from Griffith's imagination put on screen. Parades and protests began under Simmons' leaders, with these white knights on horseback riding down the street.

In 1921, the Klan progressed to a more professional mode, with paid recruiters, and enjoyed significant revenue streams from both initiation fees and costume sales. The core of its ideology? "One Hundred Percent Americanism." This resulted in a vehement prejudice against not only blacks but Catholics, Jews, and immigrants—in particular, the Italians, Russians, and Lithuanians (who brought Catholicism and Judaism with them). In short, the Klan was a staunchly white, Protestant, naturally-born American fraternity that saw all others as an infection poisoning the purity of their national blood. As logic would have it, the puritanical roots of such men condemned the use of alcohol. Thus, the Klan lobbied hard for the enforcement of prohibition laws, and when such enforcement did not come, they took violent measures into their own hands against rum runners. While such bigotry seems unattractive, the Klan had four to five million members by the mid-1920s, and the natural result of any association of that size always winds up at the same place: political influence.

At this time, the Klan began to have the issues that any sizable group is destined to have. Just who was in charge? While Simmons was the uncontested founder of the Second Klan on Stone Mountain in 1915, splinter groups grew quickly, as did struggles between state and national leaders. D. C. Stephenson, Grand Dragon of Indiana, forged tremendous political influence throughout the land, but primarily in his home state. His close affiliation with the governor and the Klan's support of his campaign gave Stephenson a sense of invincibility. In fact, it was on January 12, 1925, at the governor's inauguration party that Stephenson met a young lady who would be the proximate cause of the Klan's unmasking.

Madge Oberholtzer, a young middle-class woman, was continually approached by Stephenson at this party and solicited for a date, which was promptly refused. But worn down by the insistence of the rich, powerful, and influential man, she eventually agreed to a dinner. She ended up under his employment as a personal aid. She eventually broke off any type of personal involvement, but on March 15, Stephenson sent a message to her that if she wished to keep her employment, she must meet him at his mansion. She agreed.

Stephenson's chauffeur and two bodyguards, Mr. Gentry and "Clench," took her in the kitchen of his mansion and forced her to drink whiskey until she became sick. She was forced upstairs to a bedroom where she met Stephenson, a revolver in his hand. She was then loaded onto Stephenson's private train headed for Chicago. The moment she stepped inside the compartment, Stephenson ripped off her clothes and raped her repeatedly. He left deep and bloody bite marks all over her neck, legs, arms, and breasts. She was his captive. Although the whiskey would wear off, the bite marks would not. They became horrifically infected. Madge told him in her anger that the law would get hold of him. And he infamously told her, "I am the law of Indiana."

They checked into a hotel, and she was forced to telegram her mother to ease any concerns about her disappearance. At one point, while alone, Madge took Stephenson's revolver and considered killing herself to escape her captor but decided to not leave a stain on her mother's honor. Thus, the next day, she put on a good face for Stephenson and convinced him she needed to buy a black silk hat. Another aid by the name of Shorty, upon Stephenson's instructions, took her to do so. But while out on the errand, Madge convinced Shorty to let her go into a drug store to buy some rouge. Instead, she bought an entire box of mercuric tablets. Back at the hotel room, she swallowed six tablets and vomited blood the rest of the day. Stephenson initially refused to release her, but after fearing an unexplainable death, he concocted a story that she had swallowed too many aspirin, which would explain the internal bleeding. They eventually left Chicago and drove back to Stephenson's mansion in Indiana. In horrific pain, Madge vomited throughout the trip. She begged to be taken to the hospital. She even begged to be dropped off on the side of the road.

Upon reaching his home, Stephenson found someone standing at his front door. It was Madge's mother. Madge was finally taken home and then to a hospital where, upon being told that death was near, she made a complete statement of her abduction, rape, and attempted suicide. She died shortly thereafter from a ruthless combination of mercury poisoning and a staph infection from the bite marks.

His political clout with the governor left Stephenson overconfident in obtaining a pardon or reduced sentence. Thus, on September 9, 1927, he released a list of public officials who were or had been on the Klan payroll. The *Indianapolis Times* won a Pulitzer Prize for its interview with Stephenson and investigations into Klan's presence at all levels of government influence. The news spread like wildfire throughout the nation. While the Klan was originally thought to be a law-abiding Christian fraternity, the truth was now finally out, at least in part.

The brutal abduction and rape of young Madge Oberholtzer led to the unmasking of the Klan. Its membership dropped by a few million by the end of the 1920s, but nonetheless continued on with spikes of activity throughout the decades.

But by late 1928, the Klan was still going strong enough to hit close to home (in more ways than one) at Good Shepherd Monastery.

Isaac Newton's third law states: *For every action, there is an equal and opposite reaction*. And this reaction was particularly present in the South in late 1928. To the country's dismay, a Roman Catholic was nominated the democratic candidate for president of the United States: Al Smith, Governor of New York. Not surprisingly, the Catholic was a committed "wet" who saw prohibition as unconstitutional. This stance gained him a strong base. The German Lutherans and Southern Baptists were convinced, however, that Pius XI would control 1600 Pennsylvania Avenue from the throne of Peter. And the Ku Klux Klan was not all too happy about a papist on the ticket for the party of the South.

North and South Carolina were hotbeds for the Klan. It was something that every negro, Catholic, and Jew felt keenly, especially the negro. With the nomination of Governor Smith, however, the tension for Catholics most certainly increased along with the Klan's boldness and bluster. Articles on the Klan were piling up; marches were happening, even in the nation's capital; women and children had donned the white garb; crosses were burning. Thus, when monks went to town, the abbot found it an opportune time to heed the Gospel's directive of traveling two by two.

It was one evening, shortly after the black French telephone arrived in the recreation room, that many monks heard it ring for the first time.

"What on Earth is that?" one monk exclaimed.

"The French have always sounded weird to me," said Brother Bruno.

Haskell spoke to the telephone from across the room in the language of love: "*Silencieux, Mame*."

In disobedience, it rang out again. As porter, Brother Matthias saw it as his duty to answer. He held the receiver to his chest, camouflaging it with his habit, and asked a younger monk to retrieve the abbot immediately. Matthias's face informed Haskell and the rest of the room that the person on the other end was distraught. Everyone came to a stop, waiting for the abbot to arrive. During the interim, Abbot Gregory appeared at the threshold of the room. It was an odd sight since he rarely joined the monks in recreation. He was, at this time of evening, inevitably in his choir stall, praying before retiring early. He entered slowly and stood against the wall. He dropped his head as if in deep concentration, or perhaps prayer.

Abbot Ambrose entered the room and walked immediately to the telephone.

"Hello, Ralph," the abbot said. The only Ralph that Haskell knew of was a tenant farmer adjacent to the abbey grounds.

The abbot listened carefully and then slowly sat down in a chair next to the phone and removed his glasses.

"Are you and your family all right?" he asked, and then listened for a moment. "Your family is welcome here, if that is in any way safer. . . . Yes. Thank you. I'll turn it on right away. Thank you. God Bless you."

He hung up and took a deep breath, looking up at the room: "The Klan has gathered in the pasture just next to his. He counted twenty or so, and many more spectators. They're setting up a cross right now."

Eyes darted to and fro, particularly at Haskell.

"It's a rally against Al Smith and his nomination, but will most certainly turn to negros as they always do. The local radio station is covering it."

He went to the radio across the room, bent over, and began turning the dial. As the station cleared, Brother Bruno leaned over to Haskell. "Not a good day to be a negro Catholic."

"True, but they don't like your kind either."

Brother Bruno said with a smile, "I think we could take them by ourselves."

Haskell laughed but quickly tried to wipe the smile off his face.

A voice over the radio came in clearly:

For all of those out there who do not understand the heroic doctrines of the Klan, it is first because you are too blind to see the enemy at the gate. Let me read from the first woman Bishop in the United States, Alma Bridewell White, especially for the sake of those who say we are anti-woman. In her newest book, Heroes of the Fiery Cross, *she explains the enemies of the Klan, which brings us to the point of this here rally. Quote: "Who are the enemies of the Klan? They are the bootleggers, law-breakers, corrupt politicians, weak-kneed*

Protestant church members, white slavers, toe-kissers, wafer-worshippers, and every spineless character who takes the path of least resistance."

My friends, those are the enemy of the Klan and those are the enemy of these United States. We are the proud descendants of the old pioneer stock—the old-stock Americans, a beautiful blend of the Nordic Races of old, which have given the world its modern civilization. We are the last line of defense against the infestation, not just of Africans with the Curse of Ham on their black souls, but of so-called modernization of society, which is nothing more than mongrelized liberalism. How wrong can it be for us to represent and protect the heritage of those who have given us everything and defend ourselves against the onslaught of moral and genetic filth! Supremacy? A bad word? What has the negro done for the world! And what has the toe-kissing, wafer-worshipping Roman Catholics done for America, except try to enslave us to the pope! Just because he wears white does not make him one of us!

My brethren, we were successful in '24, stopping Alcohol Al's campaign in its tracks. But we have been too soft since then. It is a permanent stain on our nation that he is the Democratic nominee for the president of these United States, the greatest nation on Earth. But will we fill the Oval Office with an Autocrat on the Tiber, who hates democracy and public education, who fears Protestant personage and individual rights?

My friends, the greatest threat to our nation is not just Al Smith, but the rise of the Pope's Knights. Since the unfortunate and mischaracterization of Grand Dragon Stephenson's conviction, our numbers have declined as the Pope's Knights of mob and murder have increased. The Knights of Columbus are the pope's pliant tools who have bound themselves together in a secret, an unholy compact to destroy our free American public school system, our constitution and its guarantees. But their secrets are not as strong as they think. We have found circulating the oath of their Fourth Degree Knight, which includes, and I quote, "to hang, burn, waste, boil, flay, strangle and bury alive heretics." Those heretics are you and your children, the old-stock Americans, whose Protestant, God-fearing ethic has been present ever since Plymouth Rock and Roanoke Island.

My brethren, war is upon us! And the pope has sent in his General in Al Smith and his army in the Knights of Columbus.

If this papist is elected, he will admit Italian anarchists, Irish-Catholic malcontents, and all the other scum of the Mediterranean. We must not permit the infiltration of ignorant, superstitious, religious devotees that are nothing more than the festering sores of the United States politic. This great nation must remain white Anglo-Saxon Protestant if it is to remain at all! And one day, you shall thank the Klan for saving our nation. But in the meantime, we do so warn all those listening tonight, especially those papists who can't wait to run to the ballot box, be not surprised if a little bit of violence ensues in order to awaken your conscience from slumber, undoubtedly caused by your liquor and your communion wine that you so devilishly call the Blood of Christ.

Cheers were heard over the radio. And as they subsided, a chant arose: "Native, white, Protestant Supremacy! Native, white, Protestant Supremacy!" The slogan was repeated over and over, like a mind-melding spell cast upon the airways.

Abbot Ambrose stood, hands on hips, glaring at the radio dial. The room was surprised how long the station allowed the chant to continue on, as if the journalist covering the rally had nothing to say. Perhaps the producers wanted the chant to hang through the night, like a deep fog, as an omen of evil to come.

Finally, Abbot Ambrose clicked the dial off. The entire room sat perfectly still and silent. After a moment, the abbot said, "Perhaps we all have a little glimpse into what Haskell has felt his entire life."

Heads nodded. A brother reached over and patted Haskell on the back.

"Abbot," Bruno said, leaning up in his chair, "if there's only twenty of them, I'm sure Haskell and I can take them out." The monks laughed, and even Abbot Ambrose cracked a smile. A young monk from the back of the room yelled, "Hey Abbot, call the pope and ask if we can get a plenary indulgence for dying in the crusades against the Klan."

The room erupted. But there were two faces, and only two faces, in the crowded room that lacked a smile: Haskell and Abbot Gregory. The former who bowed his head at the joke and the latter who lifted his. It was as if they were of the same spirit. Abbot Gregory walked toward the center of the room, which caught the eyes of many. He approached the table at which Haskell and Bruno sat with a wooden chess set between them. He handed his cane to Haskell, and with a burst of energy never seen before, the old man grabbed the side of the table and flipped it over to its side. A bang echoed through the monastery, followed by the sound of bishops and knights rolling across the wooden floor.

"Foolish children!"

Everyone, including Abbot Ambrose, stared wide-eyed at the old man, who had a look of righteous anger.

"You are monks. There is a time for laughter. This is not one of them. I do not find it funny when a true threat is at our doorstep to laugh our way from the Gospel. Do you not see? This very night you could be called on to be true knights of the true Kingdom. You may be called to turn the other cheek, but only after being struck as hard as they can strike. You may be called to be meek in the face of wrath. You may be called to be a peacemaker in the face of violence. You may be called to pick up your cross, perhaps a burning one, and carry it. For Jesus Christ told each of you: 'The servant is not greater than his master. If they have persecuted me, they will also persecute you.'

"Look! Look up at that crucifix," and he grabbed his cane back from Haskell and pointed it like an extension of his arm above the door. "Are you ready for this? Are your hands ready to be pierced? What about those thick bones in your feet? What about the flesh that you so carefully clean with soap and water and cover up each night with a soft blanket? Is it ready to be burned? And is your soul humble enough to be stripped naked for all to see? Or would you count on the Klansmen to leave your dignity intact?

"My young monks, you may be offered this very night a glorious opportunity to be last in this worldly kingdom so that you can be first in the heavenly one. What will you choose?

"No. It is not time for laughter. It is always time for joy, but not always for laughter. We shall respond to their chants of hatred with our own chants of charity. Let us go. Let us storm the heavens with our chants and beg the Spirit to give us whatever fortitude we may need to let our sufferings be our final profession of faith."

He slouched, cast his eyes back to the floor, and with the clank of his cane, made his way out of the room.

When he was gone, everyone turned to Abbot Ambrose. He nodded, acknowledging that he had been reprimanded in front of his own community. He then led the monks to the chapel in obedience to the wisdom and charity of Abbot Gregory.

Chapter 2

A Strike

January 1, 1929

After a grueling six months of measuring, remeasuring, cutting, affixing, and sanding the sixty-foot stretch of glossy pine, painstakingly waxed with mineral oil, and painting the lane arrows guiding one toward the white pins; after enduring the laughter of the monks just as Noah endured the laughter of those who became fish food, Haskell's excitement reached a pitch. It could not have been surpassed by Odysseus's own upon seeing his Penelope after twenty years of brutal battle and tragic loss; nor could it be surpassed by Dante's upon seeing that his guide to Paradiso was none other than his beloved Beatrice; nor could it be surpassed by Edmond Dantès's excitement upon reaching the beach after his daring escape from the impregnable Château d'If following twenty-one years of false imprisonment.

No, nothing could surpass Haskell's excitement when he finally took the smooth black orb into his hands, gazing at it with amazement, like Ptolemy or Copernicus gazing upon the cosmos if they could hold it in their own hands, spinning it round and round, seeing the galaxies from every angle. Though it was only fourteen pounds, it felt that he was holding the world after the seven days of creation. He looked down that shiny lane and said to himself, *It is good.*

He had practiced countless times in the courtyard to the point of his form being flawless, but this was no substitute for the cold hard fact that he had never done the real thing, not even once. And now, the time had arrived. A row of black-robed monks lined the lane like pins ready to fall with elation if Haskell's destiny was to be fulfilled. After a few encouraging words and a few remaining skeptics shaking their heads, Haskell bowed his head, mouthed *thy will be done*, and took a small step, then another . . . and another. The ball swung back in his giant hand as if it weighed no more than a hymnal. And there it was: the sound that had been sought for six months. It was the sound of a great storm rolling in over the Greek Isles as if Zeus had gone to battle with the Titans.

Time stood still for all that were present. The past was nothing more than a memory, frozen in the depths of time, forever lost to the living; and the future was a mere fiction, a hypothetical, a speculation . . . for eternity may have found that present moment to rest upon.

As Haskell's arm raised above his head, his body leaning inward, one leg lifted behind, he watched the spinning sphere seemingly freeze in time, just right of center, calling to mind Zeno's *Dichotomy Paradox*: the clever perception that an arrow must go halfway before reaching its target, yet must also go one-fourth of the way before it gets halfway, and it must still go one-eighth of the way before it gets one-fourth of the way . . . ad infinitum. And therefore, Zeno concluded, an object can never move despite our perception thereof. As Haskell watched the ball, he worried that Zeno may have been right and that it would never reach its target.

But just as Abbot Gregory always told him, *life is larger than logic.*

It was New Year's Day. And the year 1929 began . . . with a strike!

It is a great irony of worldly life that the elite, no matter the field, are the last to know what is actually going on, despite the fact they made the policy to begin with and have countless reports and statistics and analytics to measure and grade the performance of people and production. Children often know there is a problem in the marriage before the spouses do; the line-worker sees quality degradation for the sake of profit while the white-collars think it matters not; the beat cop knows the civil unrest brewing long before the politician considers a policy change; a soldier in the trench can sense the turning tide before the general can even follow it on a map; and within the bounds of economic prosperity, laborers from main street can feel the system buckling long before the traders on Wall Street even catch a glimpse of a crack in the foundation.

Perhaps things take time to trickle up, as a tree rots at the root before the leaves fail to bloom the subsequent spring. On the other hand, it could be that pride blinds them from the facts right beneath their noses; their sense of self-righteousness convincingly says, *we can fix this whenever we have to.* Yet still, there is a more troubling possibility: perhaps those at the top know an impending doom early enough to cope, but their greed finds it is easier to capitalize on destruction than invest in restoration.

It was no different in the later part of the decadent decade of 1920. No industry more than textile felt the economic boom of post-war manufacturing, and no industry more than textile felt the strains of an unstable market in the months leading up to Black Thursday.

Brooks Textile, founded by Leopold Brooks (father of Walter Brooks), was sold just as the fabric of the community began to unwind. Perhaps it was good luck on the Brooks' part; perhaps they were more perceptive than the average tycoon. Nonetheless, they who caused the unrest escaped without a single pinprick, handing over a Gordian Knot to a gullible investor.

As one of the South's largest and most productive mills before its sale, Brooks Textiles introduced stretch weeks: double work for the same pay. If she chose to keep a paycheck, a woman couldn't care for her children if stuck in the factory for twice as long. Worse yet, children worked so many long hours that they were growing up with knock-knees. Worse still, as the production demand had steadily increased over the prior years, and the safety standards correspondingly decreased, adolescent injury became a regular occurrence, and Mr. Brooks would conveniently disappear for a few weeks until the temperature of the town settled down.

In just the past few months, the Good Shepherd monks saw firsthand the devastation of recent trends. Little Cara Connelly was brought to Mass by her parents and hoped for a blessing thereafter. She was but ten years old. Her right hand was gone. Adult hands could not fit between the small cracks to oil the machines, change bobbins, and remove loose threads from inside moving machines. And to stop the machines completely . . . well, production would have been unduly slowed, so stated the informal policy of the plant.

Another girl of nearly the same age, Kelly McDowell, came to Mass in a thick bandage wrapped around her head, with only her little face protruding. Her scalp had been ripped from her head as the loom confused her hair with thread.

Injuries such as these began to plague the small town of Capstone. Requests for safety protocols were denied as impractical. Suggestions to reduce production speeds to ensure quality were denied as ill-informed of the meaning of profit margin. The collective voice to end stretch weeks was met with an offer to resign. The pressure to institute a minimum twenty-dollar weekly wage was laughed off as communistic and growled at as un-American.

Indeed, the Great Depression was first felt by the mill workers, not by Wall Street. If the capitalists were to retain their profit, someone had to take the hit. The laborers paid the price. All the while, Wall Street suffered from Gold Sickness until the end of 1929 and either stupidly missed the signs down the economic chain or viciously looked the other way.

The conditions of Brooks Textile had caught the eye of the National Textile Workers Union (NTWU), a communist labor union, as well as the Trade Union Unity League. Such attention was largely due to the concerted effort of a certain woman named Ella May Wiggins.

Ella May was a weaver in Brooks textile and had seen the unraveling of conditions over the past several years. Rather than live in a typical neighborhood alongside most mill employees, she lived in Stumptown, a negro hamlet just outside Capstone. It was here that she could find affordable care for her children while working her ever-increasing hours.

On March 31, 1929, a community meeting of mill workers was scheduled to be held. Brother Dominic obtained permission (and encouragement) from the abbot to attend, for the abbot believed the monastery must be informed of community affairs. Upon his return home late that night, Brother Dominic was met by Abbot Ambrose and Haskell.

"I don't know, Abbot, if this is good or bad," Brother Dominic said in a flurry. "But in either case, it feels like dynamite."

"Slow down, Father. Your wheels are turning faster than a cotton gill spinner. Try to fill me in from the beginning," the abbot said, taking his seat in his parlor, waving both Haskell and Brother Dominic to take their seats.

Dominic caught his breath. "It began with this lady, Ella May Wiggins. Her story . . . so sad it broke my heart. You see, Abbot, she had nine children and lived in Stumptown to afford childcare."

"I understand," said the abbot. "Go on."

"She worked nights, which usually was a good thing so she could spend time with the kids during the day. But then whooping cough went through her house. Nearly all the children got it. She begged her supervisor to change her shift so she could care for them. She was refused time and time again. She resigned out of necessity and tried to get money in other ways. But her financial situation deteriorated quickly. She could no longer afford the medicine to treat her children. They had their mother through the torturous nights, but no medicine. Abbot, four of the nine children died! Four!"

The abbot dropped his head. "How I wish she would have come to us."

"She is not Catholic," replied Dominic.

"How I wish she would have come to us," repeated the abbot.

"Yes," said Haskell.

"Yes," echoed Dominic. "Of course. But it was this woman who somehow got up to D.C. to explain the strife to a few organizations, seeking outside help."

"The communist group?" asked the abbot.

"One of them . . . yes."

Silence for a moment followed.

"Difficult issue," said the abbot, giving voice to what was on all of their minds.

"The papal encyclicals could not be clearer on communism," Dominic said. "Haskell and I have just completed a thorough reading of *Rerum Novarum*."

"Cara's missing hand and Kelly's missing scalp could not be clearer either," added Haskell matter-of-factly.

"The stated goal of the meeting was two items: first, to agree on demand terms, and second, to get all 1,800 workers at the mill to strike tomorrow."

"Tomorrow!" the abbot said.

"Yes, tomorrow. Abbot, this is happening."

"What were the terms?" asked Haskell.

"Pretty straightforward. You see, those poor folks work twelve-hour days, six days a week, making seventeen dollars a week, whereas three years ago they worked forty to fifty hours for twenty dollars. And management says *Fine! You don't like it. There are a dozen other failed farmers who'd love your job. Just give me the word.* So, the first demand is a forty-hour work week in place of this inhumane stretch-out system. The second demand is a minimum wage of twenty dollars a week. The third is union recognition. They're also insisting on slowing the machines back down to normal speeds. Too many of the injuries, especially for children, come from the looms going too fast. Laborers are literally running up and down the mill floor to manage them. Kids are sticking their hands in more and more defective machines. If Dante were alive, the mill owners would suffer the sin of avarice in his seventh Canto, working their own sweatshops for eternity."

"Father," said the abbot with a tone of reprimand. "Be careful how you judge. You know not the entirety of the situation. The communist agitator has got your passions riled up."

"Indeed, she did, but that's not all bad."

"No. It's not all bad. But still, it is something you must watch carefully. If you do not control your passions, your passions will control you."

"Yes, Abbot," Dominic said.

"Now," said the abbot. "The question remains: What will come of this? Let us pray for peace and justice. Let us pray that the protest will not lead to violence."

The next day, reports came in that 1,800 workers refused to work. The strike was on. Reports spread throughout the nation, shining a bright media spotlight on the little town of Capstone. The people of the town sat on pins and needles, hoping for something good to come from the potentially explosive situation.

Haskell had a scheduled theology class with Brother Dominic that day, but the assigned reading seemed to fall by the wayside. They could not help but return to their previous discussion on *Rerum Novarum*, translated directly as *On New Things*, but often given the title *On Revolutionary Change*, with the subtitle *On the Condition of Labor*.

Written during the rise of industrialism and socialism in 1891, Leo the XIII penned a groundbreaking document that provided moral guidance to both employers and government as to the God-given rights of laborers. He keenly addressed the condition of the working class, supported labor unions, and condemned socialism . . . and unbridled capitalism.

Since the 1700s, the Industrial Revolution had taken hold of the modern world, especially Great Britain. Spinning gins, the steam engine, and the power loom gave birth to factories, a new phenomenon for humanity. Ever since the Garden of Eden, man and woman were accustomed to working the land, in the open sun, with fresh air to breathe and room to stretch. Factories inverted all this, taking away the natural elements from man's body and soul.

But what was it that gave rise to the sudden onslaught of needing more factories?

Just as the first sin convinced Adam and Eve to strap on fig leaves, the materialistic greed of Europe continued to spread like a virus. Every socially attuned man and woman felt the necessity of having more clothes with more colors and more styles. And if one is to make more clothes, one needs more factories filled with more looms.

Leo XIII had seen the trends throughout this life, as did Karl Marx. But these two men, who both saw the plight of laborers and the greed of capitalists, could not have come to more different solutions. It was apparent to both of them that capitalists (those who owned the means of production) were rapidly beginning to exploit the laborers (or proletariat). The man of the house, fresh in from the fields, had to adapt to lack of sunlight, the grueling hours, the poor ventilation, and the meager wages. The housing options of the inner city were of hellish conditions. City water was putrid. The compacting of families on top of each other in close living quarters led to infectious disease spreading like wildfire. Wages were barely enough to feed a family of three. On top of it all, there were no state regulations on working conditions and no other means to make a living.

The exploitation took on new levels of vileness when armies of the unemployed lined the streets willing to work for anything. Now, the power was truly in the hands of the capitalist. They increased working hours and decreased the pay. If the factory hand didn't like it, he could go look for other employment, and a starving man off the streets could replace him that very afternoon. In many cases, the woman of the house was forced to join her husband in the factory just to keep the same income stream for bread and cheese. And as if morality had nothing to do with business, for *it was just business*, the hours were stretched, and the wages were decreased yet again. Children would join the parents to support the family. These children cost a fraction of their parents, and their little hands and little bodies could easily squeeze into cracks and crevices that mom and dad could not so easily. Gruesome injuries began to occur without even a second thought from the State. Supply and demand were king.

Karl Marx and Fredrick Engels were right about a number of things. Class warfare was inevitable. Any student of history can look back and see one revolt after another, going at least back to Spartacus leading the slave rebellion in the Third Servile War, which began with gladiators fighting for their lives in the Coliseum. Nineteen hundred years later, man and woman and children were fighting for their lives in factories, being mauled not by lions but by looms.

Marx begins his *Communist Manifesto* with the all-too-true statement that man has become "enslaved by the machine" and predicted an explosion of revolt, all the more imminent the more workers were packed tighter and tighter together in the factories.

Leo the Great could agree with all of this. How could a decent man not? But every heresy contains a grain of truth. Leo stated with crystal clarity that atheism was not the answer to the plight of the working class. Whereas (in another work) Marx called religion the "opium of the people" which gave them temporary relief from the sufferings of their plight; the true illness of class oppression would not be addressed by organized religion. "The abolition of religion as the illusory happiness of the people is the demand for their real happiness. To call on them to give up their illusions about their condition is to call on them to give up a condition that requires illusions." But the supreme pontiff, in his landmark encyclical, proclaimed to the world that while Marx had a keen eye for the plight of the working class, his atheism would lead them into a pit of personal and societal darkness from which no salvation would come.

For Marx, God was the problem.

For Leo, God was the solution.

"It's astounding to me," said Brother Dominic. "It's as if Leo the Great was standing in Brooks Textile when he wrote it. Listen to this . . . paragraph forty-five," he said to Haskell. "'*If through necessity or fear of a worse evil the workman accepts harder conditions because an employer or contractor will afford him no better, he is made the victim of force and injustice.*' It's the stretch-out system! The millworkers have no other option but to take the blow on hours and the blow on pay. They've come in from the farms, they live in mill homes, they go to mill churches and shop at mill stores. Their kids even go to mill schools. If they quit, not only would they lose their jobs but their housing and their entire community."

"What's amazing to me," said Haskell, "is how similar this is to the breakdown of the feudal system since the Middle Ages. As Mark Twain said, *History does not repeat itself, but it often rhymes.*"

Dominic was scouring through the text as if having never read it before. "Every paragraph seems to fit with Brooks Textiles. Look here, paragraph seven: '*Hence, man not only should possess the fruits of the Earth, but also the very soil, inasmuch as from the produce of the Earth he has to lay by provision for the future.*' Ha! Imagine the owners of the mill reading that. Leo understood the dignity of the individual."

"The beautiful thing about this text to me, Father," said Haskell, "is the striking balance between the individual and the collective. Father Henry and I have just been through the French Revolution and the Reign of Terror—and terror it was—all in the name of individual rights, except for those Poor Clare nuns guillotined in the public square or the priests thrown in the river with ball and chain around their necks, all because of the refusal to take an oath to the State over the Church. And the same destiny awaited anyone who objected to their methods. Blood flowed like water through the streets of Paris, all for the sake of individuality. Even Notre Dame Cathedral was converted into a temple to the goddess of reason with naked women defiling the sanctuary in paganesque rituals. All for the sake of bringing down the power of the Church and the Crown.

"Leo seems to understand this evil as much as he understands the evils of communism. Man has a right to personal property, which is etched in the stone of the Ten Commandments by way of saying, *Thou Shalt Not Steal*. If the State were to take the ownership of the mills, they will have done the same evil as the millowners have done to the laborers. Thus, striking a balance through state regulation seems the only moral option before mankind."

Dominic sat in awe. He remembered back to when the quasi-literate Hack had just returned from Jefferson, asking him to explain who Plato was. He remembered the folksy *ain't* and *ya* that filled every sentence. And now, he was an articulate young man who could impress any professor in a school of Rome.

"You've come a long way," Dominic said to this student.

"How could I not with a constant flow of world-class teachers into my cell?"

"Ha! World class . . ."

"But Father, tell me: How will this play out at Brooks Textile? At this moment, 1,800 workers are refusing to take their positions. What will happen?"

"I am not a fortune teller, but I know that Aquinas would emphasize human nature in a struggle such as this."

"How so?"

"Man cannot escape his root sin, which for all mankind is pride. But going one layer above that, it seems that each person has a primary sin unique to himself. Those beset by lust or gluttony perceive the world as that which should be consumed for self-satisfaction. For others, their wrath or greed or envy see the world as something to be conquered or taken away from others. And still for others, pride demands that they be right, even if dead wrong. Consider Lucifer . . ."

Dominic went silent for a moment, and Haskell interjected.

"Yes. Lucifer's sin was that he refused to bow before God."

"Perhaps, and perhaps only in a manner of speaking."

Haskell gave him an odd look.

"Consider this, Haskell: Lucifer may have served the Holy Trinity for, what to us may seem, a million years. Of course, they are outside of time. But something changed. What was that?"

"I have no idea."

"That's because we haven't spent enough time in patristics yet. Some of the Church Fathers speculated that once God the Father announced that the Son would take on the nature of man, it was then that Lucifer announced he would never bow before flesh and blood. He would not bend his seraphic knee to a man born of a woman, who ate and drank, who needed a nap, who blew his nose, who defecated, who bled. Man was such a vile creature that he should never have been made to begin with. And now, God would become one of them? And the glorious angels would have to not only accept Him but worship Him?"

"And if the millowner's primary sin is pride," Haskell said, "then he would rather lose everything than bow before his workers."

"A lower form of being . . ."

Haskell nodded. "So the strikers will lose," he said.

"In this kingdom, probably."

Haskell shook his head.

"Always seems to come back to the two kingdoms."

Over the next two weeks, hell broke loose in the small town of Capstone. The strikers had thus far stood their ground, but some were quickly waning, feeling the urge to go back to work and protect their own livelihood. Millowners evicted families from mill homes, leaving mothers and fathers with no place to house their own children. The more zealous of the strikers armed themselves and barricaded the mill so no one could return to work, forcing the governor to call in the National Guard.

On April 18, one hundred masked men working for the owners of the mill destroyed the NTWU's headquarters, which gave rise to a tent city where evicted families lived. The leaders of the movement spent day and night spurring on the people to keep their resolution. They also responded to the violent destruction of their headquarters with equal force, arming many of the strikers with guns and baseball bats and even household knives. But many of the agitators were not even locals and had never worked a mill day in their lives. They were members of the communist party who functioned in full-time capacity taking on "the establishment" in different states. It was these outside agitators who caused the greatest ruckus of them all, but it would be locals who would forever pay the price. Not everyone, however, could be prevented from going to work. A small shift did return. Over the next few months, the professional agitators saw their cause was failing and decided they would take it to another level.

On the night of June 7, about an hour after everyone had retired for the night, a bang on the door echoed throughout the halls. Brother Mathias, in his capacity as porter, admitted a young man into the abbot's parlor. He was no more than twenty. Sweat covered his entire body as he heaved for oxygen, both from anxiety and an apparent long run. While Matthias retrieved the abbot, Hack made his way up the stairs after hearing the commotion, for everything at night traveled down the halls and down the stairs.

As Haskell walked the hall from one direction, Abbot Ambrose came from the other. The abbot gave him a paternalistic look of *shame on you* but didn't indicate at all that he should leave. In fact, he gave a little wave of the finger toward a spot next to the door, granting permission for Haskell to listen.

"I didn't mean to do it, I swear!" the young man yelled the second he laid eyes on Abbot Ambrose, his thick accent pegging him as a Jersey guy.

The abbot calmed him down and had him sit and begin anew.

"First off, son, what is your name?"

"Mark. Name's Mark."

"Do you have a last name, Mark?"

"Course I do, but I don't want you to call the coppers on me."

"Okay, Mark. Tell me nice and slow: You didn't mean to do what?"

"To kill the police chief."

The bullet itself could not have pierced the thick silence between the abbot, Matthias, and Mark. Haskell brought his hand to his mouth in shock. He folded his hands and dropped his head in prayer.

The young man explained he was an active member of the NTWU from New Jersey, bused down here for the strike. He had been here for only a few weeks, living in the tent city, repeating one-liners taught to him on the bus to the local strikers.

"The plan was to approach the mill with our band of strikers—150 of us. Some had weapons in hand; we wanted to show 'em we meant business. We called out the night shift, demanding they walk off the job and join their fellow strikers. We were real forceful with 'em, told 'em we needed a united front if the common good was going to be protected. We did our job and returned to the tent city.

"But shortly after, the coppers arrived at the tent city. The chief of police led them. He demanded we turn over our weapons. Some of the boys got angry, waving their guns saying how they had a right to carry it. There was some spitting and kicking dirt . . . but when the shoving started, it didn't stop."

The young man paused and rubbed his forehead.

"I'm not really sure what happened next."

"Try your best, son. You're doing fine."

"I was run over by the mob of people wrestling around me. Some copper tackled me to the ground. I could see everyone swinging and grappling. It was a madhouse. I've never seen anything like it. Even some ladies were fighting hard and swinging at the coppers and were being slammed on the ground. A copper got off me, and I saw his revolver laying right next to me. So I grabbed it. I thought I would shoot a warning shot in the air, putting an end to the madness . . . and then I would just throw the gun to the ground. And then I saw other strikers who had pulled their guns. I didn't even know they had them.

"And then out of the blue, a copper tackled me hard. And I think my gun went off at the same time. Multiple gun fires echoed all around me.

"The copper grabbed the gun from me and pointed it at the other strikers. But standing right next to me was the chief. He went still. And slowly, he fell to the ground. I saw two other coppers and a few strikers laying on the ground or on their hands and knees. I stood up quickly, noticed that the attention of the coppers had turned to their fallen chief . . . so I took off. I ran as fast as I could, for the last few hours. But I saw your steeple in the distance. And, well, here I am."

He buried his face in his hands and wept like a small child. "Oh, God, what have I done! What have I done!"

The abbot sat quietly. After a few moments, he finally said, "Who is at home waiting for you?"

"My mother," he said, wiping at his eyes.

"And you say you heard multiple gun shots?"

"Yes."

"How many?"

"Three or four. I don't know."

"Do you remember pulling the trigger?"

"No. I've never pulled a trigger. But as soon as he tackled me, I heard it."

"Have you ever shot a gun before?"

"Well, no."

"Did you feel the gun recoil?"

"What's that?"

"Did the gun kick back in your hand when it went off?"

"I don't think so. Why?"

The abbot smiled at Brother Matthias.

"Son, I don't think your gun even went off. If you had ever shot a gun, you would have noticed the recoil."

"Really?"

"Really."

"I think you should go home to your mother in New Jersey. I think you've had enough of this big boy world. If I think of this as God does, I see culpability for being stupid and being in the occasion of sin."

Mark nodded his head in humble agreement.

"And you are Catholic, aren't you?"

"Yes."

"So you know what an occasion of sin is?"

"Yes, or I think so: setting yourself up for sinning."

"A good way to define it, yes. You, my son, have placed yourself in a very grave occasion of sin. First, by joining a communist organization. The Church, your Church, has outright condemned such movements. And second, coming down to an unknown part of the country to stir up trouble. And third, joining those strikers at the mill tonight. And fourth, as soon as you saw the police arrive, you should have had the smarts to get the hell out of there! You are filled with so much occasion of sin, I oughta call the station right now and have you picked up."

Mark looked up wide-eyed.

"Please, no. I've learned my lesson. Really, I have."

"So what?" the abbot said. "You've broken the civil and Church law in countless ways."

The striker thought for a moment. He began to tear up again. "But my mother. She can't have her son go to jail. She can't. She needs me."

"Your mother?"

"She doesn't deserve this," he said, dropping his head.

"Ah . . . now we're getting somewhere," the abbot said, darting a little smile over at Brother Matthias. "Now you are thinking about someone other than yourself. Tell me, foolish young man, do you love your mother? What would she have thought had she seen you at the mill tonight?"

The man chuckled through his tears. "I think she'd spank my behind in front of everyone there."

"And she would be right to. Shame on you. Now let me tell you exactly what you are going to do: Brother Matthias here is going to drive you out of town—far from here—right now, and you are going to catch the first train back to New Jersey. Then you will find a holy priest up there—and pick an old one for goodness sake, one not tempted by this communist nonsense—and you will tell him everything. He will help you discern whether to turn yourself in at some point. And then you will hug and kiss your mother. Do you understand me, boy?"

The young man must have said *Yes, Abbot* a dozen times. He hugged the abbot in a most awkward way and stumbled over every word. He could not believe that he was getting out of Dodge. Matthias took him through the monastery and to the automobile. He was gone, and gone for good.

Haskell stepped into the parlor and sat with the abbot.

"Well?" said Haskell, waiting for the abbot to begin.

"The boy is just a boy."

"He's probably older than me," Haskell replied.

"But you aren't normal."

Haskell furrowed his brow, not sure of what was meant nor how to respond.

"Besides," the abbot continued, "he never intended on shooting anyone. That much was clear. And I don't even think his gun went off."

"But he was tackled at the same time."

"I know. The small possibility doesn't escape me. But help us, dear Lord, if the chief was killed."

Haskell shook his head in disbelief at the seemingly never-ending strife between people, even in this small town.

It did not end there. The monks read in the paper that a nationwide event was taking place in their backyard. Seventy-one strikers were arrested. Eight strikers and eight NTWU members were indicted for murder of the chief. A juror went insane after viewing disturbing evidence, and the judge was forced to declare a mistrial. But again, it did not stop there.

The angry townspeople who desperately desired life to return to normal—those opposed to the strike from the get-go—took justice into their own hands. A vigilante group was organized and called themselves *The Committee of One Hundred*. These men ran many of the strikers out of the county by force or threat of force. But some took it even further.

On September 14, a truck full of the strikers was chased down. Ella May Wiggins, the mother who had lost four of her nine children to whooping cough, was among them. The group of strikers was fired upon. Ella May Wiggins was shot and departed this mortal coil.

Hack's Journal

April 2, 1929

I was in the sacristy yesterday and I thought I saw my Pa in the mirror. It was me. Five years later, I am almost as tall as him. I held out my hand. It was almost as big as his. But I am much skinnier. He was as broad as Brother Bruno. And my eyebrows furrow. His never did.

I still grieve him. But mostly I am mad. I have thought over that dreadful night so many times. I have considered vengeance. Plotted it out perfectly. If I took justice into my own hands, no one would ever know. Perhaps this is why God has placed me in a basement—so that I can be His vigilante. I do not exist to the world. In that way, the world could never stop me.

I said this to Brother Bruno the other day. I thought he would sock me in the jaw. But he didn't. He dropped his head and walked out. He hasn't been back since. He even missed our bowling time.

And then Brother Mathias told me this morning that Brother Bruno got drunk again at the pub in town. This time another fella called him a dirty papist. Apparently, Brother Bruno picked him up, carried him across the room, and threw him out the window. The fella wasn't hurt too bad. But the pub owner called the police. Abbot had to get him out of jail.

Maybe he missed our bowling time because the abbot has given him penance. Maybe he got drunk because of what I told him.

Five years. It feels shorter. It feels longer. It feels like anything except five years.

Brother Henry's Journal

May 21, 1929

Edmond Dantès! What was I thinking! The boy is but seventeen, as Dantès was only nineteen. He is imprisoned unjustly, as Dantès was. He has not one Abbe as Dantès did, but many to fill his mind and spirit with the tools for accomplishing any good, or evil. How foolish of me! Of all the literature to give him . . . The Count of Monte Cristo! *The Bard was right when he said, "The fool doth think he is wise, but the wise man knows himself to be a fool."*

Lord have mercy. Spare this child from the curse of vengeance, O Lord.

The year 1929 truly was the year of strikes. It began with Haskell's strike on his homemade bowling alley and continued with the most famous labor union strike in the nation's history, with more than one dead body to show for it. Still more, the year closed out with New York stockbrokers striking the pavement after falling fifty stories from their office windows—a fall even faster than the stocks themselves.

While the mill workers of the South felt the Great Depression slowly move in like a debilitating fog, the pampered rich sucked every last breath out of the long hurrah from the close of the Great War to the end of the decade. But not every financial eye in the big cities was as blind to the impending doom. A few unpopular voices prophesied the crash with uncanny precision, though of course a prophet is never accepted in his hometown.

While a thoughtless, naive, drunken mass of partners were led to slaughter like children of the Pied Piper, slogging off to the tune of "the Market will climb forever," there were two types of prophets ignored at literally all costs.

The first, those prophets of the natural law: "What goes up, must come down," they would say. The second was closely related to the first. They saw American farmers had a glut of production yet were still suffering. They saw the southern mills—that self-sufficient ecosystem of mill towns—collapsing into disarray, resulting in even the murder of a police chief. And thus, a keen eye looking through the economy with a panoramic view showed the floor was about to fall out beneath the economy.

The skeptics included one particular young broker in New York City. He preached to all his clients that the little drops throughout the year were "natural corrections," convincing them to double down, to "buy on the margin"—a fancy way of telling them to borrow money to buy more stocks. It was, he convinced many, the perfect time to go all in. The one thing harder for this young broker than selling a husband was listening to him explain how his uneducated wife was skeptical about going into debt to gamble on the market.

On October 24, 1929, this young broker sat for four hours on the delayed ticker tape. The unthinkable happened before his eyes. There was an 11 percent drop at the opening bell. By the end of the day, sixteen million shares had been traded, which explained the deathly sluggish ticker tape. But there was a little recovery due to the vice president of the exchange getting the banks together to purchase huge amounts of U.S. Steel, to infuse not only investment in the market but, more importantly, confidence. The pesky thing about truth, however, is that it always tends to win in the end. The economy was fragile, and people were beginning to see it.

The following Monday, the DOW dropped another 12.8 percentage points. Panic reached a pitch by Tuesday. Many stocks couldn't be sold at any price. The DOW dropped another 11.73 percentage points.

The young broker was finished.

In the passing days, bodies began piling up on the sidewalks. He understood the desperation. But the only thing worse than the fall would be the sidewalk failing to finish the job.

He saw his grandmother's rosary that sat like an antique on his desk.

He pulled a revolver out from the drawer that laid beneath it. He placed it against his temple.

"God forgive me."

And he pulled the trigger.

Brother Haskell's Journal

May 21, 1934

A full decade. Each year was but a small bead on my rosary. Indeed, the decade has been a mystery. I have read many mystery novels in which a crime must be investigated. And I have prayed many mysteries of Our Lady's Rosary. One is for solving. The other—for walking, breathing, living. My decade in this abbey, with all the monks of endless entertainment, has been the best kind of mystery—one that should forever be explored but never, ever solved.

There are more mysteries and more beads to come.

The Lord has made me anew. I do not know if Brother Haskell is the same as Hack. In certain ways, Hack feels like a sibling who passed away. In other ways, he feels like the most controlling factor in my ψυχή as Plato would say, or my psyche as Sigmund Freud would say. I have recently read Freud's book, The Ego and the Id. I found it disturbing. It's as if it is wrong at the beginning, wrong at the end, but has many elements of truth sprinkled throughout. But it was like the seed sown amidst the thorns. The weeds of human frailty choked his entire work.

Anyhow . . . as I say every year . . . I miss my father. I have been thinking less about my feelings and more about the kind of man he was. He was probably my age when he had me, though I don't know how old he was when he died. I would guess 34. Yet he seemed so much older, wiser, stronger, than the 34-year-old monks upstairs.

My life seems to whimsically shift from frivolity of any given moment to extreme depth that I do not understand. I confided recently to the abbot that I can be lost in the triviality of forming a joke that will make Bruno's belly jiggle, or whipping up a funny sounding vignette on the violin that will make Mathias say, "Do it again," and then suddenly, something about the soul of the other will seem apparent. It is like a light is turned on, and I can see something they are not willingly showing. At times, this sense comes over me regarding a certain person, then I hear the footsteps, then I see the person at my door. I act surprised to see them nonetheless.

Abbot says this is a gift. I'd prefer to give the gift back. But not my will, O Lord. Not my will.

Abbot Ambrose's Journal

December 8, 1934

Hack is reaching new depths of spirituality. The Spirit dwells loudly within him. The gifts bestowed on the early Christians abound—far more than he realizes. I shall not burden him with this knowledge, for I do not know the Lord's purpose for him. His gift of prophecy makes me restless. I try, however, to keep a stoic veneer when he talks to me of his experiences.

I also must now prepare to see him before venturing down for our daily visits. I must pray and straighten out my soul. I feel obliged to visit him with poverty and purity of heart, with meekness and mercy . . . With every step down that long stone staircase, I feel called to beatitude.

I am ill-equipped to lead this young man much further, for I am terribly ordinary, and he is terrifically unordinary.

Chapter 3

1936

Brother Haskell's eyes slowly fluttered open as his recently acquired 2-Voice Big Ben alarm clock gave rise to its first voice—a gentle ring meant to soothingly lift one from slumber. It was Matins, the 2:00 a.m. hour for the monks of old, a practice abandoned by modern communities.

Not a single light penetrated the blackness of his cell. Slowly reaching his hand to the right of his bed, he felt for his candle holder. Matches rested on its ledge designed to catch melting wax. The irony of being woken by a state-of-the-art alarm clock in order to a light a wax candle did not escape him. But he had learned the hard way. He required the modern convenience of the former if he hoped to enjoy the tranquility of the latter.

He rested the candle holder on his chest, struck a match which momentarily blinded him, and with one eye squinted, lit the candle and returned it to its place on the floor. He had no sheets that begged to swaddle his body nor pillow that begged to be fluffed and swaddle his head. In fact, he had no mattress to tempt him back to soft repose as a mother's arms lull a baby back to sleep. Thus, at least in theory, getting out of bed for Haskell should have been easier than for most. But it was not.

Brother Haskell learned how quickly the human body adapted to its newly defined standards of comfort and security. To a glutton, a feast for Henry VIII was not enough, but to a prisoner in one of his towers, a fresh orange was as delicious as all the fruits of Eden. To a sloth, a vacation fit for Vanderbilt would fail to rejuvenate, but to a laboring tenant farmer in the thick of the depression, a nap under the scant shade of a cypress tree would revitalize the body, mind, and soul. And after a long day of physical, mental, and spiritual work in the monastery, a shipwrecked Odysseus could not have craved his own bed more than Brother Haskell did his plywood. Comfort was in the eye of the beholder. Even more importantly, however, Brother Haskell had learned that if a man retires with a clear conscience, a bed of nails might suffice.

And so, no matter how spartan his sleeping arrangements, that damn 2-Voice Big Ben alarm clock was unwelcome, to say the least. It was a 2-Voice because its first ring was gentle. If not turned off, a far more aggressive ring followed, like a villainous taskmaster yelling at his slave to arise and begin his day of drudgery.

Thank God that on this morning that villainous second voice would not make itself known, for Brother Haskell rolled himself off the plywood until his knees reached the stone floor. It felt cool this September morning even through the hefty habit he slept in.

"Domine, labia mea aperies. Et os meum annuntiabit laudem tuam." He began Matins by slowly reciting ten Psalms, only occasionally glancing down at the text in the dim candlelight to refresh his memory.

Upon finishing his Psalms, Brother Haskell remained in silence. He did not think about the day before. He did not think about the day to come, even though it was a day he had been greatly anticipating. He did not think about the stone beneath his knees. He simply experienced the presence of God in the present moment. For him, the presence of God was like one of those black holes Albert Einstein wrote about, which he had recently been enjoying. This black hole seemed to consume all his thoughts and feelings. It was black, not due to lack of light, but due to such immense concentration of light. If that black hole were cracked open, he would surely die, for no one shall see the face of God and live.

In a manner of speaking, he could sense the infinite within the darkness. And when one encounters the infinite, the slightest move seems rather shallow. He thus knelt perfectly still. Time stood still. Every once in a while, Brother Haskell would become aware of the complete silence enveloping his room, which was another reason he had spent good money on that Big Ben alarm clock: it was the first alarm clock ever made that was silent as the hands traveled round.

In the silence and stillness of concentration, nothing can make a man go mad faster than a "*tick, tick, tick.*" Brother Haskell had learned the hard way. His previous alarm clock's relentless and menacing tick became torturous. As he prayed to God for peace and serenity, all he could think about was slamming that *tick, tick, tick* against the stone wall.

But it was worse than that. He personified that clock, gave it a soul, and wished it to be banished to hell for eternal damnation. "What a vile imagination I have," he had thought to himself. Thus, in order to sanctify the illusions of his mind, he told himself that the purpose of banishing this accursed invention was not to punish the clock itself but to torture Lucifer for all eternity. *Tick. Tick. Tick.* A year. *Tick. Tick. Tick.* A thousand years. *Tick. Tick. Tick.* A million years. Never-ending. Never-ceasing. Is this not what Lucifer deserved for his constant pestering of humanity through all the ages? Thus, his 2-Voice Big Ben that said nothing was a sound investment with ample spiritual returns.

When he was younger, he tried so hard to remain still that at times, he found himself gasping for air. But as he matured in the ways of contemplation, he found a stillness on the far side of intentionality, resembling a feather floating in the wind more than a statue chiseled from stone.

On this early morning of September 7, 1936, the thought of a dove fluttered through his concentration, for it was Labor Day, also known as opening day for dove hunting season. The sides of Brother Haskell's mouth crept up a little. Seeing that his mind would from hereon be distracted with excitement, he thanked God for the dove hunt and looked for a way to incorporate the distractions into his prayer.

He saw many gray doves being shot down, spinning around like flower petals from the sky. But one beautiful white dove remained untouched, methodically flapping its wings. Like a conductor's wand, the wings of the dove directed his heart, when to open and when to close: *Down and up / Open and close. Down and up / Open and close.* All at once, he felt completely dependent on the wings of the dove. If those wings stop conducting, his life would surely end. But so long as they commanded, he was free, fully alive, and safe from all distress.

This sense of dependence took him deeper into contemplation. The dependence, or what he knew philosophers called contingency, became more of an emotion for him rather than a concept. He felt at that level of a single moment—that measurement of time smaller than a second, a millionth of a second perhaps—that his entire existence, not just his heartbeat, was completely dependent on God's will to keep him there. It was not as if God could take his life away, but rather that if God stopped desiring his life for a millionth of a second that Haskell would not only die, not only cease to exist, but cease to have ever been. The feeling of dependence was like someone holding your hand on the edge of a cliff, and it reminded him of the experience he had so many years ago on his first hike with Brother Bruno, when he gazed down from the top of the cliff into the black abyss. Brother Haskell had known for years that God was calling him into a deeper sense of reality, one that lay beneath all that could be seen, heard, and felt. The awareness of this power over one's own being makes palpable the very opposite attribute of He who gives you being. Haskell's focus on his own dependence shifted to God's absoluteness. God is not dependent on anyone or anything. He is solely self-sufficient and necessary.

Haskell realized the difference between him and God was not that God came first, as Aristotle's Prime Mover moved before all others; nor was it the difference between pure spirit and corporeal beings; nor even the fact that at one time, man did not exist. The difference was that man's existence, or the entire universe's existence for that matter, was contingent on an absolute. The core difference between God and all else was not time, for time is merely the measurement of change. The core difference was that of necessary versus unnecessary, absolute versus contingent.

Brother Haskell shuddered at this thought. For the first time, he understood that God was not just the creator of the physical universe. His heart ached with awe: God was something infinitely greater than this. He felt how insufficient his catechism definition of God had been: "God is the Supreme Being who made all things." Yes, he thought, but he is far more than that. Supreme Being had always led Haskell to think of God as the biggest, oldest, strongest of beings—with the longest and grayest of long beards. Haskell felt embarrassed before God. He even covered his face with his hands. "Forgive me, Lord," he whispered. The thought struck him deep at his core that we are categorically different from God. We are not smaller versions of God, and neither are the greatest of the choir of angels. No, all of us creatures are contingent, and God is not. That is the defining difference between us. Haskell recalled from Plato the notion of the demiurge—the divine entity begotten from the One. And for Plato, it was from the demiurge that the universe was born. God could have given a seraphim or principality or even a cherub the awesome power to create the universe as it is. He need not have dirtied His hands with supernovas or black holes or constellations; He need not have gotten Andromeda or Orion under His fingernails. In this sense, Plato's notion of "The One" was correct. The One was undivided, perfect unity, perfectly self-subsisting. However, Plato's One stopped short of true perfection: it was, essentially, a mysophobian—one who would be infected by coming in contact with others.

Perhaps only the grace-filled mind that has received Divine Revelation can conceive of the Incarnation.

But for Haskell on this early morning, the complete otherness of God as utterly absolute was reason for awe. Coupled with this reason for awe was the fact that God, the Absolute, still stoops down to interact with us through Scripture, through making us in some small fashion in His own image, but most beautifully in the incarnation of the second person of the Trinity.

Haskell opened his eyes and lifted his head until he gazed upon the crucifix hanging next to his bed. *And God became flesh and dwelt among us.* He emptied Himself, taking the form of a servant, born into the likeness of man . . . He humbled Himself, becoming obedient unto death, even to death on the cross.

Haskell marveled at how the Absolute could be so humble as to strip Himself of all comfort, of all appearance of dignity, to be humiliated and tortured by the contingent beings He made out of love.

It was this complete otherness of God that shed brilliant light on the beauty of the crucifix. He felt a single tear slip down his face and wiped it with a single finger. Not having any idea how long his knees had been firmly planted on the stone floor, he finally looked at his 2-Voice Big Ben alarm clock. An hour had passed. He suddenly felt the soreness in his knees. He slowly laid back down on to his plywood, rubbed his knees for a moment, and quietly whispered, "Thank you, Jesus." He was asleep within minutes and dreamed about many gray doves spinning to the ground like flower petals while the white dove slowly flapped its wings above them all.

At 6:00 a.m., it was not the 2-Voice Big Ben alarm clock that rang out but the three-thousand-pound church bell in the tallest of the two steeples that tolled for all the town to hear. The abbey had two towers of varying height meant to represent the Benedictine motto, *Ora et Labora,* Prayer and Work. The tallest represented *Ora* and the shorter *Labora,* visually depicting the prominence of prayer over work in the life of a monk, or, some would argue, the life of any Christian.

Brother Haskell had been joining the monks in choir for a number of years now. At some point along the line, the title of *Brother* became routine. Oddly enough, he had never taken vows. He was a partial hermit with limited engagement with the outside world. Enough time had passed since the incident of 1924 that the monks felt comfortable with his presence known, but only from a distance of course. If anyone ever asked where the negro monk came from, the monks would simply say, "From a sister monastery in the west" and left it at that.

By 1936, everything in America had settled down. Just as Europe had sat through the Dark Ages, so America rested quietly now in the belly of the Great Depression. But paradoxically, the Dark Ages were not all that dark; rather, they were a flourishment of philosophical and theological development. It had become a regular discussion to speculate on what good would arise from the ashes of the Depression.

Abbot Ambrose, Brother Bruno, Father Henry, Father Dominic, and Father Matthias (both newly ordained)—the group that the abbot formed twelve years ago to watch over twelve-year-old Hack—had in fact become a close-knit group of friends. An odd group to say the least.

Dominic and Matthias were rather normal, shall we say, with their own unique passions. Dominic was the philosopher and theologian who could find a heady topic of conversation anywhere. Matthias was the quintessential artist, a musician who dabbled in philosophy (but only through the vein of aesthetics). Henry was a man of letters and an ass by nature. He did not fit in with this group at all, but didn't seem to make any effort to escape. Bruno was a child stuck in a giant's body, yet a man who never met a bad guy he didn't want to fight. At one and the same time, he was as gentle as a dove and as ferocious as a lion. If the young Hack had any one caregiver, it was the Great Bavarian. But with every passing year, the roles seemed to reverse. Abbot Ambrose was the most Christ-like figure in the bunch, not due to holiness *per se*, but due to the position he held with meekness and humility. In this way, he was the most like Haskell who seemed providentially spared of aggression and pride.

They loaded up in the older Model TT truck, the same model as the one stolen twelve years ago during Bruno and Haskell's hike. This one, however, was the replacement of the replacement. It was a short two-mile drive to a field of the monastery cared for by a tenant farmer and his family. The field was covered with sunflower stalks picked over.

The tenant farmer met them as they got out of the truck.

"Mornin', Abbot. Fathers and Brothers," he said tipping his hat.

"Good morning, Mr. Smith. Thank you for prepping the field for us."

"Aw, it was nothin'. Just spread out sunflower seeds for them doves. They sure love 'em."

"We are much obliged."

"It's your land after all. I'm just thankful to work it."

"And you do a fine job," the abbot said, patting him on the shoulder.

Mr. Smith took his hat off and began to ring it in his hands. "How's the Mrs. doin' for ya, sir?"

"Oh, she's a fine cook," the abbot said. "Isn't she boys?" He looked over the group with a paternalist eye.

Father Henry diverted his eyes as if he was already tracking dove. Bruno looked down at the ground and scratched his nose as if he had to sneeze. Dominic's eyes locked on to the farmer with an awkward smile and said, "Yes."

Father Matthias, sensing the moment escaping his good abbot, said, "Boy, do I look forward to her soups. As good as any I ever had."

"Sure is," the farmer said. "She can make a mean soup."

"Mean indeed," Father Henry grumbled.

"A fine cook," the abbot repeated.

"Look here, Abbot," the farmer said as he rolled his hat into a tighter and tighter ball, "I know you didn't . . . I mean I know you don't need . . ."

"Mr. Smith," the abbot interrupted, patting his shoulder again, "She's worth every penny."

The farmer exhaled. "Thank you, sir."

After the farmer pointed out the prime real estate of entry for the doves and made his departure, Father Henry said, "You can't employ everyone in town you know."

"I'm aware. Thank you, *Father Roth*," the abbot said.

"Roth has a point," Henry replied.

"A point, yes. But God has a law. And it's called the second greatest commandment."

Dominic added, "The Depression will not last forever. There are some good signs, from what I read."

"Maybe," the abbot said. "But to add insult to injury to these poor farmers who can't sell any food, this heat has crippled their crops."

"We're gonna feel the heat today," Matthias said. "The hottest summer on record. Is that what 1936 will be remembered for?"

Ambrose said, "120 degrees through the south a few months ago. Nearly two thousand dead from heat exhaustion. Thousands of children drowned from swimming to keep cool. Yes. I'd say this year will be remembered as the summer from hell."

"No," replied Henry with his usual authoritative voice. "That's not what people remember."

It was just like Henry to leave a dramatic pause. Bruno hated such snobby tactics. "Well, spit it out!"

"History remembers war, money, and entertainment," Henry said with a tone fit for the classroom, not the sunflower field on opening day. "And that's all. Those poor people scorched to death by nature's wrath will pass from memory the moment Mother Nature sends us a hurricane or flood or ice storm. Weather is never remembered because weather is always in the now. But war . . . it leaves scars on the face of a nation seen every time we look in the mirror. And money . . . money is like water that feeds everything else. We always remember when we have it and when we don't. Oh, and we can now literally say that money is more valuable than gold since our president, in his great wisdom, took us off the gold standard."

"A monetary policy of relativism," interjected Dominic, "to match the moral doctrine of modern times."

"Indeed," agreed Henry. "And then there is entertainment. And I do not mean this in a purely negative fashion, for there are redeeming qualities of entertainment. The human spirit must escape the imprisonment of the Depression, and the heat. We are escapists by nature, even if that pertains to our flawed nature, we are indeed all escapists. And not just Americans in their self-indulgency. But mankind, throughout all times and cultures, has always placed on pedestals those heroes of war, of economy, and of entertainment, the greatest of these being entertainment. For it satisfies man's desire to be freed from life. And again, this is not all bad. The persecuted Catholics of Elizabethan England had Shakespeare's *Hamlet* and *Macbeth* to take their minds off the rack and rope. The French had Dumas's *Three Musketeers* and *Count of Monte Cristo* to distract them from both war and the poor economy brought upon them by the blood-drenched Revolution and the Napoleonic Wars. You might think of Dumas's work as fodder for France's own reconstruction period. And, of course, England had Dickens' *Oliver Twist* and countless other characters to help them escape the sweatshops of the Industrial Revolution, no matter how ironic it may be to take your mind off the horrors of factory life by reading about the horrors of factory life."

"Then what are you saying America will remember about 1936 if not the horror of roasting bodies beneath the violent sun?"

"1936 will be remembered for one thing: The masterpiece *Gone with the Wind* by a certain Margaret Mitchell."

In almost perfect harmony, Dominic, Matthias, and Ambrose said in one version or another, "I've heard of that . . ." The abbot asked, "Have you read it?"

"Indeed," replied Henry. "I finished it just last night, though it was a long journey."

"Well?" asked the abbot.

"It was a good book. Not a great one. It will be remembered as a great book, nonetheless, for it is—shall we say—innovative. It abandons many of the old tricks of storytellers and embraces new ones. It gives a psychology to the South before, during, after—even if many of those attributes are incorrect. But it is about life, and what people want in life. And it is good enough to stand the test of time. For it is as much *life* as people can stand in our modern world."

"Do you think they'll make a motion picture from it?" asked Matthias.

"Most certainly not!" protested Henry. "The movie would have to be fifty hours long.

"Why not shorten the story?" Matthias said.

"Shorten that much? To be viewable even in a single day would require writing a wholly different story. If some cockeyed Hollywood man tried, he would be racked by the book's readers. I think you will find as time goes on that movies are for entertainment, and books are for life."

"You don't read Shakespeare for entertainment?" asked Matthias.

"Not for *mere* entertainment, I should say not. Books elevate the soul. Motion pictures tickle one's fancy."

"Spectacle," interjected the philosopher, Dominic. "Aristotle wrote about the growing demand for spectacle in the *Poetics*, which he believed detracted from the deeper value of the work and was a cheap way to keep an audience engaged."

"Indeed," agreed Henry. "Spectacle indeed. Thank you, Father. That's exactly what I was looking for. Motion pictures will be used for spectacle and little else; to make a man say 'wow' or to make a lady terrified and to make her friend cry; to make the foolish boy laugh uncontrollably; to push human emotion to the fringe of morality. Books, on the other hand, will retain some level of decency, will be the medium by which moderation remains a viable guide to action, taking the reader into a journey of the human experience without reaching extremes too easily."

"*In medio stat virtus* says Aristotle," replied the philosopher.

"*Virtue stands in the means*. Yes. Yes indeed," added Henry. And motion picture will push man to the extreme of emotive response as a cheap grab at an audience, just as the dramatists tried in ancient Greece."

"Why do people say so often, 'as Aristotle said' and then speak Latin?" Haskell asked.

"Good question," Dominic said. "We do that all the time. That particular passage, *In medio stat virtus*, comes from the Angelic Doctor. And you know full well, Haskell, that Aristotle essentially said this in *Nicomachean Ethics*."

"Fair enough," agreed Haskell. "But I have another question."

There was a long pause as the group finally reached their spot in the field running alongside a strip of picked over sunflowers, strategically grown by the tenant farmer for the purpose of luring the doves. The five monks took their positions from experience about five feet apart from each other, establishing their shooting lanes. They each took rounds from their bags and loaded the chambers in the broken open barrel, ready to slam shut and shoot at the slightest flapping of a dove's wings.

"You said a few moments ago, Father Henry," continued Haskell, "that *Gone With the Wind* would be hailed as a masterpiece because it is about life and what people want out of life."

"That's right. I believe that quality is present in good literature. People instinctively respond positively to it. For they find themselves in the story. We all experience Hamlet's struggle between taking sinful revenge on his corrupt uncle who killed his father and enacting justice against an evildoer who must be stopped for the sake of the common good. Every man relates to this in some fashion. It is life. Everyone knows the pains of Aeneas who had his beloved nation burned to the ground by sacrilegious enemies yet led his people to a new home in the face of constant obstacles.

This is life, for every man wants a permanent home. Thus, Virgil stands the test of time."

"For goodness' sake!" interrupted Brother Bruno. "Is anyone looking for doves?"

"Oedipus Rex," Henry said, "how frightening a prospect to see ourselves in this man, who kills his own father and takes his own mother. Surely that German, Sigmund Freud, takes it all too far—perverting every inclination to mistakenly destroy and defile that which should be cherished by us? And as old men, do we not realize the damage caused by our pride and anger throughout our youth? And does not the sin of our youth often lay dormant during our 'reign' as it did with King Oedipus, but unfailingly returns to haunt us just as we should begin to enjoy the fruits of our labor? I think every man knows Oedipus well. It is life.

"And do not most men—even most men in the monastery—have sweet memories of their youthful romance, the tragedy of their first love, while reading *Romeo and Juliet*? When it seems that all the world is against them, all the powers of this world building barriers to their unquenchable love. And even if a man has never personally experienced this passion pounding in his chest, nature has nonetheless written an understanding of it on his heart."

"Father," Haskell said after patiently letting the monologue run its course. "I still have not asked my question, but you've taken me on a detour, which I'll address first."

Just then, a bird flew overhead. Barrels slapped shut and were raised instantly, except for Father Henry, who, upon realizing he never loaded, mumbled, "Darn." As he cracked the over-and-under open and quickly loaded.

"I'm afraid, Father," said Haskell, softly and reservedly, "that I must disagree with your reading of *Romeo and Juliet*."

"Really?" asked Henry with a mixture of surprise and contempt. "It wasn't long ago that you quite enjoyed my interpretation. If I recall, it was four or five years ago. We began Shakespeare with this play, and you marveled at not only his command of language but, vastly more importantly, at the revelation of human passion—romantic passion to be precise. You marveled at the God-given love the Greeks called eros. You explained how so much of human existence had been explained; how the species continues; how you could understand Adam's loneliness in the garden, how much self-mastery the righteous Joseph must have exercised in Nazareth."

"Well, that's true, Father, but . . ."

"You professed to understand Socrates's denial of the body, particularly as expressed in, what was it, the *Phaedo*? Yes, the *Phaedo*, in which Socrates explains how the body prevents the soul from conceiving of the ideals of nature. I must say, Haskell, you surprise me. Your first reading of *Romeo and Juliet* was visceral, and your own extrapolation was rather exalted. Tell me: How have you changed your mind?"

"And you wonder why people avoid conversations with you," snarked Bruno.

"Ha!" blurted Matthias.

"Wait a minute!" hollered the abbot. "Bird!"

All heads rose to the heavens as two doves shot across the field. Their speed was near miraculous, like a mythological creature bolting over the battlefield on the beaches of Troy, or an arrow shot from the bow of Apollo.

The speed of a dove flying for its life is faster than the conscious mind can calculate distance and lead time. And yet, it is far slower than the unconscious reaction speed of the mind. The hardest thing about dove hunting is intentionally not thinking. How ought one, particularly thinkers-of-sorts, think about not thinking? And what is the use of practicing if the unconscious mind is in control? Abbot Ambrose routinely said, "The art of bird hunting is a mystery, like the Blessed Trinity."

This particular volley of gunfire failed to hit its target. The day, however, was young.

"You're right, Father Henry," Haskell continued as if five shot guns had not just echoed throughout the field, "*Romeo and Juliet* affected me greatly. I'm surprised you remember so much of what I said about it."

"That was easy," replied Henry. "You are the first student I ever had to see the power of true love and how it is one of the greatest laws of nature causing all of nature and civilization to continue on and on." But then added with a stern look, "Don't let that go to your head, though."

"Of course not, Father. But unfortunately, I was wrong. I may have been right about the power of human love, whether called eros or something else. But I'm afraid my most recent reading of *Romeo and Juliet* reveals a radically different intent of Shakespeare."

Henry laughed. "Well then, I'm interested to hear how every Shakespearian scholar has gotten it wrong and how the pupil has single-handedly found some hidden meaning."

"Come on, Henry," the abbot said. "Don't be so touchy. Just hear him out."

Haskell said with a nod to Dominic. "Forgive me, Father, but as Aristotle said, 'Plato is my friend, but truth is a better friend.'"

"Quite right," said Dominic with a chuckle.

Henry looked away in his discomfort, as if looking out for a dove.

"Shakespeare wrote *Romeo and Juliet*," began Haskell, "in my opinion . . ."

"Do not qualify your reading," interrupted Henry. "I care not about your opinion of Shakespeare's motives, the inner workings of his soul. Bah! Pure speculation. If you have evidence, let me have it. If not, look out for birds."

"Henry," said Ambrose with the rising tone.

"Very well, Father. I will give you evidence *and* look out for birds. I'll tell you what the text says. I'll give you a clear meaning, and you can tell us just how scholars manage to render the exact opposite, just how they render this play a romance rather than a tragedy of sin."

A silence spread over the group. Even Bruno was paying attention now.

"Shakespeare's play is based on a poem by Arthur Brooke. Brooke made Juliet sixteen years old. But what did Shakespeare do? He turned her into a thirteen-year-old little girl. That was not by accident. He was telling us something. He was making her a mere child, one whose innocence must be protected, one whose violation ought to make the reader cringe, not be swooned with romantic sentimentality. And that biography on Shakespeare you gave me? You may have missed that his own daughter was around thirteen when he wrote the play. Thus, a father is envisioning a wrathful lust that ought to hit home for any parent.

"Related to this point, Shakespeare makes Romeo older than he was in Brooke's poem. And while we don't get an exact age, he is obviously not a young teenager, for he is capable of winning arguments with wit and able to defeat the villain Tybalt in a sword fight. Shakespeare was clearly emphasizing the age disparity between the two lovers in a way that should bring feelings of disgust rather than those of enchantment."

"That's gross when you think about it," said Brother Bruno.

"Exactly. Furthermore," Haskell continued, "to dive deeper into the text, as Father Henry asked of me, the most direct evidence of Shakespeare's intent is found in Romeo and Juliet's first encounter on the balcony—their first kiss. They discuss sin and how sin is passed back and forth with their lips. Juliet says, 'Then have my lips the sin that they have took.' And Romeo says, 'Sin from thy lips? O trespass sweetly urged! Give me my sin again.' And the Chorus adds to this scene by saying Romeo's old desires for Rosaline are lying in their deathbed and that new affections are replacing them. Why does Romeo turn so easily? Because, as the Chorus says, he is 'betwitched by the charm of looks.'

"And as everyone knows, the young lovers make a suicide pact, which the Church in Shakespeare's time understood to be a near unforgivable sin. And the play comes to an end with yet another sinful exchange of sin by the lips, this time passing the poison between them.

"The cleric in the play, Friar Lawrence, sums it up best for all of us: 'Violent desires have violent ends.' For the life of me, Father Henry, I cannot see how this is anything but Shakespeare expounding on the dangers of lust, resulting not in an ending of love, but of irreversible tragedy."

The silence that followed gave Haskell another moment to further consider his point. "*Romeo and Juliet* is not about human love, that God-given gift of sacramental love to which the majority of the species is called, that glorious vocation of the married life. It is about the corruption of innocence, the corruption of purity. If anything, it is about the disorder of that which is good."

Bruno slowly stood up, mounted his gun, and shot. Everyone else stood up and mounted, but by then, Bruno was walking into the field as a dove spun to the ground like a flower petal.

"Dang it!" Ambrose said, frustrated he had not focused on the task at hand.

Henry sat quietly and then said, "I'll have to review the text. It has been some years since I've studied it. But I'm rather sure it is not as simple as you present it to be."

"And why not?" asked Dominic. "Sinful creatures, tainted with darkness of intellect, weakness of will, and proneness to evil complicate everything. We, in fact, infect the truth with our own fallen nature, turning everything upside down. Perhaps this is why the Englishman G. K. Chesterton is so popular these days, especially across the pond. Everyone says he speaks upside down. But he laughs at such criticism and says he's one of the few that speaks right side up! And when I read him, well, I can't help but agree. He does with culture and ideology exactly what Haskell just did with Shakespeare. Reading Chesterton reminds me of how confused we have become about the most obvious things in life."

"Such as?" Ambrose asked.

Before Dominic could answer, Haskell spoke up. "Unity. Goodness. Truth. And most especially Beauty."

"The transcendentals," added Dominic.

"*Especially* beauty," said Matthias, having yet to speak a word.

"Yes. Especially beauty," agreed Henry, with a far gentler tone.

"Wow," said Ambrose. "A concurrence between Haskell and Matthias and Henry. Please tell me: Why *especially* beauty?"

Dominic jumped on it. "Perhaps because the passions are so strong that they constantly spot beauty, like we are spotting birds. Plato would say the senses are misleading due to being distracted with too many particulars and are thus incapable of leading us to the forms. And since the primary sense is found in the eyes, and the eyes judge based on physicality, beauty—which includes proportionality, structure, etc.—well, our senses are swept away too easily. Which brings us back to Romeo. He was swept away; incontinent, Aristotle would say. His passions screamed out 'Beauty!' while going after Juliet."

Matthias, having always been a student of beauty, felt more at home in this conversation than in any run-of-the-mill theological discourse. "I think beauty," he said, "is what elevates the soul more than any other transcendental. As a musician, I marvel that everyone on Earth likes one form of music or another. Everyone on Earth loves art in one style or another. Every culture in every land in every time looks at the Moon and the stars, at sunrises and sunsets, at lightning storms and rainbows, even at the birth of a baby and the peaceful death of an old man and says in their native tongue, 'That is beautiful.' Archeology is finding on cave walls that man has always tried to both capture the beauty of nature and even surpass it with some form of impressionism. Man cannot but help reach beyond himself, whether with his prehistoric paintbrush to bedazzle a cave wall or with the sound of his lute to entertain his village spectators.

"And the heights of art have been reached, like a man pushing up against a ceiling, by Dante and DaVinci, Michelangelo and Mozart, and . . ." he added with a smile and leaning toward Henry, "Margaret Mitchell."

Everyone laughed.

Bang!

Bruno's gun fired, shocking the other monks back to attention. Bruno was on his way again through the field as a dove glided down slowly with wings outstretched like a plane coming in for a landing.

"That's two for me," Bruno hollered behind him as he walked toward his reward.

"That's it!" Abbot Ambrose said expressing his resolve. "We've got to stop talking. I'll never hit a bird like this."

The abbot noticed Haskell with downcast eyes, lost in thought.

"Haskell? Where are you?"

Looking up slowly, he answered with a smile: "Two places, I guess, neither of which is in this here field. First, I have yet to ask my original question regarding Father Henry's comment on why *Gone with the Wind* will be so popular. But we keep taking detours in this conversation; so, secondly, my mind is lost in everyone's comments on beauty."

He paused momentarily and said, "What was said about beauty is not wrong, but incomplete."

"Go on," said Matthias.

Dominic laid his shotgun on the ground and crossed his arms, intensely focused on his young pupil, leaving the birds to Bruno.

"You all agreed," began Haskell, "that beauty was the transcendental that people mistook for worldly delights, more so than unity, goodness, or truth. And Matthias explained well that the senses detect beauty, or beautiful things we should say, and that the soul craves to create transcendent art. I agree with all of this.

"But there is something far greater about beauty, something I've been thinking about for a few years, and frankly," he said looking at Dominic, "never brought up in my lessons because I felt silly departing so much from tradition."

"We're listening," Dominic said.

Haskell took a deep breath. "Beauty is not just one of the transcendentals; it is the means by which the others are revealed to us. The one thing that lies beneath truth, goodness, and unity is existence, right? Take this blade of grass here." Haskell leaned over and gently rubbed the top of the field. "This grass is existing. It has existence, which, as Aquinas explains, is not God *per se*, for that would be the heresy of Pantheism, but the grass's existence participates in God's existence. The grass is not a little piece of God. It has its own existence, but one that is wholly contingent on God's existence and was derived from God's own existence. And when we say 'God's existence,' we know we are limited to human speech and might as well just say 'God', for all of God's attributes are infinitely united into Oneness."

"Yes, yes. Go on," encouraged Dominic.

"This small blade of grass is *being* grass. It has *being*, or existence. And it is not only being grass, but it is being grass *at* us. It is revealing itself to us, which enables us to say, 'It is good and true.' You see, I've been thinking that this is what it means *to be*. Our existence—God's existence in the Holy Trinity—is relational. Nothing, especially God, is alone. The Father is the Father because He has the Son. And the Son is the Son because He has the Father. Or better yet, the Father is Father because He is *being* a Father *to* the Son. And vice versa. And the Holy Spirit is being that . . . literally *being* that infinite unity between the Father and Son.

"And to a lesser extent, the grass here is being grass at the weeds smothering it; it is being grass at the soil from which is breaks, it is being grass at the rain drops its roots soak up; it is being grass at Bruno's empty shells lying on the ground.

"The grass's very existence, its being, has an attribute of self-revelation. This attribute is at the very core of its essence. A thing is whatever it reveals itself to be, whether the witness is able to perceive correctly or not.

"Oh, and this is the beauty of God's nature. Since God is self-revelation at His core—if we can use such insufficient terms for God, it makes perfect sense that God would desire to reveal Himself throughout salvation history as told in the Old Testament—culminating in the clearest, most simple, most pure, most direct, most unobscured, most chaste, most just, most . . . redemptive manner possible—namely, the Incarnation of Jesus Christ.

"And here is the point I struggle to explain." Everyone, even Bruno, had zoned in on Haskell. "What do we call that self-revelatory attribute of being? What do we call it in God, in us, in this blade of grass? I think the best word we have for it is beauty. Beauty is the self-revelation of being. And it perfectly coincides with the scholastic definition of beauty Dominic has kindly taught me. You see, in order for beauty—the act of self-revelation—to work, it must have structure and proportion on the metaphysical level, not just the physical. Anything that is conceivable must have form to it, or else it is formless, thus without being.

"But I digress. The point is that when we see the Moon and stars and sunrise and sunset, as Matthias wisely put it, we see a real being self-revealing. It is this unencumbered self-revealing that we find beautiful. When a singer sings, and we think it is beautiful, it is because some barrier to the singer was lifted, and we get a glimpse at the singer himself. When DaVinci's painting of Christ is said to be beautiful, what we are trying to say is that something in Christ's humanity and divinity is revealed to us . . . and something about DaVinci was revealed as well.

"And finally, bringing us home to Romeo and Juliet, those supposed icons of romance, who I believe are, rather, icons of impurity, fit this paradigm well. When one thinks they are icons of romance, one is saying it is beautiful in that Romeo and Juliet communicated their deepest selves to one another as lovers are called to do. But when one sees this play for what it truly is, you see an ugliness about it. You see Romeo smothering his God-given self with infatuation, lust, imprudence, arrogance. You see that he has given nothing more of himself than he gave to Rosaline shortly before. He gave a mere shadow of self; he gave a mere passion that burns hot but always cools. You see a hothead that barks at the Friar of God, putting up barriers between himself and the divine, so that mere fragments of his soul are presented to heaven. There is no self-revelation here, especially sitting on that balcony outside the young girl's window. No. What sits there is, 'I give myself not to you, but I demand all of you. I want your body for myself, for my own enjoyment. My lips will speak truth to you but use the words of the Father of Lies. And they will impart sin to yours. That's my revelation to you: sin. And in return, I get the enjoyment of defiling your soft, childlike skin. I want your self-revelation; I want to consume your purity, your innocence until it is no more, like a predator mauls its prey, for the thrill of it is more potent than any wine, more satisfying than any food. I will devour you, draining you of all that is good, all that is of God, until the absence of the good is all that is left. And all the while, I reveal nothing of my true self, for there is nothing of my true self left. It slowly vanished before Rosaline, during Rosaline, after Rosaline. It slowly vanished with every step as I climbed up this balcony. And so, when I opened my mouth to speak sweet nothings, there was in fact nothing left. It is with these lips and this tongue that I offer you all that is left of me, which is the absence of all good. I give you nothing, but I must have your everything.'"

Haskell paused for a moment as if to catch his breath, as if to be in that nasty character took a toll on him. He shook his head a little and came back to himself. The monks looked as still as the stone statues adorning the abbey grounds. They looked like the old scholars listening to the Child Jesus in the Temple.

"Beauty, therefore" he began again, "is the most powerful force in the world, for it is the way we see the difference between truth and falsity; it is the way we seek the good, which is our final end; it is the force by which we experience unity with God."

Bruno gazed upon his friend, his younger brother of sorts, and was proud, not just of his insight, but his assertiveness. Henry, Dominic, and Matthias saw a pupil who had perhaps surpassed his masters, and were dumbfounded. Abbot Ambrose saw a saint in the making, one who he was still obliged to care for spiritually. An uneasy sense of nervousness set in, a fear as to the weightiness of his God-given duty.

All four monks sat staring at Haskell, the black boy who had grown up in their midst. They saw him slowly rise, and without a moment's notice, mount his gun and shoot: *Bang! Bang!*

Two doves plummeted to the Earth simultaneously—a remarkable series of shots.

And they watched him slowly walk out into the open field, leaving them behind.

They returned just in time to make Vespers, which was unfortunate because the doves' activity picked up just as they were leaving. The last thirty minutes were the most active, and Bruno reached his bag limit well before the day was done.

Just as the tired monks entered the back door of the monastery, a young brother walked up quickly to Abbot Ambrose, informing him of a visitor insistent on meeting with him. "He looks rather unwell, Abbot, or perhaps nervous. And he would not agree to scheduling an appointment. He is sitting outside your office. If it were not for the Rule, I would have booted him myself."

"Very well. I will see him, but it will be after Vespers."

Haskell, who had begun to join the monks for most communal prayer, could not help but notice the odd-looking fellow in the front pew. He was in his mid-thirties, but worn out. Gaunt and antsy, he stood six feet tall, with black hair graying prematurely. His suit looked tailor-made but worn with jagged strings. It was too big in his shoulders and hung off his body, tailored for a man his height plus thirty pounds.

The man struggled to sit still. Between efforts at piety, he would have bouts of twitching and squirming that were difficult to watch, let alone endure. His shoulders would rise violently, his arm shaking as if dangling a bracelet. He turned his wrist to and fro as if it were sore. Hard blinks of his eyes and the rising and falling of his eyebrows seemed never-ending, save a few seconds here and there when he called himself back to piety.

Haskell was rarely distracted in prayer. He had, in fact, reached a point of becoming oblivious of the congregation. But this man's external struggle for comfort betrayed the raging internal struggle for peace. Haskell felt sorry for him, wanting to walk down, lay his hands upon his head, and say the words that Jesus spoke to the tumultuous seas: "Peace. Be still."

After the close of Vespers, Haskell decided to join the community in the refectory. He felt drawn to meet the troubled man who, due to invitation by the good abbot, had joined the monks for dinner.

When Haskell walked in, he saw the man sitting with some younger monks. Haskell made his way through the crowded room and, to the surprise of his brothers, sat next to the visitor.

"Welcome. My name is Brother Haskell."

The man replied softly, "I'm Thomas. Thomas Murphy."

"And what brings you here, Mr. Murphy?"

"I've asked your Abbot if I can stay here for a while."

"Why?" asked Haskell.

Thomas cleared his throat. "Well, I tried Wall Street. That didn't work. I tried women. That didn't work. I tried drinking. That didn't work . . . When all else fails, try Christianity."

Haskell leaned back in his chair, gazed up at the ceiling, and softly repeated to himself, "When all else fails, try Christianity."

Thomas looked surprised that the monk was cogitating so intently on his words.

Finally, Haskell leaned toward Thomas. "Magnificent, Thomas Murphy. Magnificent."

At that, Haskell stood up and returned to his cell.

Chapter 4

Money

1936

For Brother Haskell, fasting was a peculiar thing. It has been used throughout all of history for a variety of reasons. In the fifth century BC, Hippocrates prescribed abstinence from food and drink after observing that the sick lose their appetite; the Hellenistic healing cult of Asclepius believed that divinity would share their wisdom in dreams and visions only after the devotee emptied himself physically and detached himself from worldly affairs; Native Americans fasted before and during their sacred vision quests; and Gandhi nearly died twice in fasting strikes against violent protests.

Virtually every major religion uses fasting to make its adherents more aware of the divine voice in their lives. We are not angels. If we were, fasting would make no sense. Our bodies are part of our very being. And if we desire our being to be attuned to a mystical experience or the still small voice that resides in each of us, there must be some degree of ascetism. Not only do our bodies distract the spirit, but our desire to transcend the daily ritual of comfort and ease must be made known to both our bodies and God. Just as Christ fasted for forty days and forty nights in the searing heat of the desert, one must find some way to deny oneself in this unprecedented age of opulence and repose in order to better hear the voice of God.

Brother Haskell, however, fasted to attune himself not just to the voice of God but also to the voice of others. Even at the age of twenty-five, he was becoming a source of uncanny wisdom in the monastery. People would visit him in his hermitage, pose a question—usually one of spiritual significance—and in response, he would do the unthinkable. He would do the most unusual and yet intriguing thing possible, something that unintentionally gave rise to mystery in the community, something so mysterious that monks (particularly younger ones) came to see him as a sort of oracle from ancient times.

And what was this most unusual, intriguing, and mysterious thing? He would listen attentively until the person was done speaking, bow his head in silent consideration, and more often than not tell the person to come back in a day, a week, or sometimes a month. He would then fast and pray and even write about the issue. When the monk would return, he received clear and concise advice—truly, a rare gift if there ever was one.

Surely, Brother Haskell thought to himself, everyone on Earth must communicate like this. Why, he thought, would one answer an important question without proper consideration? He also found, to his surprise, that many people returned much more open to the advice given; for when the question was asked, the passions were at their zenith and the intellect at its nadir. Time, Haskell found, was not unlike a cold bath: it cooled the passions.

The demand on Haskell's time had become great. He had, however, been declining more and more requests for advice. His usual answer was sincere: "I am too young to have a meaningful reply. I suggest you visit Abbot Gregory." And on most occasions, the monk would say, "But Abbot Gregory sent me to you!"

"Well then," Haskell would say, "come back in a month."

And so, Brother Haskell would prepare for many of these encounters with a mild fast: the skipping of a meal, or at least reduction of a meal, or, worst of all, eating his least favorite food. This, he found, was of greater sacrifice and required far greater self-discipline than abstinence. In fact, Brother Bruno and Brother Matthias would know something important was going on when Haskell sat at table and said, "Please pass the mayonnaise."

Abbot Ambrose had informed Haskell that the twitching Thomas would be visiting him in the coming days. Haskell had not spoken with him since his first encounter but noticed that it only took a few days for the new visitor to settle into a routine. After a week or so, the twitching subsided.

But Abbot Ambrose had forewarned Haskell, "This guy is different from the others who come and go." When Haskell asked how so, the abbot just shook his head and said, "I don't mean in all good ways. He is just different. There is something different in his motives, in his reasoning, in his objectives. He is willing, but I'm not sure willing for what purpose. He feels fully here and not here at the same time. I'm hoping you can help me with that."

Thus, Haskell found ample reason to prepare for Thomas's visit with a day of fasting—except for a spoon of mayonnaise for breakfast, lunch, and dinner. If Haskell had quarried from the ground the largest boulders, built a twelve-foot-high altar, taken the fatted calf from the abbey's farm, slaughtered it with a handmade knife, built a raging fire to engulf the carcass, and drizzled incense on the flames to sweeten the smoke rising to the heavens, it would not have been as perfect a sacrifice as the three spoonful's of mayonnaise.

And so, on the appointed evening after Vespers, Haskell sat quietly in his cell with a mostly empty stomach. He sat at his little wooden table, closed his eyes, and silenced internal thoughts and passions, save one: his awareness of the presence of God in the present moment. These were his favorite moments. It was the sacrament of the present moment—and this day, it was for thirty minutes of perfect stillness and silence.

Haskell knew that Thomas's visit would be taxing, but he did not know why. He believed, he knew, that those external signs of anxiety were contagious, and while Haskell wanted to know his story, he did not want to personally know the tension Thomas carried around with himself.

Just before hearing his guest arrive, Haskell experienced an uncomfortable yet increasingly familiar sensation: he sensed him before he heard him. This was rather disconcerting. On occasion, he seemed to sense the dominant emotion of his guests. In this case, it was an extreme sense of anxiety. A wave of worry crashed into Haskell's peace of heart, causing him to sink ever so slightly in his chair.

Then he heard the fall of footsteps. He straightened back up in his chair. "Come," he said before Thomas was able to tap on the door.

Thomas slowly pushed open the door, poking his head in. Haskell sat quietly at his table and unfolded his hands toward the chair across from him. Thomas sheepishly took his seat.

Haskell sat like a statue carved from black marble. Even his eyes were still and rarely blinked. His breath was so faint that a visitor might think he sat there dead. And while Haskell's body made manifest the serenity of his soul, Thomas's tense and fidgeting body betrayed the anxiety of his.

Uncomfortable with the silence, Thomas broke it. "Abbot Ambrose said I should come see you."

Haskell made no reply.

Thomas began to chuckle but caught himself. Haskell tilted his head and furrowed his brow wondering what was funny.

"Sorry. It's just that the abbot said he wanted me to visit his resident hermit who was wise and would give good counsel. I guess I was expecting . . ."

"An old man."

"Well, yes. A very old man, frankly. Not a black man younger than me." Thomas caught himself, "Oh, but . . . but not that there's a problem with you being a negro. I mean, of course there's no problem with being a negro. I mean, I don't have a problem with you being . . . or . . . I'm happy to get advice from a negro." Thomas took a deep breath, threw up his arms and said, "Ah, rats! I'm just gonna shut up and let you do the talking."

And with that, he folded his arms and shook his head in frustration.

"Why are you upset?" Haskell asked.

While Thomas's face twisted some more, Haskell could hear his teeth clanging against each other as part of another nervous tick.

"I don't know. I'm just learning, I guess, that every time I open my mouth, something stupid comes out. And I'm sick of it."

"If you truly understand that, then you will become a saint."

"What do you mean?"

"Proverbs says, 'He that setteth bounds to his words is knowing and wise.'"

"I sure need bounds. I've always needed bounds."

"There is a simple way to find them."

"Find what?"

"Bounds."

"Oh. How?"

"By thinking before you speak. But in order to do that, you must be comfortable with the silence. Few men are. It is not that men desire to say words. It is that they fear the silence that lies between words. When you no longer fear the silence, you will have little reason to regret your words."

Thomas nodded his head and, with a mocking posture and tone of voice, said, "Mr. Murphy, think before you speak."

"Who said that?"

"Sister Mary Margaret. My eighth-grade teacher. I've been running my mouth a long time. In fact, that's exactly what ruined me."

Haskell thought for a moment: Should he inquire or remain silent? Some need a prompt to get going; others were more likely to divulge to a silent listener, as if questions stifled the thought. Thomas seemed the latter. So, he pushed his chair back, crossed his legs beneath his habit, and folded his hands, all of which communicated, *I'm in this for the long haul.*

"I was a stockbroker in New York before the crash. I started at twenty-two years old—a wiz-kid, they called me. The 'gift of gab'—as my grandmother called it—brought in a lot of business for our firm. A few years later, I wasn't the wiz-kid. I was the Rain Maker. I made the clientele and their money pour in like rain."

He stopped briefly and twitched hard for a moment, as if something he said physically tortured him. "My investors made great returns between '26 and '29. Business was booming. And I was a bachelor in New York with more money than I knew what to do with. I enjoyed all that New York had to offer, especially night clubs. They didn't call them the roaring '20s for nothing. It roared, especially . . ." he cleared his throat, "the lady lions, if you know what I mean."

"No. I don't. But proceed."

Thomas squirmed in his chair. "Jazz clubs, a new automobile every year, tailored suits, booze, lady friends. Sorry, Brother. Does this stuff bother you?"

"Your story does not bother me in the least. Your discomfort bothers me greatly."

Thomas's eyes searched for something in the room to land on other than the stoic black monk who had yet to look away.

"Anyway, I left my childhood faith in the past. All that remained was an occasional sense of guilt waking up next to a new woman on Sunday morning, knowing my grandmother never missed Mass. Ever. And one more remnant remained. Her rosary. For some reason, I kept it on my desk."

"Tell me about her," Haskell said, leaning forward.

Thomas's eyes drifted off to somewhere in the past.

"My mother died in childbirth when I was a boy, and so did a little baby girl. Then my father died, or was killed, I should say, in a shanty town, or Hooverville, as some are calling them. Just trying to help a young girl being harassed by Irish mobsters. They shot him point blank in the chest. Lived long enough to tell the doc what happened, who told me. I was twelve years old."

"Twelve," Haskell whispered to himself as he felt a cold chill run down his spine. He now understood why the abbot had sent Thomas to him. For the first time in this discussion, Haskell looked down and away, lost in memories he had not visited recently.

"Brother, are you okay?"

Haskell looked back at Thomas. "Yes. Just thoughts for another conversation. Please continue."

"So my grandmother took me in, raised me as best she could. Years later, I found myself working as a clerk in a brokerage firm and brought clients to the firm, all of whom were from church. It was an easy sell because those good people wanted to help me. They knew my story. I saw the Catholic diocese as an untapped market, and I decided to tap it. I worked referrals to different pastors. I held parish meetings. I even memorized Bible verses: 'He who soweth sparingly, shall also reap sparingly:

and he who soweth in blessings, shall also reap blessings.' And: 'The way of a fool is right in his own eyes: but he that is wise hearkeneth unto counsels.'

"At this point, I would just bring the clients to a firm partner, they would give me a little commission, but they would run with it. When I turned twenty, they promoted me to a junior broker. I expanded out to a broader market but held on to the Catholic market myself.

"Shortly thereafter, my grandmother died. I sold every possession she had, except this," and he took out her rosary from his pocket. "As I said, this became my only attachment to my upbringing, except guilt.

"For the next five years, I became the biggest producer in the firm. And I ran hard and fast the entire time. There were bumps along the road, personally and professionally, but as they say, 'Volume covers a multitude of sin.' Whatever trouble I found myself in, rainmaking solved it. Until the Babson Report."

"I'm sorry," Haskell said. "I'm not familiar."

"Almost seven years ago today, September 5, 1929, Roger Babson, the esteemed investment strategist, gave a talk at a big conference in Massachusetts. The transcript was wired to Wall Street that very day. I'll never forget the words. I read them many times throughout October, November, December, and even through the next year. 'A crash is coming, and it may be terrific . . . The vicious cycle will get in full swing and the result will be a serious business depression. There may be a stampede for selling which will exceed anything that the Stock Exchange has ever witnessed. Wise are those investors who now get out of debt.'"

Thomas looked away. "That's when I doubled down on the Bear Market. I told myself time and time again, *This is just a natural correction. Just a natural correction.* I told myself this so many times that I began to tell others the same."

He went quiet again. Haskell knew what was coming next, but headed it off, trying to put him at ease. "A prophet is never accepted in his hometown."

"But there's an irony here," Thomas said. "Wall Street listened enough for the market to slip three percent right after the Babson Report. So in a way, people listened. But on the other hand, people like me went to the opposite extreme. We doubled down. So it dropped three percent. Perfect! I called my clients and said there was an artificial dip caused by an anti-American academic named Babson. 'The market is healthier than ever,' I told them. But something, Brother, told me I was wrong. Something haunted me during those months. Instinct? A conscience? I don't know. But I felt that Catholic guilt. The same feeling when I woke up to a new lady friend."

He took a deep breath and began with twitching and violent jolts of his shoulder.

"And then October 29, Black Thursday, happened. It just . . . happened! My partners and I sat in my office staring at the ticker, which came in slow, real slow. Hours behind. Purgatory slow. The reason, and we knew it, was that so much selling was happening that the ticker couldn't keep up. It was the first time that office was silent, but it was the opposite kind of silence that you have here. It was an unhealthy silence of fear."

"Opposite extremes often have similar appearances," said Haskell.

"Well, in this case, it did. It was as silent as a hermitage. By the time the bell rang, the market had fallen 12 percent. I didn't go home. I sat at the office all night, running numbers, calculating how much my clients lost, how much I lost. The next day, the market popped back a little: propped up by big bankers buying US Steel, playing psychology with investors. But the following Monday, another huge hit happened. It was then we knew it was over.

"Babson was right. And my many clients—many of them hard-working families—suffered catastrophic financial ruin because of my advisement.

"I reread the Babson Report and concluded this was going to be a multiyear fix of an inflated market. But I wouldn't have predicted that by 1932, 80 percent of the market volume would be gone. A depression was obvious, but not a great depression.

"A rumor came up to my office that a man in Lower Manhattan, just around the corner from the Exchange, jumped out of his window. My life as I knew it was over. I was personally broke. My car would be sold.

My apartment. My shares were worthless. No one would buy even at 70 percent below value. And I couldn't bear to face the families I had ruined.

"There I sat at my desk, totally alone. I thought of my mother, who I barely remembered. I thought of my father, who died for a noble cause. I thought of my grandmother, who died trying her best to raise me. I thought of my girlfriends who had no use for a bankrupt playboy. I thought of my bankrupt partners down the hall whom I never liked anyway. There was no one left. And I envied the poor chap flattened on 23rd Street. He had escaped the hellish recovery that was to come. But I feared the sidewalk not finishing the job.

"I pulled open my drawer and stared at my revolver. I picked it up and held it to my head. I looked at my grandmother's rosary on my desk, said, 'God forgive me,' closed my eyes, and pulled the trigger."

He paused. His bottom lip quivered and eyes clenched tight as if he could hear the click of the cylinder turnover.

Haskell took a deep breath and smiled. "You must have a very thick skull."

A small smile crept onto Thomas's face. "It took me a second to realize I wasn't dead. I put the gun back in the drawer and slammed it shut. I burst into tears, dropping my head to my desk for I don't know how long. I was flooded with guilt, but also with gratitude for my grandmother. I felt that she interceded for me somehow. There's no logic to it, but I just knew she was looking out for me. I picked up her rosary and squeezed it tight. Then turned my attention back to the revolver. I couldn't make sense of it. A round must have been missing. But I didn't want to know. I didn't want to know why it didn't go off. So I walked out, taking all my cash with me. With no job and nothing to live for, I lived as a drunk. I drank all I could, every day. The money eventually dried up. The firm closed down. I couldn't have come back even if I wanted to. Over the next six years, I landed a few positions on Wall Street, but all were heavily commissioned. I made barely enough to keep the most modest apartment. At times, I stood in soup kitchen lines just to get a meal. It was not as embarrassing as you might think; believe it or not, I saw some big rollers from my previous life in line with me. We were all suffering.

"By '33, the bottom stopped falling, but I didn't. I fell for another three years until I met a man, a former stockbroker himself, who'd hit the bottom with the Crash. Bill Wilson. He had figured out a way to stay sober by helping others stay sober. A group of friends he brought together kept me on the wagon. And I think I helped some of them, too. At this time, Bill actually lived in Ohio but came to New York on occasion to meet with the groups following his system. He called it the Twelve Step Program to help with addiction to alcohol."

"Our patron, Saint Benedict, had a twelve-step program to help with addiction to self. Chapter Seven of the Rule," Haskell added.

"Really? Well, I should probably look into that too." He laughed. "Anyway, it was Bill Wilson who told me one night after a meeting, 'You're Catholic in your bones, you know. You'll never escape it.' And that was six months ago. His words resonated in a big way. I visited a few monasteries up north, but either they didn't like me or I didn't like them. So, I learned of a monastery in the South, of all places, far away from Wall Street, far away from those families I hurt. And now, I am here."

Haskell sighed after taking it all in. "Why?"

Thomas hesitated. "Why what?"

"Why are you here now? Why have you been visiting monasteries? I remember your answer in the refectory about, *When all else fails, try Christianity*. But why monasteries?"

"I want to try something that can't fail."

"Something that guarantees a—what do you call it—a rate of return?"

"Exactly. A guaranteed rate of return. Perfect."

"Do you know what the return will be?"

"I wish."

"Do you want to know?"

"Of course."

"The return is ten-fold. Jesus promised that."

Thomas smiled and said, "That's a pretty good return, so long as it's annual."

"It will compound for eternity."

"That's a hell of a return."

"No. It's a heaven of a return."

"Of course."

"But do you know what you have to invest to be guaranteed that return?"

"I guess I have to follow the commandments. But don't you worry," Thomas said assuredly. "I'm doing that now."

"If you want a guaranteed return, you must do more than follow the Ten Commandments. Those are the prerequisites for being eligible for a return. You must sell all you have and give the money to the poor. And then you must love God with all your heart, soul, mind, and strength."

"I don't have much left to sell. Just a few worthless stock certificates, which could one day be valuable, I suppose."

"But that's the easy part. You see, every monk here has taken a vow of poverty, but few live it. Every monk here loves God, but few do so with all their heart, soul, mind, and strength—as commanded."

"Come on. You guys love God all day."

"Not all day. Monks pray a few times a day, but only a handful pray without ceasing, as Saint Paul instructs. *All* is a pesky word. Would you have told a client to sell his house, car, take all his cash from the bank, and put *all* their worth in the market?"

"Never. That's crazy."

"What is it called when assets are spread around?"

"A diverse portfolio."

"Yes. That's it. Worldly investors must have a diverse portfolio. Not heavenly investors. Everything goes into one stock. Everything. One hundred percent. If you give God 99.9 percent of your heart, you're simply saying, *I refuse to give you everything. I'm hedging my bets. I put more faith in my own decision-making rather than your own. I want the future option to be my own god, just in case you fail me. I am diversifying my portfolio in order to remain secure. Your stock, God, might not bear the return you promised. And maybe my own efforts will grant me a better return.*"

"It defies all rules of sound investing," Thomas said.

"It defies all rules of worldly living. It defies everything in this life, of all the rules and regulations of the kingdom of man. But it was the very kingdom of man that collapsed by 80 percent in recent years. All the while, your investment in the kingdom of God could have begun to compound for eternity."

In the fall of 1936, as the nation turned gray in its depression, the leaves turned radiant in their slow death. Both the sadness and beauty of death was all around. And Father Vincent Roth believed that Abbot Ambrose was leading the monastery to its own slow death with his magnanimous support of all those around suffering from the depression.

Money is a peculiar thing. Scripture says not that money is the root of all evil but that the love of money is. Money is a weapon of God against the devil, and a weapon of the devil against God. Without money—or profit more precisely—there is no financial charity. There are no non-profit organizations without for-profit organizations sharing their surplus. It is too easy to say that money matters not: just ask the father of three standing in line at the soup kitchen. Truly, the only people who say money does not matter are those with tons of it, or (perhaps) those with none of it. The rest of humanity is squeezed in the middle, in the valley of reality.

Christ Himself spoke more of money than any other topic, save the kingdom of God. And, at least according to Him, the two are intricately woven together. How one treats money in this life will be accounted for in the next.

And yet, how can one give to the least of our brethren if one has no profit? It was that great doctor of the Church, Saint Francis de Sales, who defined holiness as fulfilling the duties of one's station in life, which for most of us includes making and saving money.

Likewise, a religious community has its own duties, but these duties seem to span a great length of time. A monastery has duties that go past, present, and future, just as the Church does Herself. These duties produce a patrimony in all shapes and sizes: the spiritual and theological traditions of the Church, art and music, countless devotions, priceless relics, holy vessels adorned with ancient jewels (befitting for the dwelling of the Most Blessed Sacrament), and yes, land. Lots and lots of land. So much land, in fact, that Henry VIII figured out, with whisperings in his ear from Thomas Cromwell, that the surest way to reward his aristocratic constituency following his usurping of Church authority in England (and the severing of several wives' heads), was to bequeath unto them estates of great wealth. And there was only one place to turn: the religious houses of the Catholic Church. Thus, every monastery has an inclination to hold on to its land with a defensive grip and a suspicious mind.

Even when the Church gets to keep its own land, it must be mindful not to squander the inheritance (or the means of production) of its progeny. Such a squandering could, indeed, be an affront against charity and thus a sin of the greatest magnitude.

And yet, if one is to live each day as if it were his last; if one kept his eyes fixed upon the heavens awaiting the Second Coming, why plan anything for tomorrow? Does not the Father love us more than the birds of the air? Will He not provide for our every need?

Be not anxious for tomorrow, for tomorrow will be anxious for itself.

It should come as no surprise, then, that in the thick of the Great Depression, the monks of Good Shepherd were no different in their struggle between charity to neighbor and charity to those who would occupy the choir stalls in a century. If there is one thing for certain about Benedictine monks, it is that they do not think in terms of years, or even decades, but centuries. If they have learned anything in 1,400 years, it is that the Benedictines will be huddled up in choir stalls until the end of time.

It was at a senior council meeting that Father Roth was tasked with reporting the financial status of the community, when the complex relationship of faith and money showed its ugly face. To compound the sensitivity of the moment, the abbot had begun to have Brother Haskell attend the meetings despite any official role.

"Your generosity, Abbot, is reaching an extreme, which as we know from Aristotle, leaves the realm of virtue and becomes the vice of wastefulness.

My report shows that we have increased our payroll at the monastery by 25 percent since the Crash."

"Twenty-five percent? Is that all?" asked Abbot Ambrose, genuinely surprised.

"And yet our croppers are keeping far more than ever and giving us far less than ever."

"With our permission, of course," replied the abbot.

"With *your* permission. And your permission must cease." The group of monks had become accustomed to such declarative tones from Father Roth. They had become so desensitized to such bluster that it rarely ruffled a feather.

"And our *tenants* are still giving us enough produce to live on?" asked the abbot.

"If you call the recent produce livable."

"I haven't attended a funeral recently, so I'd say livable, yes."

The room chuckled.

"And how are their pecuniary deposits to us?" asked the abbot.

"Worse than the produce. Decreasing at an unacceptable rate."

The abbot nodded. "Our savings account, how is that looking?"

"By the grace of God, we haven't had to dip into that yet. But that day is coming."

"When will that day be here?"

"I don't know but . . ."

"Estimate."

Father Roth scratched at his chin, thinking. "At the current rate of the croppers' failure, a year. Maybe less."

"The croppers' failure?" the abbot asked. "Is that what you call their work in both the greatest depression the nation has ever seen, compounded with the worst drought and hottest summer on record? Is that really what you call it?"

"Never mind what I call it. The point is . . ."

"How long would our savings last with a significantly depleted pecuniary contribution by the tenants?"

"An impossible question. I don't know."

"Estimate."

Father Roth threw his arms in the air. "Hell if I know. Three to four years, at most."

"Very good. Thank you, Father," said the abbot, calming the tension. "Now, how much land can we sell?"

Father Roth gasped. "Surely, Abbot, you would never drain the inheritance of future monks?"

"Answer the question please, Father Roth."

"Approximately two thousand acres, if anyone could ever afford it."

"Excuse me," Father Henry interjected, "but I've heard recently about some local businessmen buying up excess land from local farmers."

"Interesting," said the abbot. "I'd like to know what the going rate is per acre."

"Abbot!" yelled Father Roth. "You must not. You have a moral duty to posterity. We must preserve our core precept of stability."

The abbot said with quiet passion, "No. Our core precept is not stability. It is living the Gospel. It is to see Christ in others. It is to feed the hungry and clothe the naked. It is to love others as ourselves. Our core precept manifests in many ways, but not in stability."

Father Roth slapped the table. "We are Benedictines!"

"But first we are Christians!" yelled Abbot Ambrose, slapping the table himself.

Father Roth sat back in his chair with a look of exhaustion. He breathed heavily as he dropped his head. "You are an existential threat to this community, Abbot, which will surpass you in all things." He finally looked up. "You are a mere steward of a most sacred territory of God's kingdom on Earth. If monks of the Middle Ages had been so flippant about their moral duty to posterity, the Benedictine Order would have never saved Western civilization. All of Europe would belong to the pagans. Muhammadans would be kneeling in the great cathedrals of Italy and France and Spain worshiping their false prophet. The papacy would be nothing more than a noisy bishop, like the patriarchs of the East. And the evangelization of the New World would have never been possible.

"This land we sit upon would be filled with cow dung belonging to some illiterate anti-Catholic farmer rather than educated, prayerful monks who do the will of Almighty God. And you would sell it off for what? To fill one more empty belly of a cropper? I thank almighty God that those brave and virtuous souls who occupied your chair throughout the ages had more wits and wisdom than you."

The monks looked at Father Roth with a mixture of astonishment and horror. Brother Matthias noticed the slightest smile come over Haskell's face, as if he welcomed the showdown and relished the coming of the abbot's reply.

The abbot, who had patiently and perhaps strategically allowed Father Roth to work himself into a rage, sat still for what seemed an eternity. In such dramatic moments, ten seconds of silence can seem like one minute, thirty seconds can seem five minutes, and a full minute can feel like a life sentence to solitary confinement. The good abbot sat for a full minute with his head bowed and eyes closed. Those who knew him intimately understood exactly why such a precise time had passed. It was not that a full minute had passed but rather three slow and deliberate Hail Marys were prayed. And then, he returned to business.

Abbot Ambrose arose from the table, looking a good six inches taller than he was. He stared deep into the eyes of Father Roth. "So long as I am abbot of this monastery, the monks of this abbey will be the first to feel the pain of hunger in all of Capstone. And if it comes to it, pray God it does not, your abbot will be the first to starve to death. And you, my good prior, will be the second to starve to death. I promise you Father Roth, you will starve before any illiterate cropper on my land does. And you will do so with charity in your heart as Jesus Christ and our Holy Father Saint Benedict would command. Or will you place your holy cross on the shoulder of a more willing monk just to live on this mortal coil a few more days?"

Father Roth nodded slowly, taking it all in. "With your permission, I will take my leave."

"Granted," replied the abbot.

Father Roth rose from the table, walked out of the room, and closed the door.

The abbot chuckled and shook his head. "Money. What a peculiar thing."

The senior council looked around at each other looking for clarity, except for Haskell.

"Money is what drove Thomas Murphy to us," said the abbot, "and it is driving Father Roth away."

"How is our guest?" asked Father Henry, changing the subject.

"Haskell?" said the abbot, gesturing to him.

"He is . . ." Haskell paused, searching hard for the right words ". . . confused."

"Can you elaborate?" asked the abbot.

"Thomas is the Rich Young Man, even though he is broke. He is searching for a deal to be struck in order to find salvation. He's putting stock, one could say, in his actions, expecting an immediate return during this Earthly life. If he does not change, he will meet yet another worldly catastrophe."

The room thought for a moment over Haskell's words.

"Perhaps he could help with our finances," Father Henry said. "We could use the expertise."

"Good thinking," said the abbot.

"No," snapped Haskell. "Excuse me, Abbot." He caught himself and settled. "In my opinion, Abbot, this is the worst thing you could do to Thomas."

"And why is that?"

"Because it is that very world that drove him to the brink. It is that very world that he must escape. He must live wholly apart from the kingdom of man and wholly within the kingdom of God. He must sweep floors and wash dishes and say his prayers. And we must," Haskell gestured with his arms to show all must be on board, "praise him for such works and engage him with fellowship and speak only of heavenly things to him. I'd go so far as to hide the *Wall Street Journal* from him. He still sits in the recreation room and reads it. And for him, it is a tether preventing him from forward motion. He must break free—totally and completely free—from the kingdom of man."

"He asked me just the other day," said Father Henry, "what would happen to his stocks if he were to take final vows. You could tell he was thinking about them rebounding one day."

"Exactly," said Haskell. "Which is why we should commit here and now to never, under any circumstance, take his stocks upon final vows. They must go elsewhere, for his sake. Anything else would be a grave injustice to him."

"Money," said the Abbot. "A peculiar thing."

A few weeks later, Abbot Ambrose was working quietly in his office when he heard footsteps running through the hallway. A bang on the door followed.

"Come in."

Brother Matthias burst in. "Walter Brooks," he began to say between breaths, "is waiting for you . . . in the parlor."

"What?" The abbot rose so quickly he nearly knocked his chair to the ground. "Where is Hack?"

"I've already got him in his cell."

"Good. Good. That's good." He made his way around his desk, out of his office and down the hall. "What does he want?"

"Other than to meet with you, I don't know. But Father Roth greeted him, as if this was expected."

The abbot considered this. "Very well."

Upon entering the parlor, both Father Roth and Walter Brooks stood up to greet the abbot. There he was, the man Abbot Ambrose had prayed to never see again, to never hear his name again, standing there in his double-breasted suit and polished shoes and slicked back hair. The only exposure the abbot had to Walter Brooks these last few years was reading about him in the paper every so often as the subject of various financial successes.

"Abbot Ambrose!" Walter exclaimed with a rather artificial flamboyance, as if they were long lost friends. "So good to see you. Twelve years, I believe."

He extended his hand.

The abbot shook his hand and quietly replied, "Yes. Twelve years."

They all took their seats. The abbot made it a point to not look at Father Roth.

"How are the good monks of Good Shepherd?" Walter asked.

"Very well, thank you. And how is your family?"

"Splendid. As you may know, we sold all of our mills just as milling was slipping. That was in '28. And then we put all the cash into land. As they say, timing is everything."

Land.

That was it. The abbot now understood exactly why Walter was sitting in his parlor and exactly why Father Roth sat with him. A righteous anger welled up in his heart. But this rage was followed by the sadness of betrayal.

Betrayal. Of all the sins the human heart can muster. Of all the sins codified by Pope Saint Gregory the Great. Who does Dante Alighieri place in the deepest pit of hell, in the ninth ring of the Inferno? Who does he place not only close to Lucifer, but in his very jaws, devoured by the Prince of Darkness for all eternity? Is it the lustful or the gluttonous? Is it the greedy, the heretics, the violent?

No. It is the treacherous and the betrayers, trapped in ice, for they are the farthest from the light and warmth of the Son. Here you have Cain who killed his brother, and Mordred, the traitorous son of King Arthur. You have Antenor, the infamous Trojan soldier who betrayed his city to the Greeks. And at the very center of hell lies Lucifer, with his multiple heads, trapped in ice. He, the brightest of the angels, who betrayed God more than any other, chews on the flesh of the great betrayers of antiquity, including Brutus, who orchestrated the assassination of Julius Caesar, and, of course, Judas Iscariot.

The closer the villain is to his master, the greater the sting is felt. In the Benedictine Order, a prior's betrayal of his abbot's trust is an offense of the greatest magnitude. And it would sting an abbot more than any other failing of a monk. It was no different this day in the parlor of Good Shepherd.

"In fact," added Walter Brooks, "not one penny went to Wall Street. We saw this coming a mile away. Anyone who would have looked at the milling industry in '28 would have known Wall Street was going to take a hit. Main Street always suffers before Wall Street. Yep. We avoided the crash all together. 'A Brooks must always have impeccable timing,' my dad used to say."

"How is your dad?" the abbot asked, forcing the pleasantries.

"Oh, he died a few months back. So, I'm expanding the families' enterprise. Long overdue."

"I'm sorry to hear of his passing."

"I think it's only fitting, Abbot, that I use my good fortune to help local farmers who were unprepared for the economic downturn, which brings me to the reason for my visit."

"Go on," said the abbot.

"My real estate company is buying up excess land in your area by giving cash to those in need. Right now, land does these farmers little good. What they need is cold, hard cash. And I have it. Good ol' Father Roth contacted my company, saying you wanted to investigate the value of your acreage."

Father Roth stirred a little in his seat as Abbot Ambrose conspicuously refrained from looking at him.

"Being my Alma Mater," Walter continued, "I decided to handle this deal myself."

The abbot was quiet for a moment and then coolly said, "I'm sorry to have wasted your time Walter, but I recently decided not to sell any land." At that, he stood up. Yet with a mixture of confusion and obstinance, Walter remained in his seat, looking up at the abbot. But as the abbot stood motionless, it became evident that both Walter and Father Roth had to comply.

"I'm sorry to hear that," Walter said, slowing rising from his chair, keeping his eye all the while on the abbot. "But I hope you'll not keep me from the satisfaction of supporting my Alma Mater." He pulled out his checkbook.

"That isn't necessary," said the abbot.

"Yes, I believe it is."

"Very well. But your Alma Mater is not the abbey. It is the school, which is just across the grounds. You may remember." The abbot pointed through the window.

Walter's pen stopped moving. His eyes took a long blink. "All right then. I'll see myself out. Thank you for your time."

After Walter had left, the abbot turned his gaze upon Father Vincent Roth, who somehow managed not to bear any sign of guilt.

"How dare you," Abbot Ambrose said in a whisper.

"I followed your instructions, did I not?" asked Father Roth with his usual conceit.

"How dare you!" this time with a roar never before heard from the abbot.

"Walter would clearly offer the best price. And Haskell is tucked away. Besides, it has been twelve years. He wouldn't even recognize him. Don't overreact."

"You are no longer prior."

"What?"

"You are no longer on my senior council."

"Abbot, you can't be . . ."

"You are forbidden to have any contact outside these four walls without my express permission!"

"Outrageous!"

"If we have to consider relocation to another abbey, so be it."

"I've given my life to this abbey, you insolent fool!"

"You have given yourself to your own agenda, to your own vision of what this abbey should be, to your own notion of a paradise within these walls. I have taken your resistance in stride. I have appreciated a strong voice in opposition to my own. But this . . . this endangers not only the life of Hack . . ."

"You mean Brother Haskell? He is no longer a child. He was never your child."

"You have endangered the entire community," the abbot continued, undeterred.

"No, *you* have endangered the community all these years by thinking yourself above the Rule."

The door opened slowly. It was Abbot Gregory. He shuffled over to Ambrose, put his hand around his elbow and said, "Time to go, Ambrose." In that instant, Ambrose's rage broke. His body seemed to shrivel into exhaustion and sadness. Abbot Gregory steadily led him out of the room by the arm, like a wounded man. Father Roth was left in the parlor, alone.

Despite Abbot Gregory's feet shuffling down the hall, Ambrose looked the older of the two, fatigued beyond his years. Abbot Gregory led him to the chapel and into the choir stall. He sat in his regular stall, patting the seat next to him. Ambrose complied.

Not a word was said. They sat in silence for over an hour. Gregory breathed heavy from his age. Ambrose breathed heavy from holding back tears. Every now and then throughout that long hour, Gregory would reach over and pat Ambrose's knee. But nothing needed to be said. The older of the abbots understood everything. The younger of the abbots did not. But he was wise enough to do exactly what Gregory prescribed.

The monks, including Father Roth, poured into Vespers. The young monk who saw Ambrose in his stall simply took another seat. Ambrose noticed Hack did not attend.

And the life of monks began anew with the sweet chant, "Deus, in adiutorium meum intende. Domine, ad adiuvandum me festina."

That night, Ambrose visited Haskell in his cell. He found him sitting stoically at his table praying with his black leather journal open before him. A stack of such journals had piled up in the corner of his room over the past twelve years. One could not help but wonder about the wealth of insight jotted down on those pages.

"Are you all right?" asked Abbot Ambrose.

"It's more important that you ask yourself that question," said Haskell.

The abbot dropped his head, as if all pretense of being the leader had fallen away. "I am now. Thanks to Gregory." He paused and looked deeply into Brother Haskell's eyes. "Walter has no idea, as far as I can tell."

"I'm glad. But it is what it is. It will be whatever it will be. God's providence will reign."

"Yes."

"Maybe you should take his money. You could help a lot of families."

"Never." The abbot shook his head. "If there is one clear message from prayer, it is to stay the hell away from that man. I am completely sure. I will never change my mind."

"Well, that's that."

"That is that," the abbot repeated. He rose from the table and began to leave.

"Abbot Ambrose, forgive me," Haskell said. "But you, we, cannot escape God's providence. No matter your efforts. You must have peace of heart. Pride is the mother of anxiety; humility the mother of peace."

"When you have my responsibility, it is easier said than done."

"Not true. It is in fact done easier than said."

Abbot Ambrose gave Haskell a quizzical look. "Hack, I appreciate what you are saying, but there are things you do not understand."

"Of course, but do not change the subject. We are talking about your peace of heart, not my own level of organizational experience."

"Look, Hack, I'm only saying . . ."

"Respectfully, Abbot Ambrose, you are only saying something wrong. Your level of responsibility does not make peace of heart harder, but in fact makes peace of heart easier."

"Ha!" Abbot Ambrose burst out. "Easier? Really?"

"Really. You have been educated by the Church's finest minds. You have spent your life in prayer and fasting. You have been given the chair of a Benedictine abbot, responsible for nearly a hundred monks. Thus, peace of heart must be easier for you than nearly any other.

"You, Abbot Ambrose, have no intellectual or spiritual doubt about the omnipotence and omnipresence of God. You, Abbot Ambrose, have a lofty seat in the Church with all these monks praying for you daily, and thus you are filled with grace.

"All you must do is abandon yourself to God's will in the present moment, and the grace stored up for you will flow like a great deluge from heaven. There is no reason, no excuse, for anything other than complete peace of heart. You know, Abbot, that if you are trying to fulfill God's will at this very moment, then your life is perfect, even if the bricks of this great abbey were to crumble around your feet. Even if every monk betrayed you. Even if you were crucified out front of your abbey. The only measure of peace of heart is the desire to do God's will. So long as you possess this one truth, you possess all you need. Father Roth and Walter Brooks have no power over your relationship with God.

"In fact, if Walter were to drag me from here and string me up on the great oak tree out back, your peace of heart with God should not waver for even a second. This does not mean you would not suffer. This does not mean you should not hate the sin. But you know full well, better than I do, that your peace of heart shall never waver if your soul is desiring the will of God to reign in your life."

The abbot nodded. "Thank you, Hack." He turned to leave but turned back at the threshold. "By the way, given the fiasco with Walter, I got to thinking about which layman could be helpful at this time."

"And?"

"Eddie and Lily are coming to visit tomorrow."

Chapter 5

Lily

Lily made it a point to visit at least once a year. And for Haskell, every single visit felt too soon and yet never enough.

Lily had become the icon of femininity in Haskell's mind: the archetype of Jung, the form of Plato, or better yet, the Helen of Homer, the Beatrice of Dante.

In part, this was due to the limited experience he had with the gentler of the sexes. In part, it was due to the natural result of his time spent with her in Jefferson at a most delicate age. In part, it was because she was sublime. She was all that womanhood had to offer. She was a source of constant joy, of social charm without pomp, of grace without clout, of radiance without effort. She was a lady who could turn the heads of kings while she clasped the hand of a black servant. She was a woman who the Great Depression would never faze, for she retained in full the mountain-girl work ethic. In addition to all that, her husband said at regular intervals, "I've never heard her say a bad word about anyone."

Haskell would have not been a man had he not found her attractive on many levels. But such attraction was more difficult to put in its place when there was no other woman in his life to divert his focus. His attraction to Lily, it should go without saying, was as pure as it comes, which makes it no less difficult to put in its place.

His stomach turned as he entered the visiting parlor to meet Lily and Eddie.

"Hack!" She jumped from her seat in girlish fashion and wrapped her arms around his neck. His arms dangled to the side, uncertain of where to go.

"It's good to see you, too," he said pulling away ever so gently.

"It's been too long. But you look so good. You're bigger and stronger every time I see you. You done growing?"

"Hello there, Brother Haskell," Eddie said extending his hand.

Haskell thought that any remnant of that gangly young traveling salesmen he met in the dentist office twelve years ago was gone. Before Haskell stood a full-bodied man of premature gray, and a good ten years more on his face than time said should be there. After all, time is a relative thing—something a hermit need not be told. But this hermit had been reading about a popular physicist named Einstein who said the same thing. Haskell wondered if all that driving up and down the East Coast selling Bibles had sped up the aging process in a way similar to Einstein's theoretical spaceship that goes so fast it slows down time for its passenger. Whatever it was, it had surely taken a toll on Eddie. And the rate of this toll must have increased exponentially in the last twelve months. It was, in fact, sad for Haskell to conclude: success had vanquished youth.

But Lily had retained every bit of her youthful vigor. "Let's be sure to spend some one-on-one time after all this . . . whatever this is," Lily said grabbing on to Hack's arm.

The abbot and Henry were likewise in the room, the latter of whom was hoping to get down to business. He invited all to take their seats.

"How's business, Eddie?" asked the abbot.

"Actually, it's good. I can't take credit for such a strategic business model—dumb luck I guess—but selling Bibles door-to-door is ideal during a depression."

"Maybe not dumb luck," the abbot inserted. "Maybe Divine Providence."

"Perhaps," Eddie agreed with a tinge of reluctance.

"Sorry, Eddie," Henry said. "Can you explain how the depression is good for business?"

"First, you have the unemployed happy to work on commission when otherwise they wouldn't consider it. Second, people answer their front door now more than ever. They have less reason to go out. The decision maker, usually the husband, is home more often than not, though its nearly always the wife pressuring him to make the purchase. And third, frankly, people turn to God in difficult times."

"Fascinating," said the abbot.

"We're happy to do good and do well at the same time," continued Eddie. "But we didn't always do well. No sir. In '29, just before the Crash, ironically, when Wall Street was booming, Main Street was hurting. And so was I."

He gave a quick glance over to Lily. He corrected himself.

"So were *we*. We were growing fast but had serious logistical and cash flow issues. Printing a Bible, you know, is no cheap endeavor. Anyway, this young lady here," tapping Lily on her knee that always seemed to be moving a bit with energy, "had to pawn her engagement ring—that little spec of a diamond," he said pointing to her ring finger, "just to make payroll. But we made it. Drove together over to the pawn shop and got back the ring."

"Amazing," the abbot said.

"Ya know, Lily was one of my best reps at that time."

"I'm not surprised, with that southern belle charm of yours," said the abbot.

She giggled and shrugged her shoulders in girlish fashion.

"My dear Abbot, I thank you for the intended flattery, but I much prefer that you think of me as a mountain girl, certainly not a southern belle."

"My apologies. But can you enlighten me on the distinction?"

"A southern belle, as far as my personal experience goes, conjures up an image of, well . . ." she hesitated, "I guess it isn't uncharitable to say—given she isn't a real person made in the image of God and only a figment of one woman's imagination—but southern belle conjures up an image of that pompous and fragile character, Scarlet O'Hara, as portrayed before the Civil War toughened her up. And for the life of me, I never once met a girl from Jefferson County who walked and talked with such entitlement or that flung herself this way and that," placing the back of her hand on her forehead with the look of fainting. "No way. We mountain girls had no time to play plantation princess. We were, forgive me, too darn busy being real women to play dress up. We were as tough from our girlhood as Ms. O'Hara was after all she endured. We were too busy keeping the cocks off the chickens to attend cocktail parties, too busy milking cows to pour milk in a dainty cup at teatime. The New River Valley is no place for an aristocratic socialite. A mountain girl. That's what this chip-toothed, lanky Bible salesman married."

She smacked Eddie's arm with the back of her hand.

Hack thought to himself that if any other person on Earth had smacked Eddie, he would live to regret it.

"Fascinating," the abbot said.

Haskell took a deep breath and looked at the floor, realizing he had been staring at Lily.

"Abbot, why'd you call us here?" Eddie asked.

"Oh yes, well . . ." He sat up in his chair. "You see, while the depression has been good for Bible sales, it has not been good for tenant farmers. And we have employed a good many locals in dire straits: cooks, groundsmen, handy men, mechanics . . . I think our cars get a tune up every few weeks and it now takes two cooks to butter bread and three gardeners to pull a weed. And as the saying goes, we are land rich and becoming cash poor."

"*Are* cash poor," Henry corrected his abbot.

"A matter of perspective," the abbot said. "Nonetheless, we have discussed selling good land to a good buyer—not just any buyer. And I was wondering if you had considered getting into real estate."

Eddie sat back in his chair. Lily bit her bottom lip and looked down. Her crossed leg began bouncing a little feverishly.

Eddie slowly began, "I've been considering diversifying outside of the business, considered shopping centers, a golf course, even cattle. But until this economy picks up, it's risky business."

"I see," said the abbot.

Lily's leg stopped bouncing. She ever so slightly turned her head toward her husband without even raising her eyes at him. Eddie cleared his throat and quickly added, "But that doesn't mean a donation is not warranted."

The leg started bouncing again.

The abbot perked up. "That certainly wasn't my intent. I had hoped for a fair business transaction. But Eddie, that's very generous of you. Thank you."

Eddie smiled as he pulled his checkbook from his jacket pocket. "We'd like to give the Abbey $3,000."

"Oh! That's so generous. God bless you!"

The leg came to a screeching halt again, noticeable to all in the room. Lily looked again toward her husband and gave him a manufactured smile.

"Darling," she began, and Eddie's shoulders dropped and his pen stopped moving. It was as if the word, *darling*, was her secret weapon. It was as if *darling* was such a conspicuous code between lovers for which even the celibate monk needed no translation. It was as if *darling* was at once soft yet sharp, sensual yet strong. Any onlooker would have gotten a penetrating insight into the intricate dynamics of this marriage by simply hearing Lily say *darling*. If poetry is language surged with meaning, Lily spoke poetry like no other.

"You know that swimming pool we've discussed?"

Eddie blinked.

"We don't need it right now, do we?"

Eddie sighed. "Let's make it $5,000."

Lily's posture perked back up. The leg began bouncing again.

"Yes. Let's . . ." she said with a girlish smile and little curl of the shoulders.

The abbot threw up his hands. "I . . . I just don't know what to say. Thank you, thank you, thank you."

"This will support the extra staff we've taken on for over a year," Henry said, a rare smile creeping over his face. "Praise God."

In his exuberance, the abbot turned to Haskell. "What do you say about that?"

"I say," he paused and forced himself to look away from Lily and directly at Eddie. "Your return will be tenfold." He could see Lily's gaze out of the corner of his eye. He looked at the floor again.

As they were leaving the abbot's parlor, Lily locked arms with Haskell. "You must show me your garden so we can talk."

The abbot took Eddie for a walk around campus to show what had changed and what had not since he was last there. Meanwhile, Haskell walked Lily directly through the monastery. Later, upon reflection, he wasn't sure if he had forgotten or didn't care about how improper this was. Logically, he thought to himself, it must be one of these two. Life shows, however, a third option, one in which intentionality is not entirely removed but not entirely present. He accounted for this lapse of mental acuity as a form of intoxication.

Whatever the cause, Haskell did the unthinkable and walked a woman right through the inner sanctums of Good Shepherd. Novices tucked their heads in near embarrassment, a few middle-aged monks smiled with energetic curiosity, but as luck would have it, they passed Father Roth. He shook his head. "Despicable."

"Pay him no attention," Haskell said. Lily shrugged.

They quickly reached the garden and slowly strolled through the rows.

"The summer was too hot and too long for my zucchini, tomatoes, and beans. But the fall crops are doing okay. The melons have made it."

"The mountains never seemed to have heat waves like this past summer," Lily said. "And oh, how I miss them! I can feel them calling to me at times."

"Why don't you go back?" Haskell asked.

"The business. It's all consuming."

"I see."

"Hack, why is something so successful so depressing?"

"How so?"

"Eddie has already surpassed his own goals. He makes more money than he ever thought possible. We've just built a beautiful home. Everyone respects Eddie, compliments him, and many serve him in one way or another. But he's losing the luster in his eye that caught my attention in that Jefferson dentist office. There's a sadness in him that seems to grow with his success."

Haskell nodded but knew not what to say.

"If I water these melons too much," he said pointing to both the cantaloupe and watermelon vines crawling out in chaotic form across the ground, "the smallest crack appears. Without fail, bugs catch a whiff of the sweet scent and infest it overnight."

Lily quietly considered his words. "What kind of bugs infest us?"

"On the one hand, there are only seven. Seven bugs you could say."

"Seven?"

"The capital sins: gluttony, lust, greed, wrath, sloth, envy, and pride."

"And on the other hand?"

"There is but one bug."

She waited.

"Pride. But that goes for all of us."

"I don't think of Eddie as prideful."

"Every man and woman is prideful. But let's stay on the sadness you mentioned."

"Well, then tell me why he's sad and how he can stop being sad."

Haskell found a bench, delicately detached her arm, and sat her down. "Spiritual sadness comes on slowly. It comes as we begin to take for granted our many blessings. As life challenges us with more difficulty, we forget how blessed we are. That's why a man in a foxhole can be beaming with joy just because gunfire ceases, but a year later in the safety of his home, he gets angry at his wife for not doing his laundry. Eddie is a fighter. And he must learn to be grateful for the things for which he no longer fights."

Lily looked away, uncharacteristically silent. The silence between them on that small bench in his small garden enclosed by the walls of the monastery courtyard reminded Haskell of sitting on the riverbank in the great valley enclosed by the glorious Blue Ridge Mountains. He breathed in the moment, wishing to reach into the essence of it, making time stand still. It was eternity, he knew, that resided just on the other side of his own present moment, like another great pasture that lay on the other side of a narrow pass on the New River. If he could reach in and touch eternity, the past, present, and future would become one. He would no longer just be on the bench in the garden of a courtyard but would be thirteen years old with seventeen-year-old Lily, on the riverbank, in the valley of the mountains. And life, he thought, would be as it should be.

Abbot Ambrose, Father Henry and Brother Haskell stood outside the monastery waving as Eddie and Lily pulled away. "A wealthy man," said Father Henry.

"A good man," the abbot replied.

"Indeed," said Father Henry.

"A great woman," Brother Haskell added.

"Indeed," said the abbot.

"Indeed," said Father Henry.

"Father Henry," said the abbot, turning to face him. "You are no longer sub-prior."

Henry tilted his head and furrowed his brow.

"You are now prior."

All the monastery, including Father Henry, knew this was coming since the abbot's conflict with Father Roth.

Henry bowed his head. "I will do my best."

The abbot smiled and smacked him on the shoulder. "What do you think of our new prior, Brother Haskell?"

"I think it's long overdue. But I think Father Henry's lesson on Hamlet comes to mind."

"How so?"

Haskell thought for a moment. "Father Henry taught me that the young Hamlet had to kill King Claudius, his uncle, because Claudius had killed Hamlet's father to steal the crown. But Hamlet paused when he had the opportunity. He realized he must kill Claudius, but only for the sake of justice rather than for the sake of revenge. So I must ask: Have you killed the former prior for justice or revenge?"

Henry gasped. "Brother, it is not for you to question the abbot."

"Justice or revenge?" Haskell asked again.

Abbot Ambrose tucked his hands beneath his habit and slowly lowered his head. "Can it be both?" he asked almost childlike, almost forgetting that Father Henry was present.

"No. Not for you," Haskell said definitively. "And you wonder why your heart is without peace."

"Good God . . ." the new prior said under his breath as he rubbed the back of his own neck and turned aside.

"Is it that obvious?" the abbot said sheepishly to Haskell.

"No. Not at all. But many important truths are not obvious."

"That act is done, either way."

"The act is done, but the motive is not. Motives can transcend time on occasion. You can still decide. And must decide. There is much work to be done."

"Much work?"

"With Father Roth."

"How so?"

"Father Roth may be a wolf, but he is also your sheep. And you are the shepherd. Good shepherds smell like their sheep."

The abbot nodded, began to smile, and looked at the disconcerted prior. "Father Henry, it seems that having Lily on his arm has awoken a sleeping giant."

"Apparently," Henry agreed. "A sleeping giant indeed."

Chapter 6

Awaking the Sleeping Giant

December 7, 1941

Silence can be a beautiful thing, especially in the brick laden halls of a monastery. Silence of human speech gives birth to many other less appreciated sounds: soft footfall of young and old monks with cowls pulled over heads and hands tucked in sleeves, gently moving to and from prayer and the privacy of one's cell; the sound of monks' breath between their common chant; the clanging of dishes at a silent meal. You can tell a lot about a man, a family, a community, from what you hear during silence.

Benedictine monasteries were not the only homes of silence on this fateful day. Silence swept the nation as families gathered around their radios and strained their ears to hear any update, any death toll, any battle cry. The nation stood still and silent with terror and anger. All emotions worthy of humanity were felt for the young men butchered, burned, and buried alive beneath the waters of Pearl Harbor.

Like most families throughout the land, the Good Shepherd monks communed around the little brown radio and listened to anything they could hear. It was just after lunch.

In the back of the room stood a thirty-year-old Brother Haskell. He paid attention as much to the monks' emotional state as he did to the confused voice coming over the air waves. It was becoming increasingly rare for him to join the community in the recreation room; he was living the life of the hermit more with every passing year.

As the monks convened in smaller groups about the news coming in, Father Roth could easily be heard saying, "Do not be surprised, my young monks, when the world destroys itself. If we build a war-monger nation without the guidance of Holy Mother Church, if we continually sharpen our sword, do not be surprised or even saddened when we die by the sword."

Brother Thomas Murphy leaned toward Father Roth. "What do you know about the real world out there? Nothing. You sit in judgment of everyone and everything while you've spent your life hiding behind a brick wall."

"Hiding? If you call the supreme calling on Earth *hiding*, then you don't deserve to wear that habit."

"I wear this habit only after knowing what it feels like to be on top of the world and fall to the depths of despair. You've never stood in a soup kitchen line but have always awaited servants to bring you food. You've never stepped foot in a ghetto but only lounged about in a grotto. You've never seen a murder in the streets, but gladly murder the reputation and emotions of others. There is a real world out there, and those young sailors are getting a nasty taste of it right now. But you? You see nothing but people beneath you."

Such an exchange between the two of them was not entirely uncommon. While the younger monks elbowed each other for ringside seats, the more mature monks learned to steer clear. But Thomas eventually turned to Haskell and asked, "What do you think, Brother Haskell?"

Haskell had tuned out Father Roth and Brother Thomas by this point and had focused in on Father Matthias, who sat quietly in a chair, lost in thought.

"I think I want to know what Father Matthias is thinking about."

Shaken from his trance, Father Matthias took a deep breath. "Nothing. I'm *feeling*."

"Well, stop feeling," Father Roth said. "It's what got our nation into this mess to begin with."

"What on Earth do you mean?" Thomas said.

"Feelings. Passions. That is the problem with this cursed nation. Passions as red hot as that fire poker," he flipped his cane toward the fireplace.

"Unbridled passions raging like the devil's cavalry is precisely the problem with our broken nation. Passion for wealth caused every foolish man to bet their future on the market." He gave Thomas a little look. "And passion caused Hitler to invade Poland from the West, which caused the passions of the French and British to act like knights in shining armor coming to Poland's defense, which caused the Soviets to invade Poland from the East. You go through a dozen more spouts of passion and eventually you get those Japs attacking Pearl Harbor, which no doubt will cause FDR's passions to declare war by breakfast, which then causes our friend here," pointing to Father Matthias, "to have feelings bubbling up. A contagion, I tell you, that spreads faster and is more lethal than the bubonic plague. Spare us, Brother Matthias. Quarantine yourself so that we remain uninfected."

"But did not Aristotle, your favorite philosopher, say that passions guided by reason produce virtue?" asked Haskell. "The philosopher says that passion is not good or bad itself. You, Father Roth, lead our young monks here to think passion is bad."

"It usually is."

"Does not the shortest verse in all of Scripture prove you wrong *ipso facto?*"

"And what verse may that be?" Father Roth asked, his nose in the air, but with a hint of nervousness at what was to come.

"John 11:35, of course."

Roth remained silent.

"'Jesus wept,'" Haskell added.

Father Roth huffed and turned his attention to the radio. Matthias, meanwhile, excused himself from the room in order to weep for the sailors buried beneath the waters of Pearl Harbor.

A week later, Haskell sat reading at his small table when he heard footsteps make their way toward his cell. A knock on the door followed.

"Come."

Father Matthias stepped in.

"I was expecting you."

"Did Abbot tell you?"

"Abbot told me nothing. But his face the last few days told me everything . . . as did your melancholy."

"So, you know?"

Haskell slowly nodded. "I will miss you."

"And I you. But it won't be for long."

"It could be until I die."

"You? I'm the one shipping out."

"Let us not play games, Father. You may not ship back in. And if you don't," Brother Haskell paused as if to collect himself, "I will not see you again until my death, at which time, we will reunite outside of this vale of tears."

"You always speak truth more directly than others."

"There is no time to do otherwise."

"No. No there isn't."

"When do you leave?"

"Tomorrow. They call basic training the Chaplain Corp Army Training Program. I'll be at Ft. Benjamin Harrison, Indianapolis, for six weeks. I've known for a week but kept it private. I don't want to disrupt the community more than necessary."

"I see," nodded Brother Haskell. "And where will you be deployed?"

"The Philippines. Under General MacArthur. Since Pearl Harbor, the Japanese are doing all they can to take the Philippines. Whoever controls the Philippines will control the Southwest Pacific."

"Forgive me, Father, but I know little about such matters. What will you do as a chaplain?"

"Minister to the men. Administer the Last Rites on the battlefield. At least that's what I have in my head."

Brother Haskell shook his head. "Ordained just a few years . . . and here you go."

"I never really considered ordination until the abbot pushed me into it. And I never considered the Army, especially at forty-five years old, until the Holy Spirit pushed me in to it."

"How so?"

Father Matthias readjusted himself in his seat. "Brother, it is like I can see in my mind's eye young men lying on the ground, moaning in pain, needing to know the mercy of God in their last moment. I want their last experience to be one of charity rather than wrath."

Haskell nodded. "Taking your harmonica?"

"Of course."

Father Matthias read a note of discomfort on Haskell's face.

"What is it?"

Haskell opened his mouth to speak but nothing came out. It took another try for him to ask, "Are you ready to die?"

Matthias thought for a second. "No. Not really. But that's why I'm going."

"Good. That's what I hoped you would say."

"Why?"

"Because it is the only answer. Self-sacrifice is not an idea. It is not even a solitary act. It is a condition, a state of being. One must habituate to it, as one does with any virtue. I suspect, Father, that you will very quickly become habituated."

"I hope so."

"What is your greatest fear?"

"That's easy. Being a coward."

"Good. That's what I hoped you would say. And that's probably the surest way to be courageous when the time comes."

"I wonder if I'm willing to give my life for another. Sitting here behind these walls should make one wonder such things."

Brother Haskell looked off into the distance. "When my Pa gave his life for Catherine, he was not thinking he was brave or tough. He never thought of himself in those ways. He focused on humility. That was it. And that seemed to be enough to place himself in harm's way when the time came."

"I will write you, Brother."

"And I you."

Father Matthias stood up.

"Wait, Brother Haskell said. He cleared his throat. "You were the porter that opened the door to me the night I arrived. You took care of me. You taught me music. You taught me that all things are beautiful, save sin. You taught me friendship. You, Father Matthias, were not just an older brother to me, but a savior. You helped to give me a new life. And I will spend the rest of my life seeking to have a soul as beautiful as yours."

Father Matthias did not know how to respond. His bottom lip quivered as he took a step around the table with his arms outstretched. Haskell stood quickly and embraced him. Something in both of them knew this was the end.

"Go," Brother Haskell said. "We will meet again in paradise."

The entire community entered a state of mourning when Father Matthias departed from Good Shepherd the next morning. To combat the melancholy, Brother Bruno proposed to the abbot that a small group set aside the problems of the world for an evening and enjoy a night at the movies. *Citizen Kane*, currently sweeping the nation with fanfare, won the vote. The abbot, Father Dominic, Brother Bruno, and Brother Haskell piled into the car in plain clothes. Brother Haskell had not been to a film in several years and rarely had a desire to go, but he welcomed the distraction following Father Matthias's departure.

As they were pulling out, Brother Thomas ran outside waving down the car.

"Can I go, Abbot? This film is of particular interest to me."

Everyone in the automobile had heard that *Citizen Kane* was about a man who uses his money to buy love and revenge, about how the fleeting power of money can leave one alone and spiritually destitute. The connection was clear.

They squeezed together all the tighter and made it work.

During the movie, Haskell noticed how Brother Thomas leaned forward, as if ready to jump into the screen. The similarities between him and Kane were all too clear: a boy brought up in abject poverty, separated from his family at a young age; incredible wealth at a young age;

attempting to buy females as a source of comfort; the Crash of 1929 forcing one to admit defeat; the loneliness that followed.

The monks discussed the film on the drive home. All except for Thomas, who sat slumped against the window, looking out into the darkness with lethargic eyes.

"Is something wrong, Thomas?" the abbot finally asked from the front seat.

Still staring out the window, Thomas said, "I can relate to that poor old chap."

"Thank the Lord you were spared by the Crash," replied the abbot.

"Spared?" Thomas shook his head. "I wasn't spared. I lost everything. I was punished for being a fool. I was punished for being unfaithful and leaving my faith. And when I returned to it, I was only allowed a little reprieve from deep anxiety by locking myself away."

"You think God took your wealth away because you were unfaithful?" the abbot asked.

"Without question," Thomas said.

"And if you had been faithful while on Wall Street, would God have spared your fortune?"

"I think about that all the time. I think so. At least he would have, I like to believe, spared the families that I ruined."

"That, my friend," interjected Dominic, "is prosperity gospel. Don't fall for it."

Thomas shook his head. "Any way you cut it, I was cursed for my own lifestyle."

When they returned home, the abbot and Haskell remained outside.

"He's still a resident of the kingdom of man," Haskell said.

"But he's a good monk. No discipline issues. Does his duties. Father Henry says he is reliable, hard working. An ideal monk in many ways."

"But not an ideal Christian."

"Who is, Hack? Isn't that a little rough?"

Brother Haskell pursed his lips. "Perhaps. But he's worried more about being a monk than a Christian. We know other monks who have confused the two."

The abbot lifted his eyebrows in full recognition of the fact.

"A Christian must do his duty," said Haskell, "but with joy . . . with detachment. Matthias left this morning out of a sense of providential duty, freely walking into a storm of horror, but with a smile on his face. Thomas still has twitches from his past life on his."

"Habits are hard to break," said the abbot. "Putting on a habit is no guarantee to breaking them."

The abbot chuckled at his own play on words.

"His heart is not at peace, and his body knows it."

The abbot's smile faded. "When you speak to me like this, it's usually because you're telling me to do something."

Haskell put his hand on his abbot's shoulder, leaned toward him, and said softly, "You have a lost sheep. More lost than you know."

March 27, 1942

Dear Brother Haskell,

It is difficult for me to explain my experience of late. Both my mind and heart are bursting with the seeming contrast between the kingdom of God and the kingdom of man.

It is in the horror of broken limbs and torturous screams . . . it is in the tragedy of a virile youth crying out for his mommy . . . it is within the confines of total disregard for humanity that I find the most palpable presence of God. After the natural beauty of a landscape is blown to bits or a quaint village falls into ruins, I see the face of God. After every last shred of humanity has been ripped from this world, nothing is left to see except the Creator who will make it all new again. I see His face in the darkness.

I do not see nothing when it is all stripped away: I see all that remains, which is perfect goodness amidst the evil, truth amidst the lies, unity amidst the division, and beauty amidst the grotesque.

I have in fact, Brother, found what I was looking for. I have found beauty. I have found it because now I know how precious creation is. I have spent my life seeking beautiful sights in paintings and beautiful sounds in music. But here, I see the beauty of all that is being destroyed. One cannot defile that which is not sacred. It took total destruction for me to see the essence of all that has always been around me.

I see now that it would have been a lesser god to create a world without free will. Man's ability to do the horrific—I dare say, Brother—is a manifestation of the glory of God. God created man with the ability to reject Him and to destroy Himself. If this is not the most transcendent undertaking imaginable, I do not know what is. Indeed, the most heinous of acts shine a bright light on God's unconditional love for His flawed creatures.

Brother Haskell, my dearest friend, if you never hear from me again, know this: the evils you have witnessed in your life are manifestations of God's glory. Everything is a manifestation of God's glory. It is the purpose of man's life to train his eye to see it, to see God's face in all things . . . especially in the darkness.

Affectionately Yours,
Father Matthias

A few weeks later, Haskell sat contemplatively at his small wooden table with a little book—a gift from Abbot Gregory years ago. As every great book should be, it was frayed and worn to the point of disrepair, rubber bands holding it together. When opened, its broken spine allowed it to lay flat. And as every reader who reads at a table knows, this is the best kind of book. This little book was not just any book that cluttered the shelves of the monastery. Rather, it was the best-selling book of all time, save for the Holy Bible.

Haskell looked up from *The Imitation of Christ*. "Come in, Brother Thomas."

Thomas opened the door. "How did you know it was me?"

"Everyone's footsteps sound a little different. Come, sit."

"Abbot Ambrose said I should come see you." He sat down. "I . . . I'm not doing so well."

Brother Thomas waited quietly for a response, or for any sign of engagement. He was met, rather, with a stern look, one that was paternal in nature. A rather odd feeling for most when coming from a younger man than oneself.

"I've begun to see that God has a unique plan for everyone. And I've begun to wonder, to question, if the religious life is God's plan for me."

Haskell peered into his eyes even deeper than before, a burning look that went straight into the soul. It was not an angry look, but one of disappointment. It was the kind of look Jesus must have shot across the courtyard when Peter denied Him that third time. And whatever the pain that led Thomas to the point of questioning his vocation could not have been more discomforting than the look that he received from Haskell in that small cell.

"Who's the floozy?" Haskell finally asked.

"What?"

"You heard me."

"I . . . I don't understand, Brother."

"Yes, Brother, you do."

Thomas's face showed a desperate search for a way out of the situation. But in the end, he dropped his head in resignation.

"Shirley."

"I know of one Shirley."

"Yes, that's her."

"So that's why you spend so much time volunteering at the college library."

"It didn't begin that way."

"It never does. Nor does rot begin as rot. The wrong things have to be in the wrong place for the wrong amount of time for rot to set in."

"She's excellent at her job, and I would merely help her restock the shelves."

"Were you ever so generous to the former librarian—the one I happened to meet myself as a boy."

"Ms. Ruth?"

"Yes, Thomas. Ms. Ruth. The big one. Were you concerned about her workload as well?"

"Brother," Thomas said, "the point is . . ."

"The point," interrupted Haskell, "is that you aren't thinking clearly. You took a solemn vow just over a year ago."

"I've been thinking about a leave of absence."

"I think that may be prudent."

"You do?"

"How can one discern properly while torn within?"

"Torn within . . ." said Thomas, his energy returning and sitting up a little straighter, as if Haskell found just the right words. "Exactly."

"How long?" Haskell asked.

"Maybe six months."

"Hmm," Haskell tilted his head. "I'd make it a solid year."

Thomas nodded. "Okay, a year."

"We're in agreement then. You will take a leave of absence from Shirley for a year."

"Wait, what?"

"You will not go to the library for a year . . ."

"Brother Haskell . . ."

"You will not allow your mind to think of her for a year, and at the end of that year, I will remind you of the situation, and we will continue this conversation."

"You know full well that's not what I meant," Thomas said angrily.

"And you know we do not take a leave of absence from vows before taking a leave of absence from all else first. Imagine, Brother Thomas, a married man who tells his wife that he wants to try out his mistress for six months. What might that wife say?"

"That isn't the same."

"It isn't?" Brother Haskell leaned forward, wide-eyed, daring Thomas to say otherwise.

"A committed man," Haskell continued, easing back in his chair, "bound by sacramentality falls in love with a younger, more beautiful lady, and then questions his entire vocation. How is it different? The only difference between us, Brother Thomas, and a married man is one woman. One single woman. The other three billion women on Earth, including the floozy librarian, are off limits."

"You don't even know her. How can you call her a floozy?"

"Because any woman who flirts with, or allows a monk to flirt with her, is by definition a floozy. And Thomas, if there is one thing I know for certain, it is that while you may have been too stupid to understand what was happening, I assure you, she was not."

A look of sanity slowly crept on to Thomas's face. "Then, what do I do now? I must tell her something."

"No, you don't."

"You're saying to do nothing?"

"On the contrary, you've been doing nothing—nothing of substance—for the absence of good is evil precisely because it is *nothing*. It is outside of God's creation. It is nothing. I'm telling you to start doing something, right now: live your vocation! Pray. Work. Fast. And fast some more. Resist the thought of her at every turn. Pray a Hail Mary every time her face appears in your mind. And do not go to the library for a year. It is better to enter the kingdom of heaven as illiterate than as a brilliant monk who betrays his vocation."

Amazingly, Thomas had come around. He no longer had a look of defeatism on his face but rather of surrender to divine providence. Both are defeats, but one is by choice, and the other is not.

"Brother," Thomas asked, "how could a man with your life story know anything about women?"

"All I know about women came from one woman. And all I know about her is that femininity is one of the most powerful forces in all of God's creation. I dare not reckon with it. And neither should you."

May 25, 1942

Silence is more than just the mere absence of sound. It is, rather, the essence upon which sound relies for its own existence. Christ is the Word, the sound of the Father breaking forth from His eternal silence. But we see this reality throughout all of creation as well. Is it not right to call a great artist a master of silence?

Music relies on the spacing of silence as much as the placement of sound, as any composer knows. As God looked upon man and said *Remember you are from dust and to dust you shall return,* so too did Bach look upon his crescendos: *remember you are from silence and to silence you shall return.*

Less intuitively, the visual arts have their own silence: the subtlety of light and darkness in Thomas Cole's landscapes, the mysterious smile on Mona Lisa's face, the stillness of the Pieta's endless meanings. It is the silence of masterful art that transforms the viewer, with his own interpretations, into co-artist.

Silence between friends can mean comfort and peace or a potential storm on the horizon. In regard to saints and sinners, the most virtuous of men can be found in silence, yet so can the darkest of villains. Chatter boxes usually amount to nothing. Even for the common man, the most heroic of his decisions are made in the silence of his heart, as are the most heinous of his sins.

Life in Good Shepherd was no different. Silence could be a sign of tranquility or an omen of tragedy. And the silence that plagued the halls of the abbey now were from the latter: there had not been a letter from the beloved Father Matthias for months.

Then, finally, a letter was received. It was not from Father Matthias but from the War Department.

Abbot Ambrose assembled the monks together. They sat quietly, knowing by the abbot's look that it was not a letter they wished to receive. Without any prefatory remarks, the abbot began:

May 1, 1942

Dear Abbot Ambrose,

I regret to inform you that a member of your community, First Lieutenant Matthias O'Connor—32,209,791—has been reported missing in action in Bataan Province, Philippines, since April 9, 1942, following the fall of Bataan to Japanese forces.

Hundreds of U.S. soldiers remain unaccounted for from that engagement alone. Our hope, though difficult in itself, is that they are P.O.W.s and will be released in due course.

I realize the distress caused by failure to receive more information or details; therefore, I wish to assure you that in the event additional information is received, it will be transmitted to you without delay. If no information is received in the meantime, I will communicate with you again three months from the date of this letter.

Inquiries relative to allowances, effects, and allotments should be addressed to the agencies indicated in the enclosed Bulletin of Information.

Permit me to extend to you my heartfelt sympathy during this period of uncertainty.

Sincerely Yours,
James Alexander Ulio
Major General
The Adjutant General of the Army

A silence fell upon the room of gathered monks as the abbot finished reading the letter. Some faces were covered with hands, some with tears, some looked confused, and some looked around in their uncertainty of what to display.

But there was one face that looked angry.

"What did you . . . what did *he* expect!" Father Vincent Roth yelled, smacking the table with the palm of his hand. Buried deep beneath the anger in his voice was, in fact, a sadness—if one knew how to wade the bluster.

"Monks belong in a monastery!" he continued, looking around for concurrence. "Not a damn battlefield!"

"No!"

The sound rang out through the room like a giant bell booming in a tower. Everyone's head whipped around toward Haskell. Whispers scattered through the room like rats scurrying across a floor. Father Roth clinched his jaw and smacked his cane on the ground as if it were the whip of a lion tamer. But Haskell stood there not as a lion to be tamed but as one ready to pounce on his prey. A giant had awakened.

Abbot Ambrose cleared his voice and began to stand when Haskell shot him an eye. It was all that was needed to communicate. The abbot, to the surprise of the entire community, complied.

"No," Haskell continued. "You are wrong. Deeply wrong. You are not truly saying that monks belong in a monastery. You are saying that monks are above the work of Christians. And for that reason, you are as wrong as a man can be."

"How dare you, young man, speak to a senior monk with such a tone!"

"I'm not finished!" yelled Haskell. Roth jumped back like a frightened child. "Monks are, first and foremost, Christians. And there are certain tenets of Christianity, better yet, of being a Christian, that any Rule must bow before."

"There is nothing wrong with the Rule," Father Roth said through clenched teeth. "And you should not speak in front of the community as if the Gospel is contrary to the Rule. Your ideas, Brother Haskell, are increasingly more dangerous to the impressionable minds of our younger monks."

"There is nothing dangerous in the Gospel," said Haskell, "and there is nothing dangerous in the way my friend, Matthias, lived . . . and perhaps died. He was the most Christian man I knew, even if, according to your standards, he was not the ideal monk."

Father Roth stretched out his hands as if speaking to the whole room.

"And how might you expect these monks to understand Christianity if it is not to follow the Rule?"

"Our Rule is an ancient one," Haskell continued. "It is over 1,400 years old. It was devised by Holy Father Saint Benedict for the purpose of living out the Christian life in community rather than in the austerities of solitude in the desert. But often it has been the case that one clings to the exterior rigors of the Rule for the sake of shunning the true interior conversion that Christianity demands. This is nothing new. The Pharisees did the same thing with the Mosaic Law, and Jesus condemned them time and time again for defiling the spirit of the law.

"Father Matthias took the heart of a Christian to the battlefield. He risked his life for fellow man, for *Greater love than this no man hath, that a man lay down his life for his friends*. He placed the soul before the body at every turn. He waited for the return of Jesus rather than trying to build a kingdom on Earth. He saw beauty in all things, for all things are created by God. He had no desire in life, save aligning his life with the will of God. It was his love of neighbor, his detachment from bodily pleasures, his aesthetic eye, and his abandonment to Divine Will that led him to the battlefield.

"We should all," Haskell said, sweeping the room with his eyes, "hold Father Matthias up as a model of Christianity. And whether we are in the choir stall chanting Vespers or deploying as a military chaplain, we should seek above all else to be true Christians."

A few younger monks tapped their tables in approval, and a *Hear! Hear!* came from somewhere. Father Roth grunted in a most unattractive manner, raised himself up with his cane, and abruptly made his departure.

Brother Haskell took his seat and bowed his head, wishing to withdraw from the eyes staring at him.

Abbot Ambrose cleared his throat and sat up in his chair. "Let us pray for our dearly departed."

A sea of heads, some bald, some balding, some full of hair, instantly dropped with a reverence rarely found in the most solemn of ceremonies.

Stillness and silence became palpable again. And the most fervent of prayers ever offered in Good Shepherd stormed the heavenly courts with humility and charity, with gratitude for redemption, with the sadness of lost friendship.

By the end of 1942, the nation felt like a different place. People were busy again. Streets were bustling. Factories were wiping down cobwebs, machines were cranking up once again, and the unemployed became employed, with a paycheck and sense of purpose. The market followed, as is the nature of things. Stocks associated with the war effort boomed the loudest as a few lost fortunes were reclaimed once again. Yet again, humanity found that death and destruction brought about new life.

"If the German's fight like you play chess, they stand no chance to win the war," said Brother Haskell to Brother Bruno while the monks gathered in the recreation room.

Bruno's chin rested in the palm of his hand as he stared at the board with his usual intensity. He was too focused in his survival mode to give Haskell's friendly jab any sort of response.

Haskell noticed Brother Thomas staring solemnly at the papers. Haskell stood up from the chess board without Bruno even noticing and made his way across the room.

"What do you see in there?" Haskell asked.

"I see my timing."

Thomas dropped the paper on his lap with a loud sigh.

Haskell took a seat on the couch next to Thomas. "Explain."

"I've always had the worst timing. Look . . ."

Haskell eye's scanned over numbers stacked on top of numbers—the most recent stock prices.

"Look here . . ." Thomas said, pointing to symbols and numbers, "and here . . ."

"I'm sorry, I don't understand."

Thomas took a deep breath.

"When I entered Good Shepherd, this one stock, The Electric Boat Company, was down to three thousand dollars. They make submarines. I never sold it. It had sentimental value. My dad worked for this company. It was just about my only connection with him. But it didn't matter. I had to donate the stock to the abbey, which in turn donated them to the convent down the street, because for some ungodly reason the abbot didn't want any connection between me and my past life!"

"A decision which I endorsed," interjected Haskell.

"And now . . ."

Brother Thomas clenched his teeth and balled the edges of the paper up in a tight fist. ". . . and now it's worth over a million! It skyrocketed with the war effort."

"Brother, it looks to me that you have great timing. Or better yet, God has perfect timing."

"Great timing? Just after I take a vow of poverty, I become a wealthy man."

"Your final vows made you an incredibly wealthy man."

Thomas swatted off such a remark with his hand, like a fly had been pestering him.

"A millionaire! I'd be a millionaire. I'd be rich like Eddie O'Connell or Walter Brooks." Thomas caught himself. "Oh. I'm sorry."

"I'm perfectly glad you heard yourself say it. Walter Brooks. Yes, Thomas. He is a wealthy man. But is he worthy of your envy?"

"I wouldn't be anything like him. If I were rich, I'd give most of my wealth away."

"Of course you would," Haskell said.

Thomas shook his head. "It's as if God has played one nasty trick on me after another my entire life: the death of my mother, the murder of my father, rough knocks as a teen. I became a self-made man against all the odds because of my grit, grit that most people never dream off. And what do I get in return? A stock market crash like never before."

"Sorry," Haskell cut in. "God killed your mother? God killed your father? God broke the market?"

"Isn't everything divine providence?" The question dripped with cynicism.

"Poor God."

"Poor God?"

"He gets blamed for everything bad and gets praised for very little good. You blame God for taking your mother—and my own—and you blame Him for the sin of the man who shot your father. Yet He gets no credit for giving you a loving grandmother who sacrificed everything for you; He gets no credit for giving you a wily personality along with the grit you are so proud of; He gets no credit for the boom of the market being just at the time you stepped into the job; and yet He gets blamed for making it crash, rather than the greed and cowardice of the many thousands of investors that made it happen.

"The Greeks never treated Zeus with such gross contempt. If a ship was wrecked or a plague broke out, they assumed their own wretched deeds were deserving of such punishment. And they would double down on sacrifices and hymns of praise. The Romans never dared to put Jupiter in a lose-lose paradigm, giving themselves credit for winning a war and pointing the finger at him for losing another. Even the ancient Nordics would have seen a devastating lightning strike from Thor's hammer as justified for a reason unknown to them. But we Christians, we pervert the Revelation given us by Divine Providence into a blame game. We allow our hubris to seek a scapegoat rather than allow humility to drive introspection. Lazy . . . if you ask me. Just plain lazy. Sloth, I should say, but that sounds a bit nastier."

"But I made a deal with God."

"A deal?"

"Sure. Same as everyone here: I sign up for the religious life, I escape the troubles of the world. I ought to be freed from the troubles of the world. But here they are again, haunting me like a ghost from the past."

"A deal . . ." Haskell said, considering carefully the choice of words.

"A deal," Thomas replied emphatically. "Deals are all through the Bible. I know them. It's what brought me here. Just look at the words of Jesus Himself. John 14:23: 'If any one love me, he will keep my word, and my Father will love him, and we will come to him, and will make our abode with him.' Deal."

Haskell nodded but with limited affirmation.

"John 15:14: 'You are my friends, if you do the things I command you.' Deal."

Haskell nodded again.

"Matthew 17:19: 'If you have faith as a grain of muster seed . . . nothing shall be impossible to you.' Deal, if I've ever heard one."

Haskell sat quietly and pursed his lips.

"God offered me a deal. And I took it. But, frankly, it doesn't seem like He has kept up His side of the bargain."

Finally, Haskell said, "You are the rich young man."

"Nonsense! I've already sold all I had and given it away."

"No, you have not, Thomas. You may not possess the stock certificates anymore, but you cling to them with your heart. You're not sad because your stocks recovered. You're not sad because you cannot have Shirley. You're not sad because of your *bad timing*. You're sad because you have not yet abandoned yourself entirely to Him. That is why the rich young man went away sad. And there is nothing I can do for you, Thomas. There is nothing the abbot can do. There is nothing anyone can do except love you and pray for you. But you must let go of it all. You must die to self—past, present, and future self. You must let go of everything. And in return, in the next life, you will receive everything."

Thomas sighed and leaned forward, patting Haskell on the knee and nodding. "You've always been a friend, Haskell. Thank you."

He stood and made his way out of the room.

Haskell then noticed that Bruno had left, everyone else had left, in fact, and that he was sitting alone. There was no need to depart to his cell. He bowed his head and prayed for Thomas like never before.

There are times in life when words fail. The human mind cannot run algorithms or logical deductions to determine such times. But the human heart knows. We do know, however, that these moments are on the extreme ends of life experiences.

The young man is speechless upon seeing his beloved for the first time; the young woman when she gazes into the eyes of her newborn child; the artist staring at a sunrise; the saint in contemplation of the depths of divinity.

But the other side of the spectrum equally ties up one's tongue: witnessing the death of a child; feeling the betrayal of a spouse; alas, hearing the truth about oneself.

A wordless moment is wordless for many reasons. For one, the limits of human language to express the zenith and the nadir of human experience is evident in such moments. For another, the emotional drain in such moments takes the energy out of speech and redirects it to mere survival, such as breathing or running or mental alertness.

Most importantly, however, is a third reason for being rendered speechless. This last reason is almost always subconscious except in the most pious of souls: the awareness of Almighty God and His providence in a situation that humbles humanity to silence.

It was the latter that overcame Brother Haskell the next morning as he quietly sat at his table in contemplation. He heard Bruno's footsteps racing toward his door. He arose and began to exit the room before the door was thrown open. Breathing heavily, Bruno said, "Come quick."

They hurried down the bowling alley lane, up the stairs, and into the sacristy, past the choir stalls and the altar and past the pews and out the front entrance. Here was a place on the abbey grounds that Brother Haskell rarely came, for it was open to the public, for all to see the grand entrance and the two mighty bell towers that loomed over the surrounding town of Capstone. It was where churchgoers gathered to socialize before and after Mass with the monks, except Brother Haskell. It was where graduates gathered every year for their baccalaureate Mass. It was where brides awaited their grand entrance before being taken down the aisle. And it was where coffins and pallbearers waited before the chanting of a Requiem Mass.

A hushed crowd was gathered, standing in a circle at the bottom of the *Labora* tower. Haskell looked above them. The tower shutters were open, a glass bottle perched on the ledge.

Abbot Ambrose was kneeling in the middle of the circled monks, a stole over his neck, small book in hand, audibly praying the Last Rites in that sacred language the devil despises. A pool of dark blood ran some three feet in every direction of the head being anointed.

Upon completion, every monk in unison crossed themselves with a piety rarely known in any monastery, as if that simple sweeping of the hand across one's body had a power to call upon heavenly beings and cast unto hell the demonic prowling about the world seeking the ruin of souls.

A young monk felt compelled to say what no one believed. "He must have fallen by accident."

"Stop," the abbot said. "A Christian shall not speculate on the inner workings of a man's heart. Pray for the soul of the departed and place hope in the infinite mercy of God."

Brother Haskell slowly made his way toward the body. He squatted down and placed his hand on the dead man's shoulder. He closed his eyes and raised his head. "Forgive him his debts, O Lord. And shower upon him an undeserved return on every investment he ever made with you."

He opened his eyes and looked upon the face of his friend.

At last, the face was still.

"Be at peace, Brother Thomas Murphy."

Brother Haskell's Journal

May 21, 1944

Twenty years.

I am only realizing now how odd it is to not know one's birthday. When my mother died, Pa did the best he could. It was sometime in the summer, but that's the best I know.

Many years ago, Brother Bruno learned that I didn't know my birthday. And so, he began celebrating my arrival at the abbey.

I cannot summarize the twenty years well, other than to say that it has been a beautiful life here at Good Shepherd. How glorious an opportunity to consume the monk's knowledge of everything from theology to gardening! The monks have given me everything. Latin, Greek, Italian, French, Spanish, German, and I am teaching myself Hebrew.

Father Dominic has given me Xeno, Plato, Aristotle, Plotinus, and numerous other Platonists. He has given me Origen, Basil and his younger brother Gregory of Nyssa, their friend Gregory Nazianzus, Chrysostom and Augustine—so much of Augustine. And he has given me Peter Lombard, Anslem, Albert the Great, Bonaventure, Duns Scotus, and of course the Angelic Doctor.

Brother Henry has given me Homer and Sophocles, Cicero and Virgil, Dante and Milton, Tolstoy, Dostoevsky, Dumas and Dickens, and of course, Shakespeare.

Brother Mathias lit my heart on fire that lonely evening when he gave me Pa's harmonica, followed by a violin, followed by a recorder of all things. The harmonica is all I really care about. Oh, how I miss him. A saint. A true saint.

Abbot Ambrose, he has given me more than all the others combined. He has given me Jesus in the Gospels. And he has compounded this effect with à Kempis's Imitation of Christ, *De Sales's* Introduction to the Devout Life, *Sculpoli's* Spiritual Combat, *Ignatius's* Spiritual Exercises, *Peter Alcantera's* Prayer and Meditation, *and recently, Therese of Lisieux's* Story of a Soul.

Bruno has given me friendship and laughter, which should not go unstated. All the monks have given me a family.

The Holy Spirit has given me peace of heart.

I must give back. I must reach deeper into every moment of the day and unite with Christ on a more intimate level. It is as if I sit on a ledge of a great abyss, a depth unknown. In my mind's eye, it is the ledge at Crowder's Mountain, where Brother Bruno took me when I first arrived at the monastery (the exhilarating day the car was stolen . . .). I feel that I remain comfortably on my ledge, with my books and music and friends. A whisper seems to echo up the great abyss like the chant above echoes down the dark halls to the cell to which I return whenever I choose—in peace and comfort.

Yet the echo grows louder. "Come on," the whisper seems to say, though I do not hear the words. A leap of faith surely seems warranted, given the distinctive lifestyle God has blessed me with. I would feel ready to plunge into the depths, but for one terrifying concern: there are two whispers I hear. At times, the tranquility of God's inaudible voice says to me, "Come on." At other times, it is not so. I see Christ's face, bruised and bloodied, with His chin in the dirt, crawling on the ground toward the wooden beam of His cross with the last remnant of strength His broken body possesses. It is in the background that I hear a serpent-like hiss whispering, "Come on. Come on."

Abbot Ambrose tells me to avoid the abyss all together for this very reason.

But I feel the calling.

Twenty years ago, the most evil of things happened before my eyes. The pain ravished me for many years. But the Lord was my shepherd, and I eventually wanted for nothing. I fear no evil—neither the evil residing in my memory, nor the evil that lies deep in the abyss.

Brother Haskell's Journal

January 17, 1945

The Feast Day of Saint Anthony of the Desert

I leapt into the abyss.

Part Four

Chapter 1

1945

April 16, 1945

Sometimes death is required for new life.

Brother Haskell slowly meandered through his garden, blossoming with broccoli plants, brussels sprouts, spinach leaves, and more. All that was green grew faster and faster. No matter how many seasons a gardener tends his garden, no matter how many children a parent rears, no matter how many novices an abbot admits, one is always amazed how fast life progresses. It would be time to harvest soon enough. For now, it was the perfect time to merely enjoy nature's spectacle of bursting life.

Haskell marveled each and every year. No artist could paint the growth as our eyes see it from day to day; no musician can orchestrate a sound so sweet as a baby bird's chirping in a nest; no engineer could construct something as simple as the butterfly that landed on the tall brussels sprout plant before him. He bent down and looked closely. Blue wings with black tips slowly flapped up and down. And the antennas pointed right at his nose as he leaned closer. It was as if the butterfly was staring right at him, as interested in the large black hermit as the black hermit was interested in him.

"Do you remember being a caterpillar?" he asked.

The wings continued to slowly flap up and down.

"You went from crawling on your belly to soaring through the sky. You spun yourself up into a cocoon as if for death, but resurrected into new life."

The wings seemed to say, *Yes. I did.*

"You, my little friend, have a gloried body; the envy of every insect that crawls the Earth, the fascination of scientists, the desire of every child to see and chase in the warming sun. You are a living rainbow, a sign of God's peace with humanity."

The butterfly concurred.

"You are a symbol of life, but only because you were first a symbol of death. If the world could only see death as a symbol of new life..."

He stood up and smiled at his little friend. It took off into the air as if it knew the Benedictine monk had said all he needed to say.

The life of his garden, the tranquility of his cloistered life, and the serene silence he sought more with every passing year warmed his soul. Even so, he could not shake the thought of the countless young men from nearly every nation being slaughtered by bullets and shrapnel.

Outside of this tranquil garden, death was all around. Even the commander-in-chief, FDR, seemed to be the most recent tragedy of war, dying of a cerebral hemorrhage on April 12, the feast of Saint Sabbas the Sanctified. An easy feast for Haskell to remember since Sabbas entered a monastery at eight years old in the fifth century; he knew all the saints that began religious life as children.

Haskell agreed with most Americans that twelve years and four presidential elections was enough for FDR—not that he desired the reign to end in such a manner. On the issue of presidential terms, however, he had no dog in the fight. Rather, he listened to Abbot Gregory, who (as the most honorable of men often do) stepped down from a most coveted office. "Power is addictive," Abbot Gregory would say. "Most men cannot wean off of it like mother's milk. They must cut cold turkey, lest every reason in the world will present itself to persist a little longer."

The good abbot took to calling FDR *President Cincinnatus*—as deep a sarcasm as the old man could muster. The ancient Roman Lucius Quinctius Cincinnatus had his plow ripped from his hand and total control of the Roman Empire thrust therein. His rapid victory in this time of crisis was followed by his complete relinquishment of power, without hesitation. And he walked back to his field and picked up his plow, returning to the life of a simple farmer. An icon of civic virtue, he was matched only by

George Washington, who likewise returned to his plow on Mount Vernon as soon as the Republic could stand without him.

Such heroic precedents were not lost on the young Abbot Gregory, many moons ago, when he stepped down from the abbot's chair. If anyone had the right to question FDR's motives, Haskell thought, it was Cincinnatus, George Washington, and his very own Abbot Gregory.

Yes, outside of his idyllic garden beaming with life, death lay all around. But in the case of the ninety-seven-year-old Abbot Gregory, Haskell saw the beauty of a slow and happy death, a form of death with which Haskell had little experience. Most of the death he had witnessed had been tragic: his mother stolen by the Spanish Flu; the young girl, Catherine, and the murder of his father by the villainous Walter Brooks; the wrath of war that martyred the good Father Matthias; and the mystery that shrouded the fall of Brother Thomas Murphy. Death had consumed Haskell's life. And so, the ancient devotion to Saint Joseph, patron of a happy death, was lost on the hermit.

A happy death? It made little sense to Haskell until he finally contemplated the subject. The result of his prayer was rather simple: Joseph of Nazareth may well have died in the loving arms of both Jesus and the Virgin Mary. If such a circumstance did not lead to a happy death, perhaps nothing could.

It was this happy death that Haskell witnessed during his daily visits to the bedside of Abbot Gregory. He read to the holy old man multiple times a day—a good arrangement for all involved. Haskell had fewer monastic duties as a partial hermit, other monks felt too busy, and truth be known, Gregory would prefer no other company to that of this thirty-three-year-old black monk.

As the butterfly flew away, Haskell decided it was time to ask Abbot Gregory directly about death. It was time for the great teacher to give his last lecture.

"The truly humble man believes that everyone is better than himself, and that he is the worst of all. But are you really humble like this in your own opinion? You easily compare yourself with this one and that one, but to how many do

you not prefer yourself with the pride of the Pharisee: 'I am not as the rest of men.'"

Brother Haskell paused and looked up from the little book entitled *Humility of Heart*. Abbot Gregory breathed deeply, taking in every last word as if they were the last words he would hear.

"Why, O Lord," Abbot Gregory said faintly, "did you withhold this book from me until the end of my days?"

The book was all that Abbot Gregory had read for the last year. Now, lying on his deathbed, he had Brother Haskell read it to him throughout the day. Such requests surprised Brother Haskell considering the old abbot was the humblest of men.

He placed the book down. "What do you know of death?"

"I know that it is finally upon me, thank God."

The old abbot chuckled to himself. He saw the eyes of Haskell searching for something of deeper meaning. In a style not uncommon for him, he turned the question on Haskell. "What do you know about death?"

Haskell adjusted the pillows under Gregory's head for him, then leaned back again. "Nothing."

"Nonsense."

"I know nothing of a *good* death, that is. Only the sort that comes from evil."

"But what else do you know about death?"

"I don't know."

"You know more than you realize."

"How so?"

"What age was our Lord at His death?"

"Thirty-three."

"And how old are you?"

"The same. But what does that tell me?"

"An awful lot. It tells you that you are past your prime and have begun to die yourself." He chuckled again. "Death is just a little further down the road for you than it is for me. In the light of eternity, a handful of decades is, well, nothing. Nothing at all."

When Haskell said nothing in reply, Gregory asked, "Haven't you read Plato's *Phaedo?*"

"Many times. It is one of Dominic's favorites."

"And?"

"Well, let's see . . . Socrates sees death as an escape from the corporeal body."

"Yes . . ." Gregory said. "What else?"

"He said that all his life he was walking toward truth but that his senses were continually distracting his soul from the truth."

A little wave of Gregory's hand pulled more from Haskell.

"And that death was not just the destruction of the body but the freeing of his spirit which could then perceive truth itself, and justice and all the forms without the limiting factors forced upon us by our physical senses."

"Exactly," Gregory replied. "I've been in a knuckle brawl with this wretched body for . . . how old am I?"

"Ninety-seven."

"Ah! Far too long. I'm old. It's time to depart." The levity, however, was not an unholy one. It was, as Haskell knew full well, a healthy detachment from this world and a desire to enter the next.

Abbot Gregory coughed such that his whole body shook. Haskell helplessly rubbed his back.

When he finally recovered, Gregory said, "As I lay dying, it's a funny thing: I only think about my parents, my siblings, my youth . . . the sins of my youth. It's as if I'm coming full circle with little or no interest in my recent past." A rare look of sadness came over him.

"But you joined the monastery so young. You must not have too many sins to dwell upon," said Haskell.

"Do you think it takes very long to sin?" Gregory asked.

Haskell smiled. "I suppose not."

"And do you think one needs many sins or but a few to mourn one's past? You have seen for yourself that the brick walls of a monastery are no match for the ways of Lucifer."

"True."

"And I did not say I dwelled on my sins. I have confessed my sins. But for some reason, they keep returning to my mind."

Haskell wasn't sure, but took a leap of faith. "Do you want to talk about it?"

"I've been wondering just that. There is something I want you know."

For most people, the silence that followed would have been fraught with discomfort. But for these two unique souls, long silence was perfectly comfortable. Haskell was curious to know what the good abbot was about to reveal. But he was likewise perfectly comfortable never knowing.

"I have a story, Haskell. A story that reminds me of you. I have prayed about whether I should tell it to you. Those prayers have advised me that I should. But for one reason alone."

"What reason is that?"

"Haskell, have you forgiven the man who killed your father?"

The question hit him as if it came from a B2 Bomber 50,000 feet overhead. "What does that have to do with your story?"

Gregory shrugged. "Because there were once people in this world who would have thought I was no better than Walter Brooks."

"What are you talking about?"

Abbot Gregory lay quietly, closed his eyes, and sighed deeply.

"I was just a sixteen-year-old farm boy from Georgia working the family land, and I went by the name Solomon back then. Then one day in 1863, a strapping young lieutenant came through town recruiting for the Confederacy. He spoke in town about the glorious South, the integrity and brilliance of Robert E. Lee, the criminality of Lincoln, and the Founders' dogmatic understanding of states' rights violated by the North's invasion of our homeland. I, of course, was swept up by his rhetoric, the spotless gray uniform, his sparkling saber hanging from his side. It sure beat carrying a hoe all day, or so I thought.

"I joined on the spot. I ran home, packed a small bag, stole daddy's rifle from above the door, kissed my mother good-bye, and took off down the road before daddy could come in from the fields and stop me. Mother was yelling at me, grabbing at me, pulling me back in the door. It was awful, the more I think about it.

"Two weeks later, we were still recruiting, traveling from one town to another. The lieutenant took a liking to me and quickly began to use me as his steward. Most days I walked right next to his horse. He even purchased a new pair of boots for me in one of those small towns. I was so proud of those boots because of who had given them to me.

"But that very evening, the lieutenant told me and two junior officers to come with him." Abbot Gregory's eyes turned glossy as the emotions from so long ago resurfaced.

***

Young Solomon and the small group left the campsite and doubled back about a mile down the road. This made no sense to Solomon, for they had only passed one small negro home on the road.

As they approached that small home, the lieutenant said to the junior officers, "Boys, you've been working hard the last month, pounding the dirt road every day. Time for a little reward: the secret kind of reward we keep to ourselves." And the two officers looked at each other in confusion.

"But seniority has its privileges, so I go first."

A moment later, they saw a negro man come out the front door followed by his daughter. She was a few years older than Solomon, seventeen, maybe eighteen. She was a slender girl, wearing an apron, wiping her hands from cooking. As soon as her father saw the soldier, he turned and sent his daughter inside.

"Evening officers," he said, putting on the most respectful face he could.

The lieutenant dismounted his horse.

"Good evening, good sir," the lieutenant said with a gentlemanly tone.

"Can I help you sirs?"

"Indeed, you can, my good man," the lieutenant said, taking his belt and sword from his hip. He handed it to Solomon.

There he stood, holding the beautiful sword, the very thing he coveted. A cold chill went down his spine as he realized what was happening.

"You can help me by stepping aside with my officers."

Panic set in on the man's face.

"No, sir! No, sir!" he said as he opened his door and tried to get back inside.

Without a word of direction, the two officers grabbed him and dragged him out of the way as Solomon stood there stunned.

The father put up a hell of a fight. They tried to hold his arms, but he was too strong. One held him and the other punched. The lieutenant laughed and made his way in the house. The father got loose and tried to run inside, but the door was locked. He banged on the door and screamed.

"Run, Betsy! Run!" He tried to bust the door down.

One of the officers grabbed his rifle and pointed it right at him. The father paid no attention but kept slamming into the door. The officer flipped the rifle around and swung it like a baseball bat, hitting him square in the back. He fell to the ground. Both officers dragged him away from the door.

As if an inexplicable strength came over the man, he began to rise again. The officer with the rifle switched it from a baseball bat to an ax, swinging it from overhead straight down upon him. The other officer kicked him in the ribs in between the ax chops.

"Betsy, Betsy, Betsy," his feeble voice said over and over again.

A sound came from inside the home. Furniture was overturned and pots and pans rattled like those in a wagon on a bumpy road.

"No!" Besty yelled in a variety of volumes and pitches. It began as authoritative, like an angry mother yelling at a child. There was a ring of dignity in her voice. But the strong voice slowly turned to pleas for him to stop. And finally, there were a few moans of sadness, the fight slipping from her. Then worse still, she went silent.

All the rattling stopped. Her father breathlessly said her name over and over again, like a mad man stuck in a loop. Solomon stood there, holding the belt and sword, like Saul holding the man's cloak while Steven was stoned.

Finally, the lieutenant came out the front door, looking as polished and distinguished as ever. He walked over to the young officers wearing themselves out fighting the negro, by now beaten to a pulp, still trying to crawl toward the door, murmuring his daughter's name.

"Gentlemen. Gentlemen," the lieutenant said. "None of this barbarism is necessary. There is no need to harm this man. As officers, you must learn to use brain over brawn." And with a big smile on his face, he tapped the skull of one of his officers. They looked at each other confusedly. He clarified his meaning.

"Here's how you avoid such undesirable violence, boys." And he walked over to the father, whose face was in the dirt, and squatted next to him.

"Look here, good sir. My men need a little reward every now and then. Now your daughter is a smart girl. She's waiting patiently. I can assure you, she ain't running nowhere. Now, to prevent this brutality from continuing any farther, let us enter into a gentlemen's agreement. A compromise, I suspect it must be called given your current state of mind. But nevertheless, an agreement of sorts. You sit here patiently until my men are done, and as a sign of my sincerest appreciation for your support of our war effort, I do give you my solemn word that I will refrain from . . ."

He paused and turned to Solomon. "Come here, boy."

He gently took his belt, unsheathed his sword, and laid it bare on the ground beneath the father's nose. He continued his speech. "As I was saying, I will refrain from using your daughter's bones to sharpen this here sword."

The man's head dropped to the ground as tears welled up. He clenched his teeth. He gripped the dirt in both hands, squeezing with all his might. The lieutenant then pet the back of the father's head, like he would a small child who had fallen while playing.

"There, there, my good man. Calm down. Everything is going to be just fine." He looked up and smiled at his young officers. They were frozen, not knowing what to do or what to say. He looked back down at the father and said with a soothing voice, "You may be thinking in that monkey brain of yours that I won't do it. But see if you can follow this logic: If you are right, you probably deduce by now that we are still gonna get what we want and you are gonna get the living piss beat out of you for no productive reason at all. But if you're wrong, well, even you can follow that logic: you'll be burying Betsy before dinner. And my boys dig enough graves as it is, so we ain't gonna lend a hand."

He stood up, leaving the sword beneath the father's nose, as if daring him to take it up.

"So, do we have a deal?"

The father slowly nodded. But the lieutenant continued, "Good sir. To . . . oh, what's the right word . . . consummate! Yes. The perfect word. To consummate a deal, I need a verbal reply."

The father replied in a whisper, "Yes."

"I'm sorry," he said, cupping a hand to his ear. "All that canon blasting has done a deed on my hearing. Can you please speak up?"

And the father, lifting his head, with blood dripping from his mouth, looked him in the eyes and said, "Yes, sir. We have a deal." And he dropped his face to the ground as if he was so parched that even dirt would quench his thirst.

"Ah! Very good. Now, would you please hand me my sword?"

The father pulled himself to his knees and picked up the sword. He climbed to his feet and gripped the sword by the handle. The young officers started to move in, but a dart of the lieutenant's eye stopped them in their tracks. There was no doubt: the father could have thrust that sword right through the gut of the lieutenant. They both knew it. But for the lieutenant, this was psychological warfare.

The lieutenant fastened his belt around his waist and extended his hand to receive the sword. The father slowly handed the sword back to him, with eyes cast downward—a man defeated as much as any man could be.

As soon as the sword slipped back into its sheath, the lieutenant said to the more senior of the two officers, "You're up." And the young man entered the house like an obedient soldier.

Not a word came from the house. Solomon muttered a prayer that nothing was happening. A few minutes later, the young officers switched places without a word or look between them. All the while, the lieutenant sat on his horse not even giving a look at the father, for a complete surrender had been accomplished. Again, there was no sound that came from within the house. Just minutes of silence that seemed eternal.

Just after the second officer came through the door, the lieutenant looked at young Solomon. He merely tilted his head toward the house. Without thinking, Solomon shook his head as quickly as possible. The lieutenant squinted his eyes and gave a stare that shook the boy to his bones. He nodded his head—up and down—very slowly.

Solomon slowly walked toward the door. His hand was shaking so badly that he could barely turn the knob. He pushed the door open. It was one room. A kitchen of sorts was to his left. Pots and pans and broken dishes were scattered on the floor. There was a small fireplace with a rocking chair. And on the right were two small beds with a curtain pulled between them. On the far side of the curtain, he saw black feet on the bed. He noticed his new pair of boots as he crept around the broken dishes. Boots that he had loved, he now hated. He thought of taking them off right then and there and throwing them in the embers of the fireplace.

He walked on the far left side of the room, as far away from the beds as possible, nearly rubbing his back against the wall. And there she was. She sat on the bed, with knees pulled into her chest and arms wrapped around them. She was fully clothed, clearly the top of her dress had been torn. Solomon stood there staring. And she stared back, as if the only strength she could display was in her eyes. He whispered to her from across the room, "I'm not gonna hurt you." She nodded, as if to say thank you. He had a suspicion that the two young officers had said the same, but he did not.

Their eyes locked onto each other, affixed together amidst the terror of a war and sin and hate. And while both victims of the lieutenant, Solomon was, *de facto,* with him and she was not.

Guilt shivered down his spine. The small cabin made him think of the loving family he ran away from. Why had he run off? Why had he been enamored with the world as represented in this flashy lieutenant and his sword? He did not know.

The urge to speak to the girl welled up. He wanted to express some form of sympathy, some form of apology. Instead, he just stood there. And they looked at each other.

Eventually, he turned and exited the home, knowing that he would never see her again, never have an opportunity to make amends. As he closed that wooden door, he felt that part of his soul had died in that small cabin.

Without thinking, he took his place beside the lieutenant's horse. The lieutenant pulled the reins back to turn his horse toward the father, tipped his hat to him, and said, "Pleasure doing business with you. Good evening to you and Ms. Betsy."

And with that, the father darted inside so fast that the dirt kicked up behind him. Gregory could still hear him saying her name.

On the slow walk back to camp, the two officers and Solomon walked as far behind the lieutenant's horse as they felt was permissible. They did not look at each other. They did not say a word. It was the worst form of silence—a silence that smothered all goodness and beauty. Not a word of it was ever spoken of again.

***

Abbot Gregory's story came to an end. His head, deeply embedded in the pillow, rolled over toward Haskell. A tear was sliding through the crevasses of the old man's face.

"You were only a boy," Haskell said. "I was only a boy when I saw Catherine and my father murdered. There was nothing you could do."

"Perhaps. Or perhaps I could have taken the sword and stabbed the officer while they beat the poor man. Or I could have thrust that sword straight through the lieutenant's chest while he squatted next to him. Instead, I just stood there, like Saul. I just stood there and held that belt and sword while an innocent girl was brutalized and a petrified father had every sliver of dignity stripped from him. Truth be known, I was too afraid to do anything.

"Here I was, a Georgia farm boy just removed from the plow, thrust into an adult world filled with wrath, lust, pride. It was an introduction to the kingdom of man like none other. And as I lay here dying, I think of it often. I think of Betsy. I think of her poor old father. I even think of the lieutenant. I ask myself, and God: Have I forgiven the lieutenant?

"Haskell," he said, reaching out and grabbing his hand, "It is hard work—forgiveness. One of my final battles on this death bed is to forgive that evil man for what he did to Betsy, her father, to the junior officers . . . and yes, what he did to me.

"And so, Brother Haskell, I ask you again: Have you forgiven Walter Brooks?"

Haskell searched his memory for a time when he had said, *I forgive you.* He searched his soul for a current willingness to say the same. The answer was a good one to keep buried, as if with his father's bones. But he could not keep it from this old man he loved so much.

"No, I haven't," he said coldly.

Abbot Gregory smiled and patted Haskell's hand. "This is your fault, you know."

"What is?"

"You asked me what I knew about dying. Here's what I know. Do not let the sun go down upon your wrath. You must forgive before death . . . or after death. There is no place for the unmerciful to stand before infinite mercy."

"But does the lieutenant deserve your forgiveness? He has not asked for it. Does Walter Brooks deserve my forgiveness? He has not asked for it."

"Did the Roman soldiers ask for Jesus's forgiveness before He looked up to heaven and said, '*Father, forgive them, for they know not what they do?*'"

Haskell dropped his head.

Abbot Gregory raised his finger and said with a sharp inflection, "As we . . ."

Haskell's brow furrowed in confusion. "Sorry?'

"Do you not say the Lord's Prayer?"

"Of course."

"And how many times have you said it?"

"Thousands, I suppose."

"Then I am sorry to inform you, Brother Haskell, that you have asked God thousands of times to forgive you in the same way and to the same extent as you have forgiven Walter Brooks."

"Are you serious?"

"Deadly serious . . . since I'm dying," chuckled the old man. "'*Lord, teach us to pray,*' the apostles said. And the God-man did not mince

His words. He did not give us what we wanted to hear. He did not give poetry that was beautiful to hear or self-reflective words that were easy to say. He gave the exact words we need, you need, to gain eternal life. 'Forgive us our trespasses *as* we forgive those who trespass against us.' And I have yet to read a translation that adds 'unless he's a real son-of-a-bitch.'"

Haskell sat still, unresponsive.

"Brother Haskell, you are a remarkable man. And yet, your slightest venial sin against He who is all good, all loving, all justice and mercy, is a catastrophe. Your slightest sin, even a glimmer of thought that lacks charity, is a cosmic disaster."

"A disaster?"

Gregory adjusted himself in the bed to sit up a little more.

"What if you took a pen and poked a small hole in da Vinci's *Last Supper*. What would worldly authorities do with you? What if you chipped the tiniest stone off the *David*'s face? How would the thousands of tourists in line to see him respond? What if you stood up during the Vienna Philharmonic's rendition of Bach's *Air on the* G and blew on that good ole' boy harmonica of yours? And these masterpieces of humanity are silly little creations—like a child's finger painting—when compared to the divine artist's creation of the cosmos, of humanity, and of every neuron that carries uncharitable thoughts throughout your head.

"When you do not forgive that . . . that monster, who is a child of God nonetheless, just as when I do not forgive the lieutenant, you are poking a hole in God's masterpiece of mercy encapsulated in those two little words, *as we*."

Abbot Gregory wiggled himself back to a lying position. "That, my young friend, is all I know about death. Nothing is sweeter than dying free of resentment and thus having full hope in the mercy of Almighty God. And it cannot happen without a humble soul."

The old man reached over to the little book, *Humility of Heart*, tapped it with his finger, and rolled his head to the side, waiting.

Haskell sighed and grabbed the book, flipping to the page where he had left off.

At times, exhaustion comes from dealing with the heavyhearted and the lighthearted in too short an interval. The human heart does not seem to adjust that quickly from tears to laughter. But at Good Shepherd, with such an array of characters, one must brace oneself for the unexpected emotional rollercoaster hiding around every corner. Just as Haskell left Abbot Gregory's room having had one of the heaviest conversations of his life, Brother Bruno grabbed him around the shoulders with a big Bavarian smile.

"You won't believe what the radio just said!"

"Nor would I care what it said."

"Jackie Robinson of the Kansas City Monarchs was just seen at the Red Sox's tryouts!"

Bruno was right; Haskell didn't believe it. At least he didn't believe it was possible for him to make the team. Could this nation make such a journey in such a short period of time? In that very room, Haskell thought, lies a man who walked throughout a land clanging with the chains of slavery. And before his death, a negro could be playing in the big leagues?

A few days later, it was announced that Robinson did not make the team.

On May 1, Abbot Ambrose called the monks together in a hurried fashion. He announced that the Axis powers in Europe had surrendered and that Mussolini had been killed. Excitement bubbled up in the room.

"And furthermore," the abbot continued, raising up a piece of paper with his own handwritten notes, "I shall read you the headlines from the Cincinnati Times-Star, given to me by our Mother Abbey up there." He cleared his throat and read with a broadcaster's voice: "'Hitler is Dead, Nazis Announce. American Troops Speeding Across Austria. Peace by Week's End, Hinted by Churchill!'"

The room erupted. The monks stood and folded their hands in praise before heaven. Some shook hands. Some hugged. Some dropped their heads with sighs of relief.

There was but one person not celebrating. It was the Great Bavarian who sat quietly in his chair, happy for those around him, but possessing an interior sadness that would go unnoticed to most. Haskell, however, knew his friend. Bruno despised the Nazi movement but could not help loving the German people.

Haskell made his way over to Bruno and sat next to him.

"I am all right," Bruno said. "I am a German, but a Christian first."

Haskell patted him on the back and turned back to the joyous room.

A young monk asked, "Abbot Ambrose, does this mean the war is over?"

"I'm afraid not yet," the abbot replied. "The Japanese continue on."

"They will never surrender," said Father Henry.

"There is something admirable about that," Father Roth said under his breath.

By mid-May, the radio was delivering reports of concentration camp liberation. Soldiers were talking. Many believed it was wartime lore percolating up to big media. Walking skeletons? Gas chambers and mass graves? Rooms filled with children's shoes and women's hair? It was too much to believe.

Then images of the Bergen-Belsen liberation began making their way through periodicals. Parents hid them from their children. Businesses removed them from their waiting rooms. And abbots of monasteries questioned whether such diabolic realities should permeate the halls of a house of God. Monks still possessed the defiled human nature, with its prurient interest in the grotesque. Coupled therewith, theologians have suggested that the soul remembers everything it encounters. Neuroscientists were just beginning to concur. Good Shepherd did not need monks hidden away in their cells gawking at the diabolic results of fascism and genocide.

There is, however, little more in human nature that is as powerful as curiosity, especially in youth still trying to learn what this world is all about. A few young monks found reasons to show Brother Haskell the Bergen-Belsen images. Some guised their intent as the need for his prayers; some had the pretense of wanting to discuss the theological roots of such atrocities. Haskell had learned living with so many men from different walks of life that one thing was common to all: the need to justify opening their mouth. For Haskell, it was no different from when the monks, young and old, abusively proffered spiritual motives in order to gossip. Haskell felt a similar experience here, as if the monks were gossiping about the poor souls in Bergen-Belsen. It was as if they wanted to say *Look at their nakedness; look at their emaciation; look at their humiliation.* Haskell had seen enough. And his look of condemnation set many-a-monk straight in short order.

It was during a visit to the beside of Abbot Gregory shortly thereafter that the subject returned again.

"The images, Brother Haskell, brought to me by the monks are haunting this old man."

"Shame on them," Haskell replied.

"Perhaps. But it isn't the images themselves that are haunting me. Rather, I should say, memories they invoke are haunting me."

"Memories? How so?"

Abbot Gregory's mind wandered off into the past. He rubbed his eyes. "So much death in this world, Hack. So much death . . ."

Haskell waited.

"I have been with such death and suffering. I have even dug mass graves. I have used my bare hands—these hands that I have said Holy Mass with for more than seventy years—to push one corpse onto a pile of others."

He held his hands in front of his face, amazed at how hands could do such horrible and marvelous acts in one lifetime.

"Abbot, what on Earth are you talking about?"

"I am talking about Andersonville."

"Andersonville!" Haskell's jaw nearly dropped. "You were there?"

"I was there within a few days after the incident with the lieutenant: the story I . . ."

"Yes. I know."

The old abbot leaned his head back and closed his eyes as if traveling back in time eighty years.

***

Young Solomon had heard of Andersonville. Everyone had heard of it. There were rumors. Solomon was too green, however, to have been told anything more. He knew there was a camp but did not know what sort of camp. The small group of men with the lieutenant were headed in that direction.

His feet were hurting from the long journey until a smell slowly began to overtake his senses. He knew the smell of a latrine. He knew the smell of a rotting animal corpse. But combining the two would make any man nauseated. Being early August, the Georgia heat magnified every stench. Before they crested a hill bringing the camp into view, he saw numerous crows and vultures circling overhead, which tells any farmhand that death lay ahead.

The fortress was made of rough-hewn logs, probably fifteen feet high, with an appearance of impenetrability. The walls spanned a quarter of a mile across and half as deep. Outside of the prison, two images caught Solomon's attention, along with every man walking with him. First, a line of twenty or so prisoners being led in a side entrance under armed guard. They looked as if they had been walking for days. And they probably had. And second, another line of men about fifty yards away from the prison formed another line; they were digging a tremendous ditch, deeper than the men themselves, for dirt was seen flying out and over the trench.

It did not take the lieutenant any time to hand Solomon off to the commanding officer at camp. He merely smacked him on the back and told the officer to make good use of him. He didn't say goodbye. Solomon was grateful he didn't. And yet, he felt betrayed.

There was no greeting party. There was no orientation. While he hoped to be given quarters of sorts—at least a tent, fresh blankets, and some food—he was handed a shovel. The officer pointed to the men digging and said, "Go." That was his welcome. That was his orientation to the glories of serving the Confederacy.

Solomon joined the men. And they were men. He felt young and small next to a man with a shovel. There were no introductions. No pleasantries. In fact, the other men slacked off more because a fresh pair of hands had shown up. They talked together as if he wasn't even there, for which Solomon was grateful. A few hours later, he got a short break and some water. Even in this first assignment of his first day, he had a thirst as never before. He felt as if he were the prisoner. The splendor of military service had vanished before it ever began.

After the short break, Solomon and few of the men were led to a side entrance of the fortress. Solomon could hardly believe his eyes. Dozens of bodies were lined up next to the wall. He couldn't resist. He counted, as if telling himself it wasn't as many as it looked. But it was. One hundred and three bodies. All morning long, they had been removed from the camp. He eventually learned that since late July, the daily body count was around a hundred and increasing. One man leaned over to him and said softly, "We're gonna do this today, and tomorrow, and the next day. It might never stop." Their job was to load the bodies in the wagons and haul them over to the trench that had just been dug.

As he gazed upon the corpses, he saw them as half-naked skeletons. They looked as if death had taken them months before. Their clothes had been scavenged over. Pants were slipping off because belts had been taken, but more so because the men weighed a fraction of what they weighed upon entering Andersonville.

To imagine such men were alive just the day before was too much for Solomon to believe. To imagine that the prisoners on the other side of the wall could be alive and look like this was too much to believe.

The work began. At first, Solomon was careful with a corpse, out of respect. But out of necessity, however, he and his work partner begin tossing them like he tossed bags of grain back home. When a wagon was full, they would take them to the trench. For Solomon, this was when the horror really set in.

He heard moans. He saw eyes blink. He yelled, "Wait! Some of them are alive!" A smack came crashing in the back of his head.

"Shut up, kid. Do your job."

When he worked alone, he grabbed them under the ankles or under the arms and tried to slowly pull the bodies down the eight-foot trench. He would try to lay them flat and in a neat line. The first few he even crossed their arms across their chests. He pulled eyelids down. But eventually, due to the August heat, emotional exhaustion, and the barking orders of the older men, he ended up rolling the bodies down a few at a time. And then he would crawl down and arrange them as best he could.

When they had taken care of all hundred and three bodies, one of the soldiers took his hat off and instructed everyone else to do the same. "Let us pay our Yankee brethren the respect they deserve." Finally, a moment of civility, Solomon thought to himself. The men each took a position around on the sides of the trench and removed their hats. He had no hat, so he folded his hands and bowed his head.

Laughter was heard. He opened his eyes and was astonished: each man was relieving himself on the bodies.

Like a light shining in darkness, a sound broke through the vile laughter. A voice, calling out in the wilderness, as if it were. "How dare you! How dare you barbarians!" It was a man dressed all in black, very unconducive to the August heat. He was an old man and as skinny as some of the bodies just defiled by the soldiers' urine.

"Are you men not Christians? Does common decency have no place within your hearts?" The man pulled out a long, thin purple cloth and wrapped it around his neck and a small black book out of his pocket.

The men slowly walked away with some sly remarks about the old man. They clearly knew him, respected him, but did not take orders from him.

The old man knelt and rattled off what seemed like prayers in some unknown language to young Solomon.

Upon finishing, he took the purple cloth from around his neck and replaced his little book in his pocket as he stumbled, trying to stand. Solomon rushed over to him, grabbing his arm in assistance.

"Thank you, my boy. Thank you. These knees are not what they use to be."

Solomon said nothing, but the look of mortification could not be hidden.

"My name is Father Peter Whelan," he said as he extended his hand. It was the first act of kindness Solomon had experienced since leaving the farm. They spoke briefly but were both exhausted and both knew the other was exhausted. Father Whalen kindly walked the boy back to the commanding officer and lobbied on his behalf for a good tent and a good dinner. The officer complied out of respect for the old man.

"You've probably never met a Catholic priest before," Father Whelan said to Solomon as they parted ways for the evening.

"I don't recon I've even met a Catholic before."

Father Whelan smiled and patted him on the shoulder. "Sleep well, son," the priest said.

That night, Solomon slept harder than he had ever slept. When he awoke, every sinew in his body was screaming, begging to stay in the tent, begging to not move an inch. But worse was his fear of encountering more suffering and death. He wondered if humanity could get any darker. And yet, he also wondered why this old man, this priest, would be here doing whatever it was he was doing.

Solomon found the strength, however, to ascend from this tent, happy to find Father Whelan asking the commanding officer to assign the young boy as his assistant for the day. Solomon, at first, saw this as a glimmer of hope, but would later find it was life-changing.

Father Whelan made sure the boy got a filling breakfast. He handed him a large bag filled with bread and fruit to hang over his shoulder. "Hold steady now," he said as he hung multiple canteens around his neck. "You're loaded down like a pack mule," he chuckled. "My tired old back couldn't take much more of this. I'm grateful you've come to my aid."

"I haven't come to your aid. You've come to mine," Solomon replied.

"Well, who is keeping score, son?" the priest said. "In any event, we have a busy day ahead of us."

"What are we doing?" Solomon asked.

"We are going meet evil and Jesus, face to face, at the same time."

Solomon noticed a little smile on the old man's face.

They made their way toward the entrance of the prison camp. The old man waved to the guards at the front gate. As if routine, they opened the gate for him.

For the next few months, young Solomon spent all day in the prison with Father Whelan. It was a daily encounter with anger and violence found in riots and theft and murder. Small gangs were formed, and skirmishes had to be squelched by the soldiers on occasion. And while most men were grateful to Father Whelan for coming through, there was the occasional burst of hatred against the beloved priest simply for being a priest.

But what struck Solomon the most was the desperate voices hollering from a distance: *Father! Father Whelan!* Most of the prisoners wanted the holy man to visit them. While they knew he carried bread and water, they mostly desired a loving voice, a blessing, even a hand to hold as their end approached. It was a prison of starvation, of dysentery, of wrath and desperation. The only times the stench could be ignored was when the sight of misery consumed the mind. And the only time the sight of misery could be overlooked was when the priest's compassion engendered a glimmer of joy in the eyes of the dying.

As these men lay dying, Father Whelan would anoint them while Solomon held with tender care little vessels of oil. The most heinous surroundings could not squelch the piety of such moments. Though he did not understand the words, Solomon came to know the beauty and power of those Latin prayers, ringing out amidst the cries and moans of sin and darkness.

Father Whelan's name became *The Angel of Andersonville*. Indeed, he was. He was an angel moving through a wasteland of sin and death. He brought a little piece of heaven to any who asked for it and to many who tried their best to reject it.

A month into his time with *The Angel of Andersonville*, young Solomon asked to come into the Catholic Church. There was little pomp or circumstance. There was hardly any catechesis, other than walking him through the Creed in the evenings. It was not much different than how the earliest Christians entered the Church. It was short. It was sincere. It was a rebirth for young Solomon.

***

As Brother Haskell listened the Abbot Gregory's stories of Father Whelan at Andersonville, he thought of Father Matthias who was running from one man to the next amidst the deafening shells and explosive lights. He too must have appeared to be an angel, untouchable by the evil doings of men. And yet, something did catch him, and made him a glorious martyr.

"Thank you, Abbot, for sharing this with me," Haskell said.

"Why, Brother, have I told you this story?"

"I am not sure."

"Because you must understand that it is God's way. God allows our free will to bring about horrific death and destruction, whether at Andersonville, a German concentration camp, or violent murders on the grounds of Good Shepherd. And then, just as He did with the murder of His own son, the Father miraculously brings a redemptive good from the darkest of places. Without Father Whelan, I know not what I would have become. Without your father's murder, you know not what you would have become. While God does not desire anyone to sin, He does desire us to suffer that sin in a redemptive way. But it begins with forgiveness. You must forgive. You must forgive everyone for everything. And it is then you will find peace in your soul."

While there was celebration throughout the nation for the victory in the European theater, people sat on the edge of their seats, looking to the West Coast at the Pacific theater.

The Nazi Party was the personification of evil, no doubt. But there was something oddly utilitarian about it: the genocide of the Jewish people to make way for the Aryan race; the suppression of Catholicism to make way for nationalist doctrine; medical experiments on children for the advancement of health; looting the gold repositories of European nations and even looting the gold teeth of Polish peasants in support of the war effort. But once they had lost, they surrendered. Utility had run its course. Germans cared about winning and living.

There was something different in the Japanese. They placed no value on their own lives, as the kamikaze pilots proved to our sailors. They took a crude joy in torturing POWs, lacking even a utilitarian purpose, such as genocide. They did not care so much about winning as they cared about not losing—a far more difficult enemy to defeat. The secret to being a great fighter, in fact, is to have no fear of death. If any culture on Earth understood this, it was the Japanese, whose ancient roots continued to shape the hearts and minds of modern soldiers, politicians, and civilians.

Many in the monastery speculated that the difference between the Germans and Japanese was due to the former being a nation of baptized Christians and the later lacking any sacramental grace. Furthermore, some argued, the Japanese lacked any structured theological system. Their ancient Shintoism was little more than naturalistic pantheism. And Buddhism, which made landfall as late as 500 AD, was little more than a philosophy of life. Thus, at least according to many of the monks in the abbey, the Japanese were a nation and race indoctrinated with a philosophy: the Bushido Code, the Way of the Samurai. How is one supposed to defeat, they would ask, an entire nation of philosopher-warriors who seek the honor of a noble death?

The monks of Good Shepherd made the bold prediction that the battle in the Pacific would be waged indefinitely. Perhaps they would have been right. Perhaps not. But not one of them foresaw the world-altering event on August 6, 1945.

Named for the pilot's mother, the *Enola Gay* dropped *Little Boy* on Hiroshima, instantly killing 80,000 people. Three days later, *Bockscar* dropped *Fat Man* on Nagasaki, eviscerating an additional 40,000. Countless others would die of radiation poisoning thereafter. The Japanese nation was all but destroyed. And yet, it took another six days for Emperor Hirohito to announce his country's surrender. Some were shocked at the power of an atomic bomb. Others were shocked that the Japanese knew what the word *surrender* meant.

It was after the first bomb, however, that Abbot Ambrose preached a message of hope amidst the devastation: "Sometimes, if we are graced by God, death is followed by new life. Whether we approve of the bomb or not, let us pray for new life to spring forth in Japan, Germany, and throughout the world. Let us pray that this final act of horror will be followed by peace between all nations, between all races."

On August 29, after a few weeks of hope for new beginnings, Bruno brought Haskell a newspaper. Bruno tapped the picture on the front page. A man sat at a table signing a document.

It was not the Nazi General Alfred Jodi signing the capitulation papers of unconditional surrender in Reims, decked out in rank insignia, for that had occurred on May 6. And it was not the Japanese Foreign Affairs Minister Mamoru Shigemitsu on the *USS Missouri* signing the Instrument of Surrender with his top hat and cane. Rather, it was another kind of surrender.

Here, the picture was of the victor signing the document on behalf of an entire race of men. He sat at a small table in a suit and tie with numerous white men standing around.

Abbot Ambrose was right. New life was possible. The world was changing. This signature said something about one nation, under God, rising from its own dark past and turning the page on a dark war.

America was resurrected.

Chills ran through every vein of Brother Haskell's body. Brother Bruno couldn't believe his eyes: Haskell's lip quivered, and a tear was spilling through the thick lines of his black face.

The caption read: *Jackie Robinson signs with the Brooklyn Dodgers.*

Chapter 2

An Unsheathed Sword

May 21, 1954

For the thirtieth year in a row, Brother Bruno carried a plate of stacked pancakes to Brother Haskell, singing happy birthday. In the early years, it was a private affair with just a few friends in his cell. But as time went on, it became a community event in the refectory.

It was the worst rendition of the song ever sung. The ghastly sound was in part due to Bruno being tone deaf and in part due to his gruff German accent. It was so bad, in fact, the favorite birthday present of every monk was getting Brother Bruno in front of as many people as possible. The singing could not have been more popular if it had come from Perry Como himself. The Great Bavarian would have taken offense to the jokes at his expense years ago, but he had mellowed in his fifties, though still intimidating to look upon as ever. It could even be said that the community missed the good old days when Bruno would get arrested for bar fights in defense of Holy Mother Church. Maturity spawns boredom.

"Thirty years . . ." Bruno said. "You came to us thirty years ago. I still think of you as that little kid asking me for candy."

"Do you have any candy on you right now by chance?"

"Funny you should ask." Bruno reached behind Haskell's ear and pulled out a piece of chocolate. Haskell smiled. He stuffed it into his pocket and returned his attention to the plate of pancakes before him, cutting them up and stuffing his mouth.

"By the way," Haskell said with a mouthful. "Are we celebrating my forty-second birthday or my thirtieth anniversary?"

"You still are the first person I've ever known who didn't know their own birthday," said Abbot Ambrose shaking his head.

"My anniversary is as good as any. Pa did as good a job as he could. I guess men just aren't good at such things."

Abbot Ambrose tactfully changed the subject. "Let's play a game."

"A game?" said Father Henry with a slightly disgusted face.

"Thirtieth anniversary. Name things that go along with thirty," the abbot ordered. "Bruno . . . Go."

"Jesus was thirty when he began his ministry."

"Boo," said Ambrose. "Too obvious."

Bruno thought for a moment and added, ". . . and so was John the Baptist—that is, when Jesus started his ministry."

"Ah. Very interesting," praised the abbot. "I like it."

"The Spartans had thirty tribes and thirty senators," said Henry stoically, as if he wasn't enjoying the game.

Father Dominic put his finger in the air. "Plato was thirty when Socrates died."

"And there are thirty days in a month!" Bruno said, surprising himself. Henry smacked his shoulder with the back of his hand. "What?" Bruno objected.

"Why don't you just say thirty comes after twenty-nine and before thirty-one? And furthermore, only some of the months have thirty days," Henry said with an eye roll.

"Doesn't that count?" Bruno asked. "How the hell do you win this game?"

"No wonder the Germans lost the war," Henry said with a chuckle.

With hardly anyone noticing, Father Vincent Roth came into the room and announced, "King David's reign, the true kingdom on Earth, began when he was thirty," and let out a series of long coughs thereafter, as the eighty-four-year-old did after most sentences.

"And there were thirty curias of Rome and thirty dynasties of ancient Egypt," Henry added with a tilt of the chin that showed how impressed he was with himself.

"I have one," the abbot inserted. "Noah's Ark was thirty cubits high."

"Only thirty people to ever live know what the hell a cubit is," said Bruno.

Abbot Ambrose put up his hand to stop the laughter that ensued and turned to Haskell. "Are you drifting away from us, or coming up with the ultimate reference of thirty?"

"No. I'm here. Nothing special," replied Haskell. "But Judas sold our Lord for thirty pieces of silver."

The room went silent.

"Now why'd you have to go and do that?" Bruno barked. "Just eat your damn pancakes and don't spoil our game."

The abbot grabbed the newspaper from the side table and slid it over to Haskell.

"Have you seen this?"

Haskell read the headlines. It was from a paper a few days old, as their papers usually were. "*HIGH COURT BANS . . . ,*" he read softly to himself. But he then grabbed it with both hands from the table and read the article to himself and others hovering over his shoulder. He read the large headlines: "HIGH COURT BANS SCHOOL SEGREGATION; 9-TO-0 DECISION."

"Hear! Hear!" Dominic cheered.

Haskell continued reading aloud:

> WASHINGTON, May 17 – The Supreme Court unanimously outlawed today racial segregation in public schools.
>
> Chief Justice Earl Warren read two opinions that put the stamp of unconstitutionality on school systems in twenty-one states and the District of Columbia where segregation is permissive or mandatory.
>
> The opinion set aside the "separate but equal" doctrine laid down by the Supreme Court in 1806.

Haskell nodded with pleasure after getting through the article. A few hands patted him on the shoulder.

"I got another one for you," Haskell said. "The monks of Good Shepherd were *thirty years* ahead of the Supreme Court of the United States."

Although Father Roth grunted, everyone else gave one sound of affirmation or another.

"Whether this is enforced or not is a different story," the abbot cautioned. "The governors of southern states are not going to take this lightly."

"But does the Supreme Court get to dictate such a policy to the states?" asked Dominic.

"No," demanded Father Roth. "What part of *state sovereignty* does the Supreme Court not understand?"

"I don't know," said the abbot. "While I'm not usually in favor of federal mandates, it sure seems that something had to be done about segregation."

"But wouldn't this resolve itself in time?" continued Dominic. "Wouldn't this work itself out in the next decade? And does a Supreme Court ruling run the risk of breaking up this country again?"

"It does, indeed," said Father Henry. "Man is creative and defends his creation with a vengeance. Every time the federal government takes creative ability away from the states, conflict arises. The states are not unlike a child: they may get there a little slower than you like, but if you can let them get there on their own, the transition will be much smoother."

It was always strange to have such conversations in front of a black man, a man whose entire life was altered by racism, a man who had every right to have a loud opinion, though he was usually the last to offer one.

"What say you, Brother Haskell?" Abbot Ambrose asked.

"I think the struggle is what makes this nation great, even though it has a long way to go. When the citizens stop debating such questions, the nation will crumble."

"And what will our governor do?" asked Father Henry.

"Not *our* governor," objected Ambrose. "I refuse to say the cursed words."

Brother Haskell looked at Abbot Ambrose with a smile and shook his head. "Peace, Abbot. Peace."

To the shock of all the monks, Walter Brooks ran for and was elected lieutenant governor in 1953. While this was a grave injustice, the position was a rather meaningless one, or at least that was the hope. But a sudden heart attack that nearly killed the governor threatened to thrust Brooks into the role.

The papers had mixed reports. The first doctor who worked on the case allegedly told some of those close to him that he suspected foul play. But this doctor was immediately censured and removed from the medical team. The doctor apologized for "*allowing his imagination to run wild.*" A subsequent story in the paper, penned by a journalist with gall, mentioned rather conspicuously that the hospital's largest donor was none other than the lt. governor himself. Thereafter, that particular reporter was relegated to covering little league games and community fairs.

"Not our governor yet!" Ambrose insisted. "And by the grace of God, never!"

As appreciative of the pancakes as he was every year, as rich as the golden syrup was spilling over the side along with the melted butter, as enjoyable as it was to pretend it was a real birthday, as much as he savored the opportunity to reflect over the remarkable life he had lived with the monks, Haskell's pretend birthday and anniversary was by no means the sweetest day of the year.

That designation belonged to any and all days Lily came to visit. She was on her way that very moment, and it was no coincidence she chose that particular day. She knew the significance.

Brother Haskell walked out back where Eddie knew to park his car. He stood sweating in the hot May sun.

"Is all that sweat from this heat or the impending arrival of our guest?" the abbot teased. Haskell ignored him.

In the distance, the Rolls Royce was kicking up dirt and gravel. An alabaster arm protruded from the window and waved, like a queen's arm raised from its carriage, or a statue of a goddess waving to the Achaean army.

"Hack!" hollered Lily before the car had come to a stop. Haskell wiped the sweat from his brow. She sprang from the car, high heels and all, and wrapped those alabaster arms around his thick neck. As usual, his arms dangled to the side, not knowing where to go. It was one of those times he was eternally grateful for being black: his blush was undercover.

At forty-seven years old, her mountain girl spright contradicted the effects of age that were beginning to show. The slightest crow's feet had emerged in recent years, an indelible mark of a joyful face, for a true smile uses the eyes as much as the mouth.

But there was one most striking feature, one that drew all onlookers in, enrapturing them with wonder and awe at the perfect harmony of elegance and mature femininity. It was the silver streak of hair that fell across her face, glistening in the light. And when she pulled her reading glasses to the top of her head, the streak was tucked behind her ear, ran softly down her neck, and rested upon her shoulder.

Eddie finally emerged from the car, moving slower than his wife. He did not possess a streak of silver hair but a headful. And his face sagged. He approached the abbot in a dignified manner that seemed to increase with every passing year. Hack noticed that a certain sadness, however, seemed to grow along with his dignity.

"How is my favorite little brother?" Lily asked.

"He's doing fine," Haskell said, "and he's your only little brother, if you can even call him that."

"If I had a dozen brothers, you'd still be my favorite."

"Abbot . . ." Eddie declared with a firm handshake.

"Good to see you, my friend," said the abbot.

"Brother Haskell . . ." Eddie extended his hand.

As Haskell shook his hand, he remembered seeing him so many years ago in the dentist's office, star struck at Lily as she left the room. "*I'm gonna sell a million of them for her*," Eddie had said. And that's exactly what he had done. A thousand sales reps knocked on thousands of doors throughout the great nation, selling the Good Book. Looking at Eddie now, quickly approaching fifty, you would have thought he personally knocked on all those doors, made all those presentations, overcame all those objections, closed all those valuable sales.

As they made their way to the abbot's parlor, Lily insisted to Haskell, "You must show me your garden again."

"It isn't my garden," Brother Haskell objected.

"Ha!" Lily burst out. "We know the truth, don't we, Abbot?"

"In the case of the garden, Brother Haskell is a radical individualist who knows nothing about community."

"Abbot!" Haskell replied with disbelief.

"Brother Haskell," the abbot replied, "it is common practice in our novitiate to warn all those young men to steer clear of your den, lest they incur your wrath."

"Wrath? Me?"

Haskell was genuinely surprised at the use of such a term.

"And how is Brother Daniel's broken nose," Lily asked with a smirk.

"Now wait a minute, that's not fair. I didn't break his nose. The rake did."

Everyone laughed, even Eddie.

"Well," Lily smiled, locking arms with Haskell, "we have concluded that you strategically placed that rake, spikes up, in that exact location as a booby trap for anyone intruding on *your* garden."

Once in the parlor, Lily accepted coffee from a novice, as did the abbot. Haskell took nothing while Eddie helped himself, as if in the comfort of his own home, to some Scotch residing on a small table in the corner of the room. It was not yet 2:00 p.m. Lily's eyes pulled away from her husband as he poured, looking down in her coffee.

Abbot Ambrose asked about their only child, the miracle baby, Janey, who came to Lily at forty years old after twenty-two years of infertility.

"She's perfect," answered Eddie.

"Yes, she's wonderful," Lily added. "The joy of a child in the house . . ."

"She is her mother's daughter, with all the spunk that comes with it," Eddie said with a rare moment of affection in his voice.

"How old is she now?" asked the abbot.

"Seven," Brother Haskell answered on Lily's behalf. "She'll be eight on All Saints Day."

"See!" Lily said, smacking Eddie's arm with the back of her hand. "I knew he'd be a good godfather."

"I pray for her every day. Though I wish I could see her more."

"And I will be sure to fix that. It's just been so busy . . ." Lily said showing an unusual melancholy.

Eddie sipped on his Scotch and Lily continued to stir the cream in her coffee.

"So, Eddie," the abbot said. "Have you kept up with politics recently?"

"I try not to. But it's hard to avoid. Especially now. God rest the governor's soul."

Abbot Ambrose looked briefly at Haskell before turning back to their guests. "The last thirty-six hours have been some of the quietest we've ever had."

"Rather peaceful, if you ask me," Haskell quipped.

"Not surprising that Brother Haskell is at peace with this more than anyone else who knows," the abbot added.

Lily reached out and squeezed Hack's hand. "When I heard that Walter Brooks would be stepping up as governor, I prayed harder for you than I've ever prayed."

Haskell nodded. "I'm at peace."

"Well, I'm not!" belted Abbot Ambrose.

Lily jumped. Eddie's glass stopped midway to his mouth. Brother Haskell dropped his head, shaking it slowly.

"Abbot, we must not . . ."

"We must indeed!" he interrupted.

"We must what?" Lily asked.

"We must do something," the abbot answered. "He'll serve for a year and then run himself for reelection. We must beat him at the ballot box in one year's time."

Lily quipped, "Why, Abbot, are you running for governor?"

"No. But Eddie is."

Everyone froze, like a ghost just floated through the middle of the room. Even Haskell was shocked. Was this a calculated move? Or had the Spirit moved him spontaneously? He did not know. But within seconds, the brilliance of the idea settled in.

Haskell leaned back in his chair and softly said, "Of course," as if the solution to the problem had been right beneath their noses the entire time. Lily's eyes darted back and forth to each person in the room.

The next word belonged to Eddie. He leaned forward and put his glass down on the table before him. He sat up straight, tugged a little at his suit jacket, cleared his throat, and finally said, "I'm a Catholic."

". . . who sells more King James Bibles than King James did himself," the abbot responded.

Eddie looked away. He crossed his arms. He uncrossed them. He rubbed his face. A few loud exhales followed. "I could never win."

Abbot Ambrose crossed his own arms and furrowed his brow.

"It's a shame a small shepherd boy with a leather sling had more faith than you."

Eddie remained stoical, unaffected.

Seeing he achieved no reaction, the abbot decided to unsheathe his sword. "Eddie, if you don't have the courage to . . ."

"Now wait just a God-damn minute!" Eddie yelled.

Everyone in the room tensed, but Eddie did not go on.

"If you don't have the courage to fight Goliath," the abbot said, "an evil, evil man, then I suggest you rely on your woman's courage, for I assure you, she has enough for the both of you."

He sat back in his chair.

Haskell marveled at the trap. If Eddie argued, he would be admitting a lack of faith or denying that of his bride's, which was beyond reproach.

It was at times like this that Haskell was glad to be a monk withdrawn from the world. And even though he loved Lily's visits, the tension in the air made it so stuffy for him that he wished he could retreat to the seclusion of his cell.

Eddie's breathing increased and the anger on his face was present for all to see. He began to reach for his drink, but resisted. After a few deep breaths, he finally said, "I will make some inquires."

At that, Abbot Ambrose returned his sword to its sheath.

Just as she had grabbed Hack's hand early, Lily reached to her other side and gripped even more tightly her husband's hand with both strength and affection. Her face said it all: their lives would never be the same.

Chapter 3

Barriers . . . and Death

1954

"Barriers are made to be broken," Abbot Ambrose said as he waved a newspaper above his head.

The assembly of monks reacted not unlike the general public: the youngest generation was filled with aspiration that all things were possible with grit and tenacity; the middle-aged had grown cynical and hard-nosed; and the oldest, especially the octogenarians, enjoyed a renaissance of hope and conviction.

There were, of course, exceptions to the general rule. Father Dominic, though middle-aged, was perpetually filled with hope. "*Brown v. Board of Education*," he exclaimed to the room filled with over sixty monks, "was a barrier to be shattered in all forty-eight states—one nation, under God. If that can happen, anything can happen."

The other exception was one who had passed the octogenarian mark four years ago but seemed to lack any of the peace of heart that usually comes with that privilege. Father Roth expressed his habitual pessimism, which seemed to Brother Haskell was due to living a long life as a contrarian. "It will never happen. Don't be so altruistic. It's one thing to put negro kids in a classroom and another to put a papist in a governor's mansion in the South."

"Seems to be a year of breaking barriers," said Brother Bruno, never one to pass up the chance to argue with Father Roth in public. "Just a few weeks before *Brown*, that Englishman Roger Bannister broke the four-minute mile. Hell, if that can be done, anything can be done."

This was indeed the sentiment of every athlete and sporting fan in the English-speaking world during 1954. It was the Holy Grail of the athletic world. It was considered impossible. Countless runners had bumped up against it, but there was something elusive about that cold, hard line drawn in the abilities or the psyches of mankind. Feet could only move so fast; lungs could only pump so hard, or so the world thought.

Father Roth was far from a sports fan. He rolled his eyes so widely that his head made a near circle, hoping all the younger monks would see the old and wiser monk's disapproval. "Nonsense," he grumbled.

Abbot Ambrose saw Brother Haskell had joined the assembly, leaning up against the back wall with hands tucked into his sleeves. It was becoming a rare treat for the abbot to see Haskell with the community. He had been withdrawing more and more. He cared little to hear the news about Eddie's political moves; he preferred to pray for him and Lily in the quiet of his cell.

One particular reason Brother Haskell avoided the assemblies was that the abbot looked for every opportunity to put him on the spot. The abbot wanted him to share his unique insights as much as Haskell wanted to keep his thoughts to himself.

"What say you, Brother Haskell," the abbot hollered to the back of the room. A sea of heads spun around, except Father Roth's.

Haskell considered his words carefully. "The beauty of breaking a barrier does not reside in itself; the beauty resides in its effect on others."

Many heads nodded, even those which did not comprehend his meaning.

Abbot Ambrose motioned his hand as if pulling more out of him, like a conductor pulls the oboe soloist from the thick of the orchestra. "And . . ."

Haskell did not want to elaborate, but humble obedience won the day.

"Forty-six days after Bannister did the unthinkable, on June 21, the Australian John Landy shattered Bannister's record with a 3:58 mile. The beauty of Bannister's feat was that it gave permission to Landy. Every runner in the world took their heads out of the sand and said, *it can be done* . . . and so it was done again. And it will be done many more times in the very near future. Perhaps the first to break a barrier is so strong-willed that he refuses to accept the expectations; or perhaps he is too stupid to recognize an obstacle when he sees one. But the second and third and the fourth person to break the barrier, which is no longer a barrier, clearly possesses the courage to follow in the leader's footsteps—all two-thousand of them in the case of a mile."

"You know a thing or two about color barriers, don't you, Brother?" the abbot asked.

"A thing or two, yes."

"Such as . . . ?"

"Jesse Owens took home four gold medals from Adolf Hitler's 1936 Olympics; Jackie Robinson signed with the Dodgers in 1945; Chuck Cooper was drafted by the Boston Celtics in 1950. And more and more will be coming as this decade unfolds precisely because the first person did it. Not only was Jackie Robinson the first negro to play in the big leagues, but we often forget that the Dodgers were the first team to sign a negro. This gave permission to other white team owners to follow suit, just as Bannister gave permission to Landy."

"A beautiful thing, wouldn't you all say?" the abbot asked the room.

Nearly all heads nodded in affirmation along with a few audible expressions.

"And who can tell me what happened in 1928 on the political front?" the abbot asked the room.

The young monks looked around, wondering how they were supposed to know anything about ancient political theory. The abbot resorted in his disappointment to pointing to Father Dominic.

"Al Smith, the Democratic Party's candidate for presidency of the United States," Dominic obliged.

"Exactly!" the abbot exclaimed. "While it is true he lost in a landslide, he did prove that a Roman Catholic can run for the highest office in the land. And that was twenty-six years ago! Much headway has been made in that time. Thus, it is easy for me to believe that Edward O'Connell can be elected governor of North Carolina in five months' time."

He shook the newspaper in his hands and read with a huge grin on his face, as if a paperboy on a street corner announcing the news: *Catholic Bible Salesman, Edward O'Connell, to Challenge Governor Brooks.*

The room erupted into cheers.

"I saw the whole damn thing," Brother Bruno said.

"Just start from the beginning," Abbot Ambrose advised calmly. Brother Haskell, Father Henry, and Father Dominic listened attentively.

"I had just turned the corner and was walking toward the refectory. Brother Stephen was running through the hall, on the left side, I'm sure so as to avoid people leaving their rooms on the right. And then Father Roth came around the corner. Brother Stephen startled him. And it threw Father Roth off balance. But I don't care what Roth says; Brother Stephen did not run into him. Roth was just startled, lost his balance, and stumbled against the wall. Brother Stephen then reached for him to keep him on his feet. He may well have saved Roth from going down; I don't know for sure. It was, without doubt, an act of kindness.

"But as soon as Father Roth had regained his balance, he raised that damn cane over his head and smacked Brother Stephen hard. Real hard. 'You stupid fool,' he yelled. Brother Stephen could have gotten away, but he was still trying to make sure Father Roth was secure on his feet. And when he got hit with that cane, it was like he became frozen in obedience to the slave master. He simply covered his face with his hands and committed himself to taking his beating. And Father Roth decided to take advantage of that. He just kept swinging that cane right on Brother Stephen's shoulders and head. There were probably six or seven swings. And with every swing, his rage seemed to grow and grow. I've never seen him move with such tenacity. His rage gave him thirty years back on his life for a few seconds.

"I yelled for him to stop but he kept going. I ran toward them. I stepped right between them and grabbed the cane from him. I raised it over my head and asked him what the hell he thought he was doing.

"Now . . . Abbot Ambrose . . ." Brother Bruno paused and shook his head with a deep sigh. "I swear I wasn't going to hit the old man."

"But you wanted to scare him?"

"Well . . . hell yes, I was. That . . . that bastard! I'd just had enough of him. Brother Stephen was taking a worse beating than Saint Stephen did by the self-righteous Pharisees. And I sure as hell wasn't going to be Saul and watch the whole damn thing. For Christ's sake!"

"Brother! Watch your mouth."

"But I mean it. For the sake of Jesus Christ! I will not stand by and watch that bastard take his wrath out on an innocent novice."

"All right. All right. Then what happened?"

"I guess I really did scare him. He went wide-eyed, his jaw dropped, like he had seen a ghost, or better yet, a reflection of his own nasty soul. He groaned, grabbed his chest, and fell back against the wall. I steadied him by the arms, helped him to the ground, and laid him down. I told Brother Stephen to run for help. But tell me: How is he?"

"The doctor said he had a heart attack," said Abbot Ambrose mournfully. "I don't think he has much longer."

Brother Bruno rubbed his face.

"Brother," Father Dominic said, leaning forward and patting him on the knee. "This is not your fault. You did not do this to him. Father Roth's bout of rage probably pushed his heart to its limit, and you just showed up at the wrong time."

"Agreed," said Father Henry.

"Yes. Very true," the abbot said. "This is important for all of us to remember, especially as rumors spread."

"Can I see him?" Brother Bruno asked.

"I don't recommend it," answered the abbot. "He claims that Brother Stephen bulldozed him over, and that he gave him a gentle tap with the cane as a friendly reprimand. And then you grabbed the cane from him, swung it at his head, causing him to duck and fall to the ground."

The Great Bavarian's face suddenly looked like a volcano on the verge of erupting. But Brother Haskell raised his hand toward him. "Bruno. Take it."

Bruno took a deep breath and slouched in his chair like a deflated adolescent, unable to respond. The abbot looked at Haskell, never ceasing to be surprised at the power of his words on those who knew him.

"And respectfully, Abbot," Haskell said, "Brother Bruno must go visit Father Roth immediately."

"Are you sure?"

"There was never a better time. The devil is prowling like a roaring lion, trying to devour Father Roth just before the sun goes down upon his wrath."

Everyone nodded their agreement, including Brother Bruno. He stood up and left. Brother Haskell, meanwhile, returned to his hermitage to prepare himself for his own visit to the deathbed of the man who had abhorred him for over thirty years.

He gently pushed Father Roth's cell door open. He laid motionless, staring up at the ceiling with eyes wide, like a corpse gazing into eternal darkness, the pallor of death already on his face.

Brother Haskell sat himself in the chair next to the bed. Father Roth slowly rolled his head over toward him.

"So is this how it all ends? With you, of all people, looking down at me?"

"You know that's not true."

"What part?"

"That I look down at you. And frankly, Father . . . that this is the end."

"Really?" he said with his usual smug sarcasm.

"Yes. Really. The moment you have been working toward your entire life is upon you."

Father Roth closed his eyes. "Seventeen years old. I've been here since I was seventeen. And what is there to show for it?"

He rolled his head away from Haskell.

"There is much to show for it. You have played a vital role in the order and structure of this fine monastery. Your family loves you and will miss you."

"Family . . . what an interesting word."

"How so?"

"You know, all I can think of is my youth and my family, but what do you care?"

"Abbot Gregory told me the same thing on his deathbed almost a decade ago."

Father Roth shot him a look of surprise. Then, "Ah, never mind. Go on. Leave me be."

"You know, Father, our greatest sins are but a drop of water in the ocean of God's mercy."

"Yes," Father Roth slowly nodded, "but I've spent my life focused on his justice. And I'm not about to change now."

"You need not change, but perhaps add something to your position."

Father Roth looked as if he could accept this point.

"We need not think," Brother Haskell went on, "of God's justice and mercy as two different realities. They are different attributes from our limited perspective, just as God's truth and beauty appear to us as distinct. But you know better than I do, Father, that God is one. He is perfect unity. Perfect order and structure, attributes you have been seeking your entire life. And it is in the heart of those attributes that mercy resides, for mercy is perfectly bound up with His perfection. Mercy and justice are one and the same within perfection and only take on a different face when they are considered by man."

Faintly, and with growing fatigue, Father Roth said, "Is this coming from Plato, or Anselm?"

"Either. Both. It doesn't matter. All that matters is that you, in the here and now, focus on God's mercy, and that doesn't mean you're abandoning your life's work. You are, rather, bringing it to fruition. In fact, does not God's justice demand that we give Him His due?"

"Of course."

"And does not God deserve to have His justice contemplated alongside His mercy? Most especially at the end?"

Father Roth looked up at the ceiling. "And what would you say about God's justice?"

"I would say Dismas is your guide. I would say that God's justice may hang us on a cross; surely, we deserve a death sentence as a human race. But His mercy can take us to paradise as Christ promised that good thief, who was filled with hope while he hung in agony. Justice may be contemplated through all of life. And we live with fear before it. But Dismas teaches us that we must beg for mercy at the moment of our death, no matter the life we have lived. Even if we have lived according to the Gospel, we must bow down in humility, the way a camel must be on its knees to pass through the eye of the needle. Humility is the prerequisite for mercy. The humble see themselves before God—in all their frailty, ugliness, wretchedness. And they see clearly, for indeed we are frail, ugly, and wretched before Divinity, as you know full-well."

"You speak truth, Brother Haskell. Humility is so foundational that we, I, have failed to focus upon it."

When the conversation found a pause, Father Roth slipped into sleep.

Brother Haskell sat in silence for over an hour, watching the old man sleep. He prayed for his soul. He prayed that the ultimate barrier of repentance would be broken, whether in the silence of his failing heart or the dry lips that had said so many vile things to him over the years.

After an hour, the old man stirred. "You're still here."

"Yes."

"Why?"

"Because you said earlier that all you could think about was your youth and your family."

"So?"

"I was hoping you could tell me why?"

Father Roth laid still, stared up at the ceiling, and finally a tear began to form.

"My mother. I can't stop thinking about my mother."

Haskell took the glass of water from the end table, gently put his other hand behind Father Roth's head, and held the glass up to his lips. Father reluctantly accepted the help.

". . . enough of that," he waved.

Haskell obeyed, set the glass down, and sat back in his chair.

"Your mother?"

"I see her standing there, as I walked away."

"I remember you telling me this story when I was only thirteen. You were angry at me for asking questions."

"I remember, too. And rightly so. You were a pest." His tone had the slightest hint of affection in it, and perhaps the slightest hint of laughter in the words. But then he shook his head. "I just walked away, said I was called to something greater. And I never looked back. I never wrote. I never thought of her again."

The dying man closed his eyes and his bottom lip moved up and down without making any sounds.

"I did think about her though. When I laid my head down each night . . ." His eyes remained closed. His voice became fainter. "Yes. It was when I was drifting off. Her face would come to me."

"My mother's face comes to me then as well." After a pause, Haskell asked, "Are you sorry for how you left her?"

A tear fell down on Roth's pillow.

"Are you sorry for how you left her?" Haskell repeated.

Finally, the old monk nodded.

A fit of coughing came immediately upon him. Drool began to seep from both sides of his mouth. Brother Haskell grabbed a cloth on the end table, leaned toward him, and gently wiped the drool from his face.

Father Roth reached up and grabbed Haskell's hand. He held it for a few seconds. Haskell remained still and could have sworn that he felt Father Roth's thumb move up and down against his skin. Just as soon as he felt a sliver of tenderness, Father's Roth's hand fell back onto the bed and his head dropped to its side.

Brother Haskell retrieved the abbot immediately. By the time they returned, Father Vincent Roth, former-prior of Good Shepherd Monastery, monk of sixty-three years, was dead. He had broken the ultimate barrier, not in death, but in repentance.

January 5, 1955: The Epiphany

Brother Haskell could hear the abbot's footsteps, which had changed with age. There was a sluggishness to his walk in his advancing years. The canter had lost its rhythm. It was a more belabored shuffle. But this day, something about it was even more belabored than usual. Haskell knew something was wrong.

"Come in," Haskell announced.

The look on the aging abbot's face instantly reminded him of the look from over thirty years prior, when the young abbot informed him that the police were in search of him as the culprit, rather than in search of Walter Brooks.

"Thy will be done," he said before the abbot could open his mouth. He knew something hard was coming.

The abbot slowly took his seat at the same small table that they had been sitting at for three decades, discussing the most important matters that can be discussed in this life.

The look on the abbot's face engendered a stream of thought in Haskell's mind.

You need not tell me.

The details do not matter.

Suffering must be endured.

Grave injustice has been done.

I must wait for heaven.

It shall not be present in this life.

The details are of little consequence.

I am a mere stranger among those of this world.

"Hack," the abbot said, using his childhood name. "Eddie and Lily . . ."

And that was all that it took. Hack's head dropped, along with his shoulders, along with his soul. He was not ready for that moment, despite his previous thoughts. He could have lived a thousand years, he felt, and never have been ready for that moment. But the abbot had to continue.

". . . they were driving back from a fundraiser in Raleigh. He . . . he had too much to drink. He went off the road and flipped the car over and over. Hack . . . Lily didn't make it."

Hack's arms, tucked into his sleeves, fell by his side. His mouth opened but nothing came out. A feeling of emptiness came over him. He began to sway in his chair as if he would fall to the ground. Instead, he slipped himself on to his knees, onto that cold, hard, stone floor. He folded his hands and said, "Thy will be done. Not mine, O Lord. Not mine."

The abbot came around the table. "I'm so sorry, Hack," as he began to help him up. But Hack gently pushed him back. The abbot slowly walked out of the room and gently closed the door.

Brother Haskell knelt alone and prayed aloud. "My heart is restless, O Lord, until it rests in you alone. Alone. Alone."

He remembered sitting in the dentist office in Jefferson, right next to Lily, who had turned her attention to the young Bible salesmen, and how alone he felt next to the two love birds. He remembered sitting in Mr. Grey's living room as a child, cleaning out the fireplace, and how the betrothed Lily brought in two fishing poles to the lonely father. He remembered how alone he felt when they walked out. He remembered how alone he felt walking next to the river after she finally moved away.

He felt as alone in his cell as he had that night his father was taken from him. He stared at the crucifix that had been staring back at him ever since that night. He saw Christ on the cross, but his mind played back every image he had of that mountain girl who had flooded his heart with innocent and pure love. It was as if he had stored every possible image of her in his mind, beginning with the first time she came bounding down the back steps from the kitchen. He remembered the last time she gripped his hand, sitting in the abbot's parlor.

He did not feel anger. But he did feel sadness. Yes, sadness for himself, but even a deeper sadness for the injustice that the world would lose such a magnificent creation of God. The world seemed worse off for every one of its inhabitants. The sun would never shine as bright. The birds would never sing so sweet. The mountains would never be so serene.

When all thoughts had lost their meaning and all words had lost their ring, there was but one thought and one line of language left for Brother Haskell. And he said it over and over and over again—like a saint . . . like a madman . . . "Thy will be done. Not mine. Not mine."

Chapter 4

Janey

March 19, 1955: The Feast of Saint Joseph

Brother Haskell knelt down, cupped his fingers together, and softly lifted the drooping white petals of his Easter lily. Both the anatomy and the history of the flower communicated the vibrancy of life. It was a staggering reality for Haskell that the flower encapsulates within its petals and resting upon its receptacle the universal dynamic of sub-creation: the female pistil residing at the center of the flower; her stigma protruding to receive the life-giving pollen; the pollen traveling down her style and into her ovary; and the most inner sanctum, her ovule, the holiest of holies, the dwelling place of conception in which the unimaginable miracle of new life breaks forth from nothingness to somethingness, the place in which God shatters all natural logic with His divine right to create one more object of His endless love.

And the male stamen, appropriately standing at the side with his anther to produce pollen, as if in service to and awe of his lady at the center. His role is rather small but, due to God's mercy on his humble being, essential.

On this day, however, Brother Haskell was particularly taken with the lily's stigma—a word retaining its Greek origin meaning of *a mark made by a pointed instrument,* which explains the origin of our word *stick*. The botanist chose the word *stigma* for that portion of the flower sticking out that would catch the pollen as it floated by. Yet Haskell thought of the suffering associated with the word: his race had suffered a stigma for no other reason than a difference in pigment within the skin; but all the more, saints through the ages had been given that phenomenon called *stigmata*: the wounds of Jesus Christ.

Saint Paul is believed to have suffered the stigmata due to his own confession. Saint Francis of Assisi and Saint Catherine of Sienna are perhaps the most notable saints on the Church calendar believed to have suffered the pains of Christ. And rumor had spread all the way to Good Shepherd Monastery that a young Italian Franciscan priest, Father Pio of Pietrelcina, currently bore the wounds, that blood flowed from his hands during Mass, and that doctors had examined and could offer no scientific explanation. It was an odd reality to Brother Haskell that something so beautiful as his lily's stigma shared the name with a physical torture born from supernatural love. How odd was God's plan for life and death, beauty and agony.

And agony he was most surely still in. His Lily had been gone just two and a half months. Seventy-four days. He did the math quickly as he considered the stigma protruding from his lily: he had lived his life for 1,776 hours without his Lily in this world. Each hour seemed like a scourge from a Roman soldier, each day like a thorn penetrating his every thought, each week like a nail through his flesh. The agony was partly due to his own love being taken from this world, still though he suffered from the irreconcilable nature of goodness routinely being defeated by evil in this Earthly life. A small part of his suffering was also for Eddie, though Haskell had spent many a night grappling with his anger at the man who dared endanger Lily for the sake of a few drinks. But as those 1,776 hours unfolded, the sorrow for himself and the world and Eddie subsided as his sorrow for Janey, his goddaughter, increased by scales of magnitude. In fact, he was rather ashamed of himself that he did not think first and foremost of her, his spiritual child.

It was past time to change that.

Later that day, Abbot Ambrose and Brother Haskell stepped out of their car onto Eddie's drive, greeted by a plump black maid with an apron around her waist and an enormous smile on her face. The joy that beamed from her would seem to deny that tragedy had struck this house of late.

"Welcome, welcome, welcome," she said with a deep exuberance. "Good Lawd, it's good to have guests again at this here house!"

"Glad to be here, ma'am," the abbot replied. Haskell merely gave her a nod and smile, despite his fascination with the lady, for Haskell had been around very few people of his color during his adult life.

"And this here must be Hack," she said with familiarity. She grabbed both his shoulders, pulled him into her chest, and hugged him like hugs were going out of style. "Ms. Lily sure did love you. Oh, dear Lord . . . she loved you like she loved no one else."

Haskell gently pulled himself back and thanked her for the kind words.

"Excuse me, ma'am, I'm Abbot Ambrose," the abbot said gentleman like, extending his hand.

"I knows good and well who you is, too." She gripped his hand hard and long.

"I'm Ada. Been with Mr. O'Connell and Ms. Lily for going on, oh, twenty years, I reckon."

"How is Eddie?" the abbot asked.

Ada put one hand on her hip and the other went to scratch the back of her head.

"Mr. O'Connell ain't so well. He just sits in his study all day. I thoughts the drinkin' would stop given all what happened. But he's just lost in the bottle. I keeps tellin' him to come up for air. I keeps pointin' at Janey. But he just dives deeper in the bottle."

"Does he go to work?" asked the abbot.

"No, sir. Every now and then his man from the office, Mr. Chris, comes by. They talk awhiles. Look at a few papers with numbers. Mr. Chris does all he can to get him to the office. But he won't budge. Man's more stubborn than a hundred-year-old mule."

"And Janey?" Brother Haskell asked.

The exuberant smile returned to Ada's face. "Oh, she is her mama's child. She beams bright in all the darkness. She's saddened and all, but believes without flinchin' that her mama's lookin' down on her from heaven. She's the little ones; you know, the ones Jesus spoke about. But comes see for yourself."

She spun around and began heading behind the house. A large garden, Lily's garden, spread across the backyard. Rows of flowers were in full bloom with other seedlings poking through the soil. A wheelbarrow filled with weeds and a few gardening tools rested between one of the rows.

"Ms. Ada," the abbot said, stopping her in her tracks. "Why don't you take me in to see Eddie and let Brother Haskell visit with his goddaughter?"

"She nodded and changed direction, waving the aging abbot to follow her. "Ms. Janey back in them rows somewhere," she hollered back to Haskell.

He continued deeper into the garden until he saw the little girl. She wore a springtime dress but no shoes or socks. She was squatting next to a certain plant, holding the petals with one hand.

"Janey?" Brother Haskell said softly.

She looked toward him, stood up, and turned her head to the side. "Hack?"

"Yes. It's Hack."

She walked slowly toward him. He stood still. He did not want to frighten her. As she came closer to him, he noticed how curly her hair had become, a difference from her mother's. But she possessed her mother's enchanting green eyes.

She extended her hand, "Hello, Godfather."

He gently took her hand into his. "Hello, Goddaughter." When they separated hands, he asked, "What plant were you looking at?"

"I'll show you." She took his hand and led him down a row of colorful lilies.

"I was just looking at my own Easter lilies this morning," Haskell said.

"Lilies were mama's favorite."

He nodded. "Mine, too. Do you know the story of Saint Joseph and the lily?"

She shook her head.

"Well," Haskell sat down awkwardly on the ground, having to fold his large black habit. "The legend says that when the Blessed Mother came of age to be betrothed, a number of men were lined up in front of the rabbi who would choose her future husband. Joseph, however, was holding a staff, a walking stick, and miraculously, a white lily bloomed from the top, representing to all the purity of Saint Joseph. He was chosen to be her husband and, thus, the foster father of Jesus."

"What is purity?"

"Well, let's see now. I guess purity is when you have a clean soul, like your mama had. Her soul was as white as this Easter lily."

"Is my soul?"

"Oh yes. Yes, it is. The trick is to keep it that way while you grow up. Lots of things will try to make your soul dirty. But you must keep it clean."

"Hack?"

"Yes?"

"Since you're my godfather, are you supposed to teach me about God?"

"Yes."

"Okay," she said.

Haskell expected a question, but none came.

"Do you have questions about God?"

"Not right now."

"If you ever do, just ask."

"How can I ask you if you aren't here?"

"Good question. I'm not really sure."

Janey's face went into a mode of concentration, as if trying to untangle a thick knot. After a few seconds, "I know! We can be pen pals!"

"Pen pals?"

"Yes. We can write each other letters. I'm not great at spelling yet. But I've always wanted a pen pal."

"I think that's an excellent idea," Haskell said and smiled.

"What do you want to write letters about?"

"Oh, I don't know."

The little girl scrunched her face before looking back up. "What'd you and momma talk about?"

The question rushed through his mind like the rapids on the New River. He immediately went back to the valley and the long walks along the bank. He tried to recall what on Earth they talked about for endless hours.

"I'm not sure. When we were in Jefferson, we talked about the ash trees giving us shade and the cranes swooping across the surface of the water. We looked at elephants in the clouds and Greek heroes in the stars. We talked about everything that we saw, which always led us to talk about things we couldn't see."

"I like those things. Let's write about that."

"Which things? The things we can see? Or the things we can't?"

She shrugged. "Both."

"Sounds good to me."

"Hack?"

"Yes?"

"If your soul is dirty, does it make you sad?"

"Most certainly. Very sad."

"Is that why daddy is so sad? Because he has a dirty soul?"

He remembered how frustrated adults would be with his simple and direct questions as a child. And here, the tables had turned. He sat up and smoothed out the wrinkles in his habit. "I don't know, Janey. I just don't know. Your daddy is a good man. We all have a little dirt on our soul, especially people who . . ." he tried to gather his thoughts. "Look here: A little girl who stays inside all day and never goes outside to play or work in a garden, do her fingers get dirty? Does she get black soil stuck beneath her nails?"

"No."

"That's right. And does that little girl who lives inside day and night ever make a mistake in the garden? Does she ever plant the rows too close? Does she ever bury the seeds too deep, or water the seeds too much or too little?"

"No."

"Does she ever prune the leaves too close? Does she ever harvest too early or too late?"

"No. She can't if she's always inside."

"So, is that little girl a perfect gardener? After all, she has never made a gardening mistake."

"She can't make a mistake if she isn't trying to grow something."

"Exactly. You see, mistakes are made by people who are trying to do something. If your hands never get dirty, it's because you've stayed inside too long. You see?"

"I think so."

"Your daddy is a man who tries lots of things. And he gets a little dirty doing it. But that sure is better than doing nothing at all. And right now, Janey, he just needs a little more time to get clean again. It's like the dirt is deep under his nails right now. You can't get it out all at once. It takes time for the dirt to work itself out."

"Like this?" and she held up four fingers toward Hack, showing dirt deeply embedded under her little nails.

"Exactly. Just like that."

Janey nodded. She understood, probably better than Brother Haskell understood himself.

March 15, 1955

Dear Hack,

We are pen-pals now. This is my first letter. You just drov a way. My speling is not grate but I like riting. Daddy dos not help me with leters and Ada can not read. Momma helpt me lots.

I did not tel you I miss her. I miss her lots. I do not tel Daddy but I cry in bed. I do not want him to be sad becus I am sad.

Are you sad to?

Your Frend,

Janey

March 18, 1955

Dear Janey,

I am glad to be pen pals. I enjoyed my visit with you and our discussion about Saint Joseph.

Yes, I am sad. Very sad. I am so sad sometimes that the sky no longer looks blue and the grass no longer looks green. I'm so sad sometimes that the monk's chant sounds harsh rather than soothing and food has lost its flavor. I'm so sad that I want to sleep during the day and lie awake all night. I'm so sad that I cannot tell my Brothers, but can only tell you.

But I have learned how to be sad. I have had many reasons to be sad in my life. My Ma died when I was about your age. My Pa died when I was twelve. Sadness has become a friend.

Do not fight the sadness. It is part of God's love for you.

Your spelling will get better. I will help you. I have enclosed your letter back to you with red lines correcting your spelling. But please: send it back to me in your next letter. I would like to keep them.

Your Godfather,

Hack

March 25, 1955

Dear Hack,

Thank you for fixing my spelling. I'm sorry you are sad. Very very sad. How can sadness be a friend? Why dos God want me to be sad?

I saw a tertel in the clowds today.

What did you see?

Your Pen-Pal Friend,

Janey

April 1, 1955,

Dear Janey,

I am sorry I did not explain sadness better.

Sadness is not evil. It is a result of evil. God did not desire Adam and Eve in the garden to be sad. But now that sin is with us, sadness is sometimes the proper response.

Sadness is like a stranger among us.

Sadness is a stranger because it does not belong in this world, like a stranger who roams the world—a vagabond . . . a stowaway—not knowing where to go, not knowing whether to live or die. Anywhere he lays his head is the wrong place.

And so when sadness comes knocking at our door, we must answer it, welcome him, and live with him for some brief time. That is what I mean when I say sadness has become a friend. But he is not my master. Even if all the world looks dark and all the sounds of the world sound harsh, happiness will remain in my heart. I am happy because I know sadness can only be found in a world that God gave to us.

Please remember this when sadness comes knocking at your door. Welcome him in and love him with the love of Jesus Christ.

Your Godfather,

Hack

November 4, 1956

Dear Hack,

Thank you very much for the birthday gift, Journey to the Center of the Earth. *The book is very pretty. I like the gold pages.*

I wonder what the center of the Earth looks like. Maybe this book will tell me. I am glad my grandpa gave you the same book. It makes me feel like I know him.

I will read it as fast as I can.

Daddy took me to a picture film called The Ten Commandments *last week. The ticket man said I was not old enough to see it. Daddy yelled at the man and asked him if he was going to steal our bibles so I could not read them. Then Daddy said the Word of God was for all ages and that he better give me a ticket or he would give him a black eye. The ticket man let us in.*

The film was really big. I did not know Moses had a wife. I did not think priests could get married. She was as pretty as Momma was. I did not like the bad guy. He was bald and mean. I think Mama would have liked the horses and sheep, but not the snake.

Did you know Moses could turn sticks into snakes and water into blood?

You are really good, like Moses. Can you do magic tricks?

And guess what I saw last night on the television set? The Wizard of Oz. *It came on television for the first time just last night. Ada planned everything. She had snacks and ice cream. She even got Daddy to watch it. He fell asleep before the Tin Man was found.*

I liked it very much. My favorite was the lion. He was afraid like a kitty cat.

I liked Moses better. Did you know that God pulled apart a big sea?

How big is God?

Your Pen-Pal Friend,
Janey

November 8, 1956

Dearest Janey,

How big is love? How big is anger? How big is humor? How big is fear?

The most important things in life are not big or small. God is not big or small. He is other than that. He is not round or square or thick or thin. He is other than that. He is not old or young. He is other than that.

He is Other . . . with a capital O.

God is not just the first thing. He is the only necessary thing. Everything else—the Red Sea that He parted, the sticks that turned into snakes, the lions that have no heart —everything else is contingent. That is a tough word. Let me see if I can explain . . .

Contingent means that you need something else. A healthy seedling NEEDS, or is contingent upon, water and sunlight. It is not so important that water comes before the seedling. After all, often the seedling is here first and water falls from the sky. The important point is that water does not need seedlings, but seedlings need water. In this way, water is necessary for plants and plants are contingent upon water.

Likewise, water needs God. It is contingent upon Him. God does not need water, right? It is like this with everything in the universe. God is the only necessary "thing"; everything else depends on God. Everything else is contingent upon God.

So, when God decides to part the Red Sea for the Israelites, it is not because He is big, and it is not because He came before, but because He is the only necessary thing in all of the universe—and yet He is beyond the universe . . . and I do not know how to explain that.

Your Godfather,
Hack

November 23, 1956

Dear Hack,

At school today the older boys were talking about a man named Jim Crow and a lady named Rosa Parks. And then Ada said something about them when I got home. She said she would take me on every bus-ride in town because Jim Crow was dead and Rosa Parks was alive.

I asked her if she can sit with me in the front of the bus now. She said yes.

I don't know who Mr. Crow is, but he must have been a bad man if he did not let Ada sit with me. Glad he is dead. Maybe that is bad of me.

Can you sit on the bus with the white monks?

Your Friend,

Janey

November 26, 1956

Dear Janey,

Jim Crow is not a real person. He was a character that made negros look lazy and stupid and dishonest. Some negros are lazy and stupid and dishonest, just like some white people. People are just people.

Jim Crow laws refer to keeping black and white people separate. You may have heard the big word segregation. Many people are fighting to end segregation so that Ada can ride the bus with you any time and in any seat, eat with you in any diner, and shop with you in any store.

I have avoided the bus for many years now, so I do not know if I can ride with my white brothers.

I rejoice with Rosa Parks's victory. But remember this: Hatred will always be with us in this world. The problem is not that we lack the right laws but that we lack true Christianity.

As you get older, do not worry yourself so much about laws and politics. Think about one act of charity at a time. The rest will take care of itself.

Your Godfather,

Hack

November 9, 1960

Dear Hack,

Daddy is in an odd mood. He's a Republican and really hates the Democrats. But he sure was happy this morning when he read the headlines saying that John F. Kennedy, a Roman Catholic, was elected President. Part of me wonders if he secretly voted for the democrat, just because he is Catholic. Daddy would do something like that, you know.

I keep hearing his supporters on the radio and T.V. saying that Kennedy promises he does not speak for the Catholic Church and the Catholic Church does not speak for him. If I heard that once in the last few months, I must have heard it a hundred times.

But I wonder if that is the way it should be. I wonder if he would say that about Mrs. Kennedy, his pretty wife. Seems like they should speak for each other if they are married. Aren't we sort of married to the Catholic Church?

I don't like all the stuff on the news.

Hope I can come see you soon.

Your Affectionate Friend,

Janey

November 12, 1960

Dearest Janey,

Luke 22:54-62

Your Godfather,

Hack

November 16, 1960

Dear Hack,

I looked it up. Are you saying that President Kennedy has denied Jesus like Peter did?

Affectionately Yours,

Janey

November 19, 1960

Dearest Goddaughter,

Yes.

Cock-A-Doodle-Doo,

Hack

October 23, 1962

Dear Hack,

It seems like the world is going to blow up. I was in biology class today and they made us do a bomb drill. I had to climb under my desk with my big dress on. The teachers gave us this long talk that Russia might blow us up with their missiles in Cuba.

Why would they shoot a missile at little old Capstone? Maybe New York or Washington D.C. But why us? And if they shot a missile at us, how would getting under our desk help anything. I saw a desk break just the other day when a chubby kid sat on one.

Daddy does little else than read the paper and watch the news and talk on the phone. I think he enjoys politics even though he says he hates it.

I tell you what, if the bombs start coming our way, how about we take shelter in your hermitage? Must be the safest place on the entire East Coast!

Affectionately Yours,

Janey

October 26, 1962

Dearest Janey,

The kingdom of man has been trying to kill itself since Cain struck Abel. Mankind has always looked into the sky to see a storm of arrows coming down upon him, and now he looks for nuclear bombs to be dropped from planes. But man, especially girls about to turn sixteen, must keep their eyes turned upward looking for the Second Coming of Christ.

The early Christians were not scared of the Second Coming. They craved it like you and I crave oxygen.

Yes, Goddaughter, you may get blown to bits. Surely this is not what others want to tell you. But I have no problem telling you this, for the world is capable of any evil imaginable, even killing my dearest Janey. Nonetheless, we must live with joy.

If Soviet missiles come sailing across the Carolina sky, let us rejoice at our glorious opportunity to finally be freed from the kingdom of man.

And happy early birthday.

Your Godfather,

Hack

November 1, 1962,

Dear Hack,

It is nearly midnight, and I am so distressed. I had to write you. Oh, I wish I could just call you . . . or come see you.

Daddy took me to the club for a fancy birthday dinner, a "sweet sixteen." I am getting together with some girlfriends next weekend for a party . . . but anyhow . . . I was at the club with Daddy. We had just finished our meal (and Daddy was probably on his fifth or sixth drink . . . I had decided to drive home even though I didn't have my license yet, but I'm used to that).

The Governor, Walter Brooks, came in the dining room with his son who was about my age. As Mr. Brooks went around and shook hands, each person would stand up. But then he came to Daddy.

Daddy not only refused to shake his hand, but folded his arms! I couldn't believe it. Mr. Brooks asked how he had been since the accident – rather loudly and invasively if you ask me. But Daddy just said "fine" and looked away.

Mr. Brooks apparently didn't like being shunned like that. His son tapped him on the shoulder and said, "Come on, Dad. Let's sit down." He looked at me and seemed embarrassed. Mr. Brooks leaned over and said quietly in Daddy's ear, but loud enough for me to hear it: "You shouldn't act like a sore loser in front of your daughter."

Oh, Hack!

Daddy stood up so fast that he knocked his chair over. He grabbed him with both hands by the coat and pushed him so hard that he flew a foot or two in the air and landed smack on his fanny. The room gasped and two men jumped up from other tables and grabbed my Daddy by the arms.

Then Daddy growled at him like a wild animal and called him a murderer.

Mr. Brooks stood up quickly, without his son offering to help. He then tucked in his tie, straightened out his hair, looked around the room, and laughed. Then he said my daddy killed his own wife and called him a "pathetic wet papist."

Daddy looked him in the eye and called him a murderer again and said Governor Brooks knew exactly what he was talking about.

The Governor gave him a weird look, then yelled for the men who were holding Daddy to get him out. The Governor's son came over and picked up my purse which had fallen off the table in the commotion and handed it to me. It was nice of him.

Daddy shook the men off and we left. I drove home. Daddy didn't say a word.

When we got home, he poured another drink, sat down in his study and told me to sit. We sat quietly for the longest time. I didn't want to ask anything.

He told me your story, Hack. I guess he told me everything. About Catherine and your father. Now it all makes sense. But how did I not know this before? To me, you were just my Ma's adopted brother who became a hermit!

My heart breaks into a thousand pieces for you. How could I ever show you my sympathy?

Your Loving Goddaughter,

Janey

November 4, 1962

Dearest Janey,

If your sixteenth birthday was ruined for the sake of seeing a young man's small act of kindness amidst the silliness of old men, count your blessings along with your candles.

A beautiful lesson for your birthday: man must find his own path, undetermined by his father's. You are not your mother or your father. And neither is Walter's son.

Sorrow finds us all. It is just a matter of time. It found me a bit early in life, as it did you. But what is time when one considers eternity?

Your Godfather,

Hack

November 7, 1962

Dear Hack,

But how have you dealt with it? How have you lived with this sorrow? How are you not the angriest person in the world? How is your heart not filled with hate?

Your Loving Goddaughter,

Janey

November 10, 1962

Dearest Janey,

There is something in this life greater than miracles. Miracles are really not all that impressive when you think of it—at least for God, that is. Humans are so funny. We gawk at walking on water or turning water into wine. And yet, we seem unimpressed with the far more splendid miracle of creating a blade of grass out of nothing, or the blue sky out of nothing, or the warming sun out of nothing. If one understands that God made dirt from nothing, why is the multiplication of loaves and fishes something extraordinary?

Do not misunderstand: miracles are extraordinary, but to me, far less so than the flapping of a butterfly's wings. You see, Janey, we have categorized all repeating phenomenon into the class of "science" which in turn removes all marvel, for we see it as "natural." And we then have the gall to be unimpressed by it, but to strike our breasts in devotion before anything that is dubbed "miraculous" by the mere fact it falls ever so slightly outside the natural.

I ask you to consider throughout your life: Which is more impressive, unexpectedly giving sight to the blind or making the sun rise over the horizon at the perfectly predictable moment? If a miracle is less frequent, we nearly worship it. But if it is repeated daily, we cease to even call it a miracle.

I digress . . .

My point is to speak about that which is far greater than miracles, namely, grace. Grace is available to you every moment, unlike the miracles pilgrims tromp around the world to see. Miracles are just that which transcends our primitive understanding of nature. Gifts from God, yes. But grace, oh, Janey! Grace is literally divinity shared with your soul. Miracles are gifts from God, but grace is God Himself! Grace is a spark of the divine life of the Holy Trinity that glorifies your soul far beyond any natural ability. Truly, the smallest degree of grace is infinitely more valuable than the miracle of arising the dead.

You ask how I have "dealt" with it. I have not. God has. I have accepted His freely offered grace. And with the divine life within me, I can endure all things to whatever point God wills. Just as one day I will have a glorified body and will be able, as Christ did, to walk through doors, a grace-filled soul is capable of walking through sorrow: suffering the cruelty of man, dealing with his stubbornness, being unjustly accused, looking upon the sins of others with mercy, letting wrongs go uncorrected, smiling when anger is justified, being gentle when harshness is warranted, allowing the perceptions of man to go this way and that while you care for nothing except the perception of God.

Look around at the frailty of man and ask yourself which is more astounding: Giving the deaf his hearing or suffering a small injustice with humility?

You can endure all things with humility and charity if you but accept that divine life, grace, that awaits you. And all else in this life, even that which steps outside the natural order of things, will seem trivial in comparison. For all things are trivial in comparison to divinity itself.

I repeat: I do not deal with it. God does.

Your Godfather,

Hack

August 30, 1963

Dear Hack,

Everyone is talking about Dr. Martin Luther King's speech in Washington, D.C. They are calling it the "I have a dream" speech. It was indeed powerful.

What are my dreams? What do I want to do with my life? I haven't the foggiest idea. Maybe I'll work for Martin Luther King and fight for Ada's and your rights. After all, the two people I love most in this world are negro! But I can't leave town for college next year. I must stay close to Daddy. He's not doing well. The doctor says he has a weak heart, especially for a man in his early 60s.

Daddy announced the other day that he is retiring next month. I've got mixed feelings on that. He seems his best when he is solving a problem at work and seems his worst when he's got nothing to do. And he tells me about my trust fund at least once a week, as if I care. It's like he fixates on it to ensure I know he's done right by me. I tell him to his face that if he wants to do right by me, then get healthy and live longer. But it's like he's given up. He has no dreams left. No dreams at all.

All this leads to some great news I have to tell you. I've decided to attend Good Shepherd College next year! I assume you heard that it has recently gone co-ed. You and I can see each other all the time! And I can visit home every weekend to keep Daddy's spirits up.

I guess I'll have to work on my dreams in Capstone.

Love,

Janey

September 3, 1963

Dearest Janey,

Why must you have a dream for yourself when God already has a plan for you?

Dreams are tricky things. The world needs visionaries like Martin Luther King. But don't get tangled up in dreams. They are like beautiful spider webs: intricate and elegant from a distance but sticky and burdensome once they get on you.

Dreams are in the future. But the future is mere fiction. It may never come. And God is most certainly not in the future because the future never really exists. God is only in the present moment.

When your mother and I were young, we would walk along the New River. She would sling her shoes and socks over her shoulder, hike up her dress, and wade the river. She would then call out for me. I was much younger and shorter. I couldn't swim. And I was always afraid of being swept away, even by the little rapids in three feet of water. She would call for me to cross over. And I would tiptoe slowly, building courage, until finally reaching the other side.

The present moment is our side of the river. God's eternity is the other. The little currents are the past and future sweeping by, scaring us, ready to take us away if we let them.

And there stands God, calling us to walk through the currents of past and future, of resentment and anxiety.

You may look into the future, but never stare. You may look into your past, but never stare. Rather, live in your present moment, for Jesus promised us that tomorrow will take care of itself.

I think you know what I will say next. I am a hermit. I have completely withdrawn from outside affairs. Hermits do not have regular visitors, especially college girls. I am glad you will attend Good Shepherd, but our relationship will continue with letters. And you must continue to keep our pen pal relationship to yourself. Hermits try to keep a very low profile.

Regarding your father, it is admirable to care for him. But remember that you have your own life to live. Your presence will not significantly alter his state of mind. In fact, your prayers are more effective than your weekend visits will be. Do not allow your life to be hampered in order to take care of a man who refuses to pull himself up. Love him. Honor him. But do not pity him.

Your Godfather,

Hack

November 23, 1963

You know exactly what I write about today.

My Daddy got extra drunk. My girlfriends won't stop crying. Ada keeps praying out loud and singing hymns.

Everyone is worried about the nation. Communist this and that . . .

It seems like everyone thinks of him only as a president rather than as a man. I feel for his beautiful wife and darling children. The nation will get, or already got, another president. But those little ones will never get another daddy.

Caroline is six.

I was eight when I lost Momma.

I think everyone is thinking about the wrong things.

Affectionately Yours,

Janey

November 26, 1963

Dearest Janey,

As usual, the world looks at everything upside down.

The prime victim of this heinous crime is not America and is not even the Kennedys. It is Mr. Oswald himself.

I say this not because he was killed on the 24th, but because he has committed a far greater injustice to himself than he has to anyone else. His soul is the victim of his own grave sin, perhaps mortal sin. And his salvation is in question.

Surely, we must have tears of compassion for the president's wife and children. And indeed, painful memories have been resurrected in my own mind. But Janey, never follow the flock. The fact that you focused on his children rather than the nation shows you are not prone to do this, but it is still my duty to guide you. Never be too concerned with this kingdom. It keeps your eyes fixed on the non-essentials.

Mr. Oswald's soul deserves the attention.

The world is forever backwards. Never forget it.

Your Godfather,

Hack

December 7, 1963

The nation was still in mourning over the death of its president. Director J. Edgar Hoover and the FBI completed its cursory investigation, concluding that both Lee Harvey Oswald and Jack Ruby each acted alone and independently of each other. And yet, only 29 percent of Americans believed this was the case. Thus, the Warren Commission was formed.

The former first lady and her children moved out of the White House. The bodies of Patrick Bouvier Kennedy and his stillborn sister, Arabella, were re-interred at Arlington National Cemetery, next to their father. The nation wanted closure.

It was the twenty-second anniversary of Japan's attack on Pearl Harbor. The nation would never have closure on such an event.

And to those of the Catholic faith, further confusion was on the way with the second period of the Second Vatican Council closing exactly four hundred years to the day after the closing of the Council of Trent. The liturgy, the traditions, the articulation of doctrines, the languages . . . so much uncertainty was about to be unleashed not only within the walls of Good Shepherd but within the walls of every Catholic home on God's green

Earth. For Americans, political upheaval, societal chaos, and a religious revolution was more than one could take.

All such topics became fodder for discussion within the walls of the monastery, all too often creating rifts between the brothers. Brother Haskell, however, was able to transcend it all by descending into his hermitage. Not only had such disputes lost all flavor to him, but he remembered his Pa's saying that every time he went among men, he returned home less of one. It was a great pleasure to Haskell when he learned that Thomas à Kempis, author of *Imitation of Christ,* said the same. Great minds, indeed, think alike. But even greater minds put into action the wisdom of others. Thus, Haskell rarely came out of his hermitage and garden these days.

It was a constant battle, however, to find peace and quiet, for the abbot never ceased sending monks down the winding stairs for his counsel. It was a cross he had to bear, and bear it he did. He hoped, however, that some day before his end that he would find total solitude for at least a short period of time. What better way, he often thought, could there be to prepare for the great kingdom awaiting him?

Members of every generation have a few moments etched into their memories, knowing exactly where they were when their conscience was shocked. For Haskell's generation, President Kennedy's assassination would no doubt be such an event. But on December 7, the horrifying memory of the events of Pearl Harbor swept across the airwaves like a virus of grief and terror. Haskell remembered the curiosity of the monks around the room. But mostly, he remembered the reaction of his beloved friend, Father Matthias. It so moved him that he gave his life for the cause, or so they presumed. His remains had never been found.

For a few years, hope of him being a P.O.W. kept the community on its toes. But as the war came to an end and prisoners were liberated, no word of Matthias came their way. A year after the war ended, they held a funeral service in the monastery cemetery. To those close to him, Matthias was nothing short of a martyr. The abbot insisted that his name be revered. A portrait was painted and hung prominently in the theater; the newly named *Matthias Theater*.

The community celebrated Matthias's feast on December 7, the day his heart took the path of the martyr.

It was on this evening that a visitor came knocking on the monastery door.

Haskell had just finished his evening prayers when a young monk summoned him to the abbot's parlor. As he entered, the abbot slowly rose from his chair, along with Father Dominic and Brother Bruno. Everyone wore a long face.

Next to the abbot sat an Asian man in his mid-sixties, who sheepishly and nervously rose from his chair. He wore a modest suit and tie, but something indicated these were his finest clothes. Although he stood in near military attention out of respect for Haskell's entering, his eyes never rose from the floor. It was a striking display of . . . *something*, though Haskell did not know exactly what. Was it a cultural norm for him? Was it a spiritual act of humility?

"I'm Brother Haskell," he said with his hand suspended toward their guest.

The man awkwardly extended his hand, glancing up momentarily at Brother Haskell. Haskell gripped his hand firmly as if refusing to let the man cower back into his shell. He even dipped his head, like an adult trying to catch the eye of a shy child. "What's your name, sir?"

The abbot's face indicated that he was about to take on the role of moderator, a role in which he was versed and accomplished, but Haskell's darting glance showed that he had it under control and, for whatever reason, wanted to handle this himself. The abbot knew he was right. And while he already knew the reason for the man's visit, he also knew that the man must repeat himself to Haskell.

Such is often the case with redemption: Man must speak. Man must speak in order to amend his ways, to seek forgiveness (from others, self, and God), to redeem his own self-image amidst those harrowing moments of life in which we despise ourselves. Man must speak in the most powerful of human moments—not loudly or loquaciously, nor even audibly—but man must speak at least in his heart whatever truth must resurrect in the wake of destruction wrought by his actions.

"I . . ." the man began in a thick Japanese accent, slowly raising his eyes to Brother Haskell, "I am the man who killed Father Matthias."

Chapter 5

The Death March

1963

"Brother, meet Hioji Nishi," interjected the abbot.

Brother Haskell's ability to retain a stoic demeanor was not overcome by the man's claim. He knew, however, that *nice to meet you* was an insufficient if not inappropriate response under the circumstances.

"Welcome," said Haskell, after consideration.

"Please, everyone, sit," instructed the abbot.

Everyone did so. Hioji sat perfectly still with his hands between his knees and his eyes locked on the floor, as if awaiting a scourging.

The abbot cleared his throat. "Mr. Nishi, how about you begin with how you came to this country and why you are here, especially today?"

He nodded, or rather bowed, and sat forward in his chair. "I finally admit to this country five year ago. It took many year, almost ten. The Japanese, they are not admit. Not until recently. When I come here, I see how your people mourn the death of young men in the Pacific Theater on seven December, the day my nation bomb Pearl Harbor. This is a day I learn to stay indoors, to stay out of sight."

He paused as he fiddled nervously with his hands.

"The memories of my story and of my encounter with your Father Matthias, they haunt me for years, but they seem to scream out at me on seven December as I see the reruns of Pearl Harbor in flame. So I spent last year inquiring of War Department as to the home of chaplain stationed in Philippine during the Battle of Bataan, named Father Matthias.

A few month ago, my request was answered. I decided this day, of all days, was most appropriate to make amend."

He dropped his head as if the moment he had been waiting for was finally upon him.

"Thank you for being here, Mr. Nishi," the abbot said. "Why don't you start at the beginning."

The little man took a deep breath.

***

Hioji Nishi was a soldier of the Imperial Japanese Army in the war. Deployed to the Philippines in January of 1942, he fought for over three months in what would become known as the Battle of Bataan.

The carnage of those ninety days was impossible for a man to forget. In the midst of it, however, Hioji became desensitized, as most men do by necessity.

Americans are dogs. They have no honor.

It was repeated over and over again.

The fact that Americans surrender and hope to survive proved they had no honor. The only honor in battle, every Japanese was taught from childhood, is to fearlessly die for the sake of your motherland.

And so, when the Japanese won the Battle of Bataan, and both American and Filipino troops surrendered, the Japanese disrespected them all the more for their cowardly surrender.

Seventy-five thousand American and Filipino soldiers surrendered. Seventy-five thousand cowards. The Japanese generals did not know what to do with all of them. Many of them escaped into the mountains before the march began. But seemingly countless soldiers remained to be transported. Hioji heard through the ranks that the main objective was to move the soldiers from Bataan in the south to Camp O'Donnell in the north so that the Imperial Army could bring in more soldiers to take Corregidor. They knew, however, that they had very little food, water, and supplies to transport so many prisoners. But the commanding officers didn't care. So many of the prisoners were already wounded, malnourished, dehydrated. A sixty- to seventy-mile march was grueling even for Hioji with unlimited water and food.

On April 9, the Bataan Death March, as it would come to be known, began. Hioji was stationed toward the back of the line, which meant he saw every fallen soldier. Some fell from bullets, others from bayonets, others from exhaustion.

At the beginning of the march, there were mass executions for no apparent reason. The Allied soldiers were searched thoroughly. Any man who had even the smallest amount of Japanese money or any kind of possession was summarily executed based on the assumption they stole it off a dead Japanese body. Hioji saw men on their knees having their golden teeth knocked out with the butt of a rifle.

As the march progressed, Imperial soldiers viciously beat anyone who asked for food. Men were given the sun treatment, in which they were stripped naked and tied to posts, just feet away from running streams of cool water. And if they asked for water, they were shot dead. And for those who collapsed from exhaustion, the Imperial truck drivers would swerve into their path and slowly roll over them.

On the very first day of the march, Hioji saw a man dashing to one side of the road and then to other, kneeling next to fallen soldiers, dead or alive. He was sweeping his hand over their heads. He wore a cross on his collar. But the international custom of leaving chaplains and medics alone was non-existent among the Japanese. The Imperial soldiers got a good laugh if they could hit him in the back as he knelt next to a body. But they allowed him to continue, not due to any form of compassion, but out of entertainment.

Dying men on the side of the road would reach their arm up, like reaching for an angel of mercy, and yell, "Father Matthias! Father Matthias!" And despite the Japanese orders to keep moving, this man would dart over to whoever called him. He would have ten or fifteen seconds before the butt of a rifle hit him in the back. It was just enough time for him to say a few words and to rub his finger on the man's forehead. He fell back into line, each time more slouched over from pain. But with astonishing resolve, he would straighten up, and encourage the men walking next to him.

On the second day, Hioji's part of the line came upon a Filipino limping slowly. He had no shoes. And everyone knew he would be killed in due course. The chaplain ran up to him, took off his shoes, and began putting them on the man. An Imperial soldier approached the chaplain and looked deep into his eyes. The chaplain did not look back with hate, as many soldiers did. He did not look at him with despair. But somehow, despite the fatigue, he smiled at his enemy. And the smile was met with a fist. The chaplain went down and was kicked repeatedly by the soldier, who then turned and shot the limping Filipino in the forehead. Many Americans began to come to his defense. But the chaplain raised his hand. "Keep going!" he ordered them. And he slowly raised himself from the ground and continued on.

On the third day, many more dead bodies were piling up on the road. The chaplain continued waving his hand in the air at everybody he saw. And when time permitted, he would reach down and bless them. But late in the evening, they came across an American soldier on his knees begging for his life. Two Japanese soldiers stood over him, putting their rifles right in his mouth. Apparently, he had asked for water. Sun treatment was his sentence. He begged for his life. He promised he would never ask for water again.

Hioji watched the chaplain make his way through the crowd and over to the man on his knees. He stood directly next to the pleading man, put his hand on his shoulder, and looked at the two Japanese soldiers. He said calmly, as if it was no matter, "I will take his place."

The Japanese soldiers spoke little English. So, the chaplain pointed to the cross on his collar, pointed to the man on his knees, and indicated with his two fingers, *Swap*.

The Japanese soldiers laughed. One of them looked at Hioji and said, "What an idiot! Let's give him what he asks for. And let's see if his God comes and saves him." And he told the American to get off his knees and go. The American looked into the chaplain's eyes as he stumbled to his feet. His mouth opened wide in shock. He walked backwards, staring at the chaplain, and murmured, "Thank you."

The Japanese soldier next to Hioji had the chaplain take off his shirt. A metal crucifix dangled around his neck. He knelt in front of a post sticking out of the ground, a road sign pointing to the next town. The soldier had him scoot back until he was flat against the post. He tied his hands behind the post. He stepped back in front of him, laughing. He picked up the crucifix in the palm of his hand. "Here," he said, cramming it into the chaplain's mouth. "See if Jesus gives you water."

Hioji looked deeply into the chaplain's eyes. The chaplain did not drop his head in despair like many of the other soldiers tied down for sun treatment. No. He was praying. His parched lips were moving. Hioji stood there for a few moments watching. Many Americans walking by yelled out, "God bless you, Father! We love you, Father Matthias!" But the chaplain kept his eyes closed in prayer. Hioji wondered what he was praying.

***

"I always wonder what he pray," Hioji said quietly, almost to himself.

"For forgiveness," Abbot Ambrose said. "He was probably asking his heavenly Father to forgive them, for they knew not what they were doing."

"For strength," Brother Bruno added, with a small shake of his head. "He prayed for strength to not cower at the last minute."

Brother Haskell shook his head. "I don't think so," he said. "Father Matthias knew that beauty is the binding force that holds all things together in this life. He knew that beauty lay beneath the horrors of sin, the ravages of war. He knew that the darkness was only dark because it was removed from the light. He knew that every suffering of this world was to be felt only because of our distance from the glories of paradise that await us. For Father Matthias, suffering was beautiful because it reminds us of that which we must love. I am sure of it," Brother Haskell said, nodding his head. "He was seeking the beauty of being tied to a post and of dying a miserable death by sun and dehydration in place of another man, for 'Greater love than this no man hath, that a man lay down his life for his friends.' And I am most certain that he found it, just as he found the crucifixion to be the most beautiful act in human history."

Hioji listened attentively. So did the others.

"Sorry," Bruno said to Hioji. "But you said that you killed him?"

Hioji was jerked out of his thinking. Grief returned immediately to his face.

"You see, I stand there for a moment, watching him. But I called forward by the other soldiers. As I walk on, I couldn't take my mind off chaplain. I knew that many Japanese soldiers pass him by, just as I pass many other Americans tied to post. I know that chaplain would survive as long as two day. The locals knew not to intervene.

"I stopped. I turn around. And I run back. It must be half mile. Maybe mile. Many Americans were still saying kind things to him, knowing if they tried to free him, they be killed instantly.

"I walk up to him. My body block sun so he could see me. He look up at me. His face was fill with a peace I am still searching for to this day. He seem ready for a long suffering. Our eyes lock on each other. And I try to let my face show a look of regret. I took one step back. I raise my rifle against his head. I look deep into his eyes, wish I could communicate somehow. A smile cross his face. He understand me. And he said, 'You are forgiven.' I not understand the words then, but somehow remember them. The look in his eyes was enough for me to know that I was indeed forgive. And before anyone could stop me, I pull the trigger."

Hioji leaned back in his chair. "I am man who kill Father Matthias."

Brother Bruno's face collapsed into his hands. Father Dominic crossed himself and folded his hands in prayer. Abbot Ambrose looked at Brother Haskell. And Brother Haskell smiled at the suffering Japanese man sitting before him. He stood up, pulled Hioji up by the hand, and hugged him as if he was a long-lost friend.

Part Five

Chapter 1

Clayton

September 4, 1964

No other college was even considered. Good Shepherd had been predestined. He resented this. First, he felt his father should have given him at least a say in the situation. Second, he would have preferred going away to the West Coast, or Europe, or Mars, rather than a mere thirty minutes down the road. Going to college in Capstone was like going to the desert for vacation. And as anti-Catholic as his father was, one would think going to a good Presbyterian college, like Davidson, made more sense. But no. He was required to follow in his father's footsteps, no matter the internal inconsistency that permeated the old man's life.

The only thing of possible interest for the young men at Good Shepherd was sports, alcohol, and the girls on campus, which was a novelty for the young men since the school had gone co-ed just a few years before. Only one of those prospects held immediate interest for Clayton Brooks: the drinking.

He had two left feet and two left hands, and so despite his father's attempts over the years, Clayton no longer played team sports. And since Clayton's mother died a year ago, he had lost all interest in pursuing the females, despite their pursuit of him. He stood at six feet tall with penetrating light blue eyes and was the heir to a sizable fortune. In a strange way, however, every beautiful lady reminded him of his mother. The pain was still too raw, having lost her only a year ago to a bottle of pills. It made less sense to him with every passing day.

The first day of orientation brought with it a string of ceremonies and the inevitable meeting of one's roommate.

"Chip is my name," the awkward boy with glasses said upon entering the small dorm room, a box in his hands. He set the box down and stuck out his hand. "Actually, I'm Alexander Warfield Smith, III. I'm the 'chip' off the old block. Get it?"

"I get it," Clayton replied, shaking his hand weakly. "I'm Clayton." He withheld his last name, not wanting extra attention brought to him.

"We should get over to the opening ceremonies, don't you think?" Chip asked. "We can unpack later."

"Sure."

"Great, let me just use the bathroom."

When Chip departed down the hall, Clayton ducked outside and set out across campus on his own.

He would have preferred to remain alone. But he was not. He suddenly found himself amidst four hundred other young men and fifty or so young women, some who looked excited to be there (like Chip) and a few who looked miserable (like himself). Still more, he felt the presence of his father's shadow. The campus had an aura of his father's legendary four-year tenure—a star athlete, a famous name, and of course, valedictorian. Every large oak tree with drooping branches may have provided shade for the young superstar as he strutted beneath them. Every brick Clayton stepped on may have been like a red carpet for the celebrity of Capstone. Every classroom chair may have been a throne for the backside of this future king of North Carolina.

As he entered Matthias Theater, Clayton saw over a hundred freshmen piled into the stadium-like seating. About twenty-five were female. He saw a few empty seats in the middle of the rows but decided to hide in a back corner. But a stuffy professor with a bowtie gave him a simple point of the finger, indicating he must sit. For almost an hour, he suffered through various talks. The president of the college spoke on the value of the liberal arts, an abstract sales pitch that failed to actually be heard by any of the students, based on their disinterested faces.

Next, a senior who served as a residential director in the dorms spoke of the culture of fellowship within the structure of rules. Clayton heard nothing, for he wanted no friends and no structure.

Then, lastly, an old monk took the stage, his hunched body needing help from the residential director to ascend the stairs. He shuffled his feet slowly to the podium. When he introduced himself, Clayton realized he had heard of this Abbot Ambrose. He was made abbot when his father was a senior. But now, he was in his mid-seventies. A large golden crucifix dangled around his wrinkled neck. He struggled to lift his eyes to the crowd but did so for just a moment. Then he lowered them again to their natural resting place and held the microphone close to his mouth.

"Let me tell you, my sons and daughters, why you are here," he began with the soft whisper of an old man. "After the crafty Odysseus outwitted the Trojans with his ingenious Trojan Horse and the Greek warriors descended from its belly to take the impenetrable city, there was another hero at work. His name was Aeneas. He led his people from the burning city to the boats in search of a new life. The great Virgil tells us that Aeneas carried his aging father on his back while leading his son by the hand. This, my young friends, is a leader: one who carries tradition on his back while he leads the future generation by the hand. And as our corrupt society is turning to ash from the flames of immorality, you are called to be such leaders. This is what you are to learn at Good Shepherd. This is why you are here."

He turned and shuffled toward the edge of the stage and, with help, descended the steps slowly, heading straight out the door.

There was a slight murmur amongst the students. For the first time all day, Clayton was captivated by something, or by someone. There was no pretense, no agenda, no polish. Just the raw sincerity of an old man. It was the first thing on campus that Clayton appreciated. For that matter, it was the first thing that Clayton appreciated anywhere for the past year.

After the remarks, the students were separated into small groups, led by a senior. Clayton joined nine other freshmen as they gathered around awkwardly in the theater chairs awaiting the remarks of their leader, a senior with a loose tie around his neck, disheveled hair, and face dripping with cynicism.

"Welcome, everyone. I've been given the unfortunate job of pretending that I have loved the last three years here. And I receive financial aid to bold-face lie to you that you will enjoy it as well."

A few of the freshmen smiled, others laughed out loud.

"Let me tell you the truth about this place, for the truth shall set you free. Most of your professors are socially retarded monks who lecture for an hour to themselves while the students ignore them. The food tastes like it came from a Nazi concentration camp. And, oh, if you haven't noticed, there's only one girl for every four guys. You will have to fight to the death for even the fattest one.

"The monks are freaking nuts. Father Leo speaks crazy languages to you as if you understand what he's saying and carries around Mickey Mouse comic books in those languages. Another is a big creepy German who limps all funny. I heard he was an escaped Nazi soldier. Definitely looks like one. Don't cross him or he'll cuss you out . . . in German. And then there's Father Dominic, my theology teacher. Mr. Naïve himself. He thinks his lectures are the answers to all the world's problems. Doesn't have a clue about the real world out there."

"Who's that?" Clayton asked, pointing to a large portrait hanging on the wall of the auditorium just a few feet away from their seats.

"Well, if you can read, moron, you could see the name, 'Father Matthias.'"

"I can read," Clayton answered. "But who was he and why does he have such a huge portrait in here?"

"He was killed in World War II. That's all I know. What's it matter to you?"

"Just curious."

The senior rolled his eyes before continuing.

"And then there's the *Phantom Monk*," he said in a deep hollow voice, like one telling a ghost story to little kids, lifting both arms straight in front of him, apparently confusing a phantom with a zombie. "A colored monk who walks around at night. He's been seen occasionally in choir with the others. He's real all right, but no one has ever spoken to him. The monks call him a hermit."

"Where does he walk?" Clayton asked.

"Hell if I know," the senior replied. "The only people who see him at night are drunk students breaking curfew. Not very reliable resources."

Clayton would believe a drunk man over a sober one any day, which is precisely why he preferred drunks to regular people. People spoke the truth when drunk. They told you and, more importantly, showed you what they really believed when their fake façades were removed. And this was precisely why he had been drinking so much of late: he was desperately trying to know the truth about himself.

He wanted to interrogate the senior more about the Phantom Monk, but figured he better let it rest, lest he be perceived as weird. He would have demanded more information, and probably gotten it, if he were drunk.

Curfew was 11:00 p.m. Noise continued in the dorms for another hour. Chip would not shut up. In a way, Clayton wasn't bothered by his rambling. He felt no need to respond even when asked a direct question. And Chip did not seem to mind being completely ignored.

Eventually, the stream of consciousness flowing from Chip's mouth stopped and Clayton heard snoring a minute later. It was 12:30 a.m. Clayton had the sense that he would lay there all night. Thirty minutes later, he knew he was right. As he laid there looking at the upper bunk just two feet from his face, and as he turned over in his mind all the reasons he did not want to be there, he felt trapped. The bed sheets felt heavy. He felt the upper bunk getting closer and closer to his face, as if a coffin lid was closing.

He remembered his mother telling him that men used to be accidentally buried alive when doctors were unable to accurately detect death. When there was any uncertainty, a little string was inserted through the coffin and run up above ground, tied to a bell. If the buried man awoke in his coffin, he need only pull the string, and those among the living would hear the bell ringing and, assuming they liked him enough, dig him back up. Thus, the saying "Saved by the bell" was a favorite of his mother's. He thought about tying a shoelace to the underside of Chip's bed.

A minute later, he had a fresh box of cigarettes in his jacket pocket and was quietly creeping through the hall so as to not stir the RD whose bedroom was adjacent to the entry doors.

He felt the cool air on his face and felt it more the faster he walked. His mind was flooded with emotions on this, the first day, or night rather, of the rest of his life at college. His resentment toward his father seemed rekindled all day long as he moved about campus. His abiding sadness over missing his mother seemed to make everything feel damp and gray.

But he kept walking. He felt relieved to be completely alone. It was a beautiful sight to see no one, a beautiful sound to hear no one. He could breathe.

At half past one, Clayton found himself standing in front of the abbey church. He stopped his brisk pace and stared at the moonlight breaking through the clouds like a spotlight on the taller of the two bell towers. He wondered for just a second why one tower was taller than the other. But the moonlight itself stole his mind away.

As a boy, he believed that when sunlight shines its rays down upon the Earth that a soul was being taken up to heaven. Did his mother teach him that, he wondered. He wondered, too, if a beam of moonlight was the opposite, if some heavenly being was descending upon Earth. Perhaps it would be a heavenly being—an archangel, Elijah in a fiery chariot, or Saint Benedict himself—to prove to him that God was real, that God cared, and that God was not a cosmic taskmaster with an ax to grind.

Perhaps . . . perhaps . . . he closed his eyes in deep sadness . . . perhaps it would be his mother, hidden within the moonlight, not to stay, but to just look him in the eye with a single look of love that would give him all he needed to persevere to the end of his days.

But then a swarm of negative emotions blitzed his heart: *If there is a God, He has only taken away, not given. If my mother's faith as a God-fearing Methodist cannot even preserve her from suicide, what good is it? I will keep my faith to myself. If you want my faith, God, make the first move. Where are your signs? If you are so powerful and want my faith, show yourself!*

"Show yourself!" he shouted at the moonlight.

He shook himself out of his trance and sighed as he felt that familiar feeling wrapping around him, that feeling of contradiction—being alone yet bothered, being restricted yet abandoned, being scared yet apathetic . . . all at the same time.

He looked back up at the bell tower, still illuminated with a beam of moonlight.

"Thanks for nothing," he said. He clenched his fists, his jaw, and finally turned his head away. Then he noticed, ever so briefly, something pull itself behind one of the many large trees that spanned the grounds adjacent to the church. He could barely see but felt certain he saw something. He thought for a moment he might get in trouble on his very first day of college for so blatantly violating curfew. But this figure, if it was a figure, was not approaching him. Was it another student escaping a sleepless night as well? He walked toward the trees, one of which he thought hid the figure.

Suddenly, after closing half the distance, a huge figure in a Benedictine habit, with a pointy hood atop his head, shot quickly from behind the tree, and walked quickly back toward the chapel. Without thinking, Clayton walked in a direction as to cut off the monk before he reached the abbey. He felt drawn.

Clayton reached the side of the chapel first, but somehow lost him. He realized then that the monk had fooled him. He was not actually heading to the chapel but to the monastery that lay behind and to the right of the chapel. Clayton was impressed how deceptive his movements had been, and it was at this moment that a memory from earlier in the day returned to him.

The Phantom Monk?

He took off in a mad sprint to the right of the chapel and toward the monastery. The left side connected up to the back of the chapel so that monks could pass to and from without ever stepping outside. Clayton knew the campus enough to know that just around that far corner was a gate where the cloister began and all outsiders were prohibited. Even family could not enter certain areas of the monastery.

He ran and ran hard. His feet pounded the brick walkway in front of the monastery and wrapped around the corner to the cloister. He ran so fast that his feet slipped from beneath him on the worn brick as he turned the corner at full speed. He slid as if into home plate, skinning his elbow and tearing his pants. No matter. He popped up immediately and looked ahead.

There was the entrance, with a single light shining directly on the sign hanging on the swinging wrought-iron gate reading "Cloister." Just behind the gate, just outside of the light, stood the monk, perfectly still, awaiting his approach rather than continuing on his way into the seclusion of the cloister.

With no reason now to run, Clayton walked slowly toward the monk. He paused just a few feet from the gate, staring at the monk through the wrought-iron gate.

"What are you looking for?" the monk asked.

Clayton almost said, *Nothing*, but did not. He almost said, *You*, but did not. He finally stammered out a soft response. "I don't know."

A long moment of silence followed.

"Step into the light," the deep voice commanded.

Clayton obeyed.

The monk's face was still invisible in the darkness and further shrouded in mystery by the giant cowl covering his eyes. But he leaned toward Clayton, as if to inspect him. He slowly pulled his hand out from behind the long black scapular donning the front of his habit and pulled his hood behind his head. He took one small step into the light.

Clayton could now see a black man, seemingly in his fifties, who peered into his face with squinted eyes. And then, the black man's face went still. It was as if a motionless death seized him for solitary moment.

Then, his still face slowly dropped and stayed there for yet another long moment of silence. But it rose again a moment later. He lifted his head just enough for his dark brown eyes to gaze up at Clayton.

"Follow me," he said, and turned around, walking into the cloister.

Brother Haskell's Journal

September 5, 1964

I have not had a problem falling asleep in many years. It is 4am. 2 hours ago, I was caught. Not by young Clayton who hunted me down, but by the web of divine providence. Your ways, O Lord, are inexplicable. Please explain them to me anyway.

Your still, small voice made me pause. I could hear you, telling me that your will was chasing after me. I turned and waited for this silly boy to slide around the corner. But as he stepped into the light, so did my understanding of your plan for me.

You are wondrous, my God. . . . You are wondrous. Heavenly Father your only Son said, "Do not be anxious for tomorrow, for tomorrow will be anxious for itself." And yet, He begged you to let a certain cup pass from Him.

I dare not flee your will, but, dearest Lord, let this cup pass from me.

CHAPTER 2

A Meeting

September 5, 1964

Clayton opened the gate and entered the cloister. The monk moved quickly. With his feet not visible beneath the Benedictine habit, it seemed that he glided across the brick walkway, indeed, like a phantom. He took a tight left turn and quickly descended a staircase, entering an old wooden door that stuck badly to the concrete frame as it was yanked open. Clayton was now right behind him and pulled the door shut.

It was pitch black, no light of any kind. Clayton froze. As far as he knew, he could have been on the edge of a cliff or falling into a den of vipers. The monk could have been two feet or two hundred feet from him at that point.

"Do not fear," the monk said softly. "Walk straight and do not fear."

Clayton reached left and right, looking for a wall. But there was none. He took a small leap of faith with a small step, then another, and another. He kept walking until he saw a dim light in the distance. As he got closer, he saw the light was a line on the floor, squeezing out beneath a door. The monk opened the door and said to Clayton, "Enter."

Clayton cautiously broke the threshold, walking into a small room with walls of stone. The mortar looked as if it had been picked away, with deep crevices between each stone. The room was simple, with a wooden table and two wooden chairs in the center. One wall was lined with custom bookshelves from floor to ceiling. A few lamps rested in the corners, one of them on. A sheet of plywood lay on the floor along with a stack of blankets. A basin and pitcher of water rested on a small table, as if from an entirely different era. There was no mirror. No sink. No toilet. A crucifix hung on the wall next to the bed, and thus was only a few feet from the floor—an odd location for a crucifix, he thought. A tall stack of black journals lay in one corner nearly three feet high. Ribbons cascaded out of the yellowed pages.

He stood at the threshold of the room, unsure what to do or where to go. Then in a whisper, the monk told him to enter a second time.

Clayton took a few more steps and heard the door close behind him. He turned and saw the monk's face clearly for the first time. It was a face that demanded staring. He had large brown eyes, with deep crow's feet on each side. Deep crevices ran down each cheek, like the crevices between the stones of the walls surrounding him. And his skin looked as hard as those stones, yet as smooth as marble. Large black spots decorated his face like mysterious jewels encrusted in the dark marble. The corners of his mouth rested naturally with a slight smile. He stood perfectly still, with a strong but gentle looking face, hands tucked beneath his habit. He did not blink.

Clayton stepped back and let out a little chuckle. He spun around as if to look around the room again, but really just to escape the deadlock of eyes.

"Do you live here?" he asked, though he felt silly asking the obvious.

"Yes," the monk answered with his normal toned voice, no longer whispering.

"Why?"

"More importantly, why are you here?"

Clayton dodged. "Are you the Phantom Monk they talk about?"

"I suppose I am."

"What's your real name?"

"More importantly, sit down and tell me your name."

Both of them sat down.

"Clayton," he answered.

"Clayton what?"

"Clayton Brooks."

The monk looked down at the table and slowly nodded his head.

Clayton felt the need to fill the silence. "Why do you live down here in the basement?" he asked again.

"I am a hermit."

"Are you a monk?"

"Not everything in life fits neatly into categories. I am a hermit, which is enough to be at any given point in life."

"Okay, well, what does a hermit do?"

"Hermits pray in solitude and silence and stillness."

"Don't all monks pray?"

"Most assuredly not!"

"I don't understand."

The hermit paused to organize his thoughts. "Do all students go to class?"

"Yes."

"Do all students study?"

Clayton hesitated, as if it was a trick question. "No, I guess not."

"Are all husbands married?"

"Yes," replied Clayton, wondering where this one was going.

"Do all husbands love their wives?"

Clayton shook his head mournfully.

"Do all monks go to Lauds and Vespers?"

"I don't know what those are."

"Morning and evening community prayers."

"Oh. I wouldn't know if they go. I suppose so."

"But do all monks pray?" the hermit asked, bringing Clayton back to the original point.

"I don't really know. I just wanted to know the difference between a hermit and a monk."

"A hermit is somewhat separated from the community. Again, he prays more in solitude and silence and stillness."

"And you like being alone?"

The hermit thought for a moment. "Do I *like* being alone?"

Clayton could see the struggle over this word.

"Thomas à Kempis says, 'The greatest saints avoided the company of men as much as they could and chose to live with God in secret.' I would *like* to be a saint. And I have personally found à Kempis to be accurate when he says, 'As often as I have been amongst men I have returned less a man.' I *like* to be as manly as I can be, since God made me a man. And men make it . . . difficult . . . shall we say, for men to be good men. Thus, à Kempis teaches, 'Whosoever aims at arriving at interior and spiritual things, must, with Jesus, go aside from the crowd.'"

Clayton wondered how many other quotes he had memorized from all these books in the room. "Who is Thomas à Kempis?"

"Who is à Kempis?" the hermit gasped. "He is the bestselling author of all time—unless you consider the Holy Spirit a bestselling author of the Bible."

Clayton stared at him.

"Thomas à Kempis was a religious monk in the late 1300s and early 1400s, author of the *Imitation of Christ*. He is not a saint because they dug him up from the grave, for one reason or other, and found scratch marks on the lid to his coffin."

"Scratch marks? As in . . . he was buried alive?"

"Perhaps. The Church did not canonize him due to not knowing whether he despaired in the final moments of his death."

"Seems like a rip off if you ask me."

"Me too. But if he made it to paradise, he doesn't care."

Clayton looked around the room again. "Don't you get tired of the silence?"

The hermit turned his head off to the side and closed his eyes, as if he was looking for something in his own mind. "à Kempis says, 'In silence and quiet the devout soul goes forward and learns the secret of the Scriptures. There she finds floods of tears, with which she may wash and cleanse herself every night, that she may become the more familiar with her Maker, the farther she lives from all the worldly tumult. For God with His holy angels will draw nigh to him who withdraws himself from his acquaintances and friends.'"

It was as if he closed the book in his mind, opening his eyes and looking back at Clayton. "Besides, I don't live in complete silence. The echoes of the monks' chant travel through the halls and into my cell. And I can walk down the hall and up the stairs to the main level and hear them perfectly."

"But why are you here? Why don't you just pray with them?"

"I do pray with them."

"But why not pray, you know, in the choir seats with them?"

"Because I am a hermit."

"But why are you a hermit?"

"Because God wants me to be."

"But . . . why are you *a secret?*"

"I am not a complete secret. I attend choir on occasion. And I'm certainly not a secret to my brothers. I'm not a secret to God, nor the angels, nor the saints. Nor am I a secret to the devil and his demons. I only desire to be a secret to the world. And, my young friend," he leaned forward toward Clayton with grave eyes, "it must remain that way."

"Okay, but why?"

"Clayton Brooks, I must remain a secret, to use your word, to the world. To all of your friends, to your family. To anyone and everyone you know or ever will know. If you can swear this to me, then I shall become less of a secret to you."

"I swear to keep you a secret. But who am I keeping secret? What is your name?"

"My name is Brother Haskell," the hermit said with a sense of familiarity.

"When did you come to live here, Brother Haskell?"

Brother Haskell smiled. "It is late, or early, depending on your disposition. It is time for you to depart, Clayton Brooks." He stood up and opened the door.

"But when will I see you again?" Clayton asked sheepishly.

"When the Spirit moves you to come back. Good night." He held the door open so light would spill out into the hallway and down to the door exiting to the cloister. Clayton walked out and down the hall. When he reached the exterior door, he turned and saw Brother Haskell standing perfectly still, at the threshold to his cell, hands tucked beneath his habit. Clayton turned and exited the monastery.

The next day, Brother Haskell sat at his table waiting patiently. The rhythmic sound of wood striking stone grew louder. A gentle tap at the door finally came. "Come."

Abbot Ambrose walked in slowly, visibly fatigued from the long haul down the steps and the hallway. He paused at the table and leaned against his cane. He gave Brother Haskell a long look.

"I know," Haskell said.

"You do?"

"He tracked me down last night as I was walking."

"What?" The abbot looked off at the wall, thinking, before looking back. "He must have known about you."

"He did not know. And there are no chances. Only Providence."

The old man sighed.

"And I welcomed him in," Haskell added.

"You did what?" the old man exclaimed, sitting down at the table.

Brother Haskell took his own deep breath. "A still, small voice . . ."

The abbot pursed his lips and nodded.

"You knew he was here. And you had hoped to keep it from me?" Brother Haskell asked.

"I learned about it just recently. I thought that out of four hundred students, the chances were slim."

"There are no chances. Only Providence."

"Yes. Yes. Indeed," said the abbot. "Are you all right?"

"I don't know what that means. But I believe I am aligned with God's will."

"Yes. No doubt."

"Are you . . . *all right?*" asked Brother Haskell.

"I am anxious, though anxiety at this old age comes more as fatigue than it does as nervous energy. But I am anxious for you."

"'*And which one of you by being anxious can add one cubit to his span of life?*'"

"Yes. Yes. I'm aware."

"Be at peace, Abbot. This cup either shall or shall not pass from us. Be at peace."

"But why befriend him? Of all people, Hack?"

"That still, small voice."

Abbot Ambrose nodded and raised himself slowly to his feet, turning to leave. Brother Haskell bowed his head and returned to prayer.

Abbot Ambrose's Journal

September 6, 1964

How intricate is the interplay between Providence and prudence? Before meeting Hack over 40 years ago, I would have thought, had I asked the question, that the distinction was clear. Every day since that fateful night, I have been afflicted by my ignorance on the subject.

I spoke with Haskell about Clayton arriving on campus. So many familiar emotions came flooding back.

I feel old. I feel the same tension between acceptance and our free will to change the world in which we live, but I no longer have the strength to put my thoughts into words.

Haskell is the better man to decide such things now, or always has been.

Fiat voluntas tua. Fiat voluntas tua.

I have nothing else to say.

Nothing else to do.

Chapter 3

Lazarus and Job

October 3, 1964

Homer.

Sophocles.

Plato.

Aristotle.

Clayton's reading list for first semester was daunting. It took time. Worse than that, he did not see the point. How does one's knowledge of the Greek gods practically apply to one's life?

It had been nearly a month since meeting the hermit. He had been tempted many times to return late at night.

But when will I see you again?

When the Spirit moves you to return.

With each passing day, Clayton's respect for the hermit grew, along with his curiosity about him. Out of this respect, he did not want to return until *the Spirit moved him*—whatever that meant. He eventually concluded that his nagging desire to go visit Brother Haskell was *spirit enough*. Nearly a month, he thought, was not so short a time as to wear out his welcome. And so, an hour after curfew, Clayton made his way into the cool October air.

He quietly entered the cloistered gate, hoping there wasn't some old monk having a sleepless night. He pulled the thick, wooden door open and entered the pitch-black hallway. He walked slowly and intentionally, feeling the ground with his toes and then heel, like a clumsy ballerina. He saw the dim light breaking forth beneath the door. He felt relieved that the hermit was awake, assuming he did not sleep with the light on.

Just before he tapped on the door, he heard the soft command, "Come." He pulled the door open and saw Brother Haskell. There he sat, like the same dark marble statue, perfectly still and at peace, just as he saw him during his last visit.

"Please sit," Brother Haskell continued.

Clayton sat down. "Do you ever sleep?" he asked.

"Yes."

"I mean, do you sleep at night, like all the other monks?"

"How are your studies?"

"Oh. Um." Clayton stumbled. "Well, hard, I guess. Too many of them."

"But that is not your main problem," said Brother Haskell.

"No. Not really. My main problem is that I will never use this stuff."

"What stuff?"

"Homer, for one. Plato, for two. Aristotle, for three. Or any other ancient book they have us read."

"The ancient is the most practical, otherwise it would not remain so prominent for so long."

"What could be practical about Homer?" Clayton asked, chuckling.

"Well, let's begin with *xenia*. You are practically benefiting from it right now," Brother Haskell said as he slowly waved both hands around the room.

"*Xenia*. Hospitality, right? I remember the professor saying something about that."

"It is more than just hospitality. There are many layers here. First, it is a vital societal virtue of survival. To give comfort to those lone travelers far from home was seen as fundamental to a vibrant Greek society. You, my friend, are a lone traveler, far away from home."

"My house is just thirty minutes down the road," Clayton said smirking.

"No. It is not. It is not your house. It is your father's. And you *are* a lonely traveler on a long journey, lost at sea, at war with the gods. You are seeking shelter and nourishment off the beaten path. You are in dire need of *xenia*. Just like Odysseus."

Indeed, Clayton all of a sudden felt shipwrecked. He had not been in Brother Haskell's room but two minutes and already felt Brother Haskell prying into his soul with a crowbar. No response came to mind. A bit of anger. A bit of feeling violated. But he had no response.

Brother Haskell waited a moment and continued. "*Xenia* works both ways, of course. In Greek mythology, *Theoxenia* is when one virtuously extends kindness and generosity to a stranger for no apparent return, and yet, such a stranger is a god in disguise who will thus shower glorious rewards on the giver of *xenia*. You, Clayton, might be an angel of God, like one of the angels who visited Abraham in his tent. Even if, however, you are not an angel, you are nonetheless a message from God, or for that matter, a small revelation, a theophany, of God Himself."

"I am?"

"Certainly. God sends no one to us by accident. People may sin, which God never condones. But each person we meet, in that particular moment, is present to us because of God's will, and thus is a physical manifestation of God's divine will."

Clayton shook his head. "I'm no angel, I can guarantee you that."

"It matters not *what* you are, but *how* you are at any given moment. It matters if you practice *xenia* toward God at every moment."

"But God is not a *lone traveler* or whatever you said I was. He needs no *xenia* from me."

"God needs nothing but desires much. In fact, He desires everything. For anything He does not desire is nothing at all. He does not desire sin because sin is nothing. It is the absence of good. All that He made is good. All that you are is good—though you lack much good that you should be. And thus, no matter how much good is in you at this moment, God desires you in full. Oh, yes, Clayton. Do not fool yourself. You must practice *xenia* toward God in this present moment and every present moment. There is nothing in this universe more practical than that."

Brother Haskell had not moved an inch since he began talking. He sat still, but somehow his words had fluidity of passion without flamboyance.

"How exactly do you practice *xenia* toward God in this present moment? Am I supposed to pray or something right now?"

"Of course you are. 'Pray without ceasing,' says Saint Paul to the Thessalonians."

"But you aren't praying right now."

"But I am. I am . . ."

"I don't understand. You're talking to me, not praying."

"Living in the present moment is a form of praying."

"Why won't you give me simple answers?"

"I gave you the simplest answer I know."

For the first time since Clayton entered the room, Brother Haskell shifted in his seat. He leaned forward as if to catch Clayton's eyes as they began to drift.

"Clayton, I detect that as a sojourner on a long journey, you spend all your time navigating the violent waves of the past and future, never enjoying the tranquil seas of the present. You live in time," the monk continued. "You are confined to time. God is not. But you are. Can you see that we humans break down time into past, present, and future?"

"Yes," Clayton said, recognizing that he finally was following a point, even if it was the simplest point possible.

"Well, the past happened. It really did. It was real, and thus the past as past is real. It has an actuality to it. But it is like a fossil frozen in ice. It will never change again. It will do nothing, except be a source for our minds to return to, in good ways and bad. Usually bad."

"Usually bad for me," Clayton interjected.

"Then you're normal, my young friend!" The black marble face took on a large grin. Clayton was surprised to see Brother Haskell break from his stoic demeanor.

"Most people," he continued "use the past to stoke the fire of their resentment. I've seen it in the lives of every monk in this abbey. Harboring resentment, however, is futile. It solves nothing, by definition."

"By definition?"

"*Re-sentment*. Didn't you take Latin?"

Clayton smiled. "Do all students go to class? Do all students study?"

Haskell laughed. Clayton laughed at Brother Haskell laughing.

"Very good. Very good. But do you want to know what the word *resentment* means?"

"Given that I carry it around with me every day, you'd think I would know what it means."

"Resentment comes from the Latin *sentire,* to feel. So *re-sentire* means to re-feel. The first wound comes from our neighbor or our enemy. And the reason Christ told us to love our neighbor and our enemy is because they are often the same person. They hurt us, physically or emotionally. But when we allow that pain to return to us over and over again, we are, in a limited sense, hurting ourselves. Do not misunderstand: pain inflicted by others has a lasting impact. But our sinful nature feels the need to be victimized over and over again. Those who are hurt, hurt others . . . and themselves. Left-handed pride is a devious villain."

"Left-handed pride?"

"Yes, what would you say pride is?"

"When you think you are better than others."

He pursed his lips. "Good enough for now. Horrifically incomplete, my young friend, but good enough for now. Let's call this right-handed pride."

"Okay."

"And so, what would left-handed pride be?"

Clayton wondered why Brother Haskell had to always answer a question with a question. "When you think you are worse than others?"

"Almost. In this particular case, I refer to victimization as left-handed pride. It is a pride that says to oneself, 'You have been wronged. You have been hurt. You have been martyred. And the offender is devilish.' The prideful man enjoys going through this ritual in his head. He likes to use his own mind as a sympathetic audience. You can see, then, that we harbor resentment for the purpose of feeling the pain over and over again, so that we can feel sorry for ourselves over and over again. Living in the past is a dangerous place to be."

"But how can I forget the past?" Clayton asked.

"Oh, no. Did I say *forget the past*? Never. The past is part of God's providence. Clayton, you may look at your past. But," he leaned in, opened wide his eyes, and whispered, "do not stare."

These words sunk deeply in the heart of Clayton. He did not just look at his past, but he stared at it with all his might. And Brother Haskell was right. He had become a victim in his own mind: a victim of a cruel father, a victim of a lonely life filled with all the emptiness that wealth brings into a family, a victim of his mother's death.

Brother Haskell looked as if he awaited a response. Clayton finally said, "I understand," which was all that was needed to be said.

"Good. Let's now travel to the future. The future is nothing."

"What do you mean?"

"The future, your future, does not exist yet. It may never exist. We may die. Christ may return. And this is why you should refrain from going there. Because it is nothing, your mind has nothing to grab hold of. It is like your body falling into a void of nothingness. It is terrifying. And so, we look, *you* look around your future with anxiety. What will it be? What will happen? Will this hurt? Will that hurt? You then use your creative powers to imagine a future that may not be. This, too, is prideful, for we turn ourselves into gods shaping people in whatever mold we want. We pretend to know what this person will say, or what that person will do. We put words in their mouths. We play God. And He doesn't like it, nor do our souls."

"But we must plan for the future."

"Clayton, you may look at your future. But do not stare." He smiled. "'*Nolite ergo esse solliciti in crastinum crastinus enim dies sollicitus erit sibi ipse sufficit diei malitia sua*.' I know . . . you didn't study," Brother Haskell said. "'Do not be anxious about tomorrow for tomorrow will be anxious for itself.' These are the words of Jesus, your Master."

Your Master. What an odd way of saying it, Clayton thought. He had never given much thought to Jesus, certainly not as a Master.

"All I do is think about the past and the future," Clayton said. "I'm always mad, or resentful I guess, about the past. And I am always worried about the future. I don't know what living in the present even feels like."

"It feels a little like heaven," answered Brother Haskell matter-of-factly.

"How do you know? You been there?"

"In a manner of speaking, yes."

"What?"

"Suffice to say, Clayton, that God is the eternal now. We too often expect God to come to us. Why do we not go to Him?"

"What's that supposed to mean?"

"We must try to meet God close to His home—namely, eternity. The present moment is pretty close. It is like coming up to a beautiful river, like the New River. Your present moment, Clayton, is the shore on your side. Eternity is the shore on God's side. You cannot cross over until death carries you across. But you can see across. You can hear across. Just being on the shore should bring you peace."

"Do you ever live in the past or in the future?" Clayton asked the old monk.

Leaning back and sighing, Brother Haskell said, "Much less than I used to." He turned his head and looked toward his pile of black journals leaning against the wall. "Much less than I used to," he repeated softly. He snapped back to Clayton and said, "Well. Good night, Mr. Brooks."

"Wait. Before I go, I've been wondering for the last month . . ." Clayton hesitated, but then mustered up the courage to ask, "How did you come to live here?"

"That, my young friend, does not matter. What matters is that I live here now, in the present moment. And you must now go back to the world . . . and live in the present moment."

October 5, 1964

Dear Hack,

My class with Father Dominic is going well. I have tried a few times after class to speak about you, but he mostly ignores me. He is, however, a fine teacher.

I don't know why I can't just visit you every now and then, at least in the abbot's parlor. If you would visit Momma and Daddy, why won't you visit with me? It's silly dropping these letters at the receptionist's office, as if we live miles apart. Students call you the "Phantom Monk," and I have to keep my mouth shut. It drives me crazy!

Daddy is not good. He is closing in on himself despite my weekend visits. I just see a shell of a man.

Every now and then I see the Brooks boy on campus. He waves. I ignore him. I get angry just thinking about that family.

Yours,

Janey

October 6, 1964

Dearest Janey,

I would visit with you on campus if I could. I'm sorry you do not understand.

The Brooks boy, as you call him, is not his father. He has done nothing to you. And yet you cast upon him your sinful anger?

You, my goddaughter, are better than that.

It is time I visited your father. I will have someone give you the day and time so we can visit at your house.

Your Godfather,

Hack

A week later, Brother Haskell stepped out from the car onto Eddie's driveway. A younger Brother serving as chauffer waited behind the wheel. Ada greeted Brother Haskell with the same joy as years before, but with a slower step.

"So good to see you, Mr. Hack," she said, hugging him. "Maybe you can put some life in him."

"Only God can do that," Brother Haskell replied.

As they approached the back patio, Janey came bursting through the screen door, bounding down the steps like a small child. She looked like her mother.

"Hack!" she hollered. She wrapped her arms around his neck.

"Janey," he said, gently pushing her back. "So good to see you."

"Then you ought to let me see you more often rather than just writing letters back and forth."

"Janey . . ."

"I know . . . I'll drop it. But thanks for coming today."

"We will visit after," Haskell said. "Take me to him."

She led him into her father's dark study, a small room just off the master bedroom, lined with bookshelves from floor to ceiling. Two leather chairs were tucked into corners with a reading lamp between them. A wooden table with a half-empty bottle of Scotch and a half dozen Scotch glasses on it stood between the two leather chairs. The room reeked of cigar smoke.

"Hack," a voice came from a dark corner. Eddie sat in his bathrobe, a Scotch glass in hand. He did not rise, but straightened up in the chair and folded his legs, trying to give himself a more dignified look. "This is a surprise," he added, looking at his daughter.

Hack turned to Janey. "Leave us."

For the first time in forty years, since that fateful meeting in the dentist office when Lily slipped directions to her daddy's house in Eddie's jacket pocket and disappeared behind the door, Haskell and Eddie were alone.

Haskell looked around the room, unsatisfied with the seating arrangements. He pulled the second leather chair much closer to Eddie and sat on the edge of the seat such that their legs were nearly touching.

"What brings you here?" Eddie asked.

"I'm here to keep two promises."

"Promises?"

Haskell reached into his pocket and pulled out two harmonicas.

"During your first visit to Mr. Grey's house, when you asked to court Lily, we spoke of my harmonica. You said you were too busy to learn fun stuff. You said when you turned old and gray you might find the time."

Eddie's eye locked on the harmonicas. He placed his glass on the table, leaning forward and looking down at them.

"I told you," Haskell continued, "that if I still knew you when you were old and gray, I would come and teach you."

Eddie gazed at the two small slabs of metal resting in the monk's thick hand. A small beam of light from the covered window behind Eddie's chair glistened off the harmonicas the way the Jefferson sun glistened off the purity of the New River. Both men stared quietly, as if they were looking back in time together, into a purer world, a simpler world, filled with mountain valleys and long walks . . . and falling in love. They both loved the young Lily of the New River Valley.

Eddie slowly reached out and grabbed one of the harmonicas.

"I miss her," he said, inspecting it.

He slid out of his chair and onto his knees. His head collapsed into Haskell's lap and cried. He cried for so long, as if making up for tears he had held in these last ten years.

"How? How can this be?" Eddie asked in between his sobs.

Haskell hugged him and lifted him back into his chair. "That leads to my second promise. I promised to help you see something heavenly by looking through something hellish. Here is how you do it: You must see the remnant of Lily in this life as our suffering. It is an unwanted stranger. But it is a beautiful stranger. It is a horrific reminder of something so loveable that the suffering should be desired in its absence. Embrace it, Eddie. But do not let it be your master."

Eddie shook his head. "I can't . . . I can't . . ." he moaned.

"Yes, you can. Losing Lily is hellish, I know, but suffering her loss is heavenly because it proves the beauty of her creation. It proves that love is real. It proves that God, indeed, is the Creator of all and that evil is nothing but the absence of good. Your hellish suffering, Eddie, will be heavenly if you love it as you love yourself . . . as you loved her."

Eddie looked at Brother Haskell's face as if an oncoming train was barreling down on him. He saw a force and might in that calm face, a face that had learned to suffer better than anyone Eddie knew.

But it was now time. Brother Haskell stood up: "Come with me, Eddie."

Eddie slowly stood up and asked in a childlike voice, "Where?"

"To the one you should strive to live a thousand years for, the one who is awaiting your love and repentance, the one who possesses more of Lily than any memory in your mind. Let me take you to your Janey. It is time, right this moment, to return to her, with the same vigor and gladness you brought to her mother forty years ago. It is time to enfold your suffering into your love. It is time to welcome this stranger as a neighbor and to love him as yourself."

Eddie wiped his eyes and straightened out his robe. He stood up as straight as his old frame could take him and nodded, leaving the study.

He found Janey sitting in a chair in the hallway, as one waits in a hospital waiting room. She arose quickly upon seeing him, instantly noticing that he was not the same man. Was it a miracle or something of even greater value? As Haskell had taught her before, miracles are merely the conquering of the natural order. But there is something that transcends the multiplication of loaves and fishes, walking on water, or raising the dead. Even greater is the spark of divinity, the very essence of the Creator shared with his creatures that transforms contingent beings into an image of the Absolute itself. No, Janey saw nothing so dazzling as a miracle; rather, she saw the greatest reality that can reside on this side of eternity: grace.

They embraced. A new man was born from the grace of God. And the two of them grieved together for the loss of Lily for the first time.

Brother Haskell made his way out the door and to the car, unnoticed. As the car pulled out of the drive, he felt the presence of that familiar stranger knocking at his door once again.

October 31, 1964: All Hallows Eve

Clayton's trips to Brother Haskell's cell had become a weekly occurrence. As they discussed his classwork, no matter the subject, Brother Haskell would breathe life into the drudgery of reading ancient texts. Clayton would return to class the next day with a renewed curiosity and appreciation for the work.

After numerous visits, Clayton found himself thinking about God more frequently. At times, he found himself more curious about God than about Brother Haskell. He began going to the chapel on his own. He would sit and try to feel God's presence "in the present moment," as the monk said to do. He noticed how difficult it was to keep the past and future from intruding on his thoughts and prayers. His anger began to slip away.

He had little desire for groups or close friends but no longer relished having enemies. He had spoken to his father only once the first semester. And that phone call was merely to tell him he would not come home between semesters. "Very well," his father said without emotion.

On this particular night, Halloween, Clayton had returned from the parties which he did attend briefly. Curfew would be blown by nearly everyone. This required him to make a later trip than usual. But eventually, once the dorms settled down, he made his way to Brother Haskell's cell. As usual, he saw the light at the end of the long hall. It now began to remind him of his favorite lesson of the previous semester: *Plato's Allegory of the Cave.* But it was the opposite of the allegory. He was like the prisoner chained to the wall, yet his wall was the outside world. All the outside world's pleasures and images and stimulations and relationships were but phantoms of a deeper reality. Whereas Plato's prisoner had to ascend from the cave, Clayton had to descend into it. The moment he closed the exterior door behind him, entering into the black abyss of the monastery basement, the chains of the outside world were broken. Clayton's light was not the sun of the outside world but the dim reading light of the monk's cell. And this light peaked out beneath the monk's door, calling him forth, leading him away from the phantoms of the world, and into the depths of truth.

This night, however, Clayton did not hear the monk's command to enter as usual. He wondered if the monk was out for a midnight walk or perhaps asleep with his light on.

He gently tapped on the door. There was no answer. The door pushed open a little. He stepped further in and saw Brother Haskell lying not on his plywood bed but on the cold stone floor, face down.

Clayton rushed to him. He rolled the monk over on his back and found him just coming back to consciousness. Sweat poured down his face. "Brother, are you all right?"

The monk cleared his throat. "Yes, yes. I'm all right," he said, wincing in pain. "Help me to my bed."

Clayton laid him in the bed and retrieved a towel and wet it over the basin.

"You look exhausted," he said returning to the bedside."

"Nonsense," the monk said dismissively. "I just . . . had a bad dream."

"Must have been one helluva dream. And you never sleep at this time anyway."

The monk laid in silence for a moment.

"We shall not visit tonight, my young friend. But take a book with you." He pointed to his bookshelf without looking at it. "The third shelf from the top, about one-third from the left. Take down a little black book, *The Life of Saint Antony*."

It was exactly where the monk said it would be.

When Clayton arrived back at his room, he sat at his small desk and turned on the desk lamp. Tuning out Chip's snoring, he opened the little book, no more than a hundred pages.

Antony must have had a short life to have such a small biography, he thought to himself.

He would soon learn, however, how badly he was mistaken.

A few hours later, into the earliest hours of the morning, he had finished the book. His eyes were tired, not from lack of sleep, but from tears he had shed throughout his reading of this little book. He now understood that not only did God exist, but the devil did as well.

Father Dominic's Journal

November 1, 1964: All Saints Day

Where is the logic in this? Why might you allow a holy servant to suffer like this? Has he not suffered enough? I have read it in the tradition. Dark nights . . . assaults . . . manifestations . . .

I confess, however, that it seemed to me more holy lore than actual truth. Spectacle is never reliable, nor am I duty bound to believe any of it. And yet, I am duty bound to believe Haskell, my closest friend and the holiest man I know.

I did a little research today trying to make sense of it all. Aquinas says that demons attack the holy man out of envy, for they are compelled to hinder his progress toward God. And yet, Chrysostom says the devil does not overtake us by force, but by our own sloth. Aquinas, or was it Augustine . . . questioned whether the devil can perform a miracle. In the strictest sense of the word, no, for only God can exceed the bounds of the created order. But in a broader sense, in the mere sense of exceeding man's power and experience, yes.

I never cared much for this topic, until now.

The spiritual and Earthly worlds seem to be colliding in the life of Brother Haskell.

Abbot Ambrose's Journal

November 1, 1964, All Saints Day

I have struggled for forty years to lead him. His innocence, purity, and spiritual depth have always eluded me. And that was just in the material world, a world that seemed to attack him from every angle.

And now, the powers at work have far surpassed any knowledge I possess. I know not what is imagination or reality. I know not what is of this world or the next. I know not if my words help or hurt.

All I know is that this entire life for him has been a vale of tears. The more he suffers, the more I feel the sword piercing my own heart.

Lord, Haskell has had enough. I am old and ready to die. If you need a victim, let me be your Job.

November 24, 1964: Solemnity of Christ the King

At nearly 1:00 a.m., Brother Haskell sat quietly in his hermitage, staring down at his black journal. The blank pages seemed to speak to him, like a crystal ball to a fortune teller. There was a providence in the emptiness of the page that filled the mind. He could not decide what to put on paper and what to keep in the quiet of his heart.

He closed the journal for the time being and decided to open a letter from Janey.

November 22, 1964

Dear Hack,

I'm sorry I have not written you since your visit to the house. It was so wrong of me. I should have thanked you weeks ago. You gave this family new life.

I don't know what you said to him, but Daddy is a different man. He won't let me stay at the house too much. He wants me to have fun and be with my friends. But he calls me every few days. He even had flowers delivered to my dorm room! My silly friends thought I had a boyfriend.

I still insist on coming home on the weekends. He takes me to dinner, all fancied up. He sends Ada home (with pay) on the weekends so that we must "fend for ourselves." He tried to make breakfast. It was an utter disaster. He burned his hand on the pan, spilled bacon grease all over the floor, but as if by a miracle, laughed it all off.

He's retired, but goes to the office and, from what I'm told, just visits with people to give encouragement.

He enjoyed the whole presidential election earlier this month and really rooted for Goldwater. He says LBJ is as "evil as they come," and even has a crazy theory that LBJ was in cahoots with Governor Connally to kill JFK. But he didn't drink over it like he normally would something like this. He shrugged his shoulders at the television and said, "Oh well . . ."

Best of all (and you will love this), Daddy just purchased Grandpa Grey's house. I went there once before Momma died. I barely remember it. And I remember it much bigger than it was. He took me up there last weekend to show me. He told me where you lived, but that cabin was torn down some time ago. You can still see the foundation. The house is entirely run down. The windows were boarded up; the barn is on the verge of collapse; there is even an old Ford truck rusting to death in the front yard. And yet, I found it beautiful!

I could see you and Momma on the front porch. I could see you walking by the river. I could see her working the garden behind the kitchen.

Daddy said he would spend time and money fixing it up. "A tribute to your mother," he calls it. He looked ten years younger in the mountains, I tell you. And you, my Godfather, have a standing invitation to stay there. But surely we should fix it up first. You might find Momma in the mountains as well.

Affectionately Yours,

Janey

He returned the letter to its envelope and placed it in a box filled with every letter from Janey. He closed his eyes. He could see the river winding through the mountains, the pine trees swaying with the valley breeze, the snowflakes gathering in his outstretched hand. He could hear the tranquil flow of water that gave him a chill as he saw his bare foot dip into the cold autumn rapids. He could see the lonely front porch of the great old house, filled with endless memories of the joyful Lily bounding up and down its steps. He could see endless hills and trails on which they walked hand in hand and the tiny streams through which they waded.

He took out a clean sheet of paper.

November 24, 1964

Dear Janey,

There is nothing I would enjoy more in this life than embracing the glorious Blue Ridge Mountains, witnessing the glory of the Almighty in every rolling hill, in every drop of flowing water, in every shade of color from ground to sky, all the while relishing the sweet memory of your most beloved mother, the Lily of the New River Valley.

Your Godfather,

Hack

He inserted the letter into an envelope, sealed it shut, and smiled to himself at the silly mental teasing he must have been doing to himself. He could see no viable reason to leave his hermitage, his community. Perhaps, he thought to himself, perhaps a short retreat, at some point.

He heard the door from the end of the long hall creak open. A moment later, a tap on his door.

"Come."

Clayton poked his head in.

"Shouldn't you be on break?"

"I found an excuse not to go home. So I took it."

"Why?"

"You know why. I hate him. He hates me. Why torture each other?"

"It's been awhile since you've been home. Summer?"

"Last time was a disaster."

"You didn't tell me."

"Didn't want to."

"That's fine."

"I mean," Clayton caught himself, "What I mean is that I wanted to tell you but didn't want to tell you."

"Ah, that's perfectly clear. Thank you."

Clayton thought for a moment. "What I mean is . . ."

"An idea, Clayton: Tell me or don't. I'd prefer the latter unless it helps you to do the former."

"I think it will help me but hurt you."

"That's perfectly fine."

Clayton adjusted in his seat. "Do you know what Congress did at the end of July?"

"Are you referring to the Civil Rights Act?"

The young man nodded. "And you know lots of southern governors aren't too fond of it."

"I can imagine."

"Well, just after it passed, my father had a meeting with some men at the house, some I had seen, some I hadn't. I overheard their conversation and . . ."

"You mean you eavesdropped."

"Well, yes."

"As long as you call it what it is."

"Right. Well, I heard them discussing the need for a Third Era. I didn't know at first what they were saying. I heard *nigger* an awful lot. They discussed the failure of reconstruction and of integration and that the experiment had gone on long enough. But in the end, they were talking about using force to scare the black-friendly politicians."

Clayton stopped momentarily to gather himself. Brother Haskell knew what was coming, but decided to let Clayton work it out himself. As a tear welled up, Clayton found the courage to say, "Brother, my dad is a member of the Klan."

It was not difficult for Haskell to believe, but clearly it was an Earth-shattering revelation for a son who already despised his father.

"And he sent his goons to do his bidding."

"Goons?"

"Yeah. He's had two for years. Stephens and Mr. Gentry. They leave me alone other than tipping their hat at me every so often. Always in the fanciest double-breasted suits and fedoras, like it's still 1950. Stephens is tall and skinny. Mr. Gentry is short and fat. I always thought they were mafia, but then I would remember we were in the South, and there wasn't an Italian to be found in our circles. They do everything from driving him around to running errands to intimidating political enemies.

"And in a sense, he has a third goon. His personal secretary: Ms. Beth Martin. She's in her mid-twenties, blonde, vicious as she is cute, of course to everyone but Dad. Stephens and Mr. Gentry are the muscle, but she seems to be the brains behind much of what happens. She's devious enough to stay in the background. I've always hated her, but then . . ." Clayton paused, dropped his head, and shook it for an unusually long time. "But then, shortly after Mom's death, she came up pregnant—out of wedlock of course. I just can't help but wonder . . ."

"Yes, you can."

"I can what?"

"You can help wondering. While the imagination is one of the most glorious creations of God, without which we would have no Michelangelo or Dante or Dickens, the imagination more often serves as an evil tool to mold others into our own ideas, as if we were God. Do not allow yourself, Clayton, to imagine anything about anyone. Do not speculate as to their motives or inner workings. Leave that to God; He's much better at it than you. And besides, you may find, some point far off in your life, that even the vicious Ms. Beth Martin plays a vital role in God's plan for you. You may find God uses Ms. Martin for bringing forth something or someone glorious, just as He has done throughout all of salvation history."

Brother Haskell stopped and froze. His eyes went wide. It was as if he was struck by an electric shock. Clayton was nearly frightened by the suddenness of it all. Brother Haskell closed his eyes, seemingly being swept away momentarily.

"Yes . . . yes," the hermit continued softly. "Ms. Martin may well be a vessel that brings forth something beautiful beyond all your imagination. The Lord can use the most broken of vessels to pour out the finest wine.

And . . ." he trailed off again, lost in some inner place that Clayton did not understand. "Oh, dearest Lord, the finest wine shall be poured forth from this broken vessel."

Brother Haskell dropped his head in prayer, all but forgetting that Clayton was with him.

Clayton listened in confusion. He looked around the cell as if wondering what to do next. It was as if he knew something miraculous just happened to Brother Haskell, but his confusion brought him great discomfort. He returned to his story rather quickly, hoping to move on from the awkwardness of the moment.

"Anyway, Mother hated all three of them. She would get in raging fights with Daddy about what they would do. I never knew what it was all about. But Momma didn't hate people for no reason. She must have had a good one."

He paused for a moment and gathered himself. He looked down and shook his head.

"The last time I was home, I heard Dad tell them to *take care of* some black activists. I don't know what it means, who he was referring to. But it can't be good."

Haskell nodded grimly. "I have watched the Klan come and go before. It will come again, and it will go again."

"How can I ever go home again?" Clayton asked. "How can I let this man be my father?"

"You must honor him, even if from a distance, as the fourth commandment requires."

"How do you say such a thing so calmly?"

"How else should I say it? Would it be truer if I said it with unchecked passion?"

"No. But the Klan . . ."

"The Klan is a circle of hatred. I knew a long time ago that they may kill me or my Catholic brothers upstairs. I cannot control the Klan. Neither can you. But you and I can be ready to die at any moment. If your efforts are in preparation for death, Clayton, you will not worry so much about dying. Death is not a disaster to be avoided but a mystery to be explored—all in God's time."

"Are you ready to die?".

Haskell rubbed his chin for a moment. He took a few deep breaths and looked down at the black journal which held those blank pages he decided not to fill in.

"Almost," he finally answered.

Clayton looked away to consider the answer. His face showed that his mind went in a different direction. He was discerning something intently.

"What is it?" Haskell asked directly.

"We've never spoken about how my dad got famous around here."

"Why should we?" Haskell asked.

"Everyone knows he killed a black man trying to save his girlfriend. Trust me . . ." Clayton said, rolling his eyes. "He's gotten a lot of mileage out of that whole affair."

"How so?"

"Hell, I don't even think he'd be governor without it. He's had every journalist in town refer to him as the 'boy-hero' who grew up to be governor. And now he's the victim of an insane wife's suicide."

Clayton clenched his fist and slammed it on his knee, fighting back the tears.

"I refuse to believe my mother killed herself. I don't believe anything my father says about anything. He found her dead. He found her with the bottle of alcohol and bottle of pills . . ." Clayton rubbed his face. "You know, the creepy thing is that I can tell when he's lying because it's when he looks the most sincere. When I saw him cry on television about his wife's suicide, and I heard him explain her history of mental illness and depression, I knew he was lying. I just don't know the truth. And every minute of the day, walking around this campus, I remember he's the local legend who heroically tried to save a young lady from a violent rape. But as many times as he has reveled in that story over the years . . . hell, it makes me think he's lying about something."

Brother Haskell nodded slowly but said nothing.

January 5, 1965

A decade had flown by. It was scary how fast. He noticed how he no longer kept track of the anniversary of his arrival, but only of Lily's death. It seemed the only date on the calendar that meant anything anymore. Ten lonely years for him, but ten beatific years for her. He clenched his suffering with affection, for it was proof that he still loved—and he loved now more than ever before.

A quick footfall came traveling down the hall.

"Come."

A novice slowly nudged the door open. "Brother, the abbot would like to see you in his office."

In forty years, the abbot had summoned Haskell to his office only a few times. He arose from his table and slowly followed the young novice, leading him as if he did not know the way.

Brother Haskell made his way into the retired abbot's office. The old man sat behind his desk on the telephone.

"Here he is," the abbot said into the receiver.

He handed the phone to Haskell, who placed the phone against his ear. "Hello?"

"Hack. It's Janey." The voice was shaking with sorrow.

"Janey?"

"Hack. Daddy's dead."

Chapter 4

A Still, Small Voice

January 10, 1965: The Baptism of Our Lord

Haskell sat quietly in his hermitage. He had spent the morning looking through his journals, remembering the endless number of experiences—so many recorded, so many not.

He had learned that the hardest thing in life to decipher was not a Shakespearian play or a typology in Scripture or even the inner workings of a friend's heart. Rather, he found that listening to the still, small voice within was the ultimate mystery to be explored.

It was still, and yet violent. It was small, and yet insurmountable. It was more than a feeling. It was a longing that was larger than logic. It seemed to defy logic on purpose, just to dare the created world to take it on. It was beyond a miracle. It was grace singing her sweet love song to the soul, inviting it to a new Kingdom unbound by any cosmic law. This grace was behind all, beyond all, above all. It was a speck of God in his heart—a mere speck, but it was a speck that spoke to him. And it was of greater value than the moon and the stars, all the men on Earth and all the angels in heaven.

"Go," it said to him without a voice.

He arose from his table, turned right out of his hermitage, walked down the long hall, exited into his garden, left the cloister, and made his way toward the cemetery. A semicircle of people gathered around the gravesite of Eddie O'Connell. Brother Haskell politely made his way through the crowd. Janey sat in the front row of seats, Ada holding her hand. His presence disrupted the old abbot's prayers as he sprinkled the coffin with holy water. The abbot could not believe his eyes. The other monks shot looks back and forth of near panic. But the abbot continued on, and they returned to their pious demeanor.

Brother Haskell took a seat directly next to Janey, as if he belonged there, as if he had been out in the world the past forty years. She leaned into him, burying her face in his shoulder. He wrapped his arm around her and rocked her like Brother Bruno had done to him so many years ago.

Out of the corner of his eye, he saw Clayton standing in a suit and tie. He stood next to his father. Walter stared at him attentively. Their eyes locked momentarily, and Haskell understood. He now understood that still, small voice. And thus, his heart did not sink. He looked away and turned his attention back to Janey.

At the conclusion of the service, Abbot Ambrose shuffled to Brother Haskell as quickly as possible and nudged him in the direction of the hermitage. "What are you doing?" he whispered. Brother Haskell walked slowly back to his home.

The governor shook a number of hands and said that he was glad to "pay his respects to a fine man of the community, even if he was a political rival." Clayton, who was forced to keep beside him, had a look of paranoia on his face, not wanting his father to know he was friends with this black monk being shoved off by the old abbot.

"Excuse me, sir," the governor said, walking quickly behind Brother Haskell.

Brother Haskell pulled his cowl over his head and continued walking. Abbot Ambrose said a prayer to himself.

"Let's go, Dad," said Clayton, following on his father's heels.

"Excuse me, Brother," insisted the governor. He put his hand on Brother Haskell's shoulder.

Brother Haskell stopped. He turned and looked carefully into the governor's eyes. "Can I help you?"

Walter stared into his eyes, squinting, as if looking for something. . . searching for something. "Governor Brooks," he said, returning his hat to his head, without extending his hand.

"Hello, Governor."

"Have we met before, Brother?"

"Never properly."

"I meet a lot of people, you know. What's your name?"

"Brother Haskell."

"Haskell," he repeated the name, as if trying to jog his memory. "I don't remember ever seeing you here, though I'm not around very often. I just know the oldest monks who were all very young when I attended the college."

"I would have been too young to be a monk when you were here."

"How long have you been here?"

Brother Haskell shrugged. "One loses track of time when he focuses on eternity. I must return now to my cell. Excuse me." And he spun around and walked away.

Governor Brooks watched him walk away until he was out of sight.

"What is it, Dad?" Clayton asked.

"That monk. Do you know him?"

"I know all the monks a little. Why?"

"There is something about him . . . I don't know what it is."

He turned and began walking back to his car. The abbot stood in his path. The governor stopped. "I know all the negros look the same, Abbot, but he has an uncanny similarity to Percy."

A shiver went down the abbot's old, bent spine.

"God rest his soul."

"Yes. Yes, indeed," replied the governor. He reached up and patted the abbot on the shoulder with a paternalistic hand and walked away.

As if from an urge residing within for many years, the abbot blurted out, "And Catherine's . . ."

Walter stopped and turned back around. A smile cracked his hardened countenance as he nodded. He returned to his car without another word. Stephens was in the driver's seat, and Mr. Gentry held the back door open. The governor turned one last time and looked in the direction that Brother Haskell had walked before whispering something to Mr. Gentry. He hopped in and the car sped away.

"What on Earth were you thinking?" Abbot Ambrose said.

"Thinking is overrated," answered Brother Haskell.

"Prudence is not," shot back the old man, pacing in his parlor. "Look, it's one thing for you to be seen in public. We've done that many times. But for you to sit with her like that, it will cause people to ask questions." The old abbot paused and faced Haskell. "I told you not to come out. I told you he might be there. He might know who you are. He told me you looked just like Percy."

"I have no fear."

"You have more to think about than yourself."

At this, Haskell looked off in the distance. For the first time in a long time, he was confused. Would Walter Brooks question the other monks? Would he question Janey? Could the monastery get in trouble for hiding him all these years?

"But the still, small voice was so clear," he said softly, more to himself.

Just then, the parlor door opened, and Janey entered. She looked elegant and mature in her black dress.

"Janey, my dear," the abbot said, giving her a hug.

"Everything was beautiful, Abbot. Thank you."

She turned to Haskell, who had stood to greet her. "You never cease to amaze me, Hack." She hugged him with all her might, and once again, his arms were confused as to where to go. "Thank you for being with me," she said, stepping back. "But why? Didn't you know the governor would be there?"

"It's hard to explain," answered Haskell.

"You know, it takes my father dying for you to visit me in public," she said, jabbing him with her words the way her mother was so fond of doing.

"Never mind that. How are you?"

She looked away, trying to control herself. "I feel alone."

"I'm so sorry, dear," said the abbot. "God's ways are not our own."

"Loneliness is a reminder that someone was worth loving," Haskell said. "Thank God for the loneliness. It is the salvific way to keep the lost one with you."

Janey nodded. The abbot thought about the words for a moment.

"He had just recently changed everything," she said. "He was a different man. The happiest I ever saw him. And it's like his heart couldn't take the transformation."

The three of them sat down and remained quiet for moment until the abbot broke the awkwardness. "Well, I suspect you won't be returning to campus in the spring."

"Why not?" Janey asked.

"I . . . I just assume you will have many other responsibilities now."

"The business is running fine with the trustees. I'm going to finish college just like we planned. Sure . . . I'll pay when the girls go out to dinner from now on," she said with a little smile. "But I'm not going to let the money go to my head."

The abbot shook his head. "You are your mother's daughter."

"There is one problem, though."

"What's that?" asked the abbot.

"Daddy recently bought my mother's childhood house but he never got the chance to fix it up. It's in horrible disrepair. I don't know what I'll do with it long term, but for now, it needs a caretaker. I need someone, abbot, who would be able to stay up there for a few months until I make final arrangements. Maybe they can work on some repairs. But they have to enjoy solitude. There isn't a soul around for miles—no different, Daddy said, from forty years ago."

The abbot's eyebrows raised. "Hack," he said, turning toward him. "Is this not a perfect time for you to go on retreat?"

Janey let a small smile slip. She reached down into her purse leaning against the leg of her chair. With her legs crossed and her elbow on her knee, she leaned toward Brother Haskell and flipped her hand upside down like a ballerina in a beautiful pose, with a single ring on a single keyring dangling from the tip of her finger. She smiled.

Brother Haskell dropped his head and rubbed his face. He nodded. It was as if his soul was already there; his body need only follow.

"The mountains are calling. And I must go."

January 15, 1965

"Why the hell are you leaving?"

"A still, small voice," answered Brother Haskell with a smile.

The Great Bavarian did not look so great in the small wooden chair in Haskell's hermitage. He looked tired—not sleepy, but tired. His life had been filled with battle: the Battle of Verdun, the battle of desertion from his own army, the battle to find a new life in America, the battle of his vocation, the battle against every racist and anti-Catholic drunkard in town, the battle against his own temper, the battle against Father Roth for decades, the battle to protect Haskell.

"Last time you sent me up to the mountains, I found my way home," Haskell said.

"Last time I wasn't a broken old man."

"Come on, Bruno, you've got many years ahead."

Bruno looked at the floor.

"What's going on in that German brain of yours?" Haskell asked.

"I'm thinking it would have been easier to die in the crusades. This life has been a long suffering. And you leaving . . ."

Haskell realized that minimalizing Bruno's state of mind was counterproductive. He took a deep breath. "You, Brother Bruno, have been the truest friend a man could ask for."

Bruno laughed off his emotions. "It's been a hell of a ride. Seems like yesterday I brought you in this cell to hide from the cops."

"You saved me that night. And you saved me over and over again, taking me outside at night, taking me on hikes, playing a thousand games of checkers. You were the truest of Christians."

"That was a hell of an adventure when the car was stolen, huh?"

"It was. You showed that young lady who took us in the same kindness that you showed me. You are the kindest man I know."

Bruno folded his arms and looked at the ceiling. "How many curse words do you think I said while we built that bowling alley?"

"You would have built an ark if it had made me happy."

"We sure killed a lot of doves over the years."

Haskell nodded. "Every season you looked for ways to get me out into nature. My love of nature is due to you more than anyone else."

Bruno bit his bottom lip hard. "Can't believe we made it all these years without you getting busted, or the Klan getting to us."

"You would have died a thousand deaths to protect me, and I knew it from the very night my father was killed."

Bruno searched for a place to put his hands, to avert his eyes . . . he had nowhere else to go. He was breathing heavily.

"Hell of a ride . . ." he said again.

"Bruno?"

"What?"

"Bruno, look at me."

Slowly, his eyes lifted to Haskell's. "What?"

"I love you."

At these words, despite his best effort, tears finally ran down the Great Bavarian's face.

January 16, 1965

"I never saw the house," Abbot Ambrose said, rolling down the passenger window.

Brother Haskell looked carefully through the backseat window at the dilapidated white house as the car approached.

"Is it how you remember it?" Janey asked, turning the car from the dirt road onto an overgrown driveway.

"It's beautiful," said Brother Haskell.

"Beautiful?" she asked. "It's awful run down. There's a month of cleanup to do."

"Perfect," replied Haskell. "Just perfect."

The three of them exited Janey's car. The abbot strained to lift his head, taking in the beauty of the winter sky, the snowcapped mountains in the distance, the many pine trees holding evidence of life in their needles while all else was barren.

"Do you hear that?" asked Haskell, closing his eyes.

"What?" the abbot asked.

"The river. Listen."

The three of them stood silently. The rolling of the river seemed even louder in winter, for the birds of the air had flown away, the rustling of the leaves had long since ceased, and cold air just seems to amplify the sound of flowing water.

"I'm freezing," Janey said, heading up the front porch.

The monks followed along.

The rest of the day consisted of shifting around the mess and clearing out the abandoned belongings of the former owners, all to make room for Brother Haskell's books, clothes, tools, and food. He had over a month of provisions so that he would not have to make his way to town any time soon. It was a rather long walk, but one he nonetheless looked forward to making.

The argument had been made and lost that he should take a car and learn to drive it. He planned on needing nothing, and most certainly nothing he could not walk to. The nearest Catholic church was seven miles—a perfect distance to both prepare for the Blessed Eucharist and to give thanks.

"Come," Haskell said to the old abbot, who was visibly exhausted. "We must say goodbye to each other."

They walked out the front door and found two chairs on the front porch. Haskell put them facing each other. The abbot took his seat as if obeying the younger monk. They looked into each other's eyes, both with a small smile of contentment.

"You're sure about this?" the old man asked.

Haskell nodded. "I'm supposed to be here, for now."

"From the danger of Brooks, or for quiet prayer?"

"Perhaps both. Perhaps neither. I do not know. It doesn't matter why. It just matters that I obey."

"Obey?"

"The still, small voice."

"It has grown over the years for you, Hack. It doesn't seem so still nor so small anymore."

Haskell smiled. "Abbot, you must know something before you drive away."

"What's that?"

"Bruno was my best friend. He was like a brother. But you . . . you were the only man on Earth who could replace my father."

Brother Haskell, the hermit of Good Shepherd Monastery, a man who had obtained the highest state of self-mastery a man in this life can hope to obtain, seemed to lose the slightest bit of control. Something in him slipped back to Hack, the boy who relied on the young abbot for his very life.

"I have thought, Abbot, about the greatest compliment I could possibly give to a man. Is it to say, *I love you,* or is it to say something else? *I love you* seems too self-centered, for you have been far more *to* me than just something *for* me. After the countless hours of meditation in my life, the countless spiritual books I have read, the countless poems expressing truth and beauty together, I have found one declaration, one accolade that cannot be improved upon during this life. And it is the only fitting thing to say to you."

Haskell reached out and took the old abbot's hands into his own. "Abbot," he said leaning toward him, "you have been Christ to me."

He slowly placed the old man's hands back into his lap, leaned back into his own seat, and looked at him with a smile.

The abbot looked carefully into Haskell's eyes, knowing that humility called for accepting this ultimate form of praise rather than taking issue with it.

The old man then leaned toward Haskell, took his hands into his own, and said, "And you to me."

January 21, 1965

Clayton made his way down the long hallway, feeling his way along the wall. There was no light to guide his way. He never even considered Brother Haskell could be asleep; the routine of their encounters proved that he was always awake at midnight. The fact that the light was off was all the more reason to make sure that everything was all right.

Upon reaching the door, he gave it a small knock.

There was no answer.

He gave it a louder knock.

Nothing.

He pushed the door open and flipped on the light.

The plywood bed with blankets was gone; the crucifix no longer looking over the bed; half the books had been removed from the bookshelf. An envelope rested against a small book in the center of the table, his name scrawled across it. He sat down at the table, wiped away a tear, and read:

Dear Clayton,

I am sorry I did not say goodbye in person. I much prefer the written word.

I have gone on a very long and very silent retreat. I'm sorry I cannot be more specific.

Due to my desire for complete solitude, I will not have correspondence. Thus, I do not know when we will meet again. This may upset you. You mustn't let it.

Life is filled with one moment of sorrow after another. The goodbyes we must say in this life seem incalculable at times. Every goodbye is a small death. The problem is that death is forever seen as the enemy rather than the savior. There is no resurrection without Calvary.

The purpose, Clayton, of your life is not to avoid suffering, but to embrace it with joy and charity, like one ought to take in a stranger in the cold of night. Suffering is not the enemy, but in fact a friend, for it trains you to die to self. Aristotle says that a true friend leads you to virtue. Suffering most assuredly, then, can be a true friend.

Why am I telling you this?

Because you have suffered much in this life. But I have something to share with you that you must never forget. Some of us are called to suffer in this life by losing that which is most beautiful. God has elected a few victim souls to undergo an inordinate amount of physical or spiritual suffering. And I must confess to you now, in case we never see each other again, that you, my friend, are such a soul. Your suffering has barely begun.

But there is a short-term way out.

You can reject the spiritual path laid before you. And you will be spared the unimaginable sorrow in this life awaiting you. The problem is that if you make it to paradise, you will still be far from the glory intended for you. Many saints have said that if they could return to Earth and suffer an entire lifespan again, they would do so just to increase their happiness in heaven to the slightest extent.

If you accept this path and embrace the fullness of truth, you will suffer more than you can imagine. And yet, your place within the glories of heaven will be magnificent.

I have considered for many years the primary virtue which enables one to suffer graciously, sacrificially. And while it seems trite, the answer is humility. Without humility, your suffering will be nothing but conflict with God rather than a love affair with his divine providence.

I have placed next to this letter a book for your development. I recommend you read it a dozen times . . . in the next few years. And then, return to it time and time again as the trials begin.

As you can see, it is entitled Humility of Heart, *by Father Cajetan Mary de Bergamo. It is a small, little-known book that ought to be proclaimed as one of the greatest works of humanity. It was a gift from the late Abbot Gregory, the holiest man I ever knew. And now, I give it to you. Why?*

Humility is where you must start in the spiritual life, and it is where you must always return. I know the first paragraph by heart, and so must you:

> *"In Paradise there are many Saints who never gave alms on Earth: their poverty justified them. There are many Saints who never mortified their bodies by fasting or wearing hair shirts: their bodily infirmities excused them. There are many Saints who were not virgins: their vocation was otherwise. But in Paradise there is no Saint who was not humble."*

Humility is the one, absolute prerequisite for a right relationship with God and others. Father Cajetan is clear: Humility isn't self-deprecation, but rather, it is recognizing the glory of God all around you. If you dwell with this concept, your self-perception clarifies and your opinion of others greatly increases.

The bottom line is this: every saint is humble, every poor soul in purgatory is having their pride burned away, and every damned soul is groveling in their pride for eternity, just as Lucifer is doing.

At some point, perhaps not during your first or second reading . . . perhaps it will only be once you are fully immersed in the professional world with a wife and children, experiencing praises and the glories of this life, this little book will be a bombshell to the soul. It will reveal how pride is hiding in every nook and cranny of your life. You will see how far you are from sanctity and yet how easy it is to obtain. The devil tempts us with little thoughts of superiority and little self-pities. You will play the mini-martyr in your mind. You will judge your spouse, co-workers, friends . . . for not pulling their own weight. You will fool yourself into thinking that your cross is heavier than others'. God will hate this thinking. Satan will love it. Humility of Heart *helped me see that at my personal judgment, I will be ashamed, disgusted, and humiliated at how pride so governed my daily affairs . . . so much so that I didn't even know it. I beg you, have the revelation now rather than at your judgment.*

So many of your crosses will come from relationships, as they already have. Your father, as you have shared, brings great suffering into your life. And yet, you must suffer him humbly. If you follow this book, your attention will turn from the speck in the other's eye to the beam in your own. You will see the problem is not outside of you, but within. You will look upon your enemies with compassion, your future spouse with gratitude, your future children with renewed affection, your father with mercy. If you adopted but ten percent of what this book has to offer, your marital conflict will be replaced with new-found fidelity, your struggles in parenting will be replaced with gentleness and affection, your prayer life will turn from a duty to be performed to a pleasure to be relished.

Suffering will no longer seem a tyrant, but a welcomed stranger that draws out your patient love again and again.

Until we meet again . . .

Sincerely Yours,

Brother Haskell

Chapter 5

This Cup

April 15, 1965: Holy Thursday

We survive the winter to get to spring. All is reborn.

Haskell had survived his winter. His hands had grown calloused from swinging the ax. His legs had grown stronger walking to town in the deep snow. His lungs had grown used to breathing in the cold air. A harsh winter in the river valley was no match for a man made strong by a life of adversity. And the solitude, which would have pushed many men to their wit's end, graced him with greater peace than ever before.

He missed the chants of his fellow monks echoing off the brick walls, but he had the soothing sound of the New River rushing over rocks millions of years older than the Benedictine Order itself. He missed his conversations with Dominic and Bruno and the abbot, but he had the winter wren's call, louder than a rooster's crow, reverberating through the still winter air. He missed the familiarity of the monastery, the garden, and his midnight walks, but all winter long, he had the spruce-fir forests decked in green and white, making him feel at home.

Haskell felt that so much of life was to be seen and heard during the death of winter. It was because less fauna filled the valley with their scurrying, screeching, and singing that the winter wren reminded him of Brother Matthias's recitation of poetry. It was because so much flora lay dormant that the evergreens reminded him of the everlasting life now enjoyed by Abbot Gregory. It was the bone-chilling cold of the river that made him feel the warmth of Lily's love—even if but a memory, even if from another world.

And yet, it was the spring that brought upon him thoughts of mortality. As Haskell read his Divine Office, rocking softly on the front porch, he saw blossoms blooming and thought of the Christ Child in the nativity—a death sentence for the God-man. When he saw the royal purple of the dwarf iris spanning the fields, he thought of the purple cloak wrapped around our Lord after his scourging, mocking him as a king along with his crown of thorns. When he saw the lush stalks of Solomon's seal, with their ivory flowers dangling like church bells from bowed stems, he thought of how all Earthly beauty must droop, fall to the ground, and return to the dust from which it came. When he heard chirping from the nest of mourning doves, he thought how the mother would outlive at least one squab from her brood, as many blessed mothers had.

But in all these thoughts and reflections and meditations, there was not a trace of morbidity. Death, for him, had become a sweet fulfillment of a journey endured. It was the point of birth, not its antithesis. It was its calling, not its nemesis. It was only after so much death that Haskell could see this. And his own was not something to be avoided but rather something for which he must prepare.

He picked up the most recent letter from Janey and read it in peace.

April 11, 1965

Palm Sunday

Dear Hack,

I'm sorry if my letter spoils the glories of Holy Week for you.

Just last night I returned to the house after being away for two nights. The back door was broken open. It looked like a crowbar was used. And silly me (now that I think about it) I marched right in to see what had happened. Nothing in the house was touched as far as I could initially see. I could not find anything stolen.

I called the police, nonetheless, showed them around the house, and filed a report.

And then this morning, as I sat down to write you this very letter, I noticed that someone had gone through my papers in my desk drawer. I keep my journal in the same place. It had been shoved to the other side of the drawer. The papers were a bit disheveled. Not enough for the police to have ever noticed. But I'm certain of it. Someone went through my journal and my correspondence.

Maybe they were searching for a checkbook or money. But I can't help but worry that this has something to do with you, that they are looking for you. I am informing Abbot Ambrose this very afternoon.

Please be careful, Hack.

Affectionately Yours,

Janey

Haskell lowered the letter to his lap. His rocking chair came to a stop. He breathed deeply. His eyes closed as he went into deep prayer. Spring, as he knew it, was upon him.

He walked inside to his writing desk. He took two sheets of paper for two separate letters. In just five minutes, he wrote one letter to Abbot Ambrose and another to Janey. He neatly folded them, stuffed them in a single envelope, and addressed it to Abbot Ambrose. He licked his stamp and pushed it against the corner of the envelope with his thumb, like a priest marking a forehead with chrism oil during Extreme Unction. He put on his walking boots, his walking hat, and made his way to the Post Office. Upon his return hours later, he did not retire to bed.

This night, he kept vigil—something the apostles could not do in the Garden of Gethsemane. He gazed upon the stars all night. And more than ever before in his life, more than during those long nights listening to his Pa play the harmonica by moonlight, more than when he did exercises with Brother Bruno in the courtyard by the cover of night, more than on his nighttime walks along the river bank with Lily so many years ago, this Holy Thursday night, he noticed the glory of God in the specks of light dazzling across the universe, all of which were orchestrated to shine down upon Bethlehem, Nazareth, Gethsemane, Calvary, and the New River Valley.

It was through this long night that Haskell's lips continually began to whisper the words of Jesus on that fateful night, but a still, small voice told him to refrain. He had sought peace of heart for so many years amidst the storm of suffering, and he was almost there. It was as if the kingdom that he sought to leave was almost behind him and the kingdom he sought to enter had opened wide its gates. Everything he had studied, everything he had endured, everything he had seen and imagined and prayed for was coming to fruition in this very moment, as if by a mystical web woven by the Master Weaver, the same who dangles those stars above from his fingertips to light our way in the dark.

It was almost time. He was almost ready.

The dawn's rose-colored rays burst forth from the glorious mountains, glistening off the sacred waters of the New River, as the mourning dove sang her sweet love song to the rising sun. The glory of God was in full bloom. And, as always, no dark power of this world could stop it.

A long, black car pulled up in front of the house. Two men exited the car: one short, one tall. Haskell had seen them once before at Eddie O'Connell's funeral, escorting Walter Brooks.

The short one buttoned his doubled breasted suit.

"Brother Haskell?"

Haskell stood up slowly from his rocking chair. "I am he."

"Sorry to bother you. But we've been sent by a Ms. Jane O'Connell. She has asked that you come with us."

Haskell chuckled. "Has she?"

"Would you mind stepping into the car?"

This cup shall not pass.

He walked down the steps of the front porch and paused to look at the New River, streaming along as if into eternity. He then looked back to the two men and smiled, walking toward the long, black car, and entered the back seat.

The stranger was knocking on his door one last time, and he was willing to answer, and to love him yet again.

Epilogue

July 21, 1965

Janey sat at her kitchen table, alone in a huge house built for the glamorous life of the most successful Bible salesman the nation had ever seen. She thumbed at the crinkled paper in her hands, reading the letter yet again.

Dearest Janey,

If Abbot Ambrose gave you this letter, it is because I am gone.

Thank you for being my greatest source of joy these last ten years.

My final instruction to you is this: Do not judge Clayton Brooks for the sins of his father. You are better than that. Please remember, there is as much good in him as there is evil in his father.

You will need each other.

Your Godfather,

Hack

Janey's eyes had already cried as many tears as they could. She sat quietly, thinking, and waiting for the doorbell.

It finally rang.

She opened the door.

"Hello, Janey."

She smiled. "Please, come in." She swung the great door open. "Coffee?"

"Sure. Thanks."

She was glad he drank coffee. She couldn't stand the thought of just having to sit there. For some reason, a cup in the hand made it far more comfortable.

She led him through the great hallway and into the small kitchen. She pointed to a chair at the kitchen table, poured two cups, and placed them on the table.

"Thank you," he said.

"How's summer break going?"

"Fine. Boring." Clayton paused, then, "Why'd you invite me here, Janey?"

"To talk about Hack."

"Who?"

"Brother Haskell."

"Brother Haskell? How'd you know I knew him?"

"He told me."

"Oh."

Clayton sat quietly. Hoping more would come out. But nothing followed. She sat looking at him intently, hoping it would not come across as staring.

"How'd you meet him?" she asked.

"That's a long story with an interesting beginning. How'd you meet him?"

"An even longer story with an even more interesting beginning," she replied with a smile.

He shrugged. "Well, I've got all day, and we have a full pot of coffee."

"Maybe . . ." she began to say, looking down at her letter.

"Maybe what?"

She mustered the courage. "Maybe this," as she twirled her finger around the small table at which they both sat, "is the beginning of another long story with an interesting beginning."

THE END